CONTESTED LOYALTY

THE NORTH'S CIVIL WAR
Andrew L. Slap, series editor

Contested Loyalty

*Debates over Patriotism
in the Civil War North*

Robert M. Sandow, Editor

FORDHAM UNIVERSITY PRESS
NEW YORK   2018

Fordham University Press has no responsibility for the persistence or accuracy of URLs for external or third-party Internet websites referred to in this publication and does not guarantee that any content on such websites is, or will remain, accurate or appropriate.

Fordham University Press also publishes its books in a variety of electronic formats. Some content that appears in print may not be available in electronic books.

Visit us online at www.fordhampress.com.

Library of Congress Cataloging-in-Publication Data available online at https://catalog.loc.gov.

Printed in the United States of America

20 19 18   5 4 3 2 1

First edition

Contents

Foreword

Gary W. Gallagher

The concept of loyalty often provokes extensive analysis in times of national crisis. Competing definitions of loyalty, as well as debates about how far citizens can go in opposing their national government's policies, have arisen in every war in American history. During the Revolution, American Loyalists supported Britain against colonial rebels and paid a heavy price in treasure and influence during the conflict and especially after the Treaty of Paris in 1783. When war with France loomed at the end of the eighteenth century, Federalist politicians responded with the Alien and Sedition Acts, which criminalized a broad range of political thought and action and provoked Jeffersonian Republicans to push back with the Virginia and Kentucky Resolutions. Much of New England grew so disenchanted with Republican policy during the War of 1812 that some type of internal disruption of the republic seemed possible. At the Hartford Convention in 1814, delegates argued that true loyalty to the spirit of the Constitution required a firm stance against President James Madison and the Republican majority in Congress. Thirty years later, the outbreak of war with Mexico once again spawned heated wrangling over loyalty. Did citizens owe support to President James K. Polk, whose military actions against another American republic were deemed grasping and needlessly aggressive in many quarters? Did America's long celebration of the right of self-determination, wondered many critics, require opposition to Polk?

Nothing else in U.S. history has tested boundaries of loyalty as seriously as the secession crisis of 1860–61, the creation of the Confederacy, and the chillingly brutal war that followed. Most of the attention to loyalty during the era has focused on the white South, with Robert E. Lee representing a key example of someone torn by conflicting allegiances. Too often framed as a struggle between loyalties to home state and to nation, decisions about whether or not to support secession typically involved many other levels and kinds of loyalty—something David M. Potter explored a half-century ago, to our great good fortune, in his pathbreaking essay "The Historian's Use of Nationalism and Vice Versa." Beyond the secession crisis, historians also have lavished attention on loyalty—and disloyalty—in the Confederacy. The scale of literature on unionism in the southern upcountry, the Appalachian highlands, and elsewhere, together with a long-standing scholarly fascination with bitter political fights about the tension between central expansion and civil liberties, has created a sense that wartime loyalties were more hotly contested in the Rebel states than in the United States.

Greater attention to loyalty in the Confederacy grows out of an assumption that United States victory was somehow preordained—what I call the Appomattox Syndrome. It seems plausible that the winning side suffered less from internal divisions regarding loyalty than did the vanquished Rebels. And what attention has been given to those who questioned the Lincoln administration, denounced what they saw as transgressions against basic civil liberties, and argued for an expansive definition of loyalty in wartime, traditionally has either played down the importance of the opposition or lumped all Democrats under the rubric of toxically racist Copperheads who deserve little serious notice. Indeed, reading *The Old Guard* or other Copperhead sheets cannot help but encourage an impulse to treat their editors and readers as thoroughly repellant characters out of step with the mass of the loyal population.

In fact, the citizens of the United States engaged in protracted and complex discussions of loyalty throughout the war. Every bit as heated and widespread as comparable discussions in the Confederacy, they remind us how fragile the Union cause seemed at various moments. More to the point, they underscore how much work remains to be done regarding the topic of loyalty in the United States during the conflict. There has been refreshing recent evidence of greater scholarly attention to this dimension of the war—an emerging sub-literature that promises, at last, to redress a serious imbalance in the literature. Anyone seeking an introduction to the topic now has an obvious place to go. In *Contested Loyalty: Debates over Patriotism in the Civil War North*, ten essays by an impressive group of contributors effectively capture both the dimensions and character of attempts to define, and live with, a definition of loyalty that could sustain a great war effort while also maintaining basic civil rights and liberties. The Civil War generation wrestled with timeless questions that seem as pertinent today as they did 150 years ago, reminding us that our republic always has been, and remains, a work in progress.

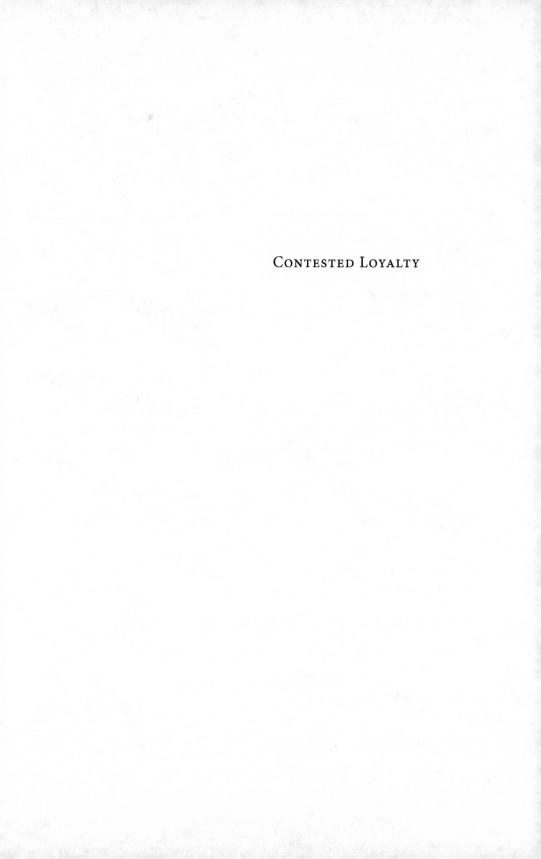

CONTESTED LOYALTY

Introduction

Robert M. Sandow

This volume explores the significance and meanings of "loyalty" in the Northern states during the Civil War. Collectively, these essays use the experiences of differing individuals or groups to illuminate the ways in which notions of loyalty were defined and contested. A number of patterns emerge. First, discussions of the term went beyond a narrow definition of loyalty as nationalism. Support for the government and for the Union cause was but one layer of potential meaning. The debate over what loyalty entailed, though, was not limited to proofs or expressions of patriotism. Strong allegiances to other social groups and their ideologies or interests coexisted with those to the perceived nation. Individuals often acted out of affinity for self, family, community, region, or ethnicity, and held principles that could work at cross-purposes to nationalism (Christian pacifism being an example of the latter). Multiple and overlapping layers of loyalty were not always mutually exclusive but the demands and suffering of war brought out inherent tensions and potential conflicts. These essays stress how such debates were not confined to the political arena. Discussions of loyalty intruded into many public and private spaces including homes, city streets, places of work and worship, and onto college campuses. Authors examine the significance of loyalty across fault lines of gender, social class and education, race and ethnicity, and political or religious affiliation. These differing vantage points reveal the complicated ways in which loyalties were defined, prioritized, acted upon, and related. Scholars of the Confederate home front have lit the way, examining in depth the pull of conflicting loyalties and their implications for Southern defeat. The Union may have prevailed but Northern society struggled with its own profound internal divisions. Historians have labored over parts of this story. We know a great deal, for instance, about political dissent and "Copperhead" opposition. This collection pushes us to see how a fractious and diverse Northern people ultimately failed to reach consensus on what loyalty meant or how citizens in times of war might demonstrate it. It also suggests that the development of American nationalism had important limitations and ambiguities that the war exposed.

Embroiled in war, Northerners wrote and spoke with frequency about the subject of loyalty. The word was common in newspaper articles, political pamphlets, and speeches; appeared on flags, broadsides, and prints; was written into diaries and letters and the stationary they appeared on; and even found its way into sermons. Its ubiquity suggests that it was an important concept but what did it mean to those who used it? The trauma and sacrifices of that bloody war gave ample reason to consider issues of what loyalty meant and how loyal people should act.

When Northerners used the word "loyalty," they most frequently invoked it in the framework of nationalism. In a broad context, loyalty implies both an individual's identity within a larger social group and actions to uphold or preserve that group and its interests against challenge. Authors have given considerable attention to the development of national identity and the accompanying claims of the nation-state on citizens. Nationalism is a product of the modern age, associated with the development of industrial-capitalism, expanding education and print culture, and centralizing institutions of government. The nation is a shared identity, or as Benedict Anderson put it memorably, an "imagined community." Nationalism gives primacy to the sovereignty and legitimacy of the nation-state and to the duty of citizens to support it. It demands that all other forms of loyalty be subordinated to the needs of the country. For this reason, among others, some scholars have described nationalism in terms of a societal disease or pathology. It holds massively destructive potential in the era of industrialized war-making.[1]

Union loyalty, however, was an ill-defined concept perceived in different ways. Northerners had no living memory of civil war to guide appropriate individual responses. The core tenet was devotion to the Union cause of suppressing rebellion. "Loyal states" were those that rejected secession and held true to the Union. Enlisting in military service offered men an undeniable expression of commitment to country. What beyond this constituted loyal behavior? People weighed other "proofs" with mixed assessments. To what degree was national loyalty dependent on visible display? Flying the national flag, incorporating patriotic elements into one's attire, writing on patriotic stationary, singing patriotic songs, or hanging popular prints with military themes were common.[2] Actions were scrutinized closely but carried differing values. Was offering charitable support for soldiers and their families regarded more highly than merely attending patriotic events in the community? Did actual labor for the war effort, such as making bandages or serving in soldiers' canteens, trump the pledging of money? Were people employed in war industries for wages, sewing uniforms or casting cannon for instance, seen as patriots?[3] Highly partisan democratic traditions added to the confusion. Could a loyal citizen criticize or disobey government policies such as the hated draft laws or the expansion of taxation? Was partisanship itself disloyalty in wartime? Some held a high bar for patriotism that required voting Republican or uttering words of support for the government and its war effort.

Scholars of American nationalism have argued that the Civil War was a watershed moment in the formation of a new national identity and loyalty. Over the course of the war, nationalists sought to perfect the meaning of the term and dispel some of the uncertainties in how it should be fulfilled. To them, military success hinged on harnessing not only the human and economic resources of the people but the psychological ones as well. Writing in the 1960s, the intellectual historian George Fredrickson devoted a chapter to this emergent "doctrine of loyalty" in his landmark study *The Inner Civil War: Northern Intellectuals and the Crisis of the Union*. Fredrickson chronicled how Northern elites, animated by the crisis of the republic, articulated this new patriotism. These influential figures deemed unconditional support for the government as both a civic and moral obligation. More than three decades later, the work of Melinda Lawson greatly expanded our understanding of how this patriotism was constructed. She interpreted it as a cultural and ideological accompaniment of larger nationalizing processes, including the centralization of power in American government, finance, industry, and institutional life. Both Fredrickson and Lawson outlined crucial elements of the campaign to shape Northern opinion. Elites established Union League Clubs in vital cities, including New York, Boston, and Philadelphia. They modeled idealized behaviors, sponsoring public patriotic events and charitable aid for soldiers and their dependents. They organized "sanitary fairs" and bond drives to raise money. They educated and enforced those norms through social pressure on peers and through distribution of propaganda to the masses.[4]

Their justifications for unconditional loyalty rested on both secular and religious foundations. The German émigré Francis Lieber was a leader in the foundation of the Union League Club of New York and its widely influential Loyal Publication Society. Authoring a number of seminal pamphlets, the staunch nationalist Lieber summed it up in one evocative title, "No Party Now; But All for Our Country." Lieber's condemnation of partisanship spoke to the political aspects of national loyalty but others dwelt on the sacred. In July 1863, the Congregational minister Horace Bushnell invoked God's favoring of the nation as grounds for a "doctrine of loyalty." Loyalty was "the religion of our political nature" in which devotion to God walked hand-in-hand with fidelity to "the State."

A man could only claim to be loyal, wrote Bushnell, "when he is devoted and true to his country." His essay provides evidence of developing national identity. "When our present struggle is over and triumphantly ended," he predicted, "we shall be no more a compact, or a confederation, or a composition made up by the temporary surrender of powers, but a nation—God's own nation."[5]

In contrast, this volume dwells at length on the limitations and incomplete nature of national loyalty. Disparate groups struggled to control its meaning. We must consider the ways in which other identities and loyalties affected personal responses to the conflict. While Lieber and Bushnell worked to forge a new national loyalty, they labored against countervailing forces in American life. Conflicting loyalties stemmed from the endemic localism and regionalism symptomatic of the young republic, as well as its many ethnic, social, and religious cleavages.[6] Nationalism was a work in progress also undercut by the entrenched and bitter partisanship of the period. Loyalty to party and ceaseless attacks on political opponents were bedrock features of the successive two-party systems that developed in the Early Republic. As the party out of power, Northern Democrats faced the dilemma of whether to oppose the government in time of war. At the outset, war fever and a "no party now" spirit stifled voices of criticism. As the conflict stretched into 1862, however, partisan campaigning and acerbic criticism of the Republican administration reemerged. Democrats pointed to conscription, emancipation, press censorship, and military arrests of civilians as evidence of Lincoln's "tyranny" and unconstitutional behavior. In this they were drawing on Revolutionary rhetoric, tapping into a wellspring of shared traditions about rights, liberty, and resistance to tyranny.

Democratic dissent and resistance has been well studied because it speaks to later generations about a vital issue. Future Americans, engaged in their own wars, have looked to Lincoln's political foes to answer questions about loyalty in times of national crisis. The tale is one of civic morality agonizing over the limits of civil liberties such as freedom of speech in wartime. In this story, antiwar Democrats can be made into villains or heroes. Those historical interpretations often tell us much about the times in which they were written and the outlooks of their authors. Historians of dissent have been especially interested in the roots of antiwar sentiment looking for social, economic, or political causes. Likewise, they have been fixated upon the extent and fundamental nature of "Copperhead" opposition and its impact on the war effort. Those studies predominantly examined Midwestern states notable for the virulence of antiwar sentiment.[7] The essay by Matthew Warshauer looks deeply into the ideology of opposition Democrats and their conceptions of loyalty. It offers an important new perspective, however, that shifts our attention to New England where the patterns learned about Midwestern dissent break down.

The essays in this collection touch upon loyalties conceived more broadly. Authors move beyond the narrow partisan debate over Democratic dissent to examine other challenges to and competing interpretations of national loyalty. In this, they connect to a larger literature on the subject that perceives loyalty as multiple and layered. Overlapping loyalties co-exist but can also be in conflict, especially under the stress of war. They are often shaped through top down processes but can also be formed from the bottom up.[8] Northern nationalists in the press and government attempted to control the message and to influence the way Americans understood local loyalties. While intellectual masters of propaganda carried tremendous influence, it is important to stress that defining and debating loyalty was a public discourse engaged in by the many. As Lawson and others point out, the Union government had no official propaganda wing nor public relations office as in later wars.[9] The outpouring of speeches, writings, sermons, and visual culture was the product of a wide range of social agents and institutions, with differing outlooks and agendas. They invoked all manner of analogies, justifications, and models of proper thought and behavior.[10] This public discourse on what loyalty meant and how it should be demonstrated is the central theme of this book.

To better understand issues of loyalty in the North, scholars can look to the Confederacy for insight. Studies of the wartime South have long examined questions of Confederate loyalty hoping to illuminate the causes of defeat. Union military occupation throughout much of the South complicated and intensified issues of loyalty in a way generally absent in the North. In the Confederate postmortem, the autopsy probed whether the patient had died of internal or external maladies. Was the war unwinnable in the face of a relentless Union juggernaut, as the Lost Cause asserted? Or was the Confederate war effort sapped by internal conflict that led to disaffection and abandonment of the cause? Coupled with that was the debate over Confederate identity and nationalism and whether Southerners were sufficiently bound by it or terminally divided along lines of race, class, region, or gender.[11]

By the late 1990s, a scholarly consensus had emerged stressing the significance of internal failures for Confederate defeat. In these works, nascent Confederate nationalism could not counteract centrifugal forces unleashed by war tearing at the social fabric. Civilian morale eroded in a context of economic despair, resentment of government policies such as conscription and taxation, and the inability to forestall widespread Union military advances. Symptoms of disaffection were strongest among the poor and yeomen classes who chaffed at the perception of "a rich man's war, but a poor man's fight." As evidence, authors pointed to speculation and trade with the enemy, endemic desertion and draft opposition, increased resistance among slaves, thorny pockets of Unionism (especially in the Appalachian uplands), and the unrest of the female underclasses exhibited in urban bread rioting or plaintive calls for soldiers to come home. The implication for the study of loyalty is whether allegiance to the Confederate nation became fatally weakened. These scholars responded that the attachments of citizens to their own selfish interests or to their families, communities, class, or region took precedence as the Confederate experiment unraveled.[12]

In the mid-1990s, a number of historians countered the "internal conflict" interpretation without denying that internal fissures did exist as they do in all societies.[13] Their work argued that despite war weariness, Confederates fashioned a durable national identity, persevered in the cause through innumerable hardships, and held common assumptions about slavery and race that mitigated class conflict. Statistics trumped anecdotes to show that Confederate civilians mobilized soldiers at high rates (much higher than their Union counterparts), encompassed men from all classes, and suffered relatively low desertion. Importantly, the outpouring of work in the last decade has broken down the binary categorization of disaffection versus national loyalty.[14]

Much of this recent work offers valuable geographic case studies, investigating how war and Union occupation strained multi-layered loyalties. Regional and community histories focus closely at the ground level of society and offer tantalizing clues about the lived reality of people caught up in conflict. A number of these authors demonstrate how the expectations of nationalists and their claims upon citizens were always undercut by the personal experiences of individuals and their local circumstances. Their interpretations warn that individuals could never achieve the total commitment demanded by nationalist rhetoric if it came at the cost of all other forms of loyalty.[15] The tug-of-war between loyalties was particularly acute in border-South communities. Residents there struggled with competing claims of nationalism and early Union military occupation. Local attachments, especially those of kinship, were an important factor mediating national identity.[16] As the war dragged on, communities on the periphery of Union advances found themselves facing difficult choices. Economic distress or opportunities for profit complicated and frequently trumped national allegiances. Illicit trading with the enemy and the swearing of loyalty oaths to receive Union protection or aid are two subjects which demonstrate this pattern. They further illustrate ways in which coercion could operate as a mechanism for generating professions of loyalty.[17] Their work cautions us to recognize the often significant difference between public words and more private deeds. Social pressures affected people's actions in numerous ways.[18]

The field of Northern "home front" studies is growing but lags significantly behind its Confederate counterparts. Scholars are considerably less interested, however, in the subject of clashing loyalty in the Union. Perhaps reading the past through the hindsight of Northern victory shapes this outcome. We perceive the North's internal conflicts as more episodic, self-contained, or even as a strength evidencing resilient people.[19] But we ought to think carefully about those internal fissures and not just because of their relation to the Union war effort. There are some noteworthy exceptions to this scholarly disinterest. Issues of loyalty do appear as small parts of broad surveys of Northern society at war.[20] The large number of works on Democratic dissent and resistance has already been mentioned. Others have addressed the Lincoln administration's handling of civil liberties and military arrests.[21] Historians have also examined the contentious policy of conscription and subsequent draft resistance. The New York City draft riots have garnered the lion's share of attention.[22] The bulk of the community studies that have trickled out focus on the urban North, leaving uncertainties about the vast swath of rural people.[23] Much of the literature is furthermore segmented in the form of essays or chapters.[24]

When scrutinized with an eye for clashing loyalties, these studies offer tantalizing observations but less sustained analysis. The first is a warning to avoid seeing the North as a monolithic block. The formation of national identity was affected by the lingering regional and local character of Northern society. Allegiances in the border-North, no less than the border-South, were complicated by cross-border ties of economics, kinship, and shared cultural values. Neither did the rural peripheries of Northern society walk in lock step with the urban centers.[25] The Union also exhibited considerably greater ethnic and religious diversity catching many people in the crossfire between allegiance to country or to their own social group and values.[26] Add to this the vast economic disparity in Northern life and the challenges faced by the laboring classes or landless agriculturalists. Economic survival and opportunity were compelling forces that weakened the call of nationalists to serve and to sacrifice.[27] As Gary Gallagher has aptly shown, the Union cause was a powerful ideology committing millions of citizens, in the ranks and at home, to a long and bloody war.[28] But loyalty to the Union cause imperfectly explains how citizens reacted to the traumas of war or the ways in which conflicting loyalties played out in everyday life. The essays in this collection are designed to point us down the path of greater understanding.

The first essays by Melinda Lawson, Matthew Warshauer, and Jonathan White examine loyalty through the familiar frame of politics at the state and national level. Scholars are indebted to Melinda Lawson for her careful research on the process and content of the war's "new American nationalism." As in her path-breaking study, *Patriot Fires: Forging a New American Nationalism in the Civil War North*, the opening chapter by Lawson focuses on key "interpreters" of war-time patriotism—Wendell Phillips, George Julian, and Abraham Lincoln—and their ideological perspectives. Lawson argues that each man was driven by a profound sense of duty and unwavering faith in America's promise of freedom and equality as expressed in the Declaration of Independence. Their loyalty to the government and to the nation, however, was contingent on its trajectory toward freedom. Could a nation supportive of slavery be worthy of such devotion? Theirs were voices of conscience, after all, pressing the country on to a future without the sin of slavery. What would have been their definition of patriotism if the reins of government, and the means of emancipation, were beyond their grasp?

Matthew Warshauer's narrative of Connecticut peace Democrats provides a counterpoint. How did the party without national power frame the meaning of loyalty? Did their opposition stem chiefly from partisanship or principles? Those Democrats who could not reconcile first the legitimacy of the war and afterward the emancipation of slaves found willing comrades in the Copperhead movement. Warshauer highlights that peace Democrats looked to the Constitution, rather than the Declaration, as the font of their political values. It shaped their condemnation of Republican government and the policies of confiscation, emancipation, arbitrary arrest, and conscription. He makes a case that Connecticut deserves further scrutiny for the intensity of its anti-war sentiment, its location outside the highly studied Midwest or border-states, and its position in the heart of New England. Warshauer also suggests how the legitimacy of their principles has been undercut by a historiography that frequently vilifies Copperhead dissent as treason.

Jonathan White investigates war victim compensation debates in the Pennsylvania Legislature to understand legal definitions of loyalty. As White describes, Northern civil and military authorities became alarmed by the rise of government opposition in its many guises and devised new methods to curb dissent. Given the stringency of treason requirements, they turned instead to prosecutions for "disloyalty" through such means as military arrests and tribunals and "test" oaths.[29] Unlike treason, however, loyalty had no clear definition in the Constitution or federal statutes. "Defining 'loyalty' and 'disloyalty,'" argues White, "thus became a bitterly contentious process in the highly charged partisan atmosphere of the Civil War North." One example of this politicized debate arose in the Pennsylvania statehouse. There legislators weighed who should receive compensation for the considerable damage done by Confederate invasions. Proposed bills highlighted that only "loyal citizens" should receive aid. But how was loyalty to be defined? White shows how the opposing political parties disagreed on the fundamental nature of disloyalty and accused each other of partisanship. In its final form, Republicans triumphed by requiring claimants to swear an oath that they had never done or said anything to give aid or comfort to the enemy. White concludes, "Republican politicians used rebel raids to conflate their conceptions of loyalty with treason and thus essentially broaden the definition of treason beyond that found in the Constitution."

In another vein, Julie Mujic and Kanisorn Wongsrichanalai examine opposing sides of the same demographic, the viewpoints of college educated men, and in Mujic's case, the women they courted. As Wongsrichanalai explains, nineteenth-century colleges were primarily elite institutions designed to form character and prepare future leaders in society. This academic climate of intellectualism and duty, as well as youth, provides a window into a small but significant subculture of American life. Wongsrichanalai traces a group of New England graduates whose choice of military service gave them unimpeachable claims to loyalty. Yet these men were highly critical of military and political leaders they deemed ineffective or misguided. Theirs was a loyalty less shaped by partisanship or unquestioned support of the administration. Instead, the author sees them reflective of an understudied Northern honor or nationalism. These young officers pursued the greater good of society without fear of individual consequences.

Mujic's essay is focused on one of the most personal relationships of all, that between young lovers. In contrast to Wongsrichanalai, Mujic looks at an outspoken antiwar Democrat, Gideon Winan Allen, studying law at the University of Michigan. The author draws on a rich base of correspondence between Allen and his future wife, Annie Cox, to examine how issues of loyalty played out in courtship. Cox was a fervent Republican and abolitionist and the young couple's disagreements over emancipation and the war are deeply illuminating. Mujic concludes that the pair's loyalties to each other, and to their relationship, overrode their disagreements about the proper stances on the conflict. She also finds that

Allen's loyalties were not based on Wongsrichanalai's sense of honor or social duty but rather on naked partisanship. Allen used his studies and his social position as an excuse to avoid military service, and his loyalty was questioned because of it.

Sean Scott next addresses the attitudes of Northern Protestant churches on issues of patriotism and loyalty. His chapter offers an instructive case of a clergyman who fell outside the patriotic, Republican, emancipationist mold. Scott examines the 1862 resignation of Presbyterian minister William S. Plumer whose Allegheny City, Pennsylvania congregation judged his sermons to be devoid of patriotic sentiment. Plumer's was the rare case of a minister who placed strict separation between political and religious spheres. Scott depicts Plumer as a man of true Christian integrity, whose ouster demonstrates the complex impacts of the "politics of loyalty." Plumer's fascinating story also illustrates the challenges of clergy in the border-states who faced divided congregations and the scrutiny of civil and military authorities. Scott's study offers a counter to a historical consensus that depicts Northern clergy as at best pro-war "cheerleaders," as Harry S. Stout described in his recent *Upon the Altar of the Nation: A Moral History of the Civil War*, or at worst callous and bloodthirsty.[30]

In writings by Judith Giesberg and Timothy Orr, the focus shifts to working class men and women in military industries. Both highlight that service in war work, manufacturing munitions and uniforms, was its own loyalty to the nation. Giesberg looks at seamstresses of Philadelphia's Schuylkill Arsenal and their petition campaign for better pay and job security. Throughout the conflict, women were targets of the campaign for loyalty. As Giesberg argues, however, the idealized female patriot generally played supporting roles for soldiering relatives and community members. Working class women who felt exploited turned the rhetorical tables by laying claim to their own service and patriotism. "Focusing on their work instead of their matrimony," writes Giesberg, "women shifted the terms of the loyalty debate to their advantage." This tactic allowed them to legitimize their labor activism in the republican language of rights and tyranny. Giesberg suggests that this was a brief window of opportunity where women challenged the formative stage of the sweatshop system. Unfortunately, while they had achieved some ameliorating success in pay, they remained vulnerable. They failed in their campaigns to uproot the hated contractor system or to establish a minimum wage.

Timothy Orr's examination of the Allegheny Arsenal in Pittsburgh reveals how employers could use a language of loyalty to take away the rights of workers. As Orr relates, political discrimination underlays the purge of fifteen factory workers for charges of disloyalty in May 1863. The men were accused by fellow workers of uttering statements critical of Lincoln and his war policies. Their dismissal following an extrajudicial inquiry sparked a heated partisan exchange in area newspapers. Here, military work alone was not satisfactory proof of patriotism. Workers were held to a higher standard that also regulated their words and behaviors. Where Giesberg described employees made vulnerable by their gender, Orr provides an example grounded in politics. Both reveal how the meaning of loyalty could be deployed for the self-serving purposes of capital and labor.

The concluding chapters by Ryan Keating and Thaddeus Romansky observe the meaning of loyalty in contexts of race and ethnicity. Looking at Irish-American communities in Connecticut and Wisconsin, Keating surveys their response to the infamous 1863 New York City draft riots. People of Irish descent faced severe discrimination and hardship. Their ethnicity and Roman Catholicism caused many non-Irish to doubt their loyalty and assimilation into American life. The many Irish migrants among the rioters were taken as "evidence of broader ethnic disloyalty," writes Keating, which "symbolically and intrinsically linked these events to larger issues surrounding the loyalty of Democrats." Keating shows, however, that there was widespread disapproval of the rioting among Irish-Americans in other communities. It indicates both the complexity of their responses to the war's divisive issues and the lack of a monolithic character to Irish immigrants living in America. They were eager to demonstrate their national loyalty through such means as military service. Keating argues that their identities became as deeply entwined with their communities and adopted nation as with a common Irish heritage.

Romansky provides our final chapter addressing definitions of loyalty among African-Americans who joined the Union army. Like Irish immigrants, African-Americans both in and out of slavery were stigmatized and thought by many to be incapable of loyalty and citizenship. The necessity of their military service opened a way to take agency in achieving emancipation while laying claim to the status of loyal men in American society. The author focuses on the subject of military protest actions in black regiments caused by abuses of their perceived rights and status as soldiers. These protests reveal their politicization and an internalization of the notions of rights, liberty, and resistance to tyranny that formed the core of republicanism. Moreover, according to Romansky, "it links the black soldiering experience more firmly to the larger trends of nationalization unleashed by the Civil War and Reconstruction." He traces a history of civic engagement in antebellum Northern black communities that influenced the actions of many. Nevertheless, the essay also contends that African-American perspectives were in other ways unique. Those who had escaped slavery, as well as others who suffered second-class status in free society, held a heightened sensitivity to discrimination and the abuse of power. Thus notions of loyalty were complicated by the issue of their race.

Notes

The editor wishes to thank Frank Towers for his insightful and thorough comments on an earlier draft. His keen analysis and deft phrasing contributed significantly to the reframing of this introduction.

1. The literature on nationalism, encompassing both theory and its historical development, is vast and interdisciplinary. A now classic starting point is Benedict Anderson, *Imagined Communities: Reflections on the Origin and Spread of Nationalism* (New York: Verso, 1983). Also valuable are (chronologically): Ernest Gellner, *Nations and Nationalism* (Ithaca: Cornell University Press, 1983); John Breuilly, *Nationalism and the State* (Chicago: University of Chicago Press, 1985); Anthony D. Smith, *The Ethnic Origins of Nations* (Oxford: Blackwell, 1986); E. J. Hobsbawm, *Nations and Nationalism Since 1780: Programme, Myth, Reality* (Cambridge: Cambridge University Press, 1990); and Leah Greenfeld, *Nationalism: Five Roads to Modernity* (Cambridge: Harvard University Press, 1992). Somewhat dated but still potent is Elie Kedourie, *Nationalism* (London: Hutchinson, 1960). For a good overview of works on the subject, consult the Oxford Reader by John Hutchinson and Anthony D. Smith, eds., *Nationalism* (New York: Oxford University Press, 1994).

2. For more on the subject of patriotic display, iconography, and popular culture, see Mark E. Neely, Jr., and Harold Holzer, *The Union Image: Popular Prints of the Civil War North* (Chapel Hill: University of North Carolina Press, 2000); Steven R. Boyd, *Patriotic Envelopes of the Civil War: The Iconography of Union and Confederate Covers* (Baton Rouge: Louisiana State University Press, 2010); Christian McWhirter, *Battle Hymns: The Power and Popularity of Music in the Civil War* (Chapel Hill: University of North Carolina Press, 2012). Alice Fahs discusses the place of patriotic literature in Northern society in *The Imagined Civil War: Popular Literature of the North and South, 1861–1865* (Chapel Hill: University of North Carolina Press, 2001).

3. Considerable thought has been given to the impact of the war on women and gender roles. There are a number of important works that address the labors and experiences of Northern women and touch upon themes of patriotism, including Jeanie Attie, *Patriotic Toil: Northern Women and the American Civil War* (Ithaca: Cornell University Press, 1998); Judith Giesberg, *Civil War Sisterhood: The U.S. Sanitary Commission and Women's Politics in Transition* (Boston: Northeastern University Press, 2000); Jane E. Schultz, *Women at the Front: Hospital Workers in Civil War America* (Chapel Hill: University of North Carolina Press, 2004); Nina Silber, *Daughters of the Union: Northern Women Fight the Civil War* (Cambridge: Harvard University Press, 2005); Judith Giesberg, *Army at Home: Women and the Civil War on the Northern Home Front* (Chapel Hill: University of North Carolina Press, 2012). Key relevant essays include several chapters in Catherine Clinton and Nina Silber, eds., *Gender and the Civil War* (New York: Oxford University Press, 1998), and Nina Silber, "The Problem of Women's Patriotism,

North and South," in *Gender and the Sectional Conflict* (Chapel Hill: University of North Carolina Press, 2008). Two excellent state of the field essays are Drew Gilpin Faust, "'Ours as Well as That of the Men': Women and Gender in the Civil War," in *Writing the Civil War: The Quest to Understand*, ed. James M. McPherson and William J. Cooper, Jr. (Columbia: University of South Carolina Press, 1998): 228–40; and Judith Giesberg, "Women," in Aaron Sheehan-Dean, ed., *A Companion to the U.S. Civil War*, 2 vols., (Malden, Mass.: Wiley Blackwell, 2014): 779–94.

    4. Fredrickson depicted this "doctrine of loyalty" (a phrase borrowed from an 1863 essay by Horace Bushnell) as a response to renewed partisan critiques by Democrats in the fall of 1862. He considered the doctrine to be "among the most interesting intellectual products of the war." He was especially focused in its diverse intellectual roots and justifications. Many clergymen, notably Henry W. Bellows and Horace Bushnell, emphasized that the government acquired its legitimacy through a fundamental element of American exceptionalism—God's blessing or "divine right." George M. Fredrickson, *The Inner Civil War: Northern Intellectuals and the Crisis of the Union* (New York: Harper and Row, 1965), 132, 136–41. Melinda Lawson's work focused on the "interpreters" of that new patriotism and their use of the sanitary fairs, bond drives, and Union Leagues mentioned earlier to engage the public. Lawson's central goal was to document how "by war's end, a 'Union' of states had become a 'nation' of Americans." Melinda Lawson, *Patriot Fires: Forging a New American Nationalism in the Civil War North* (Lawrence: University Press of Kansas, 2002), xiii, 3. For other research on the development of American nationalism in the period, consult Susan-Mary Grant, *North over South: Northern Nationalism and American Identity in the Antebellum Era* (Lawrence: University Press of Kansas, 2000); Peter J. Parish, Adam I. P. Smith, and Susan-Mary Grant, eds., *The North and the Nation in the Era of the Civil War* (New York: Fordham University Press, 2003). Paul C. Nagel addressed American national identity more broadly in *This Sacred Trust: American Nationality 1798–1898* (New York: Oxford University Press, 1971). A useful overview is Paul Quigley's entry on "Nationalism" in Aaron Sheehan-Dean, ed., *A Companion to the U.S. Civil War*, 2 vols. (Malden, Mass.: Wiley Blackwell, 2014): 1056–72.

    5. Bushnell fretted that the word "loyalty," a word that was "never till quite recently applied to American uses," had become the victim of serious misunderstanding in American society. He argued that it was not a legal concept but a moral one. He denounced partisanship and definitions of loyalty that clung legalistically to the Constitution and the laws. He argued that the nature of the crisis required all Americans to support the president and his administration: "The debates and misgivings are all over; nothing is now left us but loyalty to the cause." Bushnell asserted nothing less than unconditional loyalty as fundamental to citizenship in a God-ordained nation. Horace Bushnell, "The Doctrine of Loyalty," *The New Englander* 22 (July 1863): 560, 562, 575, 580–81.

    6. The relationship between national and local loyalties was central to the analysis of David M. Potter in "The Historian's Use of Nationalism and Vice Versa," *The American Historical Review* 67, no. 4 (July 1962): 924–50. See also the thought-provoking essay by Edward L. Ayers, "Loyalty and America's Civil War," Fortenbaugh Memorial Lecture, Gettysburg College, 2010. Ayers stressed that loyalty is not a singular thing or immutable

principle but rather a "web of relationships" and a "medium of negotiation" between conflicting interests (9). Jorg Nagler covers similar interpretive terrain in "Loyalty and Dissent: The Home Front in the American Civil War," in *On the Road to Total War: The American Civil War and the German Wars of Unification, 1861–1871*, edited by Stig Forster and Jorg Nagler, 329–56 (New York: Cambridge University Press, 2002).

7. The literature on Democratic dissent is sizeable. Scholars had largely adopted the position of "Copperhead" disloyalty until the revisionism of Frank L. Klement. His most influential work was *The Copperheads in the Middle West* (Chicago: University of Chicago Press, 1960). A complete bibliography of his many publications including a reprint of some of his most salient essays and chapters can be found in *Lincoln's Critics: The Copperheads of the North* (Shippensburg, Pa.: White Mane Books, 1999). Klement offered a sympathetic portrait (some label him an apologist) that attempted to place Democratic dissent in a social, political, and economic context. A number of studies approached this subject along similar lines, many focusing on the Midwest. Kenneth M. Stampp, *Indiana Politics during the Civil War* (Indianapolis: Indiana Historical Bureau, 1949); Richard Orr Curry, *A House Divided: A Study of Statehood Politics and the Copperhead Movement in West Virginia* (Pittsburgh: University of Pittsburgh Press, 1964); David L. Lendt, *Demise of the Democracy: The Copperhead Press in Iowa, 1856–1870* (Ames: Iowa State University Press, 1973); G. R. Tredway, *Democratic Opposition to the Lincoln Administration in Indiana* (Indianapolis: Indiana Historical Bureau, 1973); Hubert H. Wubben, *Civil War Iowa and the Copperhead Movement* (Ames: Iowa State University Press, 1980); Arnold M. Shankman, *The Pennsylvania Antiwar Movement, 1861–1865* (Cranbury, N.J.: Associated University Presses, 1980); Joanna D. Cowden, *"Heaven Will Frown on Such a Cause as This": Six Democrats Who Opposed Lincoln's War* (Lanham, Md.: University Press of America, 2001). Recent scholarship has challenged Klement's revisionism, reasserting the views of Democratic disloyalty held by wartime Republicans. Jennifer L. Weber led the way in condemning both Klement and the "copperhead" threat to the war effort in *Copperheads: The Rise and Fall of Lincoln's Opponents in the North* (New York: Oxford University Press, 2006). More recently Stephen E. Towne has echoed the potential for danger in *Surveillance and Spies in the Civil War: Exposing Confederate Conspiracies in America's Heartland* (Athens: Ohio University Press, 2014). Two indispensable works that examine the Democratic Party during the war are Joel H. Silbey, *A Respectable Minority: The Democratic Party in the Civil War Era, 1860–1868* (New York: Norton, 1977) and Jean H. Baker, *Affairs of Party: Political Culture of Northern Democrats in the Mid-Nineteenth Century* (Ithaca: Cornell University Press, 1983).

8. Two recent works written broadly on the subject of loyalty are: Simon Keller, *The Limits of Loyalty* (New York: Cambridge University Press, 2007); and James Connor, *The Sociology of Loyalty* (New York: Springer, 2007).

9. Lawson, *Patriot Fires*, 2.

10. J. Matthew Gallman's *Defining Duty in the Civil War* addressed this public discourse on loyalty in Northern print culture. He looked carefully at Northern popular literature for its messages on the proper roles of citizens during war. While addressing a number of themes, the one most relevant to this study is the discussion of enlistment and the draft. Scholars of nationalism stress that male obligations for military service are a key component of modern nationalist ideology. In contrast, Gallman found that

Northern men were expected to weigh carefully whether they could or should enlist in light of their own circumstances. Once considered, however, there was no apparent inescapable stigma for men who did not enlist. Once the draft was instituted, they were likewise expected to submit themselves manfully to the chances inherent in the system. But it was not unpatriotic to avail of commutation or substitution to avoid military service. In sum, this is a very different conception of military duty and obligation than modern nationalist thought. It is also a primary observation of Gallman's that Americans in 1860 had no experience to draw on "dictating how they should behave" (3). *Defining Duty in the Civil War: Personal Choice, Popular Culture, and the Union Home Front* (Chapel Hill: University of North Carolina Press, 2015).

11. The most comprehensive historiographical overview of this subject is Gary W. Gallagher, "Disaffection, Persistence, and Nation: Some Directions in Recent Scholarship on the Confederacy," *Civil War History* 55, no. 3 (September 2009): 329–53.

12. Gallagher identifies two waves of scholarship that established this narrative. The first was produced from the mid-1920s through the mid-1940s. A second appeared in the 1970s and 80s, "spurred in part by the new social history's emphasis on people outside the traditional power structure." Gallagher, "Disaffection, Persistence, and Nation," 333–34. Among recent works, the most significant are: Paul D. Escott, *After Secession: Jefferson Davis and the Failure of Confederate Nationalism* (Baton Rouge: Louisiana State University Press, 1978); Thomas G. Dyer, *Secret Yankees: The Union Circle in Confederate Atlanta* (Baltimore: Johns Hopkins University Press, 1999); William W. Freehling, *The South Vs. The South: How Anti-Confederate Southerners Shaped the Course of the Civil War* (New York: Oxford University Press, 2001); Victoria E. Bynum, *The Free State of Jones: Mississippi's Longest Civil War* (Chapel Hill: University of North Carolina Press, 2001); Margaret M. Storey, *Loyalty and Loss: Alabama's Unionists in the Civil War and Reconstruction* (Baton Rouge: Louisiana State University Press, 2004); Mark A. Weitz, *More Damning than Slaughter: Desertion in the Confederate Army* (Lincoln: University of Nebraska Press, 2005); David Williams, *Bitterly Divided: The South's Inner Civil War* (New York: Free Press, 2008); Michael D. Pierson, *Mutiny at Fort Jackson: The Untold Story of the Fall of New Orleans* (Chapel Hill: University of North Carolina Press, 2008).

13. As Gallagher writes: "discovering such stresses in Confederate society is roughly equivalent to finding sand on a beach. Every society in every place at every time manifests class friction. The interesting question is not whether it exists, but whether it shapes events decisively." Gallagher, "Disaffection, Persistence, and Nation," 340.

14. Gallagher encouraged historians to move beyond rigid examinations of national identity or lack thereof: "The time also has come to move beyond a binary approach to questions of disaffection, commitment to the nascent nation, and the like" (Gallagher, "Disaffection, Persistence, and Nation," 352). Gallagher's *The Confederate War* (Cambridge: Harvard University Press, 1997) became a clarion call in rejecting the "internal conflict" interpretation. A number of case studies echoed his main contentions: William Blair, *Virginia's Private War: Feeding Body and Soul in the Confederacy, 1861–1865* (New York: Oxford University Press, 1998); Robert E. Bonner, *Colors and Blood: Flag Passions of the Confederate South* (Princeton: Princeton University Press, 2002); Jacqueline Glass Campbell, *When Sherman Marched North from the Sea: Resistance on the Confederate Home Front* (Chapel Hill: University of North Carolina Press, 2003); Mark V.

Wetherington, *Plain Folks' Fight: The Civil War and Reconstruction in Piney Woods Georgia* (Chapel Hill: University of North Carolina Press, 2005); Anne S. Rubin, *A Shattered Nation: The Rise and Fall of the Confederacy, 1861–1868* (Chapel Hill: University of North Carolina Press, 2005); Peter S. Carmichael, *The Last Generation: Young Virginians in Peace, War, and Reunion* (Chapel Hill: University of North Carolina Press, 2005); Aaron Sheehan-Dean, *Why Confederates Fought: Family and Nation in Civil War Virginia* (Chapel Hill: University of North Carolina Press, 2007); Jason Phillips, *Diehard Rebels: The Confederate Culture of Invincibility* (Athens: University of Georgia Press, 2007); Joseph T. Glatthaar, *General Lee's Army: From Victory to Collapse* (New York: Free Press, 2008); Andrew F. Lang, "'Upon the Altar of Our Country': Confederate Identity, Nationalism, and Morale in Harrison County, Texas, 1860–1865," *Civil War History* 55, no. 2 (June 2009): 278–306; Michael T. Bernath, *Confederate Minds: The Struggle for Intellectual Independence in the Civil War South* (Chapel Hill: University of North Carolina Press, 2010); and Bradley R. Clampitt, *The Confederate Heartland: Military and Civilian Morale in the Western Confederacy* (Baton Rouge: Louisiana State University Press, 2011).

15. Paul Quigley's *Shifting Grounds: Nationalism and the American South, 1848–1865* (New York: Oxford University Press, 2012) cautions against accepting the view "that nationalism is the supreme form of legal allegiance and cultural identity in the modern world, and that because it is supreme it is unitary and indivisible" (5).

16. Amy Murrel Taylor's *The Divided Family in Civil War America* (Chapel Hill: University of North Carolina Press, 2005) examined the complex interplay between national and family loyalties in the border-South. It emphasized the permeable boundaries between public and private life—between home front and battle front. Taylor argued that the war which divided families and nation not only "revealed the failure of the American people to generate a common bond of national unity" but also "marked the failure of family" (9). Family loyalty had a complicated relationship to national loyalty, sometimes reinforcing and sometimes undermining it. Regardless, Taylor asserted that "the family figured prominently in their thinking about Civil War loyalty by absorbing, translating, and making understandable the divisions of the nation" (10).

17. There are a number of works on the Confederate home front that examine these peripheral regions and the complicated impacts of Union occupation. For a stimulating discussion of how Union provost marshals enforced loyalty in the Confederacy, read "The Domestic is the Public: The Occupied South" in William A. Blair, *With Malice Towards Some: Treason and Loyalty in the Civil War Era* (Chapel Hill: University of North Carolina Press, 2014): 128–59. Jarret Ruminski approached the subject of loyalty through a focus on illegal trade with the enemy in Mississippi in "'Tradyville': The Contraband Trade and the Problem of Loyalty in Civil War Mississippi," *Journal of the Civil War Era* 2, no. 4 (December 2012): 511–37. Ruminski argues that the "fluctuating hierarchy of human fidelities ensures that there is no firm connection between loyalty and identity, because no single fealty can have total influence over a person's actions. In light of circumstances, an individual can and will act on one particular loyalty without abandoning other ones" (515). Other examples include Jonathon Dean Sarris, *A Separate Civil War: Communities in Conflict in the Mountain South* (Charlottesville: University of Virginia Press, 2006); Barton A. Myers, *Executing Daniel Bright: Race, Loyalty, and*

Guerrilla Violence in a Coastal Carolina Community, 1861–1865 (Baton Rouge: Louisiana State University Press, 2009); Judkin Browning, *Shifting Loyalties: The Union Occupation of Eastern North Carolina* (Chapel Hill: University of North Carolina Press, 2011); and Aaron Astor, *Rebels on The Border: Civil War, Emancipation, and the Reconstruction of Kentucky and Missouri* (Baton Rouge: Louisiana State University Press, 2012); Stephen A. West, *From Yeoman to Redneck in the South Carolina Upcountry, 1850–1915* (Charlottesville: University of Virginia Press, 2008).

18. Robert Tracy McKenzie emphasized this point in his study of wartime Knoxville, Tennessee. Knoxville is fertile ground for study because it was militarily significant and a region of deeply divided Union and Confederate loyalties. It was also unlike many Southern communities because it was always militarily occupied by someone's enemy, first by Confederate forces and then Federal ones. McKenzie looked closely at the "moral dilemma"—how this constant pressure and observation by neighbors and soldiers affected behaviors. "What would it mean to remain faithful to their convictions," asked McKenzie, "in a town now controlled by the enemy?" (175). *Lincolnites and Rebels: A Divided Town in the American Civil War* (New York: Oxford University Press, 2006).

19. Almost as an afterthought, David M. Potter suggested that the continued working of the two-party system was a Union advantage: "Jefferson Davis and the Political Factors in Confederate Defeat," in David H. Donald, ed., *Why the North Won the Civil War* (Baton Rouge: Louisiana State University Press, 1960), 91–112. Eric McKitrick expanded on the theme: "Party Politics and the Union and Confederate War Efforts," in William Nisbet Chambers and Walter Dean Burnham, eds., *The American Party Systems: Stages of Political Development* (New York: Oxford University Press, 1967), 117–51. Mark E. Neely, Jr., rejects this Potter/McKitrick thesis and has argued forcefully for the deleterious effect of the rancorous party system in *The Union Divided: Party Conflict in the Civil War North* (Cambridge: Harvard University Press, 2002).

20. The two most significant studies of the wartime North are Phillip Shaw Paludan, *A People's Contest: The Union and Civil War, 1861–1865* (New York: Harper and Row, 1988); and J. Matthew Gallman, *The North Fights the Civil War: The Home Front* (New York: Ivan R. Dee, 1994).

21. See especially Mark E. Neely, Jr., *The Fate of Liberty: Abraham Lincoln and Civil Liberties* (New York: Oxford University Press, 1992); and Jonathan W. White, *Abraham Lincoln and Treason in the Civil War: The Trials of John Merryman* (Baton Rouge: Louisiana State University Press, 2011). William A. Blair, *With Malice Towards Some: Treason and Loyalty in the Civil War Era*, also deals at length with the ways in which the federal government enforced loyalty on the home front in frequently heavy-handed ways. See especially his treatment of government interference in elections in Chapters 6 and 7 (160–233). This is also a major theme of Jonathan W. White, *Emancipation, the Union Army, and the Reelection of Abraham Lincoln* (Baton Rouge: Louisiana State University Press, 2014).

22. On the subject of the Northern draft, consult Eugene C. Murdock, *One Million Men: The Civil War Draft in the North* (Madison: State Historical Society of Wisconsin, 1971) and James W. Geary, *We Need Men: The Union Draft in the Civil War* (DeKalb: Northern Illinois University Press, 1991). Geary has an excellent historiographical

overview; James W. Geary, "Civil War Conscription in the North: A Historiographical Review," *Civil War History* 32, no. 3 (September 1986): 208–28. The New York City draft riots are most ably interpreted by Iver Bernstein, *The New York City Draft Riots: Their Significance for American Society and Politics in the Age of the Civil War* (New York: Oxford University Press, 1990). See also Adrian Cook's excellent *The Armies of the Streets: The New York City Draft Riots of 1863* (Lexington: University Press of Kentucky, 1982). The subject of draft resistance elsewhere is often yoked to studies of Democratic dissent. One of the most thorough (yet oddly unpublished) studies is Robert E. Sterling's dissertation, "Civil War Draft Resistance in the Middle West" (Northern Illinois University, 1974). My own work encompasses draft resistance outside of the Midwest. Robert M. Sandow, *Deserter Country: Civil War Opposition in the Pennsylvania Appalachians* (New York: Fordham University Press, 2009). For a stimulating but general reflection read Peter Levine, "Draft Evasion in the North during the Civil War, 1863–1865," *Journal of American History* 67, no. 4 (March 1981): 816–34.

23. The best model for studying the urban North is J. Matthew Gallman, *Mastering Wartime: A Social History of Philadelphia during the Civil War* (New York: Cambridge University Press, 1990). Other works in the genre include Thomas H. O'Connor, *Civil War Boston: Home Front and Battlefield* (Boston: Northeastern University Press, 1997); Edward K. Spann, *Gotham at War: New York City, 1860–1865* (Wilmington, Del.: Scholarly Resources, 2002); Theodore J. Karamanski, *Rally 'round the Flag: Chicago and the Civil War* (Lanham, Md.: Rowman and Littlefield, 2006); and Earl F. Mulderink, III, *New Bedford's Civil War* (New York: Fordham University Press, 2012). Two essays that summarize the state of the field are J. Matthew Gallman, "Urban History and the American Civil War," in *Northerners at War: Reflections on the Civil War Home Front* (Kent, Ohio: Kent State University Press, 2010): 73–86; and Robert M. Sandow, "Northern Home Front" in *A Companion to the U.S. Civil War*, 2 vols., edited by Aaron Sheehan-Dean, 891–908 (Malden, Mass.: Wiley Blackwell, 2014).

24. Pertinent examples of edited collections include: Joan E. Cashin, ed., *The War Was You and Me: Civilians in the American Civil War* (Princeton: Princeton University Press, 2002); Ginette Aley and J. L. Anderson, eds., *Union Heartland: The Midwestern Home Front during the Civil War* (Carbondale: Southern Illinois University Press, 2013); Paul A. Cimbala and Randall M. Miller, eds., *Union Soldiers and the Northern Home Front: Wartime Experiences and Postwar Adjustments* (New York: Fordham University Press, 2002); Paul A. Cimbala and Randall M. Miller, eds., *An Uncommon Time: The Civil War and the Northern Home Front* (New York: Fordham University Press, 2002); Lorien Foote and Kanisorn Wongsrichanalai, *So Conceived and So Dedicated: Intellectual Life in the Civil War–Era North* (New York: Fordham University Press, 2015); and Andrew L. Slap and Michael Thomas Smith, eds., *This Distracted and Anarchical People: New Answers for Old Questions about the Civil War-Era North* (New York: Fordham University Press, 2013).

25. Two examples of border-North studies focus on Indiana and highlight community divisions in rural areas. Richard F. Nation, *At Homes in the Hoosier Hills: Agriculture, Politics, and Religion in Southern Indiana, 1810–1870* (Bloomington: Indiana University Press, 2005); Nicole Etcheson, *A Generation at War: The Civil War Era in a Northern Community* (Lawrence: University Press of Kansas, 2011).

26. A number of authors examine the complicated relationship between ethnic and national loyalties frequently in connection to military service. An excellent starting place is Susannah J. Ural, *Civil War Citizens: Race, Ethnicity, and Identity in America's Bloodiest Conflict* (New York: New York University Press, 2010). Christian B. Keller, *Chancellorsville and the Germans: Nativism, Ethnicity, and Memory* (New York: Fordham University Press, 2007) researched the subject of Germans and assimilation. In a related vein, James O. Lehman and Steven M. Nolt, *Mennonites, Amish, and the American Civil War* (Baltimore: Johns Hopkins University Press, 2007) looked at pacifist German sects. Soldiers of Irish descent are the focus of Susannah Ural Bruce, *The Harp and the Eagle: Irish-American Volunteers and the Union Army, 1861–1865* (New York: New York University Press, 2006). Multiple ethnic communities are considered in William L. Burton, *Melting Pot Soldiers: The Union's Ethnic Regiments* (Ames: Iowa State University Press, 1988).

27. Grace Palladino examined the turbulent experiences of predominantly immigrant Irish coal miners in Pennsylvania during the war. *Another Civil War: Labor, Capital, and the State in the Anthracite Region* (Champaign: University of Illinois Press, 1990). Russell Johnson explored the links between economics, class-consciousness, and military service in *Warriors into Workers: The Civil War and the Formation of Urban-Industrial Society in a Northern City* (New York: Fordham University Press, 2003).

28. Gary W. Gallagher, *The Union War* (Cambridge: Harvard University Press, 2011). For more on the ideological strength of the Union cause, consult: Reid Mitchell, *Civil War Soldiers* (New York: Viking, 1988); Earl J. Hess, *Liberty, Virtue, and Progress: Northerners and Their War for the Union* (New York: New York University Press, 1988); and James M. McPherson, *For Cause and Comrades: Why Men Fought in the Civil War* (New York: Oxford University Press, 1997).

29. White's focus on definitions of loyalty in compensation cases addresses a subject largely ignored by scholars. One important but dated work related to this is Harold M. Hyman, *Era of the Oath: Northern Loyalty Tests during the Civil War and Reconstruction* (Philadelphia: University of Pennsylvania Press, 1954).

30. Harry S. Stout, *Upon the Altar of the Nation: A Moral History of the Civil War* (New York: Viking, 2006), xvii.

"Dedicated to the Proposition"

Principle, Consequence, and Duty to the Egalitarian Nation, 1848–1865

Melinda Lawson

On September 25, 1850, six days after President Millard Fillmore signed the last provision of the Compromise of 1850 into law, Congressman George Julian reflected on the debates that had surrounded the legislation. Like many of his fellow anti-slavery congressmen, Julian had opposed the measure, facing condemnation from critics who charged that the reckless refusal to compromise would tear the Union apart. Now, in a speech delivered on the floor of Congress, he addressed those charges and spoke more generally to issues of principle, consequence, and duty.[1]

Would the rejection of the Texas Boundary Act have threatened the destruction of the Union, as his critics alleged? Julian expressed his doubts, then added "for ought I know, the *passage* of the bill may be attended with the same ultimate results . . ."[2] No one, he insisted, could know the answer with any certainty:

> The question of duty and the consequence resulting from its performance, are often entirely distinct; the former may be perfectly clear, whilst the latter may be impalpable or unknown. But the moral sense of every man, if not perverted, will tell him plainly that slavery is an outrage upon humanity, and a crime against God; and that he cannot justify himself in fastening it upon his fellow man, in the hope of thereby averting a greater evil . . . we are never justified in perpetrating an evil deed on the grounds that the end will sanctify the means.[3]

As to the charge that the refusal to compromise was a radical stance that would lead the nation into war, more than ten years before the election of an anti-slavery moderate did just that, Julian contemplated the possibility: "I stand opposed to the war spirit," he admitted, but

I will not deny that I think war sometimes necessary. I must say, too, that I believe there are things more to be dreaded. The betrayal of sacred trusts is worse
than war; shrinking from a just responsibility, when necessary to encounter, is
worse than war; the extension of slavery by the federal government, and with
the approval of the nation, I would pronounce worse than war.[4]

Weighing the comparative merits of compromise and conviction, Julian considered the unknowable nature of consequence and the compelling moral cause for
which he fought—one that might, in the end, engender war.

For Julian, the answer was clear. But the dilemma itself was one shared by patriots across the antebellum and wartime North. The Union meant many things
to many people, but for those who were truly invested in the Declaration's proposition of liberty and equality, the challenge was substantial: how best to serve
a nation founded on ideals of liberty and equality, yet held together by an acceptance of slavery? What was a true patriot's duty to this nation, and what role
should a consideration of consequence play?

This essay examines the way three men, each dedicated to the Declaration's
proposition of liberty and equality, grappled with these questions. Wendell
Phillips, George Julian, and Abraham Lincoln occupied different and, at times,
oppositional posts during the war, but each believed in a uniquely American
commitment to freedom and equality, and all three felt strongly that loyalty to
the nation was tied to the preservation and promotion of those ideals. In the end,
each man negotiated his own understanding of patriotism through the framework of duty.

Historians rarely write about duty as a political concept in the antebellum
era, but this study suggests that it played an important part in the way at least
some Americans negotiated their patriotic behavior. While today the notion of
duty has a fairly narrow usage, most frequently associated with military service
or familial responsibility, for much of American history it served as a broader
governing concept. For Puritans, duty was to be found in God's revealed will or
in His works—"by the contemplation of nature." But one need not have been a
Puritan to feel the power of duty: As John Rawls explains, by the seventeenth
century, the concept was "widely understood . . . as resting on the idea of natural
law, or divine law." Thus, Jonathan Edwards and Benjamin Franklin could agree,
writes historian Daniel Walker Howe, that "there was such a thing as natural
morality, discoverable by human reason." Fulfilling one's duty as determined by
this morality was a driving force in colonial New England; notions of duty and
its centrality to moral and political action could also be found in Scottish moral

philosophy, republicanism, and understandings of gender. Though by the mid-nineteenth century the ethic of individualism was overshadowing the notion of duty, duty continued to play an important role in American culture. Writing about Civil War soldiers, historian James McPherson notes, "the consciousness of duty was pervasive in Victorian America."[5]

Indeed, as this essay will illustrate, duty played a central role in the conceptions of loyalty set forward by the three figures in this study. Their understanding of duty was very different from the kind of unquestioning deference to an organic state that George Frederickson discovered in his study of Northern intellectuals in the Civil War. Far from a mandate for blind obedience, for Phillips, Julian, and Lincoln, duty demanded thoughtful evaluation and analysis: it suggested a discernable obligation rooted in a discoverable moral order—an obligation that was specific to one's position, and once identified, required action.[6]

Examining these three leaders' understanding of patriotism through the lens of duty contributes to our understanding of loyalty in the Civil War era in another sense. Historians have long debated the role that abolitionists played in the coming of the war, with some interpretations opposing Lincoln's prudential concern for consequences to the heedless zealotry of abolitionists and Radical Republicans. These scholars have elevated Lincoln for his restraint while disparaging those anti-slavery leaders who recklessly refused to compromise. In this view, Lincoln becomes a model of true patriotism, while abolitionists and Radicals stand as cautionary figures whose imprudence jeopardized the nation.[7] This essay suggests more commonality between the three leaders amid their differences. As each man set out to decipher his patriotic duty, he weighed principle and outcome, established a point at which he must be steadfast in conviction, and contemplated the unknowable nature of consequences. Occupying different posts, each arrived at a distinct but authentic form of patriotism. Considered together, they speak to the multiple forms that patriotism can assume, even in times of war.[8]

Wendell Phillips

For Wendell Phillips, the abolitionists' most prominent wartime orator, America had a very specific meaning: It was a celebration of the equality of humankind and its right to shape its own destiny.[9] Phillips's America had as its sheet anchor the Declaration of Independence, for "the spirit of '76, was the full liberty of each and every human being." American nationality, as he understood it, comprised the "treading under foot sex and race, caste and condition, and collecting . . .

under the shelter of noble, just, and equal laws, all races, all customs, all religions, all languages, all literature, and all ideas." It was not just America's claims of inclusiveness and equality that led Phillips to embrace his national heritage, but its commitment to the self-rule of its citizens: "American civilization" was but a "second part . . . of that same sublime confidence in the public conscience . . . which made the groundwork of Grecian democracy." Phillips celebrated "the great American idea of the omnipotence of thinking men."[10]

Loyal as he was to the ideals contained in the Declaration, for Phillips, the founders had betrayed the American promise with their Constitutional compromise with slavery. The Union, he argued, echoing the refrain made infamous by William Lloyd Garrison, had become a "covenant with death and agreement with hell."[11] The American proposition, though, lived on: "Our Revolution earned us only *independence*. Whatever our fathers meant, the chief lesson of that hour was that America belongs to Americans." In the years since the Revolution, this democratic principle had flowered, "crumbling classes into men." Its ultimate expression—one that embraced all persons regardless of race—was yet to be realized.[12]

It was this understanding of the nation that informed Phillip's definition of patriotism—a definition that was negotiated through the concept of duty. Raised in a Calvinist household, Phillips absorbed the lessons of his parents' faith. His mother urged him always to "Be good and do good . . . add other things if you may—these are central."[13] As historian James Brewer Stewart explains, at home Phillips learned that "family and faith . . . should compel an unswerving devotion to a fixed internalized code of truth and to the obligation to serve others with distinction." Even as a youth, Phillips recognized the challenges therein: in a Latin School essay he offered counsel for those hoping to follow "the perilous path of duty."[14]

As an adult, Phillips found inspiration for following that path in Calvinism: The lesson the Puritans had taught the world, he argued, was "not thought, but ACTION." In an age where "men, who called themselves thinkers, had been creeping along the Mediterranean . . . in their timidity" the Pilgrims had defied laws, and "launched boldly out into the Atlantic, and trusted God." As they faced national crises of their own, Phillips called on Americans to be the "Winthrops of today"—to lead lives "whose polar star is Duty, whose goal is Liberty, and whose staff is Justice."[15]

Phillips's understanding of duty was informed by his Calvinist upbringing; it was also shaped by republican notions of vigilant citizenship. Given the tendency of power to corruption, it was a citizen's duty to hold that power accountable. "Eternal vigilance is the price of liberty," he reminded his listeners. For abolition-

ists, the path was clear: "Now the duty of each anti-slavery man is simply this,—
Stand on the pedestal of your own individual independence, summon these institutions about you, and judge them."[16]

Moreover, in an electoral democracy such as the United States—a country
where, as he emphasized, there was "no law that can abide one moment when
popular opinion demands its abrogation"—duty assumed another form, particularly for the educated elite. As he would later counsel Harvard Phi Beta Kappa
scholars, the educated class failed in their "republican duty" if they left others
to "lead in the agitation of the great social questions which stir and educate the
age . . . in all modern constitutional governments, agitation is the only peaceful method of progress." As a privileged member of the Brahmin elite, Phillips
believed that duty was specific to position: "Where, then, is my place under a
republican government which only reflects and executes public opinion?" Phillips asked in 1852. "Where, then, is my post? I must educate, arouse, and mature
a public opinion." Such agitation served both conscience and country: It was,
Phillips argued, "the only thing which justifies us to our own consciences and
makes us able to say we have done, or at least tried to do, our duty." It constituted
patriotism in its highest form, for "out of this agitation . . . the future character of
the American government will be formed."[17]

But Phillips recognized that a powerful historical tradition circumscribed
Americans' ability to think clearly about the hard moral truths that underlay this
agitation. Americans "defiled their consciences" not so much in fear or favor to
their superiors, but rather in unthinking deference to the fathers. They looked
to the founders in awe and felt their inferiority. Obsessed with discovering the
founders' thoughts or intentions on any given subject, they were unable to examine issues objectively. Phillips thus lectured Americans on the need to look beyond the writings and deeds of the fathers, to the principles for which they stood
and the implications that those principles had for the present. As he told an audience in a speech on the Pilgrims delivered in December 1855, "The Pilgrims of
1620 would be, in 1855, not in Plymouth, but in Kansas." Thus Phillips defined an
ethical, critical, activist patriotism, rooted in conscience and dedicated to pushing America to live up to the ideals of the Declaration.[18]

And what of the consequences of Phillips' activist patriotism? On one level,
it was a patriotism that required, as Phillips wrote to British abolitionist George
Thompson, "hearts . . . that look to duty and not to consequences." In 1851, in a
speech on women's suffrage, Phillips perfectly laid out the argument for ignoring
consequences and leaving the result to God—the argument that so frustrated
politicians at the time and has served since as a foil for the wisdom of Lincoln.

"The broadest and most far sighted intellect is utterly unable to foresee the ultimate consequences of any great social change," he argued. ". . . if there be any
element of right or wrong in the question, any question of clear natural justice
which turns the scale . . . take your part with the perfect and abstract right, and
trust God to see that it shall prove the expedient."[19]

But such rhetoric—designed to encourage listeners to stake out their convictions and resist dissuasion—did not mean that Phillips ignored the impact of his
movement's actions. Time and again, he made decisions, and urged his listeners
to make decisions, that considered consequences to the fate of the American
proposition. When, in response to the Fugitive Slave Act, slave catchers headed
north to kidnap the enslaved men and women who had escaped the South, abolitionists considered counseling fugitives against leaving their country for the
safety of Canada. Why should innocent men and women have to flee the land
that was their home? If, as the founders themselves had argued, resistance to
tyranny was obedience to God, shouldn't the fugitives stay and fight? But for
Phillips, the time was not ready—if captured, the fugitive would be returned to
slavery. The public opinion that would support them and promote the cause of
freedom had not yet ripened. As he explained in an 1852 speech, it was the duty
of abolitionists to counsel slaves considering these questions that

> "There is no safety for you here; there is no law for you here. The hearts of the
> judges are stone, the hearts of the people are stone. It is in vain that you ap-
> peal to abolitionists. They may be ready, may be able, ten years hence." But the
> "Brace of Adamses" . . . if they had mistaken 1765 for 1775, would have ended
> at the scaffold instead of the Declaration of Independence and the treaty of
> 1783. We must bide our time; we must read, with anointed eyes, the signs of
> the time. If public opinion is wrong, we want to know it; know it, that we may
> remodel it.[20]

Striving to mold the public opinion that would ultimately save the American
proposition, Phillips considered the impact of efforts to this end carefully. "In
critical times, when a wrong step entails most disastrous consequences, to 'mean
well' is not enough."[21]

Still, it was not the Union as nineteenth-century Americans knew it that Phillips set out to save. In the years leading up to the Civil War, his emphatic embrace
of the American egalitarian proposition—as opposed to the Union per se—left
him far outside the mainstream patriotic discourse. If the founders had betrayed
the American promise, then any support of the Union perpetuated that betrayal:

"whoever strengthens the American Union strengthens the chain of the American slave." Phillips did not, in condemning the pro-slavery Constitution and the slave-holding Union it had engendered, view himself as any less of an American. "Seeing that all men were born equal, our first civil duty is to see that our laws treat them so," he insisted. "We are seeking the best way to get rid of a great national evil." Political anti-slavery within the context of loyalty to the constitution was misguided. "What a wreck of a noble nation the American republic is to be for fifty years! And why? Only to save a piece of parchment." Disunion, on the other hand, would result in an immediately virtuous North and within short order, cripple the Southern Slave power: "Soon, throughout all America there shall be neither power nor wish to hold a slave." For Phillips, ironic though it might appear, it was disunion alone that would redeem the national promise.[22]

Phillips understood that championing disunion would not be popular, even among those opposed to slavery. When he cursed the Constitution, he understood it would not enhance the abolitionists' popularity or enlarge their following. But such agitation was designed to have consequences: It would shock a complacent, unmindful America into thinking deeply about slavery. Indeed, a review of twenty years of abolitionist agitation suggested that it had done just that: Slavery, once barred as a topic from the halls of Congress, had entered the political discourse of the nation. "If our agitation has not been wisely planned and conducted," he assured his fellow abolitionists, "explain for us the history of the last twenty years! Experience is a safe light to walk by, and he is not a rash man who expects success in (the) future from the same means which have secured it in times past." As an agitator, it was Phillips's duty to hold American leaders accountable and mold the public opinion that would lead the nation to realize its democratic promise. He bemoaned the spread of anti-slavery politics, which he believed represented "some short act, some royal way to heaven, something else than plain, hard, duty."[23]

Throughout the antebellum years, Phillips continued to advocate disunion as the only viable approach to the fulfillment of the American proposition. But popular reaction to the attack on Fort Sumter took Phillips by surprise, and he began to consider the possibility that the war might accomplish what thirty years of abolitionist agitation had not. On April 21, 1861, four thousand people crowded into Boston's spacious Music Hall, anxious to hear what the nation's leading abolitionist had to say about the newly proclaimed war for the Union.[24]

Within minutes of speaking, Phillips made it clear that he now embraced the Union's cause. ". . . (For) the first time in my anti-slavery life," he proclaimed, "I speak under the stars and stripes . . . No matter what the past has been or said;

to-day the slave asks God for a sight of this banner, and counts it the pledge of his redemption." The declaration of war and the outpouring of support in the North had convinced Phillips that, though "hitherto (the Union) may have meant what you thought, or what I did; to-day, it represents sovereignty and justice." Abandoning disunion, Phillips yoked his dreams for the American proposition to the war and the national state.[25]

Still, Phillips maintained his insistence that loyalty to this newly egalitarian Union should be expressed not through acquiescence, but in active, vigorous terms. He reminded his listeners that precedents for this understanding of loyalty lay in classical history: "Every public meeting in Athens was opened with a curse on anyone who should not speak what he really thought." In Egypt, it was believed that souls were required to utter the following oath before admission into heaven: "I have never defiled my conscience from fear or favor to my superiors." For the first year and a half of the war, Phillips maintained this stance: "If I am to love my country," he told a crowd in December of 1861, "it must be loveable; if I am to honor it, it must be worthy of respect." It was the duty of citizens truly committed to a republican system of self-government to critically examine government policy and to express their opinions, no matter how unpopular. "Such criticism is always every thinking man's duty" he argued. "War excuses no man from this duty." Expressing a patriotism rooted in the republican assertion of conscience, Phillips urged his listeners to show tolerance toward those who disagreed with them. "No mobs . . . to silence those whom events have not converted . . . We are strong enough to tolerate dissent."[26]

But the principle toward which Phillips labored was the American promise of freedom and equality, and not all expressions of individual conscience worked to further that end. Though he initially cautioned against suppressing discontent, as the war continued and the Union's relationship to the American proposition changed, his charge to the nation's patriots changed as well. "Waste no time in showing that you are right" Phillips told his fellow believers at Boston's Music Hall two months after Lincoln issued the Preliminary Emancipation Proclamation. "Take it for granted. We are the Constitution and the patriots, everything else is treason."[27] The final Proclamation fortified this new approach. If the nation truly meant justice, and if the assertions of the war protesters threatened the fulfillment of that meaning, the prerogatives of the nation might be said to override those of an assertive citizenry.

Thus, when the administration's detractors challenged the constitutionality of the expanding national state, Phillips urged Americans to show their patriotism not through the assertion of conscience but by respecting the authority of the emerging nation-state. In this age of nation-building, Phillips told his audience that the war was "the momentous struggle of a great nation for existence and perpetuity." When, in August 1862, Lincoln suspended the writ of habeas corpus, an act that would allow the arrest and detention of war protestors, Phillips endorsed his actions. "It is necessary to do anything to save the ship," he asserted. "It is a mere question of whether you prefer the despotism of Washington or that of Richmond. I prefer Washington." "We are either a nation, or we are not," he argued in January 1863, two weeks after the Emancipation Proclamation. "If we are a nation . . . no parchment could bar us from the use of any power within our reach to save the nationality . . . . The nation knows no limits."[28]

But the changes Phillips hoped for were slow to come. In December 1863, Lincoln proposed a plan offering amnesty to any citizen of the Confederacy (some military and elected officials excluded) who swore future loyalty to the Constitution and agreed to obey all laws pertaining to the abolition of slavery. Once a mere 10 percent of any state's voting population took this oath, that state could organize a new state government. Phillips complained that this "Ten Percent Plan" made no provisions for enfranchising blacks, nor did it suggest that the government would do anything to ensure an "effectual" freedom—one that could "maintain and vindicate itself." For Phillips the plan made freedom for blacks a "sham"; it "perpetuat(ed) slavery under a softer name." Lincoln's pocket-veto of the abolitionist-supported alternative, the Wade-Davis bill, enraged Phillips, who seemed to be watching the nation he had hoped to build—a true embodiment of the American proposition—crumble before his eyes.[29]

Facing these setbacks to his hopes for an egalitarian nation, Phillips revived his notion of a conscience-based patriotic duty defined in active, vigorous terms. He became increasingly critical of Lincoln, campaigning against him in 1864. When his critics accused him of disloyalty, he defended himself in terms that made clear how far removed his understanding of loyalty was from that which his nation of "no limits" suggested:

remember Mr. President, we are American, not European. We live under the Constitution of the United States, not English or French rule; Any man . . . who raises today the war cry, "Stand by the Administration" and does not take into account that limitation . . . forfeits his franchise under the free institutions of the fathers, and binds his lips, like a vassal of the Czar, to a life-long allegiance . . . I am only a Constitutional American citizen . . . I have a right to say whether my interests shall be committed to this principle.[30]

Phillips unequivocally asserted his right to oppose the administration. In light of his commitment to the egalitarian proposition, he argued, anything but opposition was, in fact, disloyalty. He contrasted his own actions to those of Democratic war protesters on the grounds that he supported the war that was to create a nation true to the principles of the Declaration, while they opposed it.[31]

This, then, was the governing principle behind Phillips's definition of his patriotic duty: In his role as agitator he would work to shape public opinion and thereby promote the interest of the American proposition and its embrace of liberty and equality. Such uncompromising agitation was the finest expression of patriotism. As the war drew to a close, in December 1864, he underscored this point:

> In my nationality there is but one idea—the harmonizing and equal mingling of all races. . . I would leave no stone unturned until the ideas of Massachusetts kiss the gulf of Mexico . . . when that is accomplished, we shall be the strongest, noblest nation on earth, and every one of us will be proud to say, I am an American citizen.[32]

George Julian

Like Phillips, George Julian grew up in a devout household, absorbing lessons of faith and responsibility at an early age. His father died when he was six; his mother, an orthodox Quaker who struggled financially and raised six children on her own, read him the Bible at night and taught him that life's hardships were to be expected and overcome. As a young man Julian became troubled by many of the tenets of orthodox Quakerism, including original sin and the doctrine of grace. He discovered Unitarianism through the works of William Ellery Channing, reading all six volumes of his work.[33]

Channing embraced the doctrine of good works: His God was a benevolent God who created humanity as fundamentally good and capable of reason. It was thus the duty of man to use his reason to distinguish between good and evil, and then work for good. As Channing explained in a sermon on Unitarian Christianity, "We believe that all virtue has its foundation in the moral nature of man, that is, in conscience, or his sense of duty." Channing elaborated the point in an 1835 book titled *Slavery*: "Duty must be primary, prominent, most conspicuous among the objects of human thought and pursuit." Indeed, duty lay at the heart of a moral life: "No judgment can be just or wise, but that which is built on the conviction of the paramount worth and importance of duty. This is the fundamental truth, the supreme law of reason; and the mind which does not start from this, in its inquiries into human affairs, is doomed to great, perhaps fatal error."[34]

For Julian, who took to heart his mother's exhortations yet was burdened by the implications of orthodox Quakerism, Channing's approach was "like one coming out of a fearful darkness into the full light of day." His abhorrence of slavery along with his belief in the need to do good—his belief in duty—led this very serious and shy young man into reform politics. In 1849, he was elected to Congress as a Free Soil Democrat from Indiana.[35]

As a Congressman, Julian rooted his understanding of national loyalty in the egalitarian ideals espoused by the nation's founders. But if for Phillips, the founders' commitment to liberty and equality had been betrayed with the Constitution, for Julian, that commitment found clear expression elsewhere in the nation's founding documents. The founders had determined it necessary to compromise with the slave interest but had established "no more slave states, and no slave territory" as the doctrine of the Republic. Jefferson's 1774 "Review of the Rights of British America," the prohibition of slavery in the Northwest Territories, and the eschewal of the word itself in the Constitution made clear the founders' intentions for the ultimate demise of slavery. The nation's fathers, Julian argued, would have been astonished at the subsequent spread of the institution and the rise of an unapologetic slave power.[36]

Slavery was now deeply embedded in the nation. Thus, it was not individual action but politics that constituted the most powerful route to reform. Calling the belief that slavery could ever be ended through moral suasion alone a "mistake," he argued that political action was "the highest and most responsible form of moral action because it 'is that which, above all others, bears directly on the present and permanent welfare of the great masses of humanity.'" Americans needed to understand not just the *wrong* of slavery, but what they should do about it. "One may indignantly brand slavery as the sum of all villainies . . . and yet if the platform to which he subscribes teaches him that he has nothing to *do* with slavery . . . his words are but as sounding brass or a tinkling cymbal." Through politics, then, Julian sought to provide both an assessment of Americans' relationship to slavery and a constitutional strategy for bringing about its end.[37]

Together, that assessment and strategy would point the way toward duty. "We are taught by the great lights of the world," Julian explained, ". . . that doctrine goes before duty . . . we must first find out the truth, and then duty, or the practical service of truth, will result as its crowning flower and fruit. As a general proposition I subscribe to this, and I apply it to politics." Throughout his career, Julian set out to first "understand the true features of politics at this time in their various complications" in order to "thence determine the path of duty for the future."[38]

One of the hallmarks of politics, of course, was compromise. Clearly, the founders had compromised American ideals in the process of founding the nation. As a politician, Julian did not condemn nor did he challenge the enforcement of the founders' concessions to the slave South. Acknowledging the legitimacy of the state, accepting his duty as its officer, he disavowed any intention of interfering with slavery where it existed and acknowledged the South's constitutional right to retrieve escaped slaves under the *original* fugitive slave act.[39]

But for Julian, the founders had made their intentions for the *future* of slavery clear: "Not chains and stripes, but *freedom* was the dominant idea, the great thought of our founders . . . it was to be *tolerated* and *endured*, until measures could be taken for its final extirpation from the land." By the 1840s, the time to take those measures had arrived. As sectional tensions escalated, Julian insisted that not compromise, but a firm commitment to America's egalitarian principles was the only ethical course of action; it was also the truest form of patriotic duty. "It is impossible to escape this conclusion," he insisted, "without contradicting the truth of history, and branding the founders of the government as hypocrites, who, after having paraded the rights of man before the world, and achieved their own freedom, deliberately went to work to found an empire of slaves." Thus, it was the duty of American patriots committed to the principles of the American ideal to assert themselves: "If truth is incendiary, we shall still proclaim it; if our constitutional acts are firebrands, we shall nevertheless do our duty."[40]

At the heart of the issue—as it had been for Phillips—was the relationship of the Union to the American proposition. Julian was committed to the Union, not as an entity unto itself, but in its role as an instrument of liberty—a role he believed had been established by the nation's founders. "If we assure them that we love the Union," he told an Indiana crowd in 1857,

> let us not fail to inform them that we mean the Union contemplated by our fathers, with the chains of the slave falling from his limbs as the harbinger of "liberty throughout all the land, to all the inhabitants thereof," and that only by restoring their policy, and reanimating the people with the spirit of 1776, can these States be permanently held together.

Convinced that the Union as conceived by the founders represented freedom, Julian did not go the way of Phillips: He rejected disunion, holding out hope that the Union of the fathers could yet be realized. But he made clear that his attachment was, in the end, conditional. "I am for the Union, simply as a servant of liberty," he wrote Thomas Wentworth Higginson in 1857, "And I shall go for its dissolution the moment I become convinced that it can be preserved only through the perpetual enslavement of four millions of people and their descendants."[41]

But Julian and his fellow Radicals faced harsh condemnation from critics who charged that their unwavering commitment to egalitarian policies was ill-considered, irresponsible, and disloyal: Their refusal to compromise would tear the Union apart and might even lead the nation to war. In response to those charges, Julian turned the tables on his critics: The slaveholders' attacks on freedom and the conciliatory attitude of Northern politicians formed the real disloyalty, for these parties had abandoned the most fundamental principles of the republic: "He is not the friend, but the real enemy of the Union, who smil-ingly tells the slaveholders that all is well." Too often, Northerners acted out of fear—fear of upsetting the South, fear of rending political parties, fear of dis-union, fear of war—then cloaked these fears in patriotic garb. But real patriots kept their eyes on the prize. Thus Julian declared the Wilmot Proviso, which sought to ban slavery from the Mexican cession, a "peculiarly . . . American prin-ciple" to which "devotion . . . should be as honorable to an American citizen as his abandonment of it should be disgraceful." By turning their backs on such fun-damental American principles, the mainstream political parties of the 1840s and 1850s were "politically and for that very reason *morally* . . . guilty of . . . levying war against the institutions of their fathers."[42]

And what of the consequences of such unwavering conviction to the national ideal? Charged with promoting principle while ignoring the longer-term im-pact on the Union, Julian pointed out that duty and consequence were often distinct—one might clearly discern the former, while the latter could be impos-sible to predict. When his duty-driven decision to oppose the Compromise of 1850 came under attack from moderates fearful that such opposition would lead to war, in what could now be considered a strikingly prescient observation, Ju-lian noted that in the end, the *passage* of the Compromise might itself result in war. Moreover, such fears, he argued, appeared rooted in a refusal to consider the enormity of the moral wrong that was slavery—a wrong that might, in the end, *justify* war.[43]

Throughout the 1850s, Julian promoted the cause of anti-slavery politics, first as a member of the Free Soil Party, then as a Republican. But if for many mid-nineteenth-century Americans, party membership suggested a larger partisan identity or participation in a party culture, for Julian, such membership was solely a vehicle for the realization of a principle. In an 1855 speech on the state of political parties, he made this clear: Recognizing that the Democratic and Whig parties had both been formed for the achievement of "cherished doctrines" he argued that the parties had now "attempted to lengthen out their life beyond (their) appointed time. They have tried to live after the original source of their life was withdrawn." Held together by partisan ambition and reciprocal antagonisms, the parties' refusal to take a position on slavery—the most pressing issue of the day and one central to any understanding of the American ideal—rendered them obsolete. Julian looked forward to the day when Americans, "no longer blinded by the assumed necessity of choosing between two evils, shall march over their ruins to the ballot box with an eye single to the highest good of their country."[44]

The antislavery parties offered that alternative: In an address to his home state in 1857, he urged Indiana, which had catered to its moderate element and entered the Republican National Convention as the "People's Party," to pick up the Republican Banner: "Instead of deprecating radical measures, disavowing 'abolitionism,' and fulsomely parading our devotion to the Union, let us declare ourselves the unqualified foes of slavery." The defeat of these parties at the polls did little to discourage him: The "grand aim" of the Republican Party was not to win office, but to spread anti-slavery principles and promote anti-slavery policies: "If thus honestly fighting for our principles, we had yet failed at the ballot box, we should have been consoled by the consciousness of having done our duty." His message was consistent: in this nation founded on ideals of freedom and equality, slavery was inimical; thus loyalty to the nation required the active, constitutional pursuit of anti-slavery principles. The time for compromise was over.[45]

The Republicans' victory in the presidential election of 1860 marked a new phase in Julian's fight for the American proposition. To Julian, for whom the sole purpose of party was to advocate for principle, Lincoln's election on a Republican platform of non-extension represented a mandate for anti-slavery. "The triumph of the Republican party . . . was the triumph of freedom over slavery" he declared. Thus it was the duty of the administration to follow that mandate without compromise or conciliation. Visiting the new President in Springfield in 1861, Julian found Lincoln "more emphatic" on the subject of slavery than he had expected. He hoped that "his courage would prove equal to the emergency," and left Springfield "determined to sustain him to the utmost in facing the duties of his great office."[46]

That task proved more difficult than Julian had hoped. In the months between the inauguration and the attack on Fort Sumter, Julian found little to distinguish Lincoln's approach to the crisis from that of his predecessor, James Buchanan. When the war came, it was, for Julian, a war for anti-slavery principles—"a war of ideas, not less than of armies"—to be fought with the same unwavering focus: "no servant of the Republic should march with muffled drums against the foe." Clearly, that foe was slavery. In the early months of the war, with Lincoln and the moderates focused on keeping the Border States in the Union, Julian traveled his district, urging his constituents to keep slavery always at the center of the war. If it was not a message his constituents wanted to hear—if he risked his reelection by promoting it—Julian was not dissuaded. "I have no desire to continue in office by keeping mum on vital issues," he wrote in his journal in September 1861. Like Phillips, Julian had long argued that it was "not only our right but our duty to give utterance to our cherished moral convictions."[47]

But duty was specific to position, so as Congressman, Julian recognized his obligations to an administration committed to stopping the spread of slavery. It was, he explained, his "first duty" to "sustain their policy wherever I can honestly do so." Julian weighed consequences in determining this support: He conceded, for example, the notion of payment to loyal slaveholders, not as compensation, but "as a means of procuring a settlement of our troubles, and securing a lasting peace." Later, in spite of the fact that he shared Phillips's unhappiness with Lincoln's pocket veto of the Wade Davis bill, fear of a Democratic victory led Julian to support Lincoln in the 1864 presidential election.[48]

Still, Julian was a radical, committed to pursuing a war for freedom. If, as a government official, it was his "first duty" to sustain administration policy, nonetheless, he explained, it was his "second . . . to point out its errors whilst avoiding, if possible, the attitude of an antagonist." So when it appeared that the Lincoln administration did not share his view of the war, it would be Julian's duty to pressure the administration to pursue the ideals whose triumph had ushered it into office.[49]

In December 1861, Julian was appointed a member of the Joint Committee on the Conduct of the War, established to investigate the failures of the early war effort. The committee published a series of reports detailing the results of its investigations into government corruption, rebel atrocities, and the failings of Democratic generals.[50] Though Julian's involvement in the Joint Committee was peripheral, he shared both its commitment to a war informed by Republican ideals and its frustration with Lincoln's seemingly endless urge to conciliate Democrats. For Julian, that urge flew in the face of the logic of the war: "Democratic policy not only gave birth to the rebellion," he argued, "Democrats, and only Democrats, are in arms against their country. . . . Not only is it true that rebels are Democrats, but so are Rebel sympathizers, whether in the North or South. On the other hand, Loyalty and Republicanism go hand-in-hand throughout the Union, as perfectly as treason and slavery." Julian opposed all efforts to appease the Democratic party, labeling it "the great nursing mother that had fed and pampered (the rebellion)." When Republicans sought to make room for Democrats in their wartime organization, temporarily merging its identity into a new, allegedly nonpartisan "Union party," Julian objected. "Republicanism is not like a garment, to be put on or laid aside for our own convenience" he argued, "but an enduring principle, which can never be abandoned without faithlessness to the country." The Union party movement was "utterly preposterous" to Julian; ". . . simply a shallow expedient for dividing the spoils of office, at the cost of the practical surrender of the principles for which Republicans had so zealously contended."[51]

   In January 1862, increasingly frustrated with what he believed to be the administration's pandering to both the Democrats and the slave power, Julian delivered a speech on "The Cause and Cure of Our Nation's Troubles." As he had before the war, Julian assessed the situation, establishing "the true features of politics at this time in all their complications," and then pointed the way toward duty.[52] Like the nation's founders, who had exhibited a "'decent respect for the opinions of mankind'" by laying their logic before the world, Julian set out to uncover the truth about the origins of the Union's travails and present that truth to the nation. "Stern work has to be done," he declared, "and our appeal must be to the enlightened judgment and roused moral sense of the people." "The cause and cure of our troubles," he explained, "are inseparably connected." Though the founders had believed "they were yielding to slavery a transient sufferance," slavery had instead "systematically trampled the constitution under its feet in its ruthless march towards absolute dominion over these states." The Louisiana Purchase, the Missouri Compromise, the Fugitive Slave Act, and the Dred Scott decision together testified to the triumph of that dominion. As the record of the Lincoln administration suggested, even the Republican Party was complicit in the coddling of the slave power: "To pet and please it seems to have been the work of our lives." Thus it was not, as Southerners and some Northerners were wont to claim, "jealousy of the federal power" that had provoked secession, "but their inability longer to rule the national government in the interest of slavery."[53]

   The rebellion had "its source and life in slavery . . . no fact is better understood throughout the country, both by loyal and disloyal men." Nevertheless, the government claimed the war was for Union, and Julian would not argue the point: "The Union must be kept in view as the grand purpose of the war," he allowed. But even if the war was viewed solely in terms of the Union, it was slavery and slavery alone that threatened that Union. Thus "Slavery and treason, in this struggle, are identical." Emancipation had not been the Administration's initial purpose—but neither had independence been the founding fathers'. Much as events in the era of the Revolution had driven the people to demand separation, so events in Julian's own time were driving the people to demand emancipation, for "our national life and liberty can only be saved by giving freedom to all."[54]

It was clear to Julian that the federal government had the authority to grant that freedom. The nation was in a state of war, and both the President and Congress could, if they chose, assert war powers enough to declare emancipation. "Our power to destroy slavery now, I believe, is not questioned" Julian assured his audience—though he emphasized that lack of such power need not stop that destruction. The Constitution was not "so entirely sacred" that it could not be discarded. "We had a country before we had a Constitution," he pointed out, "and at all hazards we must save it. The Constitution was made for the people, not the people for the Constitution. Cases may arise in which patriotism itself may demand that we trample under our feet some of the most vital principles of the Constitution, under the exigencies of war."[55]

What, then, was the duty of a patriot? Americans at that moment had "leave to do what the great body of people have hitherto excused themselves from doing"—emancipate the slaves. They must insist that their government move: "Failure to act would be as criminal as the blessings of liberty would be priceless . . . our responsibility cannot be evaded . . . our failure to give freedom to four million slaves would be a crime only to be measured by that of putting them in chains if they were free." Though Lincoln moved slowly, with "studious tenderness . . . toward . . . slavery," it was a patriot's duty to urge him instead to mount an aggressive attack on the institution: "All tenderness towards such a foe is treason to our cause, murder to our people, faithlessness to the grandest and holiest trust ever committed to a free people . . . ." Julian recognized that this position might meet resistance. "I do not stop to inquire how many will agree with me, because I am not willing to 'put duty to the vote.'"[56]

When Julian, along with other Radicals, was accused of discounting the potentially dangerous consequences of emancipation, he had little patience. Ignoring consequences, he suggested, was a charge leveled selectively. "It will not do to talk about consequences," he contended,

> for no possible consequences of emancipation could be worse than destroying the government and subverting our free institutions. Do you ask me if I would "turn the slaves loose?" I reply, that this rebellion, threatening to desolate our land with the greatest assemblage of horrors ever witnessed on earth, is not the consequence of "turning the slaves loose," but of holding them in chains.

Do you ask me what I would do with these liberated millions? I answer by asking what will they do with us, if we insist on keeping them in bondage? Do you tell me that if the slaves are set free they will rise against their former masters, and pillage and lay waste the South? I answer that all that, should it happen, would be far less deplorable than a struggle like this, involving the existence of a free nation of thirty millions of people, and the hope of the civilized world. If therefore, our policy is to be determined by the question of consequences, the argument is clearly on the side of universal freedom.[57]

Julian spent the remainder of the war advocating for such causes as the arming of black men and the granting of land to freedmen.

In February 1865, as the war appeared to be nearing an end, Julian stood before Congress and reflected on the lessons that could be drawn from it. He returned first to the unknowable nature of the consequences of action: "At the beginning of this war . . . neither of the parties to it comprehended its character and magnitude. Its actual history has been an immeasurable surprise to both, and to the whole civilized world." Still, within the North, Julian argued, it was the Radicals, not the moderates or the conservatives—who had most clearly discerned the nature of the conflict: "We knew it was at its heart about slavery and would have to kill the slave power." Much as Julian had suggested fifteen years earlier that the Compromise of 1850 might in the end produce disunion and war, now he suggested that it was the conservative conduct of the war—not the Radicals' demands—that had protracted it. Far too cautious and conciliatory, the administration's policy of an "inoffensive war" had "vastly prolonged the struggle, and greatly augmented its cost in blood and treasure."[58]

But Radicals like Julian had not given up. They had embraced their duty to assert their consciences and shape both the thinking of the public and the policy of the administration. "The moral appeals and persistent criticism of these men" had "saved our cause and saved the country." The war was at last being fought on Radical grounds: "Abolitionism and loyalty are now accepted as convertible terms, and so are treason and slavery."[59]

Julian understood that much work remained to be done, and he urged his listeners to stay the Radical course—one devoted to the American proposition of liberty and equality. He reiterated his own commitment to that course and to his understanding of loyalty: "I believe religiously in freedom of speech. From the beginning I have exercised the right to frank, friendly and fearless criticism of the conduct of our rulers, wherever I believed them to have been wrong. Criticism has dictated the present policy of the government, and it is still a duty."[60]

Abraham Lincoln

Like Phillips and Julian, Lincoln located his understanding of personal patriotic conduct within the context of duty. Over and over, as a Congressman, as an anti-extension Republican, and, ultimately, as President, Lincoln emphasized the importance of commitment to and careful deliberation of duty. In his 1850 eulogy for Zachary Taylor, for example, he expressed deep admiration for Taylor's "unostentatious, self-sacrificing, long enduring devotion to his *duty* . . . he was always at his post."[61] Taylor's example offered a moral to Americans: it illustrated the value of "treading the hard path of duty." For Lincoln, discerning that path was a complex process involving a careful consideration of principles and consequence, and fitted to one's specific position. Lincoln repeatedly suggested this when he used phrases like "my duty as I conceive it" and "I felt it my duty."[62]

At the heart of Lincoln's notion of patriotic duty was his conception of the American nation. Like Phillips and Julian, Lincoln had a profound vision of the republic he believed Americans had inherited from the founding fathers—a vision that found its roots in the Declaration of Independence and that formed the basis of his sense of political self. As he told a crowd gathered at Independence Hall in February, 1861, "I have never had a feeling politically that did not spring from the sentiments embodied in the Declaration of Independence." Though the founders had established as the governing principle of the nation a maxim that slavery by definition contradicted, Lincoln believed that the founders understood this contradiction: Knowing slavery to be a "cancer" on the body politic, they had established equality as a *proposition:* a moral imperative asserted within the context of the existence of slavery, with a promise to the future for the decline of slavery and the expansion of freedom. That promise had been given not just to Americans but to the world: As a challenge to hereditary privilege and the divine right of kings, the United States represented a fragile experiment in republican government. The Declaration had given "liberty, not alone to the people of this country, but hope to the world for all future time." Thus, the Union was not just one vehicle for the ultimate realization of freedom and equality; it was the *only* available vehicle. For Lincoln the Union held a powerful and profound significance—one that would bring him to forgive its trespasses far longer than would either Phillips or Julian.[63]

But there were limits to Lincoln's embrace of the Union. Since the founders' assertions of liberty and equality were propositions toward which Americans must strive, the nation could remain true to the ideals of the Declaration only so long as it moved toward, not away from, those ideals. Thus, slavery must be contained and the territories guaranteed to freedom; only then could the Union remain on track to realize its promise. When the Kansas Nebraska act, with its revocation of the Missouri Compromise, threatened to derail that national promise, Lincoln called on Americans to hold firm in opposition: "Let us re-adopt the Declaration of Independence," he told his audience in Peoria, "and with it, the practices, and policy, which harmonize with it . . . If we do this, we shall not only have saved the Union; but we shall have so saved it, as to make, and to keep it, forever worthy of the saving."[64]

What then was the duty of a patriot dedicated to a Union with a slave-free future? With so much at stake, discerning duty was a complicated task, weighted with significance. If the Union was the only vehicle for the ultimate realization of freedom and equality, even an imperfect equality was better than none, and the patriot's duty *might* involve compromising principles to keep it on track. This Lincoln had made clear as early as 1845, when he wrote Liberty party leader Williamson Durley, "I hold it to be a paramount duty of us in the free states, due to the Union of the states, and perhaps to liberty itself (paradox though it may seem) to let the slavery of the other states alone." But if the nation should move *away* from its founding principles, a patriot's duty would change: "I hold it to be equally clear," he added, "that we should never knowingly lend ourselves directly or indirectly, to prevent that slavery from dying a natural death."[65]

Three years later, Lincoln made explicit his commitment to a deliberative duty that carefully considered principle and consequence. Campaigning for the Whigs in Worcester, Massachusetts, he took the Free Soil Party to task for undermining the electoral prospects of Zachary Taylor. Though the Free Soil principle was sound, the party had not thought through the consequence of its campaign, which was to aid in the election of the pro-popular sovereignty candidate, Lewis Cass. As the Boston Daily Advertiser later reported, Lincoln argued that "In declaring that they would 'do their duty and leave the consequences to God,'" they were simply providing "an excuse for taking a course that they were not able to maintain by a fair and full argument." For Lincoln, such a pronouncement did *not* establish duty. "If it did," Lincoln maintained, "we should have no use for judgment, we might as well be made without intellect, and when divine or human law does not clearly point out what *is* our duty, we have no means of finding out what it is by using our most intelligent judgment of the consequences."[66]

In Worcester, Lincoln applied his commitment to deliberative duty to the Free Soilers; twelve years later, at Cooper Union, he used that same commitment to hold firm against moderate Republican compromisers. Indeed, it is at Cooper

Union, the speech historian Harold Holzer has argued "made Abraham Lincoln president," that Lincoln's process of deciphering duty can perhaps be seen most clearly. Lincoln laid the groundwork for his argument by first establishing the principles of the nation: The founders had been committed to a slave-free future. Then Lincoln turned to calculating what, given the nation's anti-slavery essence, a patriot's duty entailed. If, in 1848, Americans committed to liberty and equality had a duty to tolerate slavery where it existed, by 1860—post Kansas-Nebraska, post Dred Scott, post John Brown—was the order of the day still compromise? Lincoln considered Americans' obligations to save their Union: "It is exceedingly desirable that all parts of this great Confederacy shall be at peace, and in harmony, one with another," he argued. "As Republicans we should do our part . . . Even though the Southern people will not so much as listen to us, let us calmly consider their demands, and yield to them if, in our deliberate view of our duty we possibly can." Delivering a markedly similar speech a few days later, Lincoln emphasized the solemnity of the process: "Let us do our duty, but let us look to what our duty is, and do nothing except after due deliberation."[67]

What, then, would satisfy the South and thus work to keep the Union together? Lincoln considered the options, then concluded that, in truth, there was little the North could do toward this end. The South wanted but one thing: active Northern approval of slavery. "This, and this only: cease to call slavery *wrong*, and join them in calling it *right*. And this must be done thoroughly—done in *acts* as well as in *words*. Nor can we justifiably withhold this, on any ground save our conviction that slavery is wrong."[68]

For those Americans who shared that conviction, and believed further, as Lincoln did, that the founders had committed the nation to freedom, the patriotic path was clear. Republicans owed it to their country to compromise with slavery where it was, but no further: "can we, while our votes will prevent it, allow it to spread into the National Territories, and to overrun us here in these Free States? If our sense of duty forbids this, then let us stand by our duty, fearlessly and effectively."[69]

And what of the consequences of such assertion in the context of a Union held together by an acceptance of slavery? How should patriots respond to those who advocated further compromise, wielding images of the Union's destruction if Northerners refused? Much as there had been for Phillips and Julian, for Lincoln there was a point at which principle trumped consequence in determining patriotic duty. The nation could not be allowed to move backwards. Those Americans truly dedicated to the Union's promise of equality must not be swayed by

sophistical contrivances . . . such as groping for some middle ground between
the right and the wrong. . . . Neither let us be slandered from our duty by false
accusations against us, nor frightened from it by menaces of destruction to
the Government nor of dungeons to ourselves. . . . LET US HAVE FAITH THAT
RIGHT MAKES MIGHT, AND IN THAT FAITH, LET US, TO THE END, DARE TO DO
OUR DUTY AS WE UNDERSTAND IT.[70]

At Cooper Union, calling on his fellow Republicans to steel themselves against
charges of extremism and warnings of dire consequences, Lincoln sounded remarkably like Julian.

Once elected president, Lincoln continued to weigh principle and consequence as he sought to determine patriotic duty. Repeatedly reminded that the
consequence of asserting non-extension of slavery as a binding national principle might be disunion, he struggled to work out his own understanding of the
relationship between ideals of liberty and equality and the value of the Union. In
private musings he termed the assertions of the Declaration an "apple of gold,"
the Union a "picture of silver," designed to "*adorn* and *preserve* it. The *picture*
was made *for* the apple—*not* the apple for the picture." Lincoln would keep this
precept in mind as he processed his patriotic obligations through a new lens:
official duty.[71]

Historians have long noted Lincoln's concern with the limits of his own authority: As national executive, he frequently asserted the parameters of presidential power. But for Lincoln, position shaped not just his rightful power, but
also his own patriotic duty—with all its moral and deliberative implications. If
he admired Taylor for keeping "always at his post," Lincoln would do the same.
He would, as he told a (visiting) delegation, "do his duty in the place to which he
had been called."[72]

In 1861, that duty was monumental. Departing Springfield for his inauguration, Lincoln told his audience, "A duty devolves upon me which is, perhaps, greater than . . . any other man since the days of Washington." At first
glance, his responsibility appeared fairly straightforward. At his inauguration,
he declared it a "simple duty" on his part to see that "the laws of the Union be
faithfully executed . . . as the declared purpose of the Union that it *will* constitutionally defend and maintain itself." As executive, he was called on "to admin-
ister the government . . . and to transmit it, unimpaired by him, to his successor." Once war broke out, Lincoln saw things equally clearly: "It is my duty, as I
conceive it," he wrote, "to suppress an insurrection existing within the United
States."[73]

But as the war progressed, Lincoln's "hard path to duty" grew more difficult to discern, complicated by his personal feelings, pressure from others, wartime dissent, and the ambiguity of executive wartime power. He had long made clear that he would not allow his personal feelings to cloud his political judgment: As he explained to his friend Joshua Speed in 1855, "the great body of the Northern people do crucify their feelings, in order to maintain their loyalty to the constitution and the Union." Nine years later, in the midst of war, he told Albert Hodges, "to this day, I have done no official act in deference to my abstract judgment and feeling on slavery."[74]

If Lincoln would not allow his personal feelings to divert him from his duty to country, nor would he allow the thinking of others to do so. Inundated with advice from concerned citizens and officials of all persuasions, he regularly asserted his commitment to *his* duty as *he* saw it. More than once, delegations arrived to the White House eager to share God's intent with the President. "If . . . God would reveal his will to others on a point so connected with my duty, it might be supposed he would reveal it to me," he told a group of Chicago Christians. When Albany Democrats complained about the suspension of habeas corpus, he responded with a long letter defending his acts against "the censures systematically cast upon me for doing what, in my view of duty, I could not forbear." When Illinois Congressman Issac Arnold urged Lincoln to dismiss General Halleck, Lincoln replied that he was "compelled to take a more impartial and unprejudiced view of things . . . my position enables me to understand my duty in all these matters better than you possibly can . . ." Lincoln argued that it was his job to listen to others, to learn from them, and then make decisions. "The radicals and conservatives, each agree with me in some things, and disagree in others," he told Charles Drake, a Radical Republican Senator from Missouri. ". . . I do not question their right. I too shall do what seems to be my duty . . . it is my duty to hear all; but at last, I must, within my sphere, judge what to do, and what to forbear."[75]

Because he believed so strongly in a deliberated individual duty based on principle and defined by position, Lincoln could be tolerant of others' views of *their* patriotic duties: He was careful not to impugn the patriotism of those who supported the war to save the Union but disagreed with him on policy. In a statement explaining his position on the draft, he addressed skeptics of this policy: "You who do not wish to be soldiers, do not like this law. This is natural; nor does it imply want of patriotism." Lincoln did not suggest, as did many Republicans, that there could be no patriotism outside the Republican (or Union) party. He did not, he told his supporters on election night, believe that they "embrace all the patriotism and loyalty of the country." And he did not, as historians for generations charged, freely arrest any man or woman who dissented from his wartime policy. As Mark E. Neely, Jr. has shown, the majority of Northern civilians arrested under Lincoln's suspension of the writ of habeas corpus were suspected deserters or draft evaders.[76]

There were, however, limits to individual interpretation of patriotic duty in a country at war. For Lincoln, words or actions that threatened to *jeopardize* the war effort—it was, after all, a *civil* war undertaken by rebels who sought to break the Union—fell outside the purview of a patriot. Defending the arrest of accused traitor Clement Vallandigham, Lincoln argued that the Ohio Copperhead had not been arrested "because he was damaging the political prospects of the administration," but rather "because he was damaging the army" laboring to preserve the Union. Lincoln similarly defended the arrest of those who encouraged soldiers to abandon their military duties: "Must I shoot a simple-minded soldier boy who deserts, while I must not touch a hair of a wiley agitator who induces him to desert?" Lincoln justified his administration's actions by pointing to the constitutional duties and powers of a wartime executive.[77]

But wartime presidential prerogatives were not always clear. In Lincoln's dealings with emancipation, we can see his continuing commitment to the process of discerning patriotic duty in an increasingly complex context. From the outset, Lincoln insisted that the Civil War was not a war for abolition, but for the restoration of Union and with it hope for the ultimate realization of freedom for all. Lincoln actively supported voluntary compensated emancipation with colonization, in part because he feared the consequence of compulsory abolition would be the secession of the border states. When, in January 1863, Lincoln issued the Emancipation Proclamation, freeing the slaves in the states under rebellion and providing for the enlistment of black troops, he immediately faced criticism, both from Democrats and from within his own party. In an April 1864 letter to Kentucky Unionist Albert Hodges, Lincoln laid out the process by which he had arrived at his decision. He understood well that he was not to "indulge (his) primary abstract judgment on the moral question of slavery," but his oath to preserve the constitution *had* imposed on him "the duty of preserving, by every indispensable means, that government—that nation—of which that constitution was the organic law." Lincoln had thus determined "that measures, otherwise unconstitutional, might become lawful, by becoming indispensable to the preservation of the constitution, through the preservation of the nation."[78]

Concerned with both the consequences and the constitutionality of emancipation, Lincoln had been exceptionally cautious in calculating the point at which

it was deemed indispensable. As he explained to Hodges, he had on many occasions turned back Radical measures aimed at freeing the slaves. It was only
after the border states had refused to consider his 1862 proposal for compensated
emancipation that Lincoln had determined that his duty mandated emancipation. Because by then, he was faced with a larger consequence: "I was, in my best
judgment, driven to the alternative of either surrendering the Union, and with it,
the Constitution, or of laying strong hand upon the colored element. I chose the
latter." At the Baltimore Sanitary Fair he reiterated this theme: "At the beginning
of the war, and for some time, the use of colored troops was not contemplated"
he told his audience. It was only "upon a clear conviction of duty (that) I resolved
to turn that element of strength to account."[79]

Lincoln justified emancipation and the enrollment of black troops through his
duty to preserve the constitution; as a part of his calculation of duty, he weighed
consequences. But by now, Lincoln acknowledged that such calculations involved a significant element of uncertainty, and like Phillips and Julian, he began
to concede the unknowable nature of consequence. As he explained to Hodges,
"In choosing (emancipation), I hoped for greater gain than loss; but of this, I was
not entirely confident." How had it gone? "More than a year of trial now shows no
loss by it in our foreign relations, none in our home popular sentiment, none in
our white military force,—no loss by it any how or any where. On the contrary, it
shows a gain of quite a hundred and thirty thousand soldiers, seamen, and laborers." But Lincoln would not claim credit for the success of what he conceded had
been, on some level, a gamble: "In telling this tale I attempt no compliment to my
own sagacity. I claim not to have controlled events, but confess plainly that events
have controlled me. Now, at the end of three years struggle the nation's condition
is not what either party, or any man devised, or expected. God alone can claim
it." The war had made clear what Julian, defending his opposition of the Compromise of 1850 over 14 years earlier, had asserted: Though duty might be clear,
consequences were often impalpable. Lincoln repeated this theme in a speech at
the Baltimore Sanitary Fair: "When the war began, three years ago, neither party,
nor any man, expected it would last till now . . . But here we are; the war has not
ended, and slavery has been much affected . . . So true is it that man proposes,
and God disposes."[80]

On March 4, 1865, as the Civil War drew to a close, Lincoln delivered his
second inaugural address. In this speech, deemed by many to be his greatest,
he revealed much about principle, consequence, and duty to the egalitarian nation. Though the speech suggested his differences with Phillips and Julian—both
of whom would support a radical reconstruction—it also revealed the common

ground the three men had come to share. "All knew," Lincoln argued, that slavery "was somehow, the cause of the war." The South was determined to "strengthen, perpetuate, and extend" the institution, while the North, committed to a slave-free future, "claimed no right to do more than to restrict the territorial enlargement of it." Still, the war and its consequences had surprised everyone. "Neither party expected for the war, the magnitude, or the duration, which it has already attained . . . Each looked for an easier triumph, and a result less fundamental and astounding."[81]

Would Americans dedicated to the proposition have made different decisions had they known the devastation the war would bring? Would they have determined that freedom for four million slaves and their descendants could not justify the carnage? Julian had argued that there were "things more to be dreaded" than war. "The betrayal of sacred trusts is worse than war; shrinking from a just responsibility . . . is worse than war; the extension of slavery by the federal government, and with the approval of the nation," he had pronounced "worse than war."[82]

In the Second Inaugural, Lincoln suggested a similar conclusion: If American slavery was "one of those offenses which, in the providence of God, must needs come, but which, having continued through His appointed time, He now wills to remove," then this "terrible war" was "the woe due to those by whom the offense came" and God deemed it just. Indeed, though all hoped the "mighty scourge of war" would "speedily pass away," if God chose otherwise—if He willed that the war "continue, until all the wealth piled by the bond-man's two hundred and fifty years of unrequited toil shall be sunk, and until every drop of blood drawn with the lash, shall be paid by another drawn with the sword," Americans could not question His justice. They must, Lincoln told his audience, instead continue to discern their duty—a perceptible duty rooted in a discoverable moral order—and carry it out as they understood it: "with firmness in the right, as God gives us to see the right, let us strive on to finish the work we are in."[83]

For nineteenth-century Americans truly dedicated to the proposition of liberty and equality, loyalty to a nation held together by its tolerance of slavery presented a distinct challenge. Phillips, Julian and Lincoln responded differently to that challenge, but their similarities are instructive. Each understood that the Union without its commitment to the American proposition was hollow; each calculated a point at which movement away from that proposition equaled its abandonment; each weighed principle against consequence and, in light of his post, deciphered duty. In the end, as they worked to shape a nation true to its commitments to liberty and equality, each employed a complex understanding of the notion of duty. Together, these men remind us of the multiple forms that loyalty to nation can assume, and the importance of a thoughtful and deliberative patriotism.

Notes

1. George W. Julian, *Speeches on Political Questions 1850–1868* (1872; reprint, Westport, Conn.: Negro University Press, 1970), 36.

2. Ibid., 36; italics added.

3. Ibid., 36.

4. Ibid., 37.

5. Perry Miller, *The New England Mind: the Seventeenth Century*, vol. 1 (1939; reprint, Cambridge: Harvard University Press, 1983), 210; see also 21, 212, 398–99, and vol. 2, 291; John Rawls, *Lectures on the History of Moral Philosophy* (Cambridge: Harvard University Press, 2000), 6–7; Daniel Walker Howe, *Making the American Self: Jonathan Edwards to Abraham Lincoln* (Cambridge: Harvard University Press, 1997), 36–37, 14; E. Anthony Rotundo, *American Manhood: Transformations in Masculinity from the Revolution to the Modern Era* (New York: Basic Books, 1993), 12–13, 20; James McPherson, *For Cause and Comrades: Why Men Fought in the Civil War* (New York: Oxford University Press, 1997), 22.

For duty and Scottish moral philosophy, see Knud Haakonssen, "From Natural Law to the Rights of Man: A European Perspective on American Debates," in *A Culture of Rights: The Bill of Rights in Philosophy, Politics, and Law 1791 and 1991*, ed. Haakonssen and Michael J. Lacey (Cambridge, U.K.: Cambridge University Press, 1992): 19–61. For republicanism, see Gordon Wood, *The Creation of the American Republic* (Chapel Hill: University of North Carolina Press, 1969). For duty and gender, see Linda Kerber, *Women of the Republic: Intellect and Ideology in Revolutionary America* (Chapel Hill: University of North Carolina Press, 1997); Rotundo, *American Manhood*; McPherson, *For Cause and Comrades*, 22–27; and Andrea Foroughi, *Go If You Think It Your Duty: A Minnesota Couple's Civil War Letters* (St Paul: Minnesota Historical Society Press, 2011).

6. George M. Fredrickson, *The Inner Civil War: Northern Intellectuals and the Crisis of the Union* (New York: Harper and Row, 1965). For more on notions of Civil War patriotism, see Melinda Lawson, *Patriot Fires: Forging a New American Nationalism in the Civil War North* (Lawrence: University Press of Kansas, 2002).

7. Recent examples of works that cast Lincoln, the abolitionists, and/or the Radical Republicans in this light include William E. Miller, *Lincoln's Virtues: An Ethical Biography* (New York: Alfred A. Knopf, 2002); Allen Guelzo, *Lincoln's Emancipation Proclamation: The End of Slavery in America* (New York: Simon and Schuster, 2004); and Andrew Delbanco, "The Abolitionist Imagination," in *The Abolitionist Imagination*, ed. Delbanco (Cambridge: Harvard University Press, 2012). Miller roots his interpretation in Max Weber's 1919 essay "Politics as a Vocation," arguing that Lincoln's success lay in part in his embrace of Weber's "ethic of responsibility," which contrasted with abolitionists' and Radical Republicans' self-righteous moral simplicity. Similarly, Delbanco portrays the abolitionists as extremists who operated "without compunction and without restraint," moving the country away from the "shrinking center" that Lincoln occupied, hasten-

ing the onset of an enormously destructive civil war. Challenges to this interpretation include James Oakes, *The Radical and the Republican: Frederick Douglass, Abraham Lincoln, and the Triumph of Anti-Slavery Politics* (New York: Norton, 2008); Elizabeth Varon, *Disunion!: The Coming of the American Civil War, 1789–1859* (Chapel Hill: University of North Carolina Press, 2008); Caleb McDaniel, *The Problem of Democracy in the Age of Slavery: Garrisonian Abolitionists and Transatlantic Reform* (Baton Rouge: Louisiana State University Press, 2013); Eric Foner, *The Fiery Trial: Abraham Lincoln and American Slavery* (New York: Norton, 2010); and Manisha Sinha, *The Slave's Cause: A History of Abolition* (New Haven: Yale University Press, 2016).

For the Weber essay, see Max Weber, "Politics as a Vocation," in *Essays in Sociology*, ed. Howard Garth and Cynthia Mills (New York: Macmillan, 1946), 26–45.

8. The tension between principle, consequence, and duty (or responsibility) is among the themes addressed in Weber, "Politics as a Vocation."

9. For major works on Phillips, see Richard Hofstadter, *The American Political Tradition* (New York: Vintage Books, 1948); Irving H. Bartlett, *Wendell Phillips: Brahmin Radical* (Boston: Beacon Press, 1961); James Brewer Stewart, *Wendell Phillips: Liberty's Hero* (Baton Rouge: Louisiana State University Press, 1986). For major works on the abolitionists, see James Brewer Stewart, *Holy Warriors: The Abolitionists and American Slavery* (New York: Hill and Wang, 1997); James McPherson, *The Struggle for Equality* (Princeton, N.J.: Princeton University Press, 1967); Timothy Patrick McCarthy and John Stauffer, eds., *Prophets of Protest: Reconsidering the History of American Abolitionism* (New York: The New Press, 2006); Bruce Laurie, *Beyond Garrison: Antislavery and Social Reform* (New York: Cambridge University Press, 2005); McDaniel, *The Problem of Democracy in the Age of Slavery*; and Sinha, *The Slave's Cause*. For more on Phillips's patriotism, see Lawson, *Patriot Fires*.

10. *National Anti-Slavery Standard (NASS)*, July 13, 1861; Wendell Phillips, *Speeches, Lectures and Letters*, vol. 1 (1863; reprint, Boston: Lee and Shepard, 1902): 243, 268, 50.

11. Phillips, *Speeches 1*, 282.

12. Ibid., 348. As political scientist George McKenna writes, the abolitionists "celebrated an America that did not yet exist." See McKenna, *The Puritan Origins of American Patriotism* (New Haven: Yale University Press, 2007), 137.

13. Phillips, in Stewart, *Wendell Phillips*, 9.

14. Stewart, *Wendell Phillips*, 9; Phillips, in Stewart, *Wendell Phillips*, 10.

15. Phillips, *Speeches 1*, 229–30. See also Wendell Phillips, *Speeches, Lectures, and Letters* 2nd Series (1891; reprint, Boston: Lee and Shepard, 1905), 295.

16. Phillips, *Speeches 1*, 52, 46. George McKenna refers to the North's "peculiar amalgamation of Puritanism and republicanism." See McKenna, *Puritan Origins*, 155.

17. Phillips, *Speeches 1*, 47; Phillips, *Speeches 2*, 349–50; Phillips, *Speeches 1*, 465–66, 110, 47. A potent force in American politics, public opinion was most notably informed by the pulpit and the press. But the church had become "but the servant of the broker and the kitchen of the factory"; newspapers, "agents of the banks and . . . slaveholders." Alternative voices were called for: "Outside of that press and that pulpit . . . there must be agitation." *NASS*, June 2, 1860. See also Phillips, *Speeches 1*, 152–53, 225, 354; Phillips, *Speeches 2*, 252–75.

For an exploration of how college-educated Northeastern officers understood their duty, see Kanisorn Wongsrichanalai's essay in this volume. For more on Phillips and his understanding of the role of public opinion, see Hofstadter, *The American Political Tradition* and McDaniel, *The Problem of Slavery*, particularly 92–112.

18. Phillips, *Speeches I*, 398, 230–31. See also *NASS*, June 2, 1860. Phillips argued that agitation was "the life of the republic." Phillips, *Speeches 1*, 53.

19. Phillips, *Speeches 2*, 8; Phillips, *Speeches 1*, 18.

20. Phillips, *Speeches 1*, 79–80.

21. Ibid., 147.

22. Phillips, *Speeches 2*, 60; Phillips, *Speeches 1*, 347, 364–65, 370. For the role that the idea of Disunion played in the coming of the war, see Varon, *Disunion*.

23. Phillips, *Speeches 1*, 153; Phillips, in Stewart, *Wendell Phillips*, 143. For more on Phillips and the importance of agitation in promoting abolition and saving democracy, see McDaniel, *The Problem of Democracy*.

24. *NASS*, April 27, 1861; James McPherson, *The Struggle for Equality*, 50.

25. Phillips, *Speeches 1*, 396–414.

26. Phillips, *Speeches 1*, 398, 419–20, 464–67.

27. *NASS*, November 22, 1862.

28. *NASS*, May 17, 1862; Phillips, *Speeches 1*, 423; *NASS*, January 12, 1862. See also, *NASS*, January 17, 1862.

29. *NASS*, November 5, 1864.

30. *NASS*, May 14, 1864. See also, *NASS*, June 18, 1864.

31. Phillips, *Speeches I*, 464–67.

32. *NASS*, December 10, 1864.

33. Patrick Riddleberger, *George Washington Julian, Radical Republican: A Study in Nineteenth Century Politics and Reform* (Indianapolis: Indiana Historical Bureau, 1966) 1–44. See also, Lydia Maria Child, "Introduction," Julian, *Speeches*, v–xvii.

34. William Ellery Channing, "Unitarian Christianity," in *Unitarian Christianity and Other Essays*, ed. Irving H. Bartlett (New York: Liberal Arts Press, 1957), 30; Channing, *Slavery* (1835; reprint, New York: Arno Press, 1969), 1.

35. Julian, quoted in Riddleberger, *George Washington Julian*, 35; Riddleberger, *George Washington Julian*, 1–44.

36. Julian, *Speeches*, 4, 40, 13.

37. George W. Julian, *Political Recollections 1840–1872* (1884; reprint, Westport Conn.: Negro Universities Press, 1970), 25; Julian, *Speeches*, 78, 143. Italics in original.

38. Julian, *Speeches*, 143, 126.

39. Ibid., 7–12.

40. Ibid., 13, 14, 10.

41. Ibid., 153; Julian to Thomas Wentworth Higginson, in Riddleberger, *George Washington Julian*, 127.

42. Julian, *Speeches*, 26–27, 154, 17, 42, 78.

43. Ibid., 36–37.

44. Frederick J. Blue, *No Taint of Compromise: Crusaders in Antislavery Politics* (Baton Rouge: Louisiana Statue University Press, 2005), 9–10; Julian, *Speeches*, 86–88.

45. Julian, Speeches, 139–40, 134, 150–52. For more on the Radical Republicans, see Hans L. Trefousse, The Radical Republicans: Lincoln's Vanguard for Justice (New York: Alfred A. Knopf, 1969) and Blue, No Taint of Compromise.

46. Julian, Speeches, 192; Julian, Political Recollections, 182–83.

47. Julian, Political Recollections, 188–89; Julian, Speeches, 154; Julian, in Grace Julian Clarke, George W. Julian (Indianapolis: Indiana Historical Commission, 1923), 217; Julian, Speeches, 6. For more on Julian's belief in the war as one of ideas, see Julian, Speeches, 186, 233.

48. Julian, Speeches, 169, 175; Riddleberger, George Washington Julian, 199.

49. Julian, Speeches, 169.

50. The newest study of the Joint Committee, Bruce Tap, Over Lincoln's Shoulder: The Committee on the Conduct of the War (Lawrence: University Press of Kansas, 1998) argues that Committee members were generally unqualified to intervene in military matters and that the Committee had an "uneven" effect on the North's war effort.

51. Julian, Speeches, 196, 195. For works on loyalty and democrats who opposed the war, see Frank Klement, The Copperheads in the Midwest (Chicago: University of Chicago Press, 1960); Klement, Lincoln's Critics: The Copperheads of the North (Shippensburg, Pa.: White Mane Books, 1999); Jennifer L. Weber, Copperheads: The Rise and Fall of Lincoln's Opponents in the North (New York: Oxford University Press, 2006); Robert M. Sandow, Deserter Country: Civil War Opposition in the Pennsylvania Appalachians (New York: Fordham University Press, 2009); and Matthew Warshauer, "Copperheads in Connecticut: A Peace Movement that Imperiled the Union," in This Distracted and Anarchical People: New Answers for Old Questions about the Civil War-Era North, ed. Andrew L. Slap and Michael Thomas Smith (New York: Fordham University Press, 2013).

52. Julian, Speeches, 126.

53. Ibid., 155–59.

54. Ibid., 157, 162–63.

55. Ibid., 164–65.

56. Ibid., 165, 169, 175, 177.

57. Ibid., 177. Pointing to the example of the West Indies, he suggested that emancipation would likely, in fact, prove profitable to the freedmen and the slave-owners. Julian, Speeches, 179.

58. Julian, Speeches, 229–32.

59. Ibid., 237.

60. Ibid., 241.

61. Roy P. Basler, ed., The Collected Works of Abraham Lincoln, vol. 2 (New Brunswick, N.J.: Rutgers University Press, 1953–55), 89. Italics in original.

62. Basler, Collected Works, 4:444, 202. See also, 2:47; 2:112; 8:304.

63. Basler, Collected Works, 4:240; Garry Wills, Lincoln at Gettysburg: The Words That Remade America (New York: Simon and Schuster, 1992), 100. See also, Richard Current, "Lincoln, the Civil War, and the American Mission," in The Public and Private Lincoln: Contemporary Perspectives, ed. Cullum Davis (Carbondale: Southern Illinois University Press, 1979), 137–46; George M. Fredrickson, "The Search for Order and Community," in The Public and Private Lincoln, 86–98; Daniel Walker Howe, The Political Culture of

the American Whigs (Chicago: University of Chicago Press, 1979), 263–298; James M. McPherson, "Abraham Lincoln and the Second American Revolution," in *Abraham Lincoln and the Second American Revolution* (New York: Oxford University Press, 1990), 23–42; McPherson, "Lincoln and Liberty," in *Abraham Lincoln and the Second American Revolution*, 23–42; Philip Shaw Paludan, *The Presidency of Abraham Lincoln* (Lawrence: University Press of Kansas, 1994); Mark E. Neely, *The Last Best Hope: Abraham Lincoln and the American Promise* (Cambridge: Harvard Universtiy Press, 1995); Lawson, *Patriot Fires*, 160–78.

The relationship between Union and emancipation in Lincoln's political thought is a subject of ongoing debate among historians. Important recent works that suggest Lincoln's evolving commitment to emancipation include Foner, *The Fiery Trial*, and James Oakes, *Freedom National: The Destruction of Slavery in the United States* (New York: Norton, 2012.) Recent works that argue that the Union played a larger role in Lincoln's wartime decisions include Harry S. Stout, *Upon the Altar of the Nation: A Moral History of the American Civil War* (New York: Viking, 2006); Dorothy Ross, "Lincoln and the Ethics of Emancipation: Universalism, Nationalism, Exceptionalism," in *The Journal of American History* (September 2009), 379–99; and Gary Gallagher, *The Union War* (Cambridge: Harvard University Press, 2011).

64. Basler, *Collected Works*, 2:276

65. Basler, *Collected Works*, 1:348.

66. Basler, *Collected Works*, 2:3–4.

67. Harold Holzer, *Lincoln at Cooper Union: The Speech That Made Abraham Lincoln President* (New York: Simon and Schuster, 2004); Basler, *Collected Works*, 3:547; Basler, *Collected Works*, 4:8; Miller, *Lincoln's Virtues*.

68. Basler, *Collected Works*, 3:547.

69. Ibid., 553.

70. Ibid., 550. For an interpretation of this speech in terms of Weber's "Politics as a Vocation," see Miller, *Lincoln's Virtues*, 375–84.

71. Basler, *Collected Works*, 4:169.

72. Basler, *Collected Works*, 5:279. William Miller, *President Lincoln: The Duty of a Statesman* (New York: Alfred A. Knopf, 2008) continues the "ethical biography" Miller began in *Lincoln's Virtues*, examining Lincoln's balance of various moral imperatives, including his duty as executive. See also, James Underwood, "Lincoln: A Weberian Politician Meets the Constitution," *Presidential Studies Quarterly* 34, no. 2 (June 2004), 341–65.

73. Basler, *Collected Works*, 4:190, 265, 270, 444. Italics in original. The version of the farewell speech cited is one of three. While the wording varies among them, this point is made in each.

74. Basler, *Collected Works*, 2:320; 7:281.

75. Basler, *Collected Works*, 5:420; 6:262, 231, 504.

76. Basler, *Collected Works*, 6:445; 8:96. Mark E. Neely, *The Fate of Liberty: Abraham Lincoln and Civil Liberties* (New York: Oxford University Press, 1992). Lincoln's "Opinion on the Draft" was never delivered.

77. Basler, *Collected Works*, 6:266. For works on the Copperheads and loyalty, see Frank Klement, *The Copperheads in the Midwest* (Chicago: University of Chicago Press, 1960); Klement, *Lincoln's Critics: The Copperheads of the North* (Shippensburg, Pa.:

White Mane Books, 1999); Jennifer L. Weber, *Copperheads: The Rise and Fall of Lincoln's Opponents in the North* (New York: Oxford University Press, 2006); Robert M. Sandow, *Deserter Country*; and Matthew Warshauer, "Copperheads in Connecticut: A Peace Movement that Imperiled the Union," in *This Distracted and Anarchical People*, ed. Slap and Smith.

78. Basler, *Collected Works*, 7:281. For Lincoln and the war for Union see Basler, *Collected Works*, 2:247–83 and Basler, *Collected Works*, 5:388–89. For Lincoln and the border states, see Foner, *The Fiery Trial*, 166–205.

79. Basler, *Collected Works*, 7:282, 302.

80. Ibid., 282, 301.

81. Ronald C. White, *Lincoln's Greatest Speech: The Second Inaugural* (New York: Simon and Schuster, 2002); Basler, *Collected Works*, 8:332–33.

82. Julian, *Speeches*, 37.

83. Basler, *Collected Works*, 8:333.

Connecticut Copperhead Constitutionalism

A Study of Peace Democratic Political
Ideology During the Civil War

Matthew Warshauer

In mid-summer 1861, following the Confederate bombardment of Fort Sumter in Charleston Harbor, South Carolina, New Englanders and those throughout the North came to understand the seriousness of the constitutional crisis that faced the Union.[1] How to resolve that crisis, however, became an immediate point of dispute. Many in the North rallied in the nation's defense, forming regiments and preparing to march south. The little state of Connecticut revealed a surge of patriotism. President Abraham Lincoln's call for 75,000 men required Connecticut to field a single regiment. Unionist enthusiasm instead provided three and Lincoln gladly accepted them. Yet not all Connecticut men supported the call to arms. On July 2, Mexican War hero, three-time Democratic governor, and former ambassador to Russia, Thomas H. Seymour rose as a representative in the Connecticut General Assembly, offering a set of peace resolutions and words of stern counsel to his colleagues.[2] Acknowledging that a third of the "sovereign states heretofore composing the United States have withdrawn from the Union, and the effort to compel their return, and to enforce, within their limit, the laws of the United States, have assumed the proportions of a civil war of vast magnitude, threatening the people of the country with the burdens of enormous taxes and public debt, but the destruction of thousands of men in deadly combat," Seymour resolved,

> That while we are in favor of maintaining the Constitution in the true spirit of its founders, and of upholding the government organized in consonance therewith, we believe it to be the duty of Congress now soon to assemble, to adopt the resolutions known as the "Crittenden Compromise," or some other plan of adjustment of similar design, for a fair and honorable termination of the present troubles; and in any event stoutly protest against any interference by any warlike movement upon the institution of slavery when it is recognized

by the Constitution of the United States, or for the purpose of disparaging the equality of the several states as united by the Federal Constitution.

Seymour further advised that there existed "a growing sentiment among the people for a peaceful settlement—and honorable peace." He insisted that the South could not be forced back into the Union: "There seems to be a radical mistake on the part of many people. They appear to think the South can be conquered. Sir, this is impossible. You may destroy their habitations, devastate their fields and shed the blood of their people, but you cannot conquer them."[3]

Thomas H. Seymour's statements defined two important facts about Connecticut Copperhead Constitutionalism during the American Civil War. First, Seymour outlined many of the essential Democratic criticisms, both within Connecticut and nationally, that remained constant throughout the war. That it would lead to burdensome taxes, public debt, and the death of thousands. Antiwar Democrats further worried that disruption of commerce with the South would destroy the American economy. There were also important constitutional principles at stake. The Southern states were "sovereign." They had "equality" within the Union and, therefore, the right to defend that sovereignty. Seymour's insistence that he and other Democrats were "in favor of maintaining the Constitution in the true spirit of its founders" was of critical importance. That spirit, and the document forged from it, was one of compromise and a clear recognition of slavery. Seymour "stoutly protest[ed] against any interference by any warlike movement upon the institution of slavery when it is recognized by the Constitution of the United States." This was, arguably, the Democrats most unshakable assertion, from the years immediately preceding the conflict well through to the end of the war. They declared at every opportunity that Lincoln and the Republican Party were abolitionists bent on the destruction of the institution, and in the process revolutionizing the Constitution created by the Founders. In place of states' rights, the Union would be characterized by arbitrary rule from a centralized despotism.

Connecticut Peace Democrats remained remarkably consistent on these points, and in doing so reveal the party's commitment to a distinct, conservative political ideology.[4] Viewing themselves as the heirs to Jeffersonian strict construction and small government, Peace Democrats bristled at the notion of an expansive federal government that forced the states to fall in line and simply accept decrees from above. Much like Southerners, who believed that the long-brewing battle over slavery was the ultimate attack on states' rights, these Northern peace men saw Republicans, and especially Abraham Lincoln, as the greatest threat to the nation's future and a distinct change in course from the Union created by the Founding Fathers.[5]

Peace Democrat arguments during the war, then, represent an important expression of political philosophy, one that has been largely dismissed both in their own day, by Republicans who branded Democrats as little more than disloyal traitors, and by many scholars who came to much the same conclusion, even insisting that they represented a fifth column, a secret conspiratorial movement that undermined the war effort.[6] To be sure, Democrats were on the wrong side of history when it came to Lincoln's ideals about the Declaration of Independence and a new birth of freedom. That, however, does not diminish the seriousness or consistency of their political views, nor what they believed was their duty in defending the Constitution and their own long-held political ideology. In many ways, men like Seymour speak to the notion of duty addressed in Melinda Lawson's essay in this volume, as well as Julie Mujic's chapter, which focuses on the idea of loyalty. She notes that Gideon Winan Allen's patriotism was defined by the Democratic Party's belief in Union, the Constitution, and the intentions of the Founding Fathers; that continuity, not change, characterized his wartime perspective. This was certainly the case for Peace Democrats in the state of Connecticut. Their views were based on philosophical beliefs expressed through the normal rough and tumble politics of nineteenth-century America.

That expression was most widely circulated through party newspapers. It was via the partisan presses that both organizations did their best to influence the electorate. The editorial combat was severe and provides a remarkable window into how mainstream party politicians framed their ideological views and how they were in turn acted upon by voters. In this sense there was an almost symbiotic relationship between what the political leaders said and what the electorate did, and vice versa. Democratic peace men maintained a consistent fight against what they saw as misguided, radical Republicanism.[7] Republican newspapers, in turn, ridiculed peace men as unprincipled rebels, often no better than those manning Confederate lines, labeling them "traitors," "disloyal," and "Copperheads." To Republicans, there could be no accepted notion as a loyal opposition, no honor in party consistency.

What is even more certain is that Connecticut peace men did not represent any sort of radical phalanx that attempted to undermine the war effort through secret or underhanded machinations. Although there was always the fear that something of this nature was afoot, and this fear was expressed almost universally by Republicans who wanted to place Democrats in the worst possible light, there is no proof that plots existed or that organized violence was perpetrated against the federal government. In reality, the fairly small scale unrest in Connecticut was almost always at the hands of those attempting to force allegiance to the Union; Republicans engaged in more violence and coercion than Democrats. The Democratic Peace movement in Connecticut actually represented a generally conservative action, holding rallies and, most importantly, appealing to the electorate through the democratic process to force change at the polls.

Utilizing the natural course of elections was the key Democratic strategy in the state, focusing on local, gubernatorial, and presidential elections to force the political change that was necessary to change the direction of the Republican war and allow what Democrats believed could be a return to civility with the South that might result in compromises based on the precedents established by the Founding Fathers. There were, therefore, distinct phases through which the movement traveled: 1) initial organization and opposition to war in the aftermath of Fort Sumter; 2) a reinvigoration of the anti-war movement following Lincoln's preliminary Emancipation Proclamation and the release of the final proclamation on January 1, 1863, which primed Democrats for that year's gubernatorial election; 3) a hard-fought contest over the 1864 presidential election, which revealed, as it did nationally, the last opportunity for peace men.[8] That the timing of the most focused and spirited dissent revolved around elections reflected the natural pulse of politics in a republic that was remarkable for its party organization and activity. In this sense, dissent against the war did not merely make a difference in mainstream politics—it was mainstream politics. Elections and the partisan battles that went with them were the cornerstones of the democratic process and amazing during the Civil War primarily because they were not postponed or canceled.[9] Indeed, it is striking to consider what Democrats may have been willing to do had normal elections been suspended. That may very well have been, in the eyes of Democrats, the crowning act of Lincolnian despotism and cause for a true political/military uprising according to revolutionary standards.

The extent to which Connecticut Democrats remained conservative in their approach to fighting the political ideology of the war is worth noting. Rarely can one find an editorial or speech that advocates open defiance of the Lincoln administration, such as a refusal to abide by the draft or speeches encouraging soldiers to desert. Thomas Seymour was a true conservative in fighting on behalf of a political principle. He rarely made his attacks personal, and this may be one reason that, though highly regarded by Democrats in the nation, he never became so outspoken in his criticism that his remarks urged arrest by Union authorities. Indeed, Seymour watched carefully the ebb and flow of the Peace wing's activities and his own role within it, opting at certain times to not run for governorship and ultimately refusing to be considered as a presidential candidate in 1864.[10]

Ultimately, the Peace movement in Connecticut stands out as a particularly fitting example of the Civil War political debate over patriotism and constitutionalism specifically because the state is in the heart of New England. Most studies of Copperheads have focused on the Midwest, believing that the Old Northwest, with its geographic proximity to border states and the significant generational emigration from the south, was particularly ripe of Southern leanings.[11] Early historians assumed the Peace movement was a Midwestern phenomenon, even asserting that "the Peace Democrats undoubtedly believed the War was one of New England making."[12] The story in Connecticut does not bear out such assumptions. The state's peace movement was immediate and explosive.[13] It also revolved around a deeply held party ideology, a Jeffersonian conservatism that likely transcended state borders and aligned with the earliest philosophies espoused by the party, and which held sway throughout the Jacksonian era, when the party's leaders did all they could to avoid conflicts over slavery. Thus Democrats constantly appealed to the citizenry that the Democracy was more loyal to the Union and Constitution than the new and radical Republican Party.

The seriousness of Connecticut's peace movement can be revealed not only in a consistent ideological stance from the beginning of the war to the end, but perhaps most importantly in Thomas Seymour's nearly successfully bid for governor in 1863; he was one of the few Peace Democrats in the midst of the war who came close to unseating an incumbent Republican governor.[14] The state also revealed a lower margin of victory for Lincoln in 1864 than any other New England state and lower than anywhere else in the nation except where the president actually lost to McClellan.[15] Thus, there is something important about Connecticut's experience, something that cannot be chalked up to any sort of surmised cultural affinity as with the Midwest. Connecticut had always been referred to as "the land of steady habits," conservative in its outlook and Puritan in its origins, even as the 1850s brought serious change in the form of European immigration that demonstrably altered the reality of the state.[16]

Connecticut had always been a hard fought state throughout the ante-bellum period, with Democrats and Whigs gaining and losing governmental control on an almost annual basis. In the 1830s and 1840s, the battles had centered on Andrew Jackson. In the 1850s, Connecticut's party structure changed as did the rest of the nation's, with the death of the Whigs and the rise of Know Nothings and Republicans.[17] Abolitionism reared its head, but in a spotty and disputed way, one that reflected no distinct region or county that was more opposed to slavery than another. William Lloyd Garrison, the famed abolitionist once referred to the state as "that Georgia of New England," and he knew Connecticut well, having been married in Brooklyn, Connecticut, where his wife's family resided.[18] Republicans ultimately gained control of the state in 1858 with the election of William Alfred Buckingham, a well-respected Norwich business man who never left any doubts about where he stood on Union and Abraham Lincoln. He supported both and came to view the war in an almost messianic way, a divine purging of slavery by the lord.[19]

Democrats in Connecticut were divided and weakened, but hardly dead. The party remained adamant and outspoken, fueled in part by devoted politicians and a robust party organ in the form of the *Hartford Times*. Editor Alfred E. Burr had begun his apprenticeship in the business at age twelve with the *Hartford Courant*, and was even offered ownership of the well-established paper in the 1830s. The requirement, however, necessitated joining the Whig Party, an action he refused to take. Instead, Burr chose the far more difficult path of joining the *Times* and rebuilding it from the ground up. In that capacity, along with Thomas Seymour, Burr became the Democratic constitutional voice of Connecticut.[20]

Democrats had argued since the mid-1850s, when the Republican Party first emerged out of the Second American Party System's disintegration, that these new Northern politicians were abolition fanatics who endangered the very bonds of Union because of their relentless attacks upon Southern slavery. Connecticut had deep business ties with the South and worried that they would be disrupted in the event of war. In the aftermath of the John Brown raid, for example, businessmen from throughout the state gathered in Meriden to craft a public response that might soothe the South.[21] To be sure, not all Republicans were abolitionists, but their insistence on legislating against the western expansion of the peculiar institution was viewed as sectional and highly inflammatory.[22] Democrats, especially those who later became Peace Democrats, maintained that the Constitution recognized the legality of slavery, insisted that it was a states' rights issue, and maintained that the federal government had no authority to interfere. The 1857 Dred Scott decision defined their ideological stance. The cannon smoke floating over Charleston harbor in April 1861 did nothing to change this view.

Following the attack on Fort Sumter, the Democratic *New Haven Register* bemoaned, "we have no heart for the sickening spectacle that presents itself to the mind, brought upon the country by Northern injustices and Southern resistance—higher law heresies, contempt for national obligations, and the indulgence of partisan prejudices."[23] On the same day, April 13, the *Hartford Times* declared, "The blackest day ever seen by America dawned yesterday, when the first clash of arms commenced between the two Governments into which our wretched country is now divided." The author pointed the blame for the conflict squarely at the feet of Lincoln and his party, insisting, "A few brief weeks ago this horrible drama could have been stopped. The troubles could have been settled as Washington, Franklin, Jefferson, Madison, and Adams, would have settled them—by the expression of kindly feelings among brethren—by the adoption of peace measures, of conciliation."[24]

As the armies of both sections prepared for war, Peace Democrats in Connecticut consistently defined their position. "The Constitution of the United States—indeed, 'The Constitution!' 'the Constitution!' is the rallying cry of the whole North," announced the *New Haven Register* on May 6, 1861. "But that very Constitution," continued the paper, "recognized the right of slaveholding in the different States of the Union." The author challenged that the nation's founding document also promised to suppress insurrections, "from whatever quarter they may come," and charged that the real source of the war was Northern Republicans bent on invading the South and abolishing slavery.[25] This accusation was coupled with the allegation that Republicans were the real traitors. "The men who are urging that this war be waged to destroy the domestic institutions of the South—who plead against guarantees, the rights of the border States, in order that the ill-conceived design of ultimate Abolitionism may be accomplished—are greater traitors to the cause of Constitutional Liberty, than the Secessionists themselves,—are doing more efficient service in the work of destroying the Government. Let us have an end to the Abolition humbug," announced the *Register* on June 7.[26]

The paper also outlined the Jeffersonian, states' rights underpinnings that historian Joanna Cowden identified, warning readers that "the greatest danger we had to fear was that the people would be induced to adopt explicit ideas of the old Federalists, that we must have a 'strong' government; that the state lines should be obliterated, and the whole country consolidated into one individual mass, under a supreme central power." The *Register* specifically noted that "Thomas Jefferson was elected, and in him States Rights and limited constitutional government triumphed." Yet, continued the author, "The fanatical North willingly risked war with all its horrors, the utter prostration of business, setting the country back a quarter of a century in the scale of all material prosperity and even a dissolution of the Union itself, for the sake of the Utopian idea of Abolitionism. Make the Central Government Supreme—make it the master, instead of the creature of the States."[27]

It was in the midst of this deepening crisis, as the drums of war grew louder and thousands of Union troop descended on Washington, that Thomas Seymour rose to the floor of the Connecticut General Assembly and presented his resolutions calling for compromise and outlining the ideological ground upon which Democrats viewed the conflict. Within weeks of his efforts, the first major battle of the war revealed for many what Seymour believed to be true. The Confederacy could not be defeated. The loss shocked state residents and inspired an even more robust anti-war movement.[28] Peace meetings appeared throughout Connecticut, where Democrats continued to blame the conflict on Republican abolitionists, and denounced the war on both patriotic and constitutional grounds. At an August gathering in Bloomfield, one Elisha Moore delivered a set of resolutions identical to Thomas Seymour's July 2 statement in the General Assembly. By August, these resolutions had become the standard peace position. William W. Eaton, a close friend of Seymour's, a representative from Hartford, and another leading peace advocate, then spoke. The *Hartford Times* reported that his remarks "were calm and patriotic," that the meeting was the largest ever held in the town, and that "no expression was made" and "no sentiment was entertained . . . that was not friendly to the government of the United States and the Union."[29]

At a meeting only a day later, held in Cornwall, the resolutions were brought forth again. They blamed the "mad policy" of the Republican administration for the war, called for a peaceful settlement through the Crittenden Compromise measures, complained that "the Black Republican war party" had already determined the existence of an irrepressible conflict, and that the nation would be saddled with a great war debt. The Democratic position also further reflected the larger ideological concerns over dangers to Jeffersonian republicanism, declaring, "That we view with anxiety and alarm the prospect of a large standing army, as inconsistent with republican institutions, and dangerous to their existence. . . . The prospective increase in the military powers of the Administration should admonish every Democratic citizen that a military despotism is death to American liberty." The final resolution noted that "to the cry of 'traitors,' 'secessionists,' and threats of mobs and terrorism, raised by Black-Republicans, who have destroyed our noble Union, let us respond with the shout of 'PEACE! PEACE!—if this be *treason*, make the most of it.'!"[30]

To Seymour's principled stance, Republicans responded with scorn and charges of disloyalty. The ex-Governor surely meant his statements to be pro-Union, conciliatory, and instructive. He undoubtedly believed that many in Connecticut opposed war; this was evidenced by the raising of peace flags throughout the state in the aftermath of Fort Sumter.[31] He also sincerely believed both that the South could not be conquered and that great constitutional principles were at stake. Yet the primary Republican newspaper in the state, the *Hartford Courant*, responded to Seymour's entreaties with ridicule and accusations of treason. The article announcing his peace resolutions included the subtitle, "Ex-Gov. Seymour's Sympathy with Traitors." Just a few days later the *Courant* announced "that Thomas H. Seymour has made himself an object of suspicion and distrust is saying but little. His legislative career went out in a blaze of infamy. He achieved, in one day, a political damnation from which there can be no resurrection." The paper continued,

> once an honored son of this good old State, a son upon whom she has not hesitated to heap her honor and praises, a man who has represented his country abroad, who has defended its flag on the battle-field, from who it had a right to expect unqualified support in the hour of its agony, rose in the House on the last day of its session, and proposed that the representatives of the people of the State of Connecticut should stultify themselves before the world, by declaring that it was wrong to defend our blessed, God-given government from the attacks of traitors, and that it was wrong to resent the indignity offered to the National Flag, that it was wrong not to confess that the men who love their country are the aggressors, and that it is their duty to offer terms of peace. Thomas H. Seymour did this.

The *Courant* then decried both Seymour and seventeen other Democrats who voted in favor of his peace resolutions, declaring, "Let them be remembered. Here is the black list."[32] Later that year, during a special October session of the General Assembly, Senate Republicans vented their anger toward Seymour and another Democratic ex-governor, Isaac Toucey (who also served as President James Buchanan's Secretary of the Navy), by cutting their portraits from the frames, which were left empty on the wall for half a day before they, too, were removed from the Senate chamber.[33]

Republicans charged anyone who opposed the war with treason to the Union. Every effort was made to suppress war opposition and come down hard on the dreaded "Copperheads." The *Hartford Courant* declared unequivocally, "This is no time for the North to talk about Peace with the South!" The paper repeatedly denounced such an idea, insisting, "*this quarrel must be* FOUGHT OUT!" "There never was a more ill-timed movement," continued the *Courant*, "than that of Eaton & Co. at Bloomfield, and of some scheming politicians at Cornwall . . . Let no well-meaning man be therefore deluded by Eaton's sophistics, honied [honeyed] over and made plausible as he knows how to prepare them."[34]

Democrats, of course, responded to the Republican charge that anyone who dissented against the war was an unpatriotic turncoat and anti-Union. In an article entitled, "Philosophical," the *New Haven Register* insisted, "It is of no use to cry, 'treason,' 'traitors,' at every man who thinks it advisable to save the country from utter demoralization and exhaustion, by securing peace short of a long and bloody war."[35] The paper attempted to reverse the notion of who was the true traitor, pointing the blame directly at abolitionists. "The most detestable traitors are those who hate the Union and have been working for its overthrow for the quarter of a century," continuing, they "now have the hypocrisy and audacity to pretend that they are in favor of the Union, and the Constitution on which it rests."[36]

As tempers continued to flare so, too, did the rhetoric and action of the parties. Nathan Morse, Democratic editor of the *Bridgeport Farmer and Advertiser*, displayed true venom, deriding the "grand army" that "ran back" from Bull Run, and jeering that "the heart of the Abolitionists heaved with sorrow at the blasted prospects of their fanaticism, and the diminished hope of a speedy gratification of their bloody will."[37] The animosity quickly led to Republican charges of Democratic conspiracy. A. A. Pettingill, the editor of the *Bridgeport Republican*, wrote to Governor William Buckingham, "I am becoming alarmed at the condition of things in this part of the State. Rebels—& very active ones—can be found without going south of the Mason & Dixon line. In other words we have *open traitors* at home." Pettingill complained that the *Bridgeport Farmer* was partially responsible, and "the consequence is that we are now threatened with a *Peace party* & a formidable one." He warned further, "There are secret organizations—one in this city—the members of which have *armed themselves for some purpose*—not a patriotic one."[38]

There is no evidence that secret societies were at work in Bridgeport, or elsewhere in Connecticut, but the threat, combined with the outspoken Democratic anti-war sentiment boiled over into violence. As a peace meeting was organizing in Stepney, just nine miles from Bridgeport, pro-Union men and returned soldiers from their three months service were led by the legendary showman P. T. Barnum to break up the affair. They chased peace men into the nearby cornfield, tore down a peace banner, and then regrouped and sang "The Star-Spangled Banner." When they returned to Bridgeport, the crowd swelled to several thousand, went to the offices of Morse's *Farmer*, battered down the door and destroyed everything in sight. Morse escaped by fleeing across the rooftops.[39]

Mark Howard, one of the state's Republican Party leaders, wrote to Secretary of the Navy Gideon Welles: "In no part of the free States is treason more malignant, defiant and insidious than in Conn., and Hartford is the seat of its influence. The feeling here is becoming intense on both sides—many of the traitors now go around armed, and the loyal portion of our community will have to do so, in self-defense. And but a spark is now necessary to kindle a flame that can only be extinguished in blood."[40] George A. Oviate, a Congregational minister from Somers, Connecticut, issued similar warnings to Governor Buckingham. "In Conn. there are many who favor the South, and such men, in the rural districts talk of secession openly and do much in demoralizing the people," wrote Oviate. He insisted that Alfred Burr's *Hartford Times* was largely responsible, noting, "Those who read this paper so exclusively are emboldened in their sympathy with the seceders. If this state of things continues, what is before us?" Oviate advocated shutting the *Times* down and implored the governor, "I hope in order to avoid bloodshed an [*sic*] Civil War, . . . [by] your Constitutional authority you would by Proclamation or otherwise would forbid the raising of peace Flags, and also peace gatherings in our area."[41]

Governor Buckingham acted quickly, issuing a proclamation on September 1 outlawing "the public exhibition of *peace-flags* falsely so called." Although acknowledging that "the Constitution guarantees liberty of speech and that of the press," he insisted that "the very exercise of our government, the future prosperity of this entire nation, and the hopes of universal freedom, demand that these outrages be suppressed." He continued: "I call upon the officers of the law to be active, diligent, and fearless in arresting, and instituting legal proceedings for the punishment of, those who disturb the public peace, or those who are guilty of sedition and treason, and of those who are embraced in combinations to obstruct the execution of the laws."[42] U.S. Marshal David Carr subsequently announced that traitors would "be summarily dealt with."[43] Arrests ensued, and prisoners were transported to Fort Lafayette in New York.[44] Barnum wrote to Lincoln that these actions "have rendered secessionists so scarce, I cannot find one for exhibition in my museum."[45] The back of the peace movement was broken, at least temporarily.[46] The papers reported few meetings throughout the remainder of 1861 and well into 1862.

The Democrats were not, however, silenced. The *New Haven Register* announced,

Governor Buckingham evidently believes that there are combinations of people in this State to 'obstruct the execution of the laws,' etc. We have not the remotest idea of any such thing . . . There is not a democrat in Connecticut but would be prompt to expose, and to condemn, the slightest approach to anarchy, or even confusion, in our good old State.

The paper followed in another article just a few days later, "Tens of thousands of our citizens must have been astonished on reading this announcement of the Governor . . . We are not aware that any secret organizations of a political character existed in this State."[47] Such accusations have been a steady point of dispute among historians. Was the Republican charge of conspiracy and secret societies enough to substantiate their reality? In combing through Connecticut newspapers and archives no evidence has been found to support the argument that secret Copperhead movements were afoot. This was true even in the immediate aftermath of the famous 1864 Colt factory fire, when charges of conspiracy abounded.[48]

The only "plot" executed by Peace Democrats was a steady, consistent attack on Republican principles, especially their alleged abandonment of the Constitution and dedication to abolition. This issue was always at the core of Democratic criticism and rose like a wave following the August 30, 1861 action by General John Fremont issuing a military emancipation decree in Missouri. Lincoln quickly rescinded the order, but it was too late.[49] Democrats saw what they had always believed to be true. A radical abolitionist revolution dedicated to the freeing of slaves, granting blacks social and political equality, and in the process destroying both the Constitution and the law of nature which placed whites above blacks. The *Register* put the matter plainly:

> There is no time like the present for examining the sincerity of men's desire for a restoration of the Union. To wish for the conquest of the Southern states, and the extermination of the slave-holding population there, and a new Constitution, which shall ignore slavery, is not to wish for the restoration of the Government or the supremacy of the Constitution, but is actually to desire a revolution which shall found a new government on the ruins of the old.[50]

The *Hartford Times* provided considerable space to the Fremont issue, condemning his action and faintly praising Lincoln for rescinding the order. The paper made note of an abolitionist speech delivered by Massachusetts Senator Charles Sumner, and questioned why Republican papers like the *Hartford Courant* would take exception at being charged with abolitionism. The *Times* announced, "It is impossible to misunderstand the purport of these things. There is an active, bitter, powerful element in the Republican party who are radically hostile to everything that savors of Conservatism, of an adherence to the Constitution, and especially of an approval of the President's patriotic course with General Fremont."[51] The *Times* continued in another article, acknowledging, "We are fully aware that all Republicans are not Abolitionists . . . But if the *Courant* will speak its honest sentiments, it will agree with us that they have had a very great, and too often a controlling influence in the councils of the Republican party. Does the *Courant* assume that it is wrong to sound the alarm in view of the progress of their strength and influence?"[52]

The question was an important one. Peace Democrats fully embraced the view that they were sounding the alarm on a host of issues connected to the war, most importantly the destruction of the Constitution. Again, the *Times* put the matter simply: "We do not believe the Government and Union can be sustained by, breaking the Constitution, which is the Government. It is no way to save the Constitution, to break, destroy, or violate any part of it. These are our views."[53]

The year 1862 was devoted to ramping up what many in the North now realized was a long and bloody struggle. Democrats in Connecticut, as elsewhere in the nation, split into opposing wings. War men sided with Lincoln while Peace Democrats maintained that the conflict was a grand mistake. As always, Thomas Seymour's convictions were crystal clear. When a meeting of War Democrats was announced in Hartford on July 10, 1862 and it was erroneously reported that Seymour served as vice president, he utterly rejected the idea, insisting in a letter to newspapers that such a meeting "ignores peaceful remedies of any sort, as a means of restoring the Union, and calls loudly for men and means to aid in the subjugation and consequent degradation and overthrow of the South. I follow gentlemen, in no such crusade, neither will I contribute, in any way, to the accomplishment of such bloody purposes."[54]

With the lull in anti-war activity at the outset of 1862, Democrats had rather lamely attempted to unseat Governor Buckingham in the April gubernatorial election, nominating War Democrat James C. Loomis, who lost by 9,148 votes.[55] Many in the North were confident of a quick Union victory and the demoralization initiated by the great bloodletting to come had not yet materialized. Of Buckingham's victory, Republican newspapers gleefully announced the death of Democratic opposition: "In no northern state has the spirit of secessionism been so rampant and malignant as in Connecticut. In none has its rebuke, since the war began, been so signal and overwhelming. . . . And if the party is buried, it cannot complain that we have not given it a splendid funeral."[56] Democrats, in turn, insisted that the party "is on a solid foundation. Your principles are just.

You sustain the Constitution, which *is the government* of the United States, as you have ever sustained it. You oppose those who make war upon that Constitution, no matter where they belong—whether they are secessionists in arms, or abolitionists with wily talk and insidious ways, ever encroaching upon its principles of compromise and of justice."[57] Even in defeat and at a low ebb, Peace Democrats clung to the belief that it was they who were the true adherents of Constitution and Union. Abolition and war were the real threats.

And 1862 revealed ample evidence for the Democratic belief that a great abolitionist conspiracy undergirded the entire war. On March 13, the Republican-controlled Congress enacted a new article of war forbidding army officers from returning escaped slaves to their masters; this was essentially an official extension of General Benjamin Butler's contraband policy. In that same month, President Lincoln sent a special message to Congress urging a joint resolution offering "pecuniary aid" to "any state which may adopt gradual abolishment of slavery." Lincoln had also been encouraging the border states to enact gradual emancipation plans. In April, Congress abolished slavery in the District of Columbia. The *Hartford Times* lamented that such measures would make matters worse, arguing, "It is important, *if our Union is really to be preserved*, to impress upon the minds of the people of the South—those who are not uncompromisingly dissolutionists— the fact, if it is a fact, that this is *not* an abolition war."[58]

When Lincoln announced the preliminary Emancipation Proclamation in September, following the Battle of Antietam, Democrats exploded. The *Hartford Times* blasted, "the President's act *is in violation of the Constitution* . . . it is a REVOLUTIONARY act! . . . that so far as the *Times* is concerned—and in this we can speak for all Democrats as well—we shall never approve, or attempt to justify such a measure!" The paper insisted that "The rebellion can be quelled, if at all, only by measures that accord with the Constitution. The Union can only be saved or restored under that paramount law. A war in violation of the Constitution can never restore the Union; it would endanger our system of government.[59] The *New Haven Register* announced, "The Republicans having now so generally taken the Abolition ground, openly and even boastingly, cannot any longer find fault, as they have in the past, if they are known as, and called, Abolitionists. Our future divisions must therefore be Constitutionalists and Abolitionists."[60]

In many ways, Lincoln's proclamation was exactly what Democrats needed to revitalize and unify their beleaguered ranks. Having been beaten down by Republican patriotism in late 1861 and well into 1862, they now had a rallying cry. As historian J. Robert Lane noted, "only through victory at the polls could the Democrats hope to change the administration's plans." The first step to Democratic political control in Connecticut was winning the upcoming November town elections, which provided a springboard to the April 1863 gubernatorial campaign. Democrats succeeded in capturing several important towns, including Hartford, New Haven, and Bridgeport.[61] The party presses crowed with victory. "The ballot box has proven that the North is not *all* abolitionized, and the UNION MAY YET BE RESTORED," trumpeted the *New Haven Register*, adding, "there is great joy throughout THE NORTH! Joy among friends of the Constitution and the Union, for the RIGHT HAS TRIUMPHED and the evil sectional party of abolition, and so called Republicanism, *has received its death blow*." The *Hartford Times* declared, "The result is a most gratifying one as it rebukes the Abolition Proclamation."[62]

The Democratic victory sparked a reinvigorated protest of the war. From abolition to violations of habeas corpus and conscription, Democrats lashed out. In an article entitled, "States Rights Vindicated," the *Times* insisted, "Under the pretence of 'necessity' and 'the war powers,' Abraham Lincoln has resorted to open and destructive violations of the Organic Law, and initiated a system of Centralization which would, if he and his party were permitted to carry it out, unchecked, soon extinguish the altar fires of Liberty, and plunge the country into a military despotism."[63] Democrats also complained of crushing debt and taxation, and continued to mock Republican charges of disunion. In an article entitled "Republican Estimate of Treason," the *Times* noted, "The only arguments of the Black Republican presses, are these—'traitor,' 'copperhead,' 'ought to be suppressed,' 'served him right,' &c. So indiscriminate had been their epithet of 'traitor,' that it has become meaningless."[64]

The primary Democratic aim was victory in the April 1863 gubernatorial election. So resurgent was the Peace faction of the party that it succeeded in nominating Thomas Seymour, rather than James Loomis, who had been the War Democrat nominee for the two preceding campaigns. Seymour's inclusion on the ticket promised a ferocious partisan contest. Historian J. Robert Lane noted that Republicans and Democrats "expressed such venomous hostility towards each other that experienced politicians considered the campaign the bitterest ever conducted in the state."[65] One cannot read the Democratic newspapers of the time and fail to sense the level of party excitement in Connecticut. Meetings and rallies were held all over the state. The *Times* announced "A GREAT MEET-ING. *Outpouring of the Democracy!* IMMENSE ENTHUSIASM. 'Seymour and the Constitution.'"[66] Republicans fully understood the threat posed by this surge of Democratic action. The Republican State Central Committee published a lengthy appeal to the people, declaring, "A State Election is soon to take place more important than any which has occurred since the foundation of our Government. Connecticut is to declare on the first Monday in April, whether she is in favor of a *dishonorable peace—submission to the demands of armed traitors*, and a *dissolution of the Union*, or whether she is determined at every hazard, to defend the honor of our National Flag and the Union of these States."[67] The *Hartford Evening Press* charged that Democrats "have put themselves squarely against the war, and picked out as their candidate about the only public man in New England who has been from the first openly and notoriously *with* the South and *against* the North in this struggle. It is not possible to show that he occupies any different ground than Jeff Davis, except in daring."[68]

The election was also closely watched by Connecticut's soldiers in the field, many of whom expressed grave concerns over what was happening at home. The *Courant* and *Times* engaged in a duel of soldiers letters, publishing dozens upon dozens over the course of a month, along with formal resolutions from Connecticut regiments. "Do not elect T. H. Seymour, for I do not want to come home to Connecticut and have such a man as that holding the position that those anti-war Democrats—those slimy copperheads—do to a State which ought to be loyal. For Heaven's sake, what is Connecticut coming to?" Some men even threatened to turn their regiments around and march on their home state.[69] One of the most significant resolutions, purely because of what it represented, was a statement from the Ninth Army Corps, comprising the 9th, 12th, 13th, 23rd, 24th, 25th, 26th, and 28th Connecticut Regiments, all then stationed in the Louisiana area: "You sent us here (did you not?) to bear onward the stainless folds of Connecticut's flag, side by side with the glorious Stars and Stripes, until perjured Secession shall be ground to powder beneath the iron heel of war. And we will do it; but do not place us between two fires. To-day treason is more dangerous in Connecticut than in Louisiana."[70]

The *Times* responded, charging that the *Courant* fabricated the true sentiments of soldiers and that many were coerced into adopting regimental resolutions. A soldier from the 22nd claimed: "Almost to a man, rank and file, HEARTILY ENDORSE THE NOMINATION of Gov. Seymour, and daily wish and pray that he may be elected. I never saw in my life a set of men so unanimous for Seymour." He noted that a group of state Republican Party leaders had suddenly appeared in camp to talk about the election and, he wrote, "to unmask this vile Niggerhead plot, with its underground work arrangements . . . to make it appear that the soldiers endorse niggerism." He concluded that the regiment's resolutions are "a willful, DELIBERATE LIE." Another soldier from the same regiment stated that the men had held an informal ballot, with Seymour the victor.[71]

Democratic Party leaders met at Touro Hall in *Hartford* on February 17–18, where they were regaled with speeches of Union, political victory, and denunciations of Lincoln. William W. Eaton declared, "The Democrats of Connecticut will not sustain war waged for the destruction of the Union. We will tell Lincoln that he cannot come into Connecticut, and take men from their homes; that he cannot come into Connecticut and compel men to serve in the army."[72] Henry H. Barbour insisted, "*We are against the War. The elections of other States have not been understood by the President. There have been too many War Democrats chosen.* When Thomas H. Seymour is elected, *the President will understand what that means*."[73] Democrats prepared a new set of resolutions, drafted by Eaton: "The time has now arrived when all true lovers of the Constitution are ready to abandon the 'monstrous falacy' [*sic*] that the Union can be restored by the armed hand, and are anxious to inaugurate such action, honorable alike to the contending factions, as will stop the ravages of war, avert universal bankruptcy and unite all the State upon terms of equality, as members of one confederacy."[74] Seymour pledged himself to negotiation with the South.

He lost the election by a remarkably narrow margin, just 2,634 votes.[75] Consider that Loomis had been defeated in 1862 by 9,148 votes, and the following year, 1864, Democrats again shifted to a War candidate, Origen Seymour (cousin to Thomas), who lost by 5,658, and one understands the amazing shift of sentiment that had hit Connecticut in the midst of the conflict. The people seriously considered peace. There had never been any doubt where Seymour stood on the question of war. Indeed, Peace Democrats remained remarkably consistent in their views throughout the entirety of the war. Moreover, it is entirely likely that they lost the 1863 election solely because of the soldier vote: primarily Republican men who had been furloughed to return home and vote the Buckingham ticket (by 1864 Connecticut passed a law allowing soldiers to vote in the field).[76] Democrats, of course, cried foul. The *Times* insisted that "The Democracy of Connecticut gallantly contended on Monday against all the virulent Abolitionists, the haters of the Union," yet Republicans utilized "the whole power of the federal administration; with MONEY in unlimited quantities . . . with over 2,000 *selected* soldiers from the army sent home to vote."[77]

The 1863 gubernatorial election was the crest of the Connecticut Peace movement. The peace men were never able to muster enough strength to again nominate one of their own. Still, they refused to back down or temper their rhetoric against what they viewed as an unconstitutional war against slavery, a war that was sapping both the life blood and resources of the nation, a war that was destroying the old Union and building upon its foundation a central despotism mortared by executive usurpation. Rather than slackening their efforts, Democrats increased their cries. "The States made the Union. They gave no authority to the general government, or any branch of it, to abolish slavery or to destroy any other purely State institution," complained the *Times*, "the Union could not have been formed without this contract. When a portion of the States, by force of arms, under any pretext, destroy that contract by abolishing slavery in any of the other States, the Union is broken—the bond that made the Union is violated and severed . . . If this Proclamation is sustained, the Union will be broken."[78]

The Democratic press continued to pose questions to its readers: "What sort of Union are we to have? A Union of force? A Union of centralized government, which dictates terms to States, and disposes of State institutions at pleasure? Is this the sort of a Union we are promised? It is of the Austrian kind." The papers promised devotion to the law and, as always, challenged Republican notions of disunion: "All Democrats are ready to give the last dollar and the last man to maintain the Constitution and restore the Union; but not a dollar nor a man, unless legally compelled to do so, to aid in a war for the abolition of slavery—a war for the destruction of the Union. If this is treason, make the most of it."[79]

Democrats also pointed out the vast inconsistencies in Lincoln's position on the issue of slavery. They had made this point throughout the war, but as Republicans in Congress worked to pass the Thirteenth Amendment abolishing slavery, Democrats addressed the issue with a new vigor. The President had been painfully clear in his inaugural address; he had no authority and promised no intention of touching slavery where it existed. "A change took place," declared the *Times*. "Mr. Lincoln and his friends determined to disregard what they knew and had solemnly declared to be the law of the land; and they determined to trample the Constitution and their own construction of it underfoot."[80]

The last possible opportunity for Democrats was the 1864 presidential election. If they could defeat Lincoln, Democrats believed the Union might be saved and the excess of government power rebuked by the people. Early in the year the chances seemed slim at best. As noted, Peace Democrats failed to nominate one of their own for the gubernatorial election, and when War Democrat Origen S. Seymour went up against Governor Buckingham he lost by a wide margin. Democrats also lost the New Haven city elections for the first time in eight years, and, more significantly, William W. Eaton of Hartford, one of the most outspoken peace men, lost his House seat in the General Assembly.[81] This series of losses no doubt influenced Thomas Seymour's refusal to accept the possibility of the party's nomination for president in 1864.[82] The results represented a solid victory for Republicans, and they claimed it as such. "Throw high the cap of liberty! Connecticut has spoken in thunder tones to the nation and the world," announced the *Courant*. "Copperheadism in Connecticut has received its death wound." The *Hartford Evening Press* announced that the Democrats were "finally nailed up and sent home in a box . . . Union triumphant—no compromise with treason."[83]

The Republican tide, however, had not yet risen fully. The summer of 1864 went poorly for the Union military. The North expected a quick end to the war with newly appointed General Ulysses S. Grant at the head of the Army. What they received instead was bloodshed not previously imagined and what seemed like the army's constant inability to defeat Robert E. Lee or take Atlanta.

In the midst of this gloom peace negotiations swirled about in the summer heat. Democrats made all they could of the news. The *Hartford Times* announced, "For the first time since this reign of horrors began, *there is a gleam of light* through the black storm clouds which have rested like a funeral pall upon our afflicted country. The South proposes to RESTORE THE OLD UNION!" Yet, continued the paper, "it seems that the proposition of the South is not satisfactory to Abraham Lincoln. This man, whom an inscrutable Fate inflicted upon our unhappy land as its chief magistrate . . . demands as a *condition* precedent to its [the Union's] restoration, that the South shall abolish negro slavery! This arrogant usurpation of dictatorial power, and most wickedly unpatriotic use of it, will, if persisted in, be duly attended to by the American people. Abraham Lincoln must not be permitted to stand in the way of a restoration of the Union."[84] The reality is that there were no real peace negotiations. The entire matter had been got up by New York *Tribune* editor Horace Greeley, who so wanted to believe rumors that he publicized them and insisted upon meeting Jefferson Davis's emissaries in Canada. Nothing came of the matter, except an opportunity for Democratic newspapers to lambaste Lincoln once again.[85]

As the November election neared, the Southern stalemate lifted when William Tecumseh Sherman captured Atlanta. New life was breathed into the North; Republicans were buoyed by the news from the front. Democrats pinned everything on the presidential election. It was their last opportunity to defeat the tyrant Lincoln. They focused on the war's duration, promising that reelecting Lincoln would guarantee many more years of bloodshed and, as they had always insisted, that the South could never be subjugated. The *Hartford Times* asked readers, "How many more years of war are we to have? How many more drafts? How many more thousands of millions spent? How long are our institutions to be crushed by military rule? How long is labor to be drained by the exhaustion of men and means?"[86] The day before the election, the paper posed the most simple of Democratic questions, and one that defined their ideological position from the start of the war. "A Republic or a Monarchy," declared the *Times*, "this is the question. If Fraud and Force prevail tomorrow, and the honest voice of the People be stifled in the unfair re-election of Abraham Lincoln, farewell to the Liberties of America. The work of the Patriot Fathers will be destroyed. This is no idle talk. Everything points to the inevitable result. Abolitionism is tyrannical and arbitrary in all its measure and works."[87]

The *New Haven Register* offered an equally dire choice for the nation:

> The argument is closed—the case is made up, and tomorrow the jury will render its verdict,—a verdict upon which rests the fate of the country. Should it pronounce in favor of the election of General McClellan, we shall speedily have restored the Union, with peace reigning throughout our now distracted land; and we can then apply our energies to the work of restoring the happiness and prosperity which prevailed before the fell spirit of sectional fanaticism became a power in the land. Should it pronounce for Lincoln,—it will be an endorsement of the usurpations, corruption and outrages of which the Administration has been guilty—a declaration in favor of uncompromising war for Abolition—for unrelenting conscription and ruinous debt and taxation to carry out the policy of Garrison, Greeley, and Co. Was there ever a more momentous issue committed to the judgment of any people?[88]

Nationally, Abraham Lincoln won a resounding victory. In Connecticut, he barely defeated his former general. Out of almost 90,000 votes cast, Lincoln won by a mere 2,405—a victory almost certainly secured by the fact that the General Assembly had passed an amendment to the state constitution authorizing soldiers to vote in the field.[89] Lincoln's meager win in the state was the lowest margin, a mere 51.38 percent, than any state in New England and the lowest in the nation next to the three states that the president actually lost to McClellan.[90] What had been true at the war's outset and throughout the conflict remained true at the end of 1864: Connecticut was deeply divided. From the beginning of the conflict Connecticut Peace Democrats had been outspoken in their defense of the Union, the Union they believed had been created by the Founders. It was a Union that recognized slavery and states' rights and provided for a limited federal government that did not interfere with state sovereignty. It was a nation based on Jeffersonian ideals. Democratic loyalty, then, was defined by an unalterable conception of states' rights, limited government, and strict constitutional interpretation. Democratic loyalty was rooted in a far more stringent political conservatism than was most of the North's conception of Union. While much, if not most, of the North was hostile to abolition at the outset of the war, even those who had been resistant came around to the idea of emancipation primarily because it promised a quicker end to the conflict. Peace Democrats never embraced such a notion. Indeed, they attacked the war as an abolitionist plot from the outset and railed against the unmasked scheme once Lincoln issued the preliminary Emancipation Proclamation. There should be no wonder why "Copperheads" viewed themselves as loyal to the Constitution first.

They continued to espouse such views throughout the war, even in its darkest hours when their political future seemed most in doubt. Whether this was sheer stubborn partisanship or principled ideological conviction requires further research and consideration. It was, however, remarkably consistent. It also met with serious backlash from Republicans, who labeled Democrats with the notorious epithet "Copperhead." At times, Democrats embraced the criticism and challenged the very notion of treason, insisting that it was actually the Republicans who had destroyed the Union and Constitution, that they had forced a new revolution upon the nation. Gone was the limited government of the Founders, replaced instead by a powerful central authority. It is hard to argue that the Democrats were wrong on this count. The Civil War was a revolution, both socially and governmentally.[91]

Peace Democrats during the Civil War were on the wrong side of history. They embodied an anti-black racism that is anathema in contemporary America. They may very well have been content to allow Southern secession and with it destruction of the Union. Abraham Lincoln has been rightly recognized as the nation's savior, one of our greatest presidents, and the great emancipator who remade America by envisioning the Declaration of Independence as the true cornerstone of democracy. Democrats, however, believed his new birth of freedom was entirely unconstitutional, as were many of the means he utilized to achieve it. Democrats never wavered in their ideological convictions regarding constitutional authority over slavery, or over the stringent power utilized to secure Northern victory. As historian Joanna Cowden rightly recognized, Thomas Seymour "and his followers should not be dismissed as hopelessly nostalgic, out of touch with reality. In fact, they grasped only too well the meaning of the war, that it was a revolutionary conflict that would bring fundamental changes to the Union."[92] Historians can ultimately judge the Democrats wrong in their views on race and humanity, but their views on constitutional authority and states' rights versus a powerful federal government have continued to rage in American society.

Given the level of rancor that existed throughout the war, it is particularly interesting to note how the political animosity in Connecticut began to wane as the
armies of the South surrendered and peace returned to the land. The *Hartford
Times* reported on April 29, 1865 that the portraits of ex-governors Seymour and
Toucey had been returned to the Senate Chamber wall, explaining that a Senate
resolution authorized their return "satisfied of the 'loyalty' of their originals." The
Times expressed what was now standard Democratic astonishment: "we do not
understand why these gentlemen should have been denounced as disloyal four
years ago, and pronounced loyal now. Their devotion to the Constitution and the
Union, and to law and order, has been constant and unswerving."[93]

Notes

1. Democrats and Republicans certainly recognized the seriousness of secession, but
until, and shortly after, the bombardment of Fort Sumter, many hoped that a peaceful settlement via compromise would resolve the situation before extensive bloodshed
occurred. This is discussed in some detail in Matthew Warshauer, *Connecticut in the
American Civil War: Slavery, Sacrifice, and Survival* (Middletown, Conn.: Wesleyan
University Press, 2011), 48–51.

2. "Obituary: Ex-Gov. Thomas H. Seymour, of Connecticut," *The New York Times*,
September 4, 1868; Thomas H. Seymour, biographical information, National Governor's
Association, http://www.nga.org.

3. "Connecticut Legislature: Senate Peace Resolutions Afternoon Session Evening
Session House," "Ex-Gov. Seymour's Sympathy with Traitors," *Hartford Courant*, July 3,
1861; see also, "Gov. Seymour's Peace Offering," *Hartford Weekly Times*, July 22, 1861.

4. For more on a consistent Democratic ideology, see, Joel H. Silbey, *The Partisan
Imperative: The Dynamics of American Politics Before the Civil War* (New York: Oxford
University Press, 1997); Jean H. Baker, *Affairs of Party: The Political Culture of Northern
Democrats in the Mid-Nineteenth Century* (New York: Fordham University Press, 1984).
See also, Richard O. Curry, "The Union as It Was: A Critique of Recent Interpretations of
the 'Copperheads,'" *Civil War History* 13, no. 1 (1967): 25–39; Richard O. Curry, "Copper-
headism and Continuity: the Anatomy of a Stereotype," *Journal of Negro History* 57, no. 1
(1972): 29–36.

5. Joanna Cowden noted that Peace Democrats in Connecticut were "committed to
an inflexible brand of Jeffersonianism" and had throughout the 1850s been in favor of
granting the Southern members of their party concessions and compromise, especially
in support of the fugitive slave act and the Dred Scott decision. Joanna D. Cowden, "The
Politics of Dissent: Civil War Democrats in Connecticut," *New England Quarterly* 56,
no. 4 (December 1983): 538–54. See also, Joanna D. Cowden, *"Heaven Will Frown on Such
a Cause As This": Six Democrats Who Opposed Lincoln's War* (Lanham, Md.: University
Press of America, 2001).

6. For a detailed discussion of Civil War dissent, see Matthew Warshauer, "Northern
Dissent," *A Companion to the U.S. Civil War*, ed. Aaron Sheehan-Dean (Boston: Blackwell Publishing, 2013).

7. John Tallmadge understood the essential nature of the antebellum political culture and the interplay between politicians and the public, explaining that Thomas Seymour was heartened by the spontaneous hanging of peace flags and banners, and that he mentioned this in his July 1861 speech. Tallmadge also questioned, "Were the Connecticut peace demonstrations a spontaneous outburst of this anti-Abolitionist feeling? They had all the appearances of a grass-roots movement: beginning in widely separated villages and spreading rapidly to larger towns and city suburbs. The men who raised the first flags may well have acted on their own impulses, but their hostility to the war undoubtedly intensified by the bold editorials of [Bridgeport *Farmer* editor Nathan] Morse and the unyielding stand of Seymour." John E. Tallmadge, "A Peace Movement in Civil War Connecticut," *New England Quarterly* 37, no. 3 (September 1964): 306–21.

8. Jennifer Weber makes a similar point about the rhythm of Peace Democrat activity, noting that it began at the start of the war, expanded with Lincoln's Emancipation Proclamation, and peaked with the presidential election of 1864. For Connecticut, the peak was the gubernatorial election of 1863, though the 1864 election was an excellent indicator that the movement was not dead. See Jennifer L. Weber, *Copperheads: The Rise and Fall Lincoln's Opponents in the North* (New York: Oxford University Press, 2006).

9. Mark E. Neely, Jr., *The Union Divided: Party Conflict in the Civil War North* (Cambridge: Harvard University Press, 2002); Adam I. P. Smith, *No Party Now: Politics in the Civil War North* (New York: Oxford, 2006).

10. For more on Seymour's political wariness and conservatism on going forward in office, see, Cowden, "*Heaven Will Frown on Such a Cause As This*," 51–53.

11. Wood Grey, *The Hidden Civil War: The Story of the Copperheads* (New York: Viking Press, 1942); George Fort Milton, *Abraham Lincoln and the Fifth Column* (New York: Vanguard Press, 1942); Elbert J. Benton, *The Movement for Peace Without Victory During the Civil War* (Cleveland: The Western Reserve Historical Society, 1918). Frank L. Klement, *The Copperheads in the Middle West* (Chicago: University of Chicago Press, 1960); Robert H. Abzug, "The Copperheads: Historical Approaches to Civil War Dissent in the Midwest," *Indiana Magazine of History* 6, no. 1 (March 1970): 40–55.

12. Benton, *The Movement for Peace Without Victory During the Civil War*, 19. One theory for the Midwestern peace movement was an alleged western conception of states' rights democracy.

13. Peace Democratic opposition in Connecticut seems to have been more immediate following the outset of the war than in other places in the North, at least as described by Weber in *Copperheads*. John E. Tallmadge argued that "only in Connecticut did the protests coalesce into what might be called a peace movement and threaten, briefly, to set off a minority rebellion north of the battle lines." He surmised that the flood of anti-war protest was caused by outspoken Democratic newspaper editors and prominent peace men, like Thomas Seymour. See Tallmadge, "A Peace Movement in Civil War Connecticut." Certainly, a more comparative study of Peace Democrats throughout the North is needed to better understand how the movement began and the extent to which there existed continuity in strategy and ideology.

14. Seymour's election bid in 1863 will be discussed later in the essay, but consider that he lost by a mere 2,600 votes, compared to Vallandigham's loss in Ohio by 100,000 votes.

15. A far more comprehensive investigation of the peace movement throughout the North is needed, and more consideration needs to be given to why Connecticut was so unlike her New England sisters. Part of the reason may have been because of significant economic ties with the South, but also due to a significant and viral racism within the state. Discussion of the 1863 gubernatorial and 1864 presidential election appears later in this essay.

16. The point here is not to argue that Connecticut maintained in the 1850s some sort of cultural consistency that influenced dissent during the war, except in that the Democratic Party remained strong and advocated a long-held political ideology. A discussion of state demographics goes beyond the focus of the essay, but it is worth knowing that in 1850 only 10.3 percent of the population were recent immigrants, mostly Irish Catholics, whereas ten years later the population was 17.4 percent, 80 percent of which were Irish. This caused a temporary gain to the Know Nothing Party. The impact on Democratic Peace ideology, if there was any at all, was likely minor. See Carroll John Noonan, *Nativism in Connecticut, 1829–1869* (Washington: Catholic University of America Press), 249–56; John Niven, *Connecticut for the Union: The Role of the State in the Civil War* (New Haven: Yale University Press, 1965), 9.

17. Jarvis Means Morse, *A Neglected Period of Connecticut's History, 1818–1850* (New York: Octagon Books, 1933). See also, J. Robert Lane, *A Political History of Connecticut during the Civil War* (Washington: Catholic University of America Press, 1941).

18. For a detailed discussion of Connecticut's history of slavery and race, see Warshauer, *Connecticut in the American Civil War*. New research is coming to light on regions of the state that may have leaned more toward abolitionism. See Carol Patterson Martineau, "Patriotism and Abolitionism in Civil War Era Windham County," in *Inside Connecticut and the Civil War: Essays on One State's Struggles*, ed. Matthew Warshauer (Middletown, Conn.: Wesleyan University Press, 2013).

19. For more on Buckingham, see Warshauer, *Connecticut in the American Civil War*; Samuel Giles Buckingham, *The Life of William A. Buckingham: The War Governor of Connecticut* (Springfield, Mass.: W. F. Adams Company, 1894).

20. James Hammond Trumbull, ed., *The Memorial History of Hartford County, Connecticut, 1633–1884*, vol. 1 (Boston: Edward L. Osgood, 1886), 617–20.

21. "The Manufacturers' Convention at Meriden," *Hartford Daily Courant*, January 19, 1860.

22. Michael F. Holt, *Political Crisis of the 1850s* (New York: Norton, 1978); Michael F. Holt, *Political Parties and American Political Development from the Age of Jackson to the Age of Lincoln* (Baton Rouge: Louisiana State University Press, 1992); Eric Foner, *Free Soil, Free Labor, Free Men: The Political Ideology of the Republican Party Before the Civil War* (New York: Oxford University Press, 1970).

23. "The Culmination," *New Haven Register*, April 13, 1861.

24. "Beauregard opens fire on Ft Sumter, Civil War Begins," *Hartford Times*, April 13, 1861.

25. *New Haven Register*, May 6, 1861.

26. *New Haven Register*, June 7, 1861.

27. "Toryism," *New Haven Register*, June 13, 1861; Cowden, "The Politics of Dissent: Civil War Democrats in Connecticut," 538–40.

28. For examples of Republican shock following Bull Run, see "Forward! Once More," *Hartford Evening Press*, July 23, 1861; Horace Bushnell, *Reverses Needed: A Discourse Delivered on the Sunday After the Disaster at Bull Run, in the North Church, Hartford* (Hartford, Conn.: L. E. Hunt, 1861); "Editorial," *Hartford Daily Courant*, July 29, 1861; "Push on the Column!" *Hartford Daily Courant*, August 10, 1861; "The War is Necessary," *Hartford Daily Courant*, October 5, 1861.

29. "PEACE MEETING IN BLOOMFIELD," *Hartford Times*, August 7, 1861.

30. "Another Peace Meeting in Cornwall," *Hartford Times*, August 7, 1861.

31. A white "peace flag" appeared in Ridgefield, where two men were shot while attempting to tear it down. Other peace flags were raised in Avon, New Milford, New Preston, West Hartford, and Windsor. See "News Items," *New Haven Register*, May 7, 1861; *Hartford Times*, June 3 and 6, 1861; William Croffut and John Morris, *The Military and Civil History of Connecticut during the War of 1861–1865* (New York: Ledyard Bill, 1869), 103; Cowden, "The Politics of Dissent: Civil War Democrats in Connecticut"; Tallmadge, "A Peace Movement in Civil War Connecticut"; Warshauer, *Connecticut in the American Civil War*, 55.

32. "The Seymour Resolutions," *Hartford Courant*, July 8, 1861.

33. "It will Stand," *Hartford Daily Courant*, October 19, 1861; "Toucey and Seymour," *Hartford Courant*, October 29, 1861; "CONNECTICUT DISGRACED," *Hartford Times*, October 16, 1861. The *Times* announced that the act "will not fasten upon Governors Toucey or Seymour stigma of 'treason' or 'disloyalty.'" Rather, it was "the indecent assaults of petty malice." The resolution allowed the portraits to be restored when satisfied of Toucey and Seymour's loyalty to the Union. See Croffut and Morris, *The Military and Civil History of Connecticut During the War of 1861–1865*, 136.

34. "Push on the Columns!" *Hartford Courant*, August 10, 1861.

35. "Philosophical," *New Haven Register*, June 16, 1861. See also, "Traitors to the Administration," *New Haven Register*, June 20, 1861.

36. "Traitors," *New Haven Register*, July 5, 1861.

37. Quoted in Croffut and Morris, *The Military and Civil History of Connecticut during the War of 1861–1865*, 106.

38. A. A. Pettingill to William A. Buckingham, August 24, 1861, RG 005, Governor William A. Buckingham, Connecticut State Library.

39. Croffut and Morris, *The Military and Civil History of Connecticut during the War of 1861–1865*, 100–10, provides an excellent account of the peace movement and the reactions to it. See also, Tallmadge, "A Peace Movement in Civil War Connecticut"; Cowden, "The Politics of Dissent."

40. Quoted in Lane, *A Political History of Connecticut during the Civil War*, 180.

41. George A. Oviate to William A. Buckingham, August 27, 1861, RG 005, Governor William A. Buckingham, Connecticut State Library.

42. "A PROCLAMATION: BY HIS EXCELLENCY THE GOVERNOR," *Hartford Daily Courant*, September 2, 1861.

43. On September 3, Carr wrote to Secretary of War Simon Cameron that he had stopped circulation of the *New York Daily News* in New Haven. On the 11th, he reported that the order was being defied by "a noisy secessionist" named George A. Hubbard, who continued to sell the newspaper on trains of the Naugatuck Railroad. Carr requested

approval to arrest Hubbard and did so on the 20th. Hubbard's brother, however, had connections in the Republican Party, and Secretary of State Seward ordered his release. See Barruss M. Carnahan, *Act of Justice: Lincoln's Emancipation Proclamation and the Law of War* (Lexington: University of Kentucky Press, 2007), 57.

44. On August 29, Ellis B. Schnabel was arrested and charged with "making treasonable harangues at peace meetings . . . and with publicly denouncing the government" (*War of Rebellion: Official Records of the Union and Confederate Armies*, 2nd ser., 2:620). The full scope of arrests requires further study.

45. Phineas T. Barnum to Abraham Lincoln, August 30, 1861, Abraham Lincoln Papers, American Memory Collection, Library of Congress, http://memory.loc.gov/ammem/alhtml/malhome.html; Barnum also noted: "Those who one week ago were blatant secessionists are to day publicly announcing themselves as 'in for the country to the end of the war.' The 'strong arm' has a mighty influence here."

46. Croffut and Morris, *The Military and Civil History of Connecticut during the War of 1861–1865*, 110, notes that the peace movement was broken.

47. *New Haven Register*, September 13, 1861; *New Haven Register*, September 11, 1861. The *Hartford Courant* insisted, "the bold wickedness of the sympathizers with treason demands just such an out-spoken, manly call from our Executive upon all loyal men and officers of the law who put down with a firm hand the traitors that are hissing by our own hearth-stones, and right loyally will it be responded to." "Gov. Buckingham's Proclamation," *Hartford Courant*, September 2, 1861.

48. See Luke Boyd, "The Colt Armory Fire: Connecticut and the Great Confederate Conspiracy," in Warshauer, ed., *Inside Connecticut and the Civil War: Essays on One State's Struggles*.

49. James M. McPherson, *Battle Cry of Freedom: The Civil War Era* (New York: Oxford University Press, 1988), 352–53.

50. *New Haven Register*, October 25, 1861.

51. "Anti-slaveryism," *Hartford Times*, October 5, 1861. See also, "Abolition fanaticism," *Hartford Times*, September 24, 1861.

52. "Abolitionists," *Hartford Times*, October 21, 1861.

53. *Hartford Times*, October 4, 1861.

54. Quoted in Lane, *A Political History of Connecticut during the Civil War*, 205.

55. Buckingham received 39,782 votes, to Loomis's 30,634. The total votes cast were 70,416. This was a distinct drop in votes for Democrats and in overall voter turnout from previous elections. In 1860, Thomas Seymour had received 43,917 (with 88,375 votes cast), and in 1861, Loomis had received 40,986 (with 83,998 votes cast). See *The Connecticut Register: Being an Official State Calendar of Public Officers and Institution* (Hartford, Conn.: Brown and Parsons, 1859–66). Part of this reduction was undoubtedly because some 15,000 soldiers were at the front and thus unable to vote. Democrats claimed that three-quarters of these soldiers were from their party. For this claim and the health of the party, see "The State Election," *Hartford Daily Times*, April 8, 1862.

56. *Hartford Evening Press*, April 8, 1862.

57. "The State Election," *Hartford Daily Times*, April 8, 1862. For additional reactions of Republicans, see "hartford redeemed!"; Sham Democracy Rebuked. A Gain of 500 Votes!" *Hartford Daily Courant*, April 8, 1862; "Another Victory for the Union!

UTTER DEFEAT OF THE REBELS! Wm. A. Buckingham Re-Elected by from 7,000 to 10,000 Majority!! A UNION SENATOR FROM EVERY DISTRICT! Great Gains in the Legislature!" *Hartford Daily Courant*, April 8, 1862.

58. For the development of Lincoln and the Republican Congress's movement toward emancipation, see Eric Foner, *Fiery Trial: Abraham Lincoln and American Slavery* (New York: Norton, 2010); "Abolition of Slavery in Washington," *Hartford Times*, April 19, 1862. See also "Abolition in the District," *Hartford Times*, April 4, 1862; "Abolition Begun," *Hartford Times*, April 11, 1862.

59. *Hartford Times*, October 4, 1862; Lane wrote, "The proclamation not only ended harmony between the parties, but brought about change in the war aims such as peculiarly affected New England." See Lane, *Political History of Connecticut during the Civil War*, 210.

60. *New Haven Register*, September 27, 1862.

61. See Lane, *A Political History of Connecticut during the Civil War*, for additional information on Democratic victories. See also "New Haven Election," *Hartford Daily Courant*, November 29, 1862; *Hartford Daily Courant*, November 26, 1862; *Hartford Daily Courant*, December 25, 1862.

62. *New Haven Register*, November 7, 1862; *New Haven Register*, December 22, 1862; *Hartford Times*, November 27, 1862. Joanna Cowden noted that "the preliminary Emancipation Proclamation had the greatest effect in arousing the citizenry and temporarily reducing the attractiveness of the Republican party." See Cowden, "Politics of Dissent," 543.

63. "States Right Vindicated," *Hartford Times*, January 27, 1863; see also, "The President and the Constitution," *Hartford Times*, January 7, 1863; "Conscription Law," *Hartford Times*, February 26, 1863; "Something to Think of," Hartford *Times*, February 27, 1863; "The Constitution," *Hartford Times*, February 27, 1863; "A Political Jail Delivery," *Hartford Times*, December 1, 1862.

64. See "The Negro Soldier Bill," *Hartford Times*, February 6, 1863, which insisted that Lincoln had "impoverished the country, injured the National Credit, and loaded us all with a crushing weight of Debt and Taxation, whereof no living man will see the end." See also, "Republican Estimate of Treason," *Hartford Times*, February 24, 1863.

65. Lane, *A Political History of Connecticut during the Civil War*, 227.

66. "A GREAT MEETING. Outpouring of the Democracy! IMMENSE ENTHUSIASM. 'Seymour and the Constitution,'" *Hartford Times*, February 28, 1863.

67. "An Appeal from the Republican State Central Committee," *Hartford Daily Courant*, February 12, 1863. See also, Lane, *A Political History of Connecticut during the Civil War*, 221–24.

68. "The Reaction," *Hartford Evening Press*, February 20, 1863.

69. "How Soldiers Feel," *Hartford Daily Courant*, March 18, 1863; for a detailed description of the soldiers' letters, which I describe as "the most concentrated, sustained political effort of the war," see Warshauer, *Connecticut in the American Civil War*, 107–13.

70. "A VOICE FROM THE NINTH CORPS. Patriotic Appeal from Five Connecticut Regiments," *Hartford Daily Courant*, March 21, 1863. See also, "The 19th Army Corps—A Patriotic Appeal," *Hartford Daily Courant*, March 25, 1863.

71. "The Latest Dodge. REPUBLICAN MISREPRESENTATION OF THE SOLDIERS!" *Hartford Times*, March 12, 1863. "Hear the Soldiers. THE TRUTH AGAINST ABOLITION LIES," *Hartford Times*, March 20, 1863. In response to the letter concerning the 22nd, Private William Pearson wrote: "The writer is very ignorant—not much acquainted with the minds of his fellow soldiers (in Co. B, especially) or he is awfully addicted to saying and writing that which is not true" in "STILL ANOTHER VOICE," *Hartford Daily Courant*, March 19, 1863. Another soldier insisted: "I wish to say that that article is an unmitigated falsehood, and that the writer has not the courage to make his name known. . . . If a vote was taken nearly every man would vote for Buck" in "Another Voice from the 22d—The Outrageous Course of the *Hartford Times*," *Hartford Daily Courant*, March 19, 1863.

72. "The Convention," *Hartford Times*, February 17, 1863.

73. "Democratic Caucus. The Administration Denounced. The Rebels not Denounced," *Hartford Daily Courant*, February 18, 1863.

74. *Hartford Courant*, February 19, 1863.

75. There is some minor discrepancy regarding the actual number of votes. I follow *The Connecticut Register: Being an Official State Calendar of Public Officers and Institution* (Hartford, Conn.: Brown and Parsons, 1859–66), which provides the following numbers: Buckingham: 41,031 votes; Seymour: 38,397 votes; total votes: 79,428; margin: 2,634.

76. Anticipating the 1863 election, Governor Buckingham asked the state's Supreme Court justices to consider the constitutionality of a law allowing soldiers to vote in the field; he was told without qualification that it would be unconstitutional. The General Assembly passed an amendment in 1864 that allowed soldiers to vote, but this did nothing for them during the contested and very important 1863 campaign. See Warshauer, *Connecticut in the American Civil War*, 113–15; see also, Cowden, "Politics of Dissent," 547. Connecticut 1818 Constitution, Article 3, Section 5. The 1864 amendment was passed in August of 1864, Article 13, and applied solely to soldiers during the "present war." See also, Josiah Henry Benton, *Voting in the Field: A Forgotten Chapter of the Civil War* (Boston: Privately printed, 1915), 175; *Hartford Times*, January 1, 1863, makes a brief mention of the judges' determination.

77. "Unwelcome Truths," *Hartford Times*, April 8, 1863; "The 'Government' Outrage On the People of Connecticut," *Hartford Times*, April 10, 1863. See also "Connecticut Election. The Result," *Hartford Times*, April 7, 1863; "Cheated Out of It," *New Haven Register*, April 8, 1863.

78. *Hartford Times*, September 11, 1863.

79. "The Union," *Hartford Times*, October 20, 1863; *Hartford Times*, November 18, 1863. See also, "The President's Message," *Hartford Times*, December 10, 1863, in which the paper responds to Lincoln's third annual message: "Our government is the Constitution. . . .We desire that every candid man shall read and ponder upon it. We have here only attempted to call attention to the monstrous propositions, involving a most alarming assumption of power on the part of the Executive; and to point to the proclamation proposing to destroy State equality, State Constitutions, and State laws, and to impose such oath upon Southern men as will prevent a Union of States." See also, "Where, or to What, are we to Look for the Limit of President Lincoln's Power?" *Hartford Times*, March 11, 1864.

80. "Another Word With Candid Republicans," *Hartford Times*, September 17, 1864.

81. Thomas and Origen Seymour may have been cousins. Buckingham received 39,820 votes to Seymour's 34,162 (*The Connecticut Register: Being an Official State Calendar of Public Officers and Institution* [Hartford, Conn.: Brown and Parsons, 1859–66]).

82. When the Democratic Party met in convention in Chicago, Alexander Long of Ohio put forward Seymour's name for nomination. See Cowden, "Heaven Will Frown on Such a Cause As This," 52.

83. "The Result in Hartford! COPPERHEADISM ON ITS LAST LEGS! Wm. W. Eaton Defeated! A GLORIOUS DAY'S WORK!" *Hartford Daily Courant*, April 5, 1864; "BUCKINGHAM AND UNION," *Hartford Daily Courant*, April 5, 1864; "Victory Again," *Hartford Evening Press*, April 5 1864; see also, "The Great Victory," *Hartford Evening Press*, April 5 1864.

84. "Peace," *Hartford Times*, July 22, 1864; see also, "Peace Negotiation," *Hartford Times*, July 21, 1864; "Propositions for Peace," *Hartford Times*, July 22, 1864.

85. Abraham Lincoln to Horace Greeley, July 9, 1864, Abraham Lincoln Papers; "Alleged Peace Negotiations," *Hartford Daily Courant*, July 22, 1864; *Hartford Daily Courant*, July 23, 1864.

86. "How Many More Years of War!" *Hartford Times*, October, 20 1864; see also, "The Difference," *Hartford Times*, September 7, 1864; "The Difference," *Hartford Times*, September 8, 1864.

87. *Hartford Times*, November 7, 1864.

88. "Close Up the Campaign of 1864," *New Haven Register*, November 7, 1864.

89. By 1864, nineteen states had passed legislation allowing soldiers to vote in the field. In New York and Connecticut, these votes provided the margin for Lincoln's victory. See McPherson, *Battle Cry of Freedom*, 804–5; 1818 Constitution of the State of Connecticut, art. 3, sect. 5, http://www.sots.ct.gov/sots/cwp/view.asp?a=3188&q=392280. See also, Josiah Henry Benton, *Voting in the Field: A Forgotten Chapter of the Civil War* (Boston: privately printed, 1915), 175. Connecticut election results were 44,693 for Lincoln and 42,288 for McClellan (Connecticut Election Results, http://www.uselection atlas.org/RESULTS/state.php?year=1864&off=0&elect=0&fips=9&f=0).

90. Lincoln's margin of victory in New England: Connecticut 51.38 percent; Maine 59.07 percent; Massachusetts 72.22 percent; New Hampshire 52.56 percent; Vermont 76.10 percent. McClellan won Delaware, Kentucky, and New Jersey. See Atlas of U.S. Presidential Elections, 1864 Presidential General Election Data, uselectionsatlas.org.

91. James M. McPherson, *Abraham Lincoln and the Second American Revolution* (New York: Oxford University Press, 1991).

92. Cowden, "Politics of Dissent," 553.

93. "Ex-Governors Toucey and Seymour," *Hartford Times*, April 29, 1865.

"I Do Not Understand What the Term 'Loyalty' Means"

The Debate in Pennsylvania over Compensating Victims of Rebel Raids

Jonathan W. White

Treason is the only crime defined in the Constitution: "Treason against the United States, shall consist only in levying War against them, or in adhering to their Enemies, giving them Aid and Comfort." The next sentence states that treason must be an "overt Act," thus precluding judges or politicians from declaring that words or thoughts might be deemed treason. In defining treason narrowly, the Framers hoped to depoliticize a crime that for centuries had been partisan in nature. In early modern England monarchs could define treason however they chose and force judges to convict the accused simply to eliminate political opposition. This process of construing a defendant's words or nontraitorous actions to be treason became known as "constructive treason."[1]

The Founding Fathers hoped to prevent partisan and constructive meanings of treason from appearing in American politics and jurisprudence. "The doctrine of *constructive treasons*, created by servile judges, who held their office during the pleasure of the king, was used by them in such a way as to enable the sovereign safely to wreak vengeance upon his victims under the guise of judicial condemnation," wrote Solicitor of the War Department William Whiting in 1862. "If the king sought to destroy a rival, the judges would pronounce him guilty of constructive treason; in other words, they would so construe the acts of the defendant as to make them treason." The power to define treason or determine who was a traitor, under the old English law, "was in its nature an *arbitrary* power."[2] By incorporating a limited and precise definition of treason into the Constitution, the Framers hoped to keep arbitrary and constructive definitions of treason out of the United States.

One might have expected treason to have been widely prosecuted in the North during the Civil War. After all, many Northern Copperheads were suspected of "adhering" to the Confederate cause and giving the rebels "aid and comfort." But there were not many treason prosecutions during—or after—the war. Attorney General Edward Bates was wary of bringing treason cases into the federal courts. Failure to win convictions would be embarrassing to the Lincoln administration, while winning convictions might undermine the war effort by making martyrs of the accused. Bates thus discouraged local district attorneys from prosecuting too many treason cases. It would be more effective, in Bates's view, to try Northern traitors for lesser crimes. "It is far better policy I think when you have the option to prosecute offenders for vulgar felonies and misdemeanors than for romantic and genteel treason," Bates told one U.S. attorney. "The penitentiaries will be far more effectual than the gallows."[3]

Bates understood that treason trials would not be the most effective way to bring errant citizens back to their allegiance to the Union. Nor would they be the best way to stifle dissent. Instead, Republicans developed new ways to disenfranchise or otherwise punish suspected traitors without going through the time and expense of a civil trial. Suspected traitors could be punished by far less stringent standards than the Constitution necessitated for treason trials (or any criminal trials, for that matter). In short, Northern civil and military leaders established new mechanisms for testing citizens' "loyalty" to the Union—they used the military to arrest and try thousands of civilians for crimes against the Union war effort; military leaders assessed taxes upon civilians in areas plagued with guerrilla warfare; they required "test" oaths of many classes of citizens, including office holders, ministers, lawyers, and government employees; and in the postwar period, Congress stripped deserters from the Union army of the rights of U.S. citizenship.[4]

Unlike treason, the crime of disloyalty was not defined in the Constitution or any federal statute. Defining "loyalty" and "disloyalty" thus became a bitterly contentious process in the highly charged partisan atmosphere of the Civil War North. Republicans tended to define "loyalty" as adherence to Lincoln's war policies, including confiscation, emancipation, suspension of habeas corpus, legal tender, and conscription. Democrats, by contrast, believed that loyalty entailed adherence to "the Constitution as it is and the Union as it was." Crimes of disloyalty—as a replacement for the law of treason—thus became highly politicized, undermining the whole purpose the Founding Fathers had in writing a definition of treason into the U.S. Constitution.

One venue in which the definition of "loyalty" was fully articulated during the Civil War was the Pennsylvania legislature. Following rebel raids into the Keystone State, lawmakers in Harrisburg debated bills to compensate civilians who had lost property during the raids. A key sticking point in these measures was whether those seeking compensation should have to prove their fidelity to the national cause before receiving aid. The debate over compensation in Pennsylvania exposed how Republican politicians used rebel raids to conflate their conceptions of loyalty with treason and thus essentially broaden the definition of treason beyond that found in the Constitution.

Rebel Raids into Pennsylvania

Confederate troops invaded the North on several occasions between 1862 and 1864. In September 1862, Robert E. Lee brought his Army of Northern Virginia northward in a campaign that culminated in the Battle of Antietam. Shortly after Antietam, Lee sent his cavalry commander, Jeb Stuart, into Pennsylvania. Stuart's three day raid resulted in the capture of some 1,200 horses, several convalescing soldiers, and large amounts of shoes and boots. In the process, Stuart burned a railroad depot that contained Union military supplies, and he terrorized the countryside.[5] In June and July 1863, Lee mounted a major invasion into Pennsylvania, which culminated in the Union victory at Gettysburg. Then, in 1864, Confederate General Jubal Early invaded Maryland and Pennsylvania, threatening the national capital and burning the Pennsylvania town of Chambersburg. Each of these Confederate offensives would have major implications for how treason and loyalty were defined during the war.

Rebel raids into Maryland and Pennsylvania forced Northern civilians and government officials to reevaluate how they defined treason, loyalty, and disloyalty. Both political parties in the North believed the other party benefited from rebel raids. Democrats believed that the Republicans enjoyed seeing Confederate invasions into the southern regions of the North because there the rebels would strip bare the fields of Democratic farmers. Republicans, by contrast, often accused Democrats of welcoming, comforting, and feeding Southern soldiers. Along these lines, Confederate troop movements into the North revealed the awkward position in which the Democratic Party found itself as an opposition party. By 1863, as more and more Democrats opposed the Lincoln administration's apparent radicalizing of the war, Democrats came under frequent fire for actually wanting to see the South prevail. Some moderate Democrats feared that "too ultra [of an] opposition" to the Lincoln administration might end up hurting the party. As one moderate Democrat in Washington noted during Lee's invasion into Pennsylvania in June 1863, "We must put down opposition to the war and do the best we can when the enemy is at our gates."[6]

In fact, most Democrats—even Peace Democrats—believed in fighting the rebels when they came looking for a fight on Northern soil.[7] Still, rebel incursions into the North revealed some of the tensions and disconnects that existed between Northern soldiers and civilians, causing many Union soldiers to doubt whether those who remained at home were truly loyal.

Union soldiers frequently complained that Northern civilians took advantage of the troops who came to protect their homes and farms. More than a year after Gettysburg, one Union soldier stationed near Atlanta told his father that he had "no sympathy" for citizens of southern Pennsylvania who were now "very much alarmed about the 'Raid.'" He recalled that during the Gettysburg campaign some civilians just "sat upon the fences by the road side and in the doors of the Village houses 'looking at the show,'" while other "men and women inside did not know how *much* they ought to ask for a loaf of bread. I had to pay several times 50 cents for a loaf of bread, 5 to 8¢ apiece for eggs, 75¢ for a chicken &c. If men will not defend their own homes and firesides they deserve to lose them."[8]

Another soldier noted the difference between Marylanders and Pennsylvanians when Union soldiers came to protect them from rebel invaders. "In the southern part of Pennsylvania we found Dutch *animals* and once and a while a woman would shake her handkerchief," he wrote his sister. "In Maryland we found fine people who could appreciate the danger we had rescued them from, and when we asked them to sell us a loaf of bread or a pie, almost invariably their answer would be, 'Indeed, sir, we have none to sell, but will *give* you all we have got.' Is'nt [sic] there more Union in that, than in waving handkerchiefs? In Pennsylvania we were often charged 50 cents for a loaf of bread, 15 cents per quart for milk, and 40 cents for a pound of butter." This soldier concluded that he "wish[ed] Lee would go there again. . . . Copperheads had better improve the time for their day of grace is short."[9] Loyalty, to these soldiers, meant giving aid to Union soldiers when they were protecting the Northern countryside.

Others were disappointed by Pennsylvania's slow response to rebel invasions. During the Gettysburg campaign in July 1863, one New Yorker expressed his frustration to a Pennsylvania congressman, saying, "I will say nothing about the war except the Union men of our state are sadly grieved at the backwardness of Pennsylvania in bringing her troops in the field. We think the scare is over but the disgrace remains."[10] A Baltimorean visiting Philadelphia in late June 1863 noted the "most extraordinary & inexplicable calm" of many Philadelphians: "The 'invasion' not only fails to alarm the people, but I see evidences at every turn that great numbers of the people are at least indifferent to it. I assure you there is *no* excitement here. Many say 'let them come'—others say 'we are ready to trade off the scoundrels in power, for gentlemanlike enemies.'" This Democratic observer believed that the North had grown weary of Lincoln's "abolition Crusade," as was evidenced in the words he heard said in his presence.[11] The Democrats' real enemies, it seems, were the abolitionists. Many Democrats and Republicans distrusted each other perhaps more than they distrusted their common enemy to the south.

Both sides even accused the other of wanting the rebels to invade the North, and both believed that they were the better protector of the home front. According to the Bellefonte *Democratic Watchman*, the "most prominent abolitionists" in Pennsylvania hoped that Lee's troops would make it to the central part of the state to "ravage and plunder everything in their course because, as these *patriots* affirmed, they would thus be sure to burn out and destroy all the 'd—d Copperheads.'" But the Democrats protested that they were the true patriots of the North. "In order to see that class of our citizens whom they denominate 'Copperheads,' burnt out and killed off, they [Republicans] would be willing to have the country indiscriminately pillaged and ruined from Chambersburg to Bellefonte. That is what *they* call patriotism! It is, however, nothing but fanaticism, and shows the rancorous party feeling which has taken complete possession of their souls."[12]

Republicans, by contrast, claimed that the rebels had been invited into Pennsylvania by their Democratic friends. Congressman Thaddeus Stevens criticized Democrats for wanting to be conciliatory and compromising, and for referring to the Southerners as their "brethren." After describing the destruction, stealing, re-enslavement, and violence that the rebels introduced into Pennsylvania, Stevens exclaimed: "Thieves, robbers, traitors kidnappers! *They* our '*brethren of the South.*' God forbid that I should thus treat them. They are no kindred of mine. I would as soon acknowledge fellowship with the sooty demons, whose business and delight it is, to torture the damned! Let Copperheads embrace them. They will find together an appropriate place, in the great day of Accounts."[13]

Rebel raids became central to politics and elections during the war. Indeed, Confederate leaders hoped that their incursions north could influence Northern elections. The Gettysburg campaign occurred during the summer of 1863, while the Democratic Party in Pennsylvania was assembled in nearby Harrisburg, choosing its candidate for governor. One Republican congressman claimed that the Democrats "seemed to have no fear of the rebels, and I suppose had no reason to fear them."[14] But Democrats resented such accusations. When a Union League formed in Doylestown, Pennsylvania, in the summer of 1863, the local

Democratic paper complained that only seven of its 130 members went to defend the state during the rebel invasion. "It is easier to abuse Copperheads than fight rebels," concluded the Democrats.[15]

Some soldiers and Republicans hoped for more rebel raids to help bring the Democrats to their senses about the reality of the danger that they faced. Writing from Philadelphia while the battle of Gettysburg was still raging, one man told his son in the army that "the majority" of the people thought Lee's invasion "was a hoax, in fact a trick of the Government to get men to enlist for six months and thus evade the enforcement of conscription." Along these lines, many Republicans believed that rebel raids into the North would force Democrats to acknowledge the danger the nation was in and the reality of the enemy they were fighting. "There should be one raid per year to bring those infernal Copperheads to their senses," wrote one Pennsylvania cavalryman.[16]

The Pennsylvania Legislative Debate

Rebel raids into Pennsylvania caused a significant amount of destruction and loss of personal property. "You can form no idea of the losses endured by the people of these counties, and the suffering consequent therefrom," wrote one border county Democrat a few months after the Gettysburg campaign in 1863. "It extends to nearly every family."[17] "The men have cleared some farm yards," wrote one Confederate infantryman to his mother from his camp near Chambersburg in late June 1863. "This pillaging has been stopped . . . but it is almost impossible to prevent men from taking what they want." Besides, he reckoned, "the people deserve the treatment."[18] According to historian Allen C. Guelzo, "the town [of Gettysburg] and the surrounding farmlands suffered over half a million dollars in damages, including 800 confiscated horses and 1,000 head of cattle" during that rebel invasion into the state.[19] Accordingly, the Pennsylvania legislature debated several bills during the war to compensate Pennsylvanians for their losses. But because so many residents of the border counties were Democrats, these debates exposed the wide-ranging definition of loyalty that had taken root in the North during the Civil War and the connection between Republican conceptions of loyalty to many political issues.

In April 1863, the Pennsylvania legislature adopted a law to adjudicate the claims of "loyal citizens" of the commonwealth who had lost property during Confederate General Jeb Stuart's October 1862 raid into the state, and to authorize the governor to seek compensation for those citizens from the federal government (this law did not provide any actual relief).[20] In 1863, each party controlled one house of the legislature; however, in 1864, the Republicans gained slim majorities in both houses.[21] Because the southern border of Pennsylvania was heavily Democratic, future legislation of this sort would not pass so easily through the Republican-controlled state house.

On February 8, 1864, border county Democrat J. McDowell Sharpe introduced a bill in the state House of Representatives to amend and supplement the 1863 law to include Pennsylvanians who lost property during the Gettysburg campaign. Sharpe proposed that the bill be sent to a select committee of five members, to which the house agreed. The following day, Republican James R. Kelley introduced a resolution stating that because "there is reason to believe" that disloyal Pennsylvanians had encouraged the rebels to invade the state, that any persons claiming compensation for lost property must "furnish positive proofs of their loyalty." Should it be adopted, the resolution would require the select committee to incorporate such a provision into the bill.[22]

Kelley's resolution provoked a great deal of debate, and Democrats instantly raised their voices in protest. Sharpe proclaimed that there were "no disloyal constituents" in his district. Another Democrat asked "what the standard of loyalty is to be. Is a test-oath to be administered by the committee? Are they to make claimants swear that they are loyal? or must the claimants bring positive testimony?" This legislator denied the right of a legislative committee to determine just how loyalty would be defined or proved. "Some members of this House have been in the habit here of calling men disloyal who are just as loyal as themselves," he exclaimed. "It has become very fashionable now-a-days to cast imputations upon the loyalty of citizens, without any grounds for so doing," echoed Sharpe.[23]

In the course of the debate, both sides articulated highly contradictory conceptions of what it meant to be loyal. Democrat Truman H. Purdy maintained that "a loyal man is a man who is loyal to the Constitution" and "loyal to the Government of our fathers." Any person "who bases his claims to loyalty upon his adherence to the ideas of a particular individual—who bases his claim to loyalty upon the theory that if a man supports the doctrines of a certain platform, or the particular notions of a certain President or a certain Governor he is loyal—I say that such a man knows nothing about loyalty." Purdy continued, "There is no test of loyalty in this country, save that which brings a man's actions to the touchstone of the Constitution and the laws of his country."[24] Loyalty to the nation, in other words, could not be tested against party platforms and partisan creeds.

Another Democrat tried to take the offensive by arguing that it was the Republicans who were disloyal. Repeating the oft heard trope that the Republicans and abolitionists had eschewed moderation and compromise and thus brought about the war, Thomas J. Barger accused the Republicans of wanting the war to continue so that they could remain in power. "These are the 'loyal' men—'loyal' not from conviction, but 'loyal' because they are making money out of this war, and for no other reason." Barger described the great nationwide suffering the war had caused and concluded, "When the champions of that Administration rise in their places here and say to us that we are disloyal, I hurl back into their teeth and deep down into their throats the charge of disloyalty, and I say to them, recollect what you are and what you have made this once glorious country."[25]

The Republicans countered with their own definition of loyalty. Loyalty, to them, meant unconditional commitment to winning the war, regardless of constitutional niceties. James R. Kelley, the author of the resolution, mockingly noticed the "great deal of sensitiveness manifested" by the Democrats "whenever any mention is made of *loyalty*." He took the opportunity to articulate his own definition of the term:

I will say that my ideas of loyalty are these: That a man shall support and defend the Constitution and the Union at all costs and at all sacrifices. A man who is willing to sacrifice everything and to do everything in his power to maintain, preserve and perpetuate the Union of these States as cemented by the blood of the patriots of the Revolution, is, according to my idea, a loyal man. It is not for a man to stand up and quibble on certain constitutional points, saying "this is not constitutional," "that is not constitutional;" "this way of conducting the war is not constitutional and that way is not constitutional," but a man must go for the Union at all hazards, if he would entitle himself to be considered a loyal man.[26]

At root, this partisan definition of loyalty was incompatible with a republican form of government that depended upon debate, disagreement, and compromise. Knowing that Democrats believed many of the war measures of the Republican Party were unconstitutional, Kelley knew that his definition of loyalty automatically excluded the majority of the opposition party.

For this reason, most Democrats accused the Republican party of politicizing the concept of loyalty. "I do not understand what the term 'loyalty' means as it is used by the Republican party of the present day," stated one Democrat. "It is a new word, sir, in politics, and it had its birth as a political phrase in the Republican party." Did loyalty mean one is "for the Union as it was and the Constitution as it is? or, sir, does his term loyalty extend so far that a man must be for the new Union and the new Constitution, as conceived by the expounders of the Republican faith and about to be inaugurated upon an unwilling people." To Democrats like this one, loyalty meant fidelity to the Union and the Constitution as they existed prior to the war. They would not tolerate changes to the Constitution that appeared to be made only for immediate partisan purposes. If loyalty meant supporting President Lincoln and his "directions, behests and proclamations," one Democrat proudly railed, "then, Mr. Speaker, I am not loyal, and the Democratic party is not loyal; for we hold . . . that this self-same President has violated time and again—times without number—the Constitution of the United States. . . . Every man who does not entirely agree with them in all their views, is charged by them with being 'disloyal'—a 'copperhead' and a 'traitor.'"[27]

The debate raged for several days. Democrats—and even a few Republicans—feared that the vague requirement for "positive proofs" would allow partisan claims commissioners to reject all claims from Democrats. They feared, in essence, that Republican-appointed commissioners would treat Democrats the same way that the Republican press did. Beyond that, most Democrats were not willing to relinquish their political principles just to be considered "loyal" so that they could receive compensation. They opposed emancipation, conscription, legal tender, and suspension of habeas corpus, along with other Republican war measures. One Democrat surmised that to prove his loyalty he would have to swear, "I will relinquish my Democratic and constitutional sentiments—I will endorse Abraham Lincoln's proclamation—I will hereafter be an abolitionist." In other words, unless a Democrat was willing "to abandon his politics and to support the party in power," they believed they would be considered "disloyal" by those in control of the government.[28]

Most Democrats believed that a person's disloyalty ought to be a judicial question rather than one of legislative determination. Along those lines, they argued that if a person was suspected of disloyalty, they ought to be tried under Pennsylvania's state treason law, which had been enacted in April 1861. Requiring claimants to furnish "positive proofs" of loyalty would reverse "the old and well established maxim of the law" that a person was innocent until proven guilty. Moreover, Democrats argued that the resolution sought "to strike down" men from the border counties of Pennsylvania by allowing "certain partisans to draw a test of loyalty upon them." If a Pennsylvanian invited or encouraged the rebel raids, then he should be punished: "He may even be liable to have his property confiscated, and to be hung for treason." But the Democrats maintained that he should be punished in accordance with the principles of due process.[29]

The Republicans countered that there was nothing partisan about the measure, and they expressed surprise that the Democratic side of the aisle took such exception to it. One asked why the Democrats "rise in such wrath whenever a motion is broached which touches upon the word loyalty," and why they opposed "all measures, whether here or in Congress, looking to the exclusion of rebels and traitors from the benefits which we claim for loyal men." "I have tried to take them at their own word," he continued, "but when I see them rise in their places and utter upon this floor speeches more fitting for a rebel Congress than the Legislature of a free State, I am inclined to doubt their professions of loyalty to the Constitution and the Union."[30]

Republicans believed that a loyalty requirement would prevent disloyal civilians from bleeding the public treasury only to invite the rebels back into the state so that they could claim more money for their losses. The taxpayer ought to be protected, they argued, to prevent the "pay out [of] millions of public money without discrimination, as well to disloyal as to loyal claimants." Ultimately, stated one Republican, "No loyal man fears this test."[31]

The Republican members reclaimed the offensive, questioning the Democrats' devotion to actually winning the war. One Republican declared that pro-war remarks from Democrats were "mere lip-service . . . to suit the place which they are in," and that "such professions are all hollow-hearted." James Kelley underscored this point, contending that the Democrats' defensiveness in this debate had revealed them to be their own accusers. "That the Democratic party should be thin-skinned, when any question touching loyalty is mentioned, is to be expected; for their leaders have, since the rebellion began, been the allies of Jefferson Davis and the right wing of Lee's army," he said. Evidence of their treason existed in their opposition to all efforts made by the Republicans to suppress the rebellion. Claiming that Republican actions were unconstitutional was merely "the screen behind which Northern treason has continually veiled itself."[32]

Republican P. Frazer Smith of Chester County raised the stakes in the debate, arguing that loyalty to the Constitution and Union were closely linked to nationalism. American democracy, according to Smith, transcended party politics. Accordingly, a loyal citizen would not assail the government just because his candidate had lost a presidential contest. No, in the democracy of George Washington, Andrew Jackson, Lewis Cass, and Stephen A. Douglas, the "true citizens" of the country would come "up to sustain the Government under all circumstances in which it may be placed, and especially in the putting down of such a rebellion as we are now witnessing." To Smith, a truly loyal citizen would follow the elected leader when the nation was in trouble. This form of loyalty "puts the Government of the United States above every government that is formed under it" and "recognizes no pestilent heresy of State rights which would lead a man to say, 'My State

calls upon me to do so, and I am therefore a loyal man, whilst I am obeying that
State, although she may be in rebellion against the Government of the nation.'
Out such loyalty! Let us never hear of that in these halls."[33]

This "great nation" was not "a mere compact of States," according to Smith.
"We read it there as plain as A, B, C, that 'we, the people,' form this great government . . . [and] that when the government enacted laws . . . those laws were
supreme, and the man was a traitor and a scoundrel—(those were our sentiments then, and they are mine now)—who deliberately says, that any State has
rights which will put it above the government of the United States, and that we,
as citizens of this State or any other State, should obey the behests of our State
to the overturning of the government of the United States." Accordingly, loyal
men would support expelling rebels from Northern soil, they would "not throw
discredit upon the currency of the country," and they would not discourage enlistments. While conceding that the majority of the Democratic Party was loyal,
Smith argued that its leaders were not:

> You will find them prating about the Constitution, when every act shows that
> they are in sympathy, if not in co-operation, with those who are assailing it
> with armed hands. You find them glorying in the defeat of our armies, and
> you will find them rejoicing when our adversary succeeds, mourning when
> he fails. . . . The Democracy which will put the country above everything
> else is the Democracy that we all love. I care not whether the man calls him-
> self a Democrat or a Republican, if he places his party above his country—if
> he desires to grind out of the groans and tears of the people that which will
> make him rich—he is disloyal, according to the test which I think ought to be
> applied—according to the test which I am willing to be applied to myself.[34]

In closing, Smith described a hypothetical mother who had lost her son on
the battlefield. If you asked her to denounce the president she would not, but
rather would say: "My boy went into the service of his country, and love him as
I did, I love my country more." Country was more important than family, than
personal hardship, than locality, state or community, than political or constitutional principles, than life itself. This Republican version of loyalty involved
suppressing one's own desires, beliefs, comfort, or political scruples for the sake
of preserving the nation.[35]

Border county newspapers followed the debate in the house with great interest. The Republican *Franklin Repository* praised the Democrat Sharpe for
championing this issue, but stated that he "erred in resenting the motion [Kel-

ley's resolution] as an insult to his constituents, instead of accepting a just test of fidelity for his people and thus silencing all cavil on the subject."[36] The *Repository* lamented the partisan turn that the debate had taken, fearing that it would kill the bill. "The measure is free from all political bearings," stated the editors. "It applies to men of all parties: for all have suffered alike under rebel invasion."[37] How unfortunate that Democrats like Purdy had "chose[n] to make an ass of himself by an insolent, inflammatory and reckless stump speech" against Kelley's resolution.[38]

The debate in the Pennsylvania senate took a much different course. There, Republicans openly opposed the bill, while Democrats universally supported it. The Democrats argued that because border county citizens had paid their taxes, volunteered for the military, and been subject to the draft, they ought to be compensated for their losses if the government had not been able to protect them. Republicans countered that such a bill was unprecedented—that at no other time in the history of warfare had a state or a nation compensated its citizens for losses that had occurred as a result of a battle. Beyond that, they argued that while the border counties had lost whiskey and chickens and mules, the rest of the state had lost children, fathers, and husbands. "Which was the richer or which was the greater loss?" asked one Republican.[39]

Throughout the war, the Democratic Party had warned that the Civil War would bring financial devastation upon the nation. The Republicans now countered that this relief bill was intended to speed up that coming fiscal disaster. By compensating every citizen for lost property, the Democrats were seeking to saddle the state with an insurmountable debt. "The Northern allies of Southern traitors are crying down the credit of the nation and predicting financial ruin, and praying for national bankruptcy as the means of forcing us to acknowledge the independence of the traitors' confederacy," argued one Republican senator, "and by the unanimous support that this measure is receiving at the hands of that party in this Senate, we must regard this as one of the means adopted by them to bring to pass the bankruptcy which they prophesy." The Democrats, in other words, were acting on their disloyal opinions in attempting to enact this law. Moreover, another Republican argued that disloyal Pennsylvanians would now be tempted "*to invite* raids into this Commonwealth" so as to put the state into further financial trouble, all while lining their own pockets and aiding the rebels.[40]

One Republican senator, whose throat became hoarse during the debate, declared in hyperbolic language that the compensation bill was "the most dangerous piece of legislation that was ever proposed before this Legislature" and that he would rather "see this capitol in flames" and "burned by a rebel raid" than see the bill become law, for "if it passed there is nothing but destruction left for this Government." Beyond that, those Northern traitors who were willing to help rebels invade the state and pillage their neighbors would not hesitate to commit perjury to fill their own pockets with government money. "Treason," another Republican added, "is the sum of all villainies and embraces all minor crimes." Consequently, Republicans doubted that a test oath would be sufficient to ensure that claimants were loyal. "A man who will give aid and protection to the rebels against our Government," stated one Republican, "is one who will disregard his oath. The oath of such a man is of no account. To me, it would be no evidence of his loyalty, none in the least." For these reasons, Republicans believed that the bill would raise taxes on the loyal only to compensate the disloyal.[41]

The Democrats responded to these accusations with a series of novel arguments. In an extraordinary speech, one Democrat argued that if the government would not protect its citizens from rebel incursions—and later refused to compensate them for their losses—then they no longer owed it any allegiance. Citizens gave up some of their rights and paid their taxes in exchange for protection from the government, he maintained. "If it is unable to save the citizen from wrong, then it must compensate him in damages; and if the Government is unable to do that, or if it will not do it, then the citizen is released from his fealty and allegiance to that Government, which is false to its trust, and he is at liberty to look around for such other sources of reliance as will be likely to protect him, his home and his family." Justice demanded that the citizens of southern Pennsylvania receive compensation for their losses, he continued, concluding, "the Government that fails to protect its citizens ought not to exist longer among a free people."[42]

As with the debate in the lower house, the debate in the senate took on a partisan tone and breadth that extended well beyond the particular issue at stake. Hoping to unite the state senate behind the measure, one border county Democrat called on his colleagues to put party politics aside and to adopt the bill as a way to aid his constituency who had suffered so much. The bill guarded against the citizen who had "been faithless in his obligations and allegiance to his Government" by requiring an oath that stated that the claimant had never borne arms against the state or national governments, nor "given aid, information or encouragement" to the rebels, nor discouraged enlistments. Moreover, he reckoned that there was "no doubt" that the federal government would eventually reimburse the state.[43]

Politics and Loyalty in the Debate over Compensation

Having seen and experienced the devastation of Confederate invasions, the Republican press along the border tended to support compensation for losses. Although they agreed that the House resolution demanding "positive proofs" of loyalty was objectionable and too indefinite, they believed that some proof of past loyalty ought to be required of those making claims against the government.[44] Still, Democrats feared that any demand for loyalty would automatically disqualify all Democrats from receiving compensation—not because they were disloyal, but because the Republican Party said they were. "This oath is now the great test of 'loyalty' in the eyes of the party in power," wrote one Democratic newspaper. "They stigmatise [*sic*] the whole Democratic party as 'disloyal;' and as a matter of course every Democrat who presents his claim for damages must take this oath, or present other 'positive proof' of his 'loyalty.'" Moreover, the editors reiterated the Democratic concern that Kelley's resolution would invert proper judicial procedure: "In the good old times that have gone by, every man was presumed innocent until he was proved guilty; but under the new regime the citizens of the border counties are all considered guilty of treason, unless they purge themselves of the charge by 'positive proof,' before a partizan commission. And what justice can be expected from such a commission as this, with full authority to decide upon the 'loyalty' or 'disloyalty' of their fellow citizens?"[45]

Border county Democrats who had borne the full brunt of rebel raids were particularly sensitive to discussions of disloyalty. They recognized that in the debate over compensation they were being convicted of treason without a trial or any judicial procedure. They also denied that the accusations made against them were anything more than partisan attacks intended to discredit the Democratic opposition. The "council" that determines the loyalty of claimants will be "controlled by the party who have been shouting charges of disloyalty and treason against the Democratic party for the last three years," stated one Democratic legislator. "Accusations will no doubt be made from motives of political animosity. Political adversaries will make charges of disloyalty against them, because forsooth they have committed the sin of voting the Democratic ticket perhaps at the last election." (It should be recalled that there was no secret ballot in the United States at this time.) And no matter what proofs of loyalty a Democrat might bring, he will be found to be "'disloyal,' because condemnation of the acts of the [Lincoln] administration is considered a 'disloyal practice.'"[46]

Throughout the course of the debate Republicans conjured up stories of alleged acts of disloyalty on the part of border county Pennsylvanians during Lee's

1863 invasion into the state. Many of them were hearsay; one story that can be documented is that of Joseph Fisher, "a transient person," who was tried before a military court in Pennsylvania in November 1863. Fisher was charged with "lurking as a spy in behalf of the enemy" just north of Gettysburg in June 1863, and with subsequently "giving intelligence to the enemy" with the intention of aiding the rebels in seizing and destroying "arms and property belonging to the United States, and to loyal citizens thereof." Fisher was convicted of both charges and sentenced to be hanged. According to court records, he was "a drunken, loafing vagabond" who spoke broken English, had only one arm, and had lived as a beggar for three years. His death sentence was consequently commuted to imprisonment for ten years. A few months later, President Lincoln remitted his sentence.[47]

Joseph Fisher's description is hardly that of a Peace Democrat or Copperhead devoted to helping the South win its independence. It is possible that he was not even a citizen of Pennsylvania. Thus, in using stories like Fisher's, Pennsylvania Republicans relied upon evidence of questionable validity to impugn the opposition party, to embroil the relief bill in partisan controversy, and ultimately to kill border claims.

The Meaning of Loyalty in the Debate

In an ingenious argument before the Pennsylvania House of Representatives, Harry Hakes of Wilkes-Barre argued that in a strictly legal sense, it was the Republicans, and not the Democrats, who were traitors. In the process, Hakes demonstrated that Republicans had bastardized the constitutional definition of treason by infusing it with the vague, imprecise, and extra-constitutional concept of loyalty. "'Loyalty,'" he said, "as it is used here in these days, means almost anything or absolutely nothing."[48]

Hakes began his argument by criticizing the resolution that called for "positive proofs" of a claimant's loyalty. Specifically, Kelley's resolution declared that there was "reason to believe that the rebel invasions of Pennsylvania were, in a great measure, brought about through the connivance and by the encouragement of disloyal persons in our own State." These words—encouragement, connivance, and disloyal—amounted to one crime and one crime only: "treason." Hakes suggested that the framer of the resolution may have been "afraid to say here in plain terms that he means by these words 'treason,' [but] I will speak that word for him, for that is what they amount to, if they amount to anything. The persons who have done these things should be called by their proper names. A man who is a traitor, I will call a traitor. This half and half thing of calling a man 'disloyal,' a sort of half-way treason, because he chooses to differ in opinion with the administration party, seems to me entirely out of place."[49]

Hakes spent quite some time impressing upon the House why it was important to charge those who aided the rebellion with treason, rather than with disloyalty: "If the allegations of these gentlemen who propose this resolution be true, they are guilty of a high crime, for which *disloyalty* is not the proper name." In fact, any person who gave aid and encouragement to the rebels—who "connived or winked at their invasion"—was guilty of treason as defined in the Constitution and must be punished accordingly. "Disloyalty is too mild and uncertain a word," Hakes declared, for it was defined in neither the Constitution nor any other law of the land.[50]

Loyalty, according to Hakes, was "a proper and favorite word" of kings who forced their "slavish subjects [to] bow in silence" and to stand "in subjection to laws made for them and not by them." Americans were not subject to such tyranny: "The proper term for us, when we mean giving aid and comfort to the enemies of our government, is 'treason.' There is a certain meaning to that term, and there is a reason why the gentlemen on that side wish to avoid using that term, because by using the word disloyal they can pounce with iron hands upon their political opponents, and can screen the treasonable acts of their friends."[51] Republicans, in short, could use the vague concept of loyalty to punish political opponents just as English monarchs had done using the fluid and ever-changing doctrine of constructive treason.

Hakes further criticized the resolution for reversing the rules of judicial procedure. A suspected criminal was innocent until proven guilty, but by this resolution the citizen would have to stand before a "smelling court" and "political inquisition" in order to prove his innocence. The resolution, in short, would deprive suspected traitors of their day in court (in a state where the civil courts were open), of trial by jury, and of due process of law. In contrast, Hakes declared that Democrats desired a government that would not only deprive traitors of compensation, but would also punish them for their treason: "Men who have given aid and comfort to the enemies of the State are guilty of treason and must be punished for that crime." He criticized the resolution for proposing, "in an indirect manner, to cast suspicion upon a man, or rather to convict him of treason. . . . Gentlemen on the other side ought to be as willing as I am to call treason by its proper name; and when a man has been guilty of that crime they should be willing, not only to refuse payment for property that he may have lost, but to pursue him as they would a serpent, and never to stop in the pursuit till he has been punished for his crime."[52] Calling a spade a spade, Hakes argued that forcing citizens to prove their "loyalty" was a partisan and illegal way of convicting them of treason in effect.

Hakes finally turned his aim directly at the Republicans. For several days now they had loudly recited stories of traitors who lived in the districts they represented. Knowing that such traitors lived in Pennsylvania, Republicans insisted that loyalty must be tested to ensure that these traitors did not receive any taxpayer money as compensation for lost property. But Hakes was incredulous: "I was astonished that those gentlemen should reveal such a knowledge of treason and treasonable practices in this State. Yet I will venture to say that not one of those gentlemen has entered a complaint in any court against any of these men." But reporting traitors to the proper authorities was precisely what the law required! He read from Pennsylvania's treason law, adding emphasis to the relevant provisions:

> If any person, having knowledge of the treasons aforesaid . . . shall *conceal* them, and not as soon as may be, disclose and make known the same to the [government] . . . *such person shall, on conviction, be adjudged guilty of misprison of treason, and shall be sentenced to pay a fine not exceeding one thousand dollars, and undergo an imprisonment, by separate or solitary confinement at labor, not exceeding six years.*

His reading of the statute was greeted with loud applause from his side of the aisle. He feigned charity, surmising that the Republicans' stories about traitors in Pennsylvania had not been based in fact but had been mere "suspicions" and the outcome of overly excited "political feelings." But if they *did* know of treason, and they had not reported it to the proper authorities, then they had not only neglected "their duty as good and patriotic citizens," but had, in fact, committed a treasonable offence themselves. Were these the people who would save the struggling nation? Ought they to get away with such irresponsible criminality with impunity? Should they be the ones who got to define what loyalty to the nation entailed?[53]

Hakes's rhetorical tactic not only exposed the partisan motivation of the Republicans but also the inherent injustice of requiring "positive proofs" of loyalty since loyalty and disloyalty had never been statutorily defined. Therefore, not only did requiring "loyalty" neglect the constitutional requirements of a trial and conviction before one could be punished for treason (or any other crime, for that matter), but Hakes's speech also revealed how fervently Republicans spoke of disloyalty in their midst when the evidence may have been little more than circumstantial rumor mongering that took place among disgruntled and fearful neighbors. "This mere suspicion that is to be cast upon men for political opinions does not conform to the true standard of the law," Hakes declared. Traitors must be found guilty, and the innocent must be protected. And these determinations should be done according to the law and formal judicial procedure.[54]

Epilogue

After much heated debate—and many postponements—the Pennsylvania House of Representatives rejected all proposals to compensate loyal citizens for lost property and instead passed a bill to adjudicate their claims (the bill was styled as an amendment to the 1863 law that had provided for the adjudication claims of those who had lost property during Jeb Stuart's 1862 raid into the state). The measure included a provision that would require each claimant to take an oath

> that he has never directly or indirectly, by word or act, given aid, comfort, countenance or encouragement to the traitors, whether in arms or otherwise; that he has never given any information to them or any of them, which could in any way be of advantage to them; that he has not resisted or evaded, or advised others to resist or evade any law of the United States; that he will support the Constitution and the laws of the United States which shall be made in pursuance thereof, as the supreme law of the land, and will bear true faith and allegiance to the same.

The Senate, however, refused to pass the House bill.[55]

Border county civilians were sorely disappointed by the outcome of the debate. Some Democrats believed that the deeper purpose of Kelley's resolution had been "to kill the bill by engulfing it in a political whirlpool."[56] Others blamed Republican governor Andrew G. Curtin for not coming out more firmly in favor of the measure. During the gubernatorial election the previous fall, both Curtin and his Democratic opponent, George W. Woodward, had supported compensation for Pennsylvanians who had lost property during rebel invasions. Curtin won a close race in October 1863. But when the Republicans in the legislature subsequently gutted and then killed the measure in the spring of 1864, Democrats protested what they now perceived as a hollow campaign promise. "Many of our citizens were seduced into voting for Curtin under this specious, but, as it now has turned out, treacherous promise," wrote the editors of Chambersburg's

Democratic paper. "Curtin before the election, and Curtin after the election were quite different individuals."[57] (In truth, this was not exactly a fair criticism—Curtin would continue to support relief measures for border county citizens in his annual messages of 1865 and 1866.[58])

The debate in the Pennsylvania legislature mirrored the national debate over loyalty, with Republicans interpreting political opposition as disloyalty. Border county Democrats thought they had firm ground from which to fight back against such accusations since they had suffered material and financial losses in the cause of the nation. But being in the minority in both houses, and with the taint of treason infecting their party nationally, they simply did not have enough public support to carry the measure.

On July 30, 1864, less than three months after the border claims bill went down to defeat in the legislature, Confederate General Jubal A. Early sent forces into Pennsylvania with orders to burn the city of Chambersburg. This rebel raid led to even more destruction of property than the Gettysburg campaign, including 537 buildings (266 of which were private residences or businesses), and about one million dollars in damage to other private property. All told, Early's men destroyed an estimated two million dollars worth of property. Prominent Pennsylvania politician and journalist Alexander K. McClure noted that the 1864 burning of Chambersburg left most residents of the town "entirely homeless"; and even though much of the property had been insured, "the insurance was lost, as the destruction was caused by a public enemy."[59] Because of the nature of the destruction, no one could accuse the citizens of Chambersburg of having welcomed the enemy into the state, as Republicans had alleged in connection with the earlier raids.

With more than 2,000 citizens left homeless, border county legislators made a bipartisan attempt to pass a relief bill, but it failed during the 1865 session for several reasons. First, too many rural legislators from other parts of the state opposed appropriating money for residents from just one region of the state. Moreover, many legislators claimed that such a bill would set a dangerous precedent for future wasteful spending. Others pointed out that citizens from all over Pennsylvania had lost blood and treasure during the war. From this point of view, there was no reason border county citizens should receive any special treatment. These opponents further charged that it was unfair to tax the widows and orphans of deceased soldiers to compensate those who had simply lost material wealth.[60]

According to Alexander McClure, it was only through backroom dealing, lobbying efforts, turnover in the legislature, and even some corruption that enough legislators were persuaded to support the measure in 1866. The bill made its way through the state house with remarkably little debate. Unsuspecting opponents of such relief measures were shocked upon learning of its passage. "Had we believed it possible for both branches of the Legislature to pass so unwise a measure we should have raised a protesting voice against it ere this," wrote the editors of the Wellsboro *Agitator*. "This kind of legislation should be throttled at once. Kill it."[61]

The new law appropriated $500,000 for the relief of those who had lost property in Chambersburg (as opposed to all border county citizens) but explicitly excluded disloyal citizens. Each claimant was required to sign an affidavit stating that he or she had "never, directly, or indirectly, by word, or act, given aid, comfort, countenance, or encouragement, to the traitors, whether in arms, or otherwise; that he, or she, has never communicated, or attempted, or taken means, to communicate with them, or any of them, any information which could, in any way, be of advantage to them."[62] This language, as we have seen, was adapted from the 1864 House bill, although in 1864 it only used the masculine pronoun. The inclusion of both the masculine and feminine pronouns in the 1866 version recognized how loyal women had suffered during the war, underscoring that they too deserved the opportunity to make claims for relief.[63]

Republicans could be satisfied that the law required a declaration of past loyalty, which had become a staple of Radical Republican loyalty oaths during the war, such as the Ironclad Test Oath of 1862 (which had also been incorporated into the Wade-Davis Bill of 1864). Democrats may have wished such a loyalty provision had not been included because it could have been used for partisan purposes. But they chose to accept the measure in order to secure relief. Ironically enough, a requirement for an affirmation of past loyalty, which had seemed so odious during the war years, now must have appeared more palatable than the original vague requirement for "positive proofs." Even more importantly, border county Democrats recognized that a relief measure for Chambersburg could serve as an opening wedge for other border counties to gain relief. And that is exactly what happened. In 1868, the legislature enacted another measure—which included the same loyalty provision—to supply relief for the citizens of all seven border counties who had suffered from rebel incursions during the war.[64]

Notes

I thank Sean A. Scott, Frank Towers, Andrew Slap, and Robert Sandow for reading this essay and offering helpful comments and suggestions. Mark E. Neely, Jr. also offered valuable comments when I presented a version of this paper at the annual meeting of the Pennsylvania Historical Association in 2013.

1. U.S. Constitution, art. 3, sec. 3 (1787); James Willard Hurst, *The Law of Treason in the United States: Collected Essays* (Westport, Conn.: Greenwood Publishing Corporation, 1971), 3–56; William Whiting, *The War Powers of the President, and the Legislative Powers of Congress in Relation to Rebellion, Treason and Slavery* (Boston: John L. Shorey, 1862), 94.

2. Whiting, *War Powers*, 94; *The Federalist* 43.

3. Edward Bates to R. J. Lackey, January 19, 1863, in *War of the Rebellion: A Compilation of the Official Records of the Union and Confederate Armies*, 128 vols. (Washington, D.C.: Government Printing Office, 1880–1901), ser. 2, 5:190–91 (hereafter *O.R.*).

4. Jonathan W. White, *Abraham Lincoln and Treason in the Civil War: The Trials of John Merryman* (Baton Rouge: Louisiana State University Press, 2011); General Orders No. 24, in *O.R.*, ser. 1, 8: 431; Harold M. Hyman, *Era of the Oath: Northern Loyalty Tests during the Civil War and Reconstruction* (Philadelphia: University of Pennsylvania Press, 1954); *An Act to Amend the Several Acts Heretofore Passed to Provide for the Enrolling and Calling Out the National Forces, and for Other Purposes*, act of March 3, 1865, in 13 Stat. 490; Jonathan W. White, *Emancipation, the Union Army, and the Reelection of Abraham Lincoln* (Baton Rouge: Louisiana State University Press, 2014), chap. 5; William A. Blair, *With Malice Toward Some: Treason and Loyalty in the Civil War Era* (Chapel Hill: University of North Carolina Press, 2014).

5. Edward L. Ayers, *In the Presence of Mine Enemies: War in the Heart of America, 1859–1863* (New York: Norton, 2003), 322–31.

6. T. J. Barnett to Samuel L. M. Barlow, June 22, 1863, Samuel L. M. Barlow Papers, The Huntington Library, San Marino, Calif.

7. See, for example, the remarks of Clement Vallandigham at *Congressional Globe*, 37th Cong., 3rd sess., p. 1262.

8. John McCowan to Father, August 9, 1864, Anderson-Caperhart-McCowan Family Papers, Civil War Miscellaneous Collection, U.S. Army Military History Institute, Carlisle, Pa. (hereafter MHI). See also Steven J. Ramold, *Across the Divide: Union Soldiers View the Northern Home Front* (New York: New York University Press, 2013), 17–18.

9. C. R. Dart to sister, July 18, 1863, newspaper clipping, probably from Monroe *Republican*, RG-7 (Military Manuscript Collection), Box 3 (General Correspondence), Item 75 (Folder 14a), Dart Collection, Pennsylvania State Archives, Harrisburg, Pa. See also, George Henry Herbert to Jack, September 13, 1862, George Henry Herbert Papers, British Library, London, U.K.

10. Oscar Coles to Hendrick B. Wright, July 1, 1863, Hendrick B. Wright Papers, Luzerne County Historical Society, Wilkes-Barre, Pa.

11. S. M. Johnson to Barlow, June 26, 1863, Barlow Papers. Johnson still believed that the Union would be restored. He wrote, "There is in the others as with me a strong hope that by & by, the spirit of the Union may be revived; but there is no hope that it can be revived thro existing agencies—there is a solid belief that the existing government stands between the true lovers of the Union and the restoration of the Constitution. . . . My whole soul—all I am & all I hope for—is identified with the Union—I believe it can be restored; but to restore it, surely, we must first put down its real enemies."

12. Bellefonte *Democratic Watchman*, July 17, 1863; *Doylestown Democrat*, June 30 and July 21, 1863.

13. Thaddeus Stevens, "Speech on State Elections," September 17[?], 1863, in *The Selected Papers of Thaddeus Stevens*, 2 vols., ed. Beverly Wilson Palmer and Holly Byers Ochoa (Pittsburgh: University of Pittsburgh Press, 1997), 1:407–8.

14. *Congressional Globe*, 38th Cong., 1st sess., 1595.

15. *Doylestown Democrat*, June 30, 1863.

16. Fred Steffan to John Martin Steffan, July 2, 1863, Steffan Family Letters, and Paul Hersh to Jim, July 10, 1864, Paul Hersh Letters, both in Civil War Miscellaneous Collection, MHI.

One Tennessean serving in the Union army noted that Lee's raid into Pennsylvania and John Hunt Morgan's incursion into Ohio had revealed the weaknesses of the "cowardly copperheaded fraternity commonly called K. G. C." The Copperheads had had their "supplies consumed by an invading *friend*," while the rebels were forced to reckon with "the cowardise [sic] of theire [sic] northern allies." William Brunt to Martha Weir, July 26, 1863 (GLC7006.02), Gilder Lehrman Institute of American History, New York, N.Y.

17. E. Harmon to Jeremiah S. Black, September 10, 1863, Jeremiah S. Black Papers, Manuscript Division, Library of Congress, Washington, D.C.

18. Charles J. C. Hutson to mother, June 28, 1863, in Robert E. Bonner, ed., *The Soldier's Pen: Firsthand Impressions of the Civil War* (New York: Hill and Wang, 2006), 161–62.

19. Allen C. Guelzo, *Gettysburg: The Last Invasion* (New York: Alfred A. Knopf, 2013), 467.

20. An Act to Provide for the Adjudication and Payment of Claims Arising from the Loss of Horses, and Other Property, Taken, or Destroyed, in the Border Counties by the Rebels, in October, Anno Domini One Thousand Eight Hundred and Sixty-Two, and for Property and Horses Impressed for the Use of the Military of the State, in September, One Thousand Eight Hundred and Sixty-Two, act of April 22, 1863, in *Laws of the General Assembly of the State of Pennsylvania, Passed at the Session of 1863, in the Eighty-Seventh Year of Independence* (Harrisburg: Singerly & Myers, 1863), 529–30.

21. Arnold M. Shankman, *The Pennsylvania Antiwar Movement, 1861–1865* (Rutherford, N.J.: Farleigh Dickinson University Press, 1980), 100.

22. George Bergner, *The Legislative Record: Containing the Debates and Proceedings of the Pennsylvania Legislature for the Session of 1864* (Harrisburg: The "Telegraph" Steam Book and Job Office, 1864), 172–75; *Franklin Repository*, February 24 and March 2, 1864. The resolution was later amended to require "satisfactory proofs." The House *Journal* recorded this line as "to furnish satisfactory proof of their loyalty." See *Journal of the House of Representatives of the Commonwealth of Pennsylvania, of the Session Begun at Harrisburg, on the Fifth Day of January, 1864* (Harrisburg: Singerly and Myers, 1864), 165.

23. Bergner, *Legislative Record for 1864*, 173.

24. Ibid., 174.

25. Ibid., 204.

26. Ibid., 174. For a similar argument, see Abraham Lincoln to Erastus Corning and Others, June 12, 1863, in Roy P. Basler et al., eds., *The Collected Works of Lincoln*, 9 vols. (New Brunswick, N.J.: Rutgers University Press, 1953), 6:263–65.

27. Bergner, *Legislative Record for 1864*, 181–82.

28. Ibid., 174–76, 181.

29. Ibid., 182, 174. In April 1861—in the immediate aftermath of the attack on Fort Sumter—Pennsylvania enacted a treason statute that was derived almost verbatim from the state's 1777 treason law, which had been enacted during the American Revolution and was repealed in 1860. The law was enacted with little debate or fanfare. State authorities never enforced the law. See Jonathan W. White, "'Words Become Things': Free Speech in Wartime," *Pennsylvania Legacies* 8 (May 2008): 18–23.

30. Bergner, *Legislative Record for 1864*, 176.

31. Ibid., 207, 223.

32. Ibid., 177, 204–8.

33. Ibid., 222–23. See also Melinda Lawson, *Patriot Fires: Forging a New American Nationalism in the Civil War North* (Lawrence: University Press of Kansas, 2002), chapter 3; Mark E. Neely, Jr., *Lincoln and the Triumph of the Nation: Constitutional Conflict in the American Civil War* (Chapel Hill: University of North Carolina Press, 2011).

34. Bergner, *Legislative Record for 1864*, 223–25.

35. Ibid., 225.

36. *Franklin Repository*, February 17, 1864.

37. *Franklin Repository*, March 2, 1864.

38. Gettysburg *Republican Compiler*, February 24, 1864; Chambersburg *Franklin Repository*, February 24, 1864.

39. Bergner, *Legislative Record for 1864*, 781–82, 810, 995.

40. Ibid., 781–83.

41. Ibid., 781, 783, 995, 1035.

42. Ibid., 810.

43. Ibid., 783, 811, 1035–39; *Franklin Repository*, March 9, 1864; Harmon to Black, September 10, 1863, Black Papers. Several Republicans had also argued that the federal government, and not the state government, should compensate citizens who had lost their property during a rebel invasion.

44. *Franklin Repository*, February 17, 24, 1864.

45. Gettysburg *Compiler*, February 22, 1864.

46. Bergner, *Legislative Record for 1864*, 217–18.

47. Court-Martial Case file NN-1005, RG 153, Records of the Office of the Judge Advocate General (Army), National Archives and Records Administration, Washington, D.C. Fisher is mentioned in Bergner, *Legislative Record for 1864*, 175.

48. Bergner, *Legislative Record for 1864*, 213.

49. Ibid., 212.

50. Ibid., 212–13.

51. Ibid.

52. Ibid., 213–14.

53. Ibid., 214–15.

54. Ibid., 214.

55. Gettysburg *Compiler*, May 30, 1864; *Journal of the Senate of the Commonwealth of Pennsylvania, of the Session Begun at Harrisburg, on the Fifth Day of January, 1864* (Harrisburg: Singerly & Myers, 1864), 294, 795–96, 806, 818, 968, 992, 1027, 1029, 1039; *Journal of the House*, 53, 156, 165, 171, 175–76, 194, 206, 208–10, 214–15, 231, 260, 271, 491,

612, 794–98, 932, 964–65; Bergner, *Legislative Record for 1864*, 230–35, 289–91, 759–63, 958–63, 1042–43.

56. Gettysburg *Compiler*, February 22 and May 30, 1864.

57. Harmon to Black, September 10, 1863, Black Papers; S. N. Baily and J. S. Shillito to Woodward, September 15, 1863, and H. J. Stable to James F. Shunk, September 26, 1863, and Junius [pseudonym] to Woodward, September 29, 1863, all in Biddle Family Papers, Historical Society of Pennsylvania, Philadelphia, Pa.; Woodward to Jeremiah S. Black, September 24, 1863, in Jonathan W. White, ed., "A Pennsylvania Judge Views the Rebellion: The Civil War Letters of George Washington Woodward," *Pennsylvania Magazine of History and Biography* 129 (April 2005): 220; Gettysburg *Compiler*, October 12, 1863; Chambersburg *Valley Spirit* quoted in Gettysburg *Compiler*, May 30, 1864; George Edward Reed, ed., *Pennsylvania Archives*, 130 vols. (Harrisburg: William Stanley Ray, 1902), ser. 4, 8:457–58, 561–64.

58. Stroudsburg *Jeffersonian*, January 12, 1865; Philadelphia *Daily Evening Bulletin*, January 30, 1866.

59. James C. Mohr, ed., *The Cormany Diaries: A Northern Family in the Civil War* (Pittsburgh: University of Pittsburgh Press, 1982), 446n9; Alexander K. McClure, *Old Time Notes of Pennsylvania*, 2 vols. (Philadelphia: John C. Winston, 1905), 2:149; George Bergner, ed., *The Legislative Record: Containing the Debates and Proceedings of the Pennsylvania Legislature for the Session of 1866* (Harrisburg: The "Telegraph" Steam Book and Job Office, 1866), 235.

60. McClure, *Old Time Notes*, 2:176–78; Gettysburg *Republican Compiler*, March 20, 1865. For the text of the debate, see George Bergner, ed., *The Legislative Record: Containing the Debates and Proceedings of the Pennsylvania Legislature for the Session of 1865* (Harrisburg: The "Telegraph" Steam Book and Job Office, 1865), 449–50, 559–62, and Appendix pp. xxxviii–lxi.

61. McClure, *Old Time Notes*, 2:170–80; Bergner, *Legislative Record for 1866*, 173, 182, 201–2, 205, 216, 234–38, 340, 352, and Appendix ppxvii–xxviii; Wellsboro *Agitator*, February 21, 1866.

62. An Act for the Relief of Certain Citizens of Chambersburg and Vicinity, Whose Property was Destroyed by Fire, by the Rebels, on the Thirtieth of July, Anno Domini One Thousand Eight Hundred and Sixty-Four, act of February 15, 1866, in *Laws of the General Assembly of the State of Pennsylvania, Passed at the Session of 1866, in the Ninetieth Year of Independence* (Harrisburg: Singerly & Myers, 1866), 43–45.

63. Bergner, *Daily Legislative Record for 1864*, 181, 231–32. For more on this point, see Judith Giesberg, *Army at Home: Women and the Civil War on the Northern Home Front* (Chapel Hill: University of North Carolina Press, 2009), chapter 1.

64. An Act for the Relief of the Citizens of the Counties of Adams, Franklin, Fulton, Bedford, York, Perry and Cumberland, Whose Property was Destroyed, Damaged or Appropriated for the Public Service, and in the Common Defence, in the War to Suppress the Rebellion, act of April 9, 1868, in *Laws of the General Assembly of the State of Pennsylvania, Passed at the Session of 1868, in the Ninety-Second Year of Independence* (Harrisburg: Singerly & Myers, 1868), 74–76.

Several other states also contemplated government compensation for citizens who lost property during rebel raids. Kentucky, Maryland, and Pennsylvania each sent resolutions to their members of Congress requesting them to seek legislation for federal compensation.

In 1864, Ohio adopted legislation to adjudicate the claims of taxpaying victims of John Hunt Morgan's 1863 raid into that state. In 1869, the state appropriated money to pay out the claims, but the state's supreme court struck down the legislation saying that a quorum had not been present in the legislature when the second claims bill had been adopted. As in Pennsylvania, some Northerners assisted Morgan's raiders on their way through Ohio in July 1863. Edward L. Hughes, an Ohioan who had helped Morgan navigate his way through the state, claimed that he could not be punished for his actions because he had taken Lincoln's December 1863 amnesty oath. According to one historian, "The district attorney said that Lincoln did not mean it for Northern traitors, but the judge said he did and ended the case."

The state of Kansas assumed the claims of citizens who lost property during Confederate General Sterling Price's 1864 raid into the state, although the law contained no provisions regarding loyalty. Following the war, loyal West Virginians were permitted to sue former rebel guerrillas for compensation for property they had lost during the war.

For citations to these various resolutions, court cases, and pieces of legislation, see Jonathan W. White, "'To Aid Their Rebel Friends': Politics and Treason in the Civil War North," (Ph.D. diss., University of Maryland, 2008), 302–5. For a highly contentious and partisan debate over compensation for victims of Morgan's raid in Indiana, see Stephen Rockenbach, "'This Just Hope of Ultimate Payment': The Indiana Morgan's Raid Claims Commission and Harrison County, Indiana, 1863–1887," *Indiana Magazine of History* 109 (March 2013): 45–60.

"We Are Setting the Terms Now"

Loyalty Rhetoric in Courtship

Julie A. Mujic

What I meant by saying that I should personally have no objections to going to war, was, that aside from all considerations in which you were concerned—i.e., if I had never known you, I would as soon go as not. I don't want to leave you, though; and I shall not if it can be avoided . . .

—GIDEON WINAN ALLEN, APRIL 26, 1865

Gideon Winan Allen left the University of Wisconsin in 1862 and moved to Ann Arbor, Michigan to begin his studies in the law school at the University of Michigan. His love interest, Annie Cox, who later became his fiancée and wife, remained in Madison and the two commenced a vibrant and emotional correspondence. In their letters, they discussed their feelings toward each other, the events of the American Civil War, happenings in their respective towns, and, with incredible intensity, politics. Annie was a devout abolitionist and supported the Republican agenda while her betrothed pledged his loyalty to the Democrats and eventually proudly called himself a Copperhead.[1]

Their long-distance relationship spanned nearly the entire war, placing them in a unique situation. They faced the challenge of developing a relationship that could endure time and distance and could create a foundation for the future—a daunting task considering that no one knew what that future might hold. Through their letters, they negotiated the positions and expectations that would influence their relationship. Gideon Winan Allen and Annie Cox utilized the upheaval caused by the Civil War as a tool to shape their discussions of the nature of marriage. Both implicitly and explicitly, they adapted the meaning of war for their own purposes; while it may seem at first in reading their letters that they were arguing about the war's causes, nature, or consequences, in actuality, they were using it as a metaphor for their own perspectives on gender roles, marital expectations, and the balance of power in their relationship. Yet, while both seemed to represent a certain view on the war's significant questions, neither of these two young adults were willing to push their opinions on the other to a point that would jeopardize the relationship.[2]

Despite the uncertainty caused by the war, Gideon Winan Allen and Annie Cox focused on their relationship as their first priority, using the war's themes when advantageous to punctuate other debates they were having about marriage. When considering ways that Northerners contested the meanings of loyalty and patriotism during the Civil War, this example reveals the ways in which some Northerners usurped rhetoric about loyalty and treason for their own intentions. Thus, one way that Northerners contemplated and shaped the definition of loyalty was by appropriating the larger public debates for application in their personal lives, therefore articulating an interpretation of allegiance to the Union that actually turned national disputes into a microcosm for private affairs. Annie Cox worried at times that Gideon Winan Allen's politics bordered on treason and she was concerned about the impact his vocal opposition to the war might have on his future and, by extension, on hers. Her fears did not, however, decrease her desire to marry him because, as she once explained, "I did not give my heart and promise my hand to your politics." Northerners did indeed contest the meaning of loyalty and patriotism during the war but sometimes they did it for personal reasons rather than to contribute to the larger cause.[3]

Three strains of historiography inform this analysis. First, historians have acknowledged that much of the most virulent antiwar rhetoric, and therefore most fraught contestations of the definition of loyalty, occurred on the Midwestern home front. In the recent publication, *Union Heartland: The Midwestern Home Front during the Civil War*, historian William C. Davis notes that while Americans during the Civil War debated the "ever-present problem of what constitutes disloyalty in wartime [,] the hotbed of disloyalty was in the Midwest." Historians Frank L. Klement and Jennifer Weber signaled this truth in their studies of dissent in the North by focusing largely on events, politicians, and popular unrest in the Midwest. They, among others, have sought to determine how important the antiwar factions of the Midwest were to the stability, or instability, of Lincoln's war effort. Klement downplays these threats, while Weber insists upon their significance. Recent literature about the Civil War Midwest recognizes the region's central role in the war but focuses more on its economic contributions than on its identity as an ideological shaky ground. These studies help to contextualize the region of the country in which Gideon Winan Allen and Annie Cox lived. Much of the Midwest was still recently settled at the outbreak of the war, populated by large immigrant groups with allegiance to the Democratic party and a young Republican party that was quickly gaining popularity. Midwesterners understood that not everyone in their midst supported the war. Voices of dissent found confidence in the rhetoric of newness and the potential of their growing region.[4]

Second, studies regarding how Americans, Union and Confederate, debated notions of loyalty and the construction of nationalism influence the interpretation of this source base. Historians have examined whether Northerners and Southerners rallied for the war by creating new nationalisms or relying on existing ideologies. It is also unclear how important the development of nationalism was to the outcome of the war and how it affected the respective home fronts. In these debates, though, historians have focused mainly on the ways in which Americans engaged with the war as though it was an obstacle or an opportunity. For example, Melinda Lawson examines the ways that Americans who consciously wanted to shape nationalism in the North identified factors about the American experience that could be used to foster attachment to the nation. William Blair demonstrates how notions of loyalty shifted over time in Pennsylvania and eventually led to Republican definitions of patriotism that were linked with military service. Blair finds that "staying home might be acceptable as long as one helped the Union war effort." Robert M. Sandow's work on lumbermen in the Pennsylvania Appalachians reveals how concerns about the economic impact of the war and enlistment shaped their support for the war. Gideon Winan Allen did not see the war in any of these lights. Like the college-age Northerners in Kanisorn Wongsrichanalai's essay in this volume, Allen also was loyal to a cause rather than to the military or political leaders who represented it. Allen did not wish for Northern victory; he merely wanted the war to end and life to go back to the way it was before 1860. Whichever way you turn for comparison in the North or South, Gideon Winan Allen and Annie Cox surprise us; the war did not consume them. However these two young adults came to understand the demands of nationalism within the Union, it was not something that overrode other goals in their lives, and this essay highlights the reality that not everyone in the Civil War North found the war knocking at every door and influencing every step in their lives.[5]

Third, gender studies of the Civil War era illuminate the social constructions and discourse that existed at the time that these letters were written. Historians have sought to understand how women and men who stayed home during the war understood their role in the conflict and how it impacted the way that they related to each other. While LeeAnn Whites points out that white men in the Confederacy understood the war as a "threat to their manhood," Lorien Foote explains that "there was a diversity of models and patterns" in the North that influenced the "conception of manhood." Considering "both the social diversity of the region and the new class structures that accompanied modern life"—both of which were exaggerated in the nascent Midwest—one can understand how Gideon Winan Allen could avoid military service and still maintain a belief in his manliness. In her examination of Northern women, Judith Giesberg demonstrates how women overcame the constraints of gender to survive the challenges of the war. Annie Cox moved often during the war with her family but did not associate those hardships with the war itself. And, like the Confederate women in Whites's study of Augusta, Georgia, Annie Cox saw the war as an opportunity for "expanded significance" in her responsibility to shape Allen's masculinity. Despite consistent arguments in the literature regarding the impact of war on gender identities, such as Reid Mitchell's conclusion that "remaining a civilian was thought unmanly" and Amy Murrell Taylor's finding that "disloyalty to a husband's wartime convictions was tantamount to becoming his public enemy," Gideon Winan Allen and Annie Cox seemed blissfully unaware of these notions. All he cared about was whether she could love him despite his politics and all she asked was for him to not go so far with his politics as to ruin their future prospects. In late 1863, Annie warned, "If [you] should soon be influenced to dishonorable acts by them [your politics], then my duty might be different." This couple's letters reveal that one way gender shaped the home front was by absorbing the rhetoric of war as another tool in determining the composition of a private relationship.[6]

Gideon Winan Allen, called Winan by his friends, enrolled at the University of Wisconsin in 1858 after leaving his home town of New London, Ohio. Born in March 1835, Winan's mother died during his childhood, leaving him with his father and four siblings. Winan was the smallest and weakest of the three boys in the family, often plagued by "wheezing and coughing," and he preferred reading to helping on the family farm. His father grew frustrated with his intellectually driven son and increased his criticism of Winan's educational pursuits and his outspoken support of the Democratic party. Theirs was a Whig, and then Republican, household, and Winan's father saw his son's developing affiliation with the Democratic party line as further evidence of his uselessness in the family. Finally, Winan declared that he would leave the house where he was unwanted and headed off on his own, never returning to his birthplace and only seeing his father once more. In October 1862, he referred to himself in a letter to Annie as the prodigal son. He had been alienated in his home since his mother's death and set out to make a name for himself independent of his family's expectations.[7]

Winan was twenty-six years old at the outbreak of the Civil War. Despite being a few years older than most students at the University of Wisconsin, Winan took an active part in university activities. He served the student Democratic Club as secretary and participated in rousing debates with the Republican Club in the months leading up to the election of 1860. He was attracted to the Democratic party because he opposed emancipation, based on a belief that the founding fathers allowed slavery in the constitution. Winan took a strict constructionist, conservative line regarding the constitution, and failed to be swayed by any emotional appeals about the cruelties of slavery; he insisted "slavery is bad, but war and disunion are a thousand times worse." Winan saw Southerners as increasingly attacked and marginalized and he sympathized with their plight. Or perhaps it was the Republicans' quest for change that scared him. He explained, "I oppose the policy of the administration which seeks to form a new union by the abolition of slavery . . . because it involves an unwarrantable assumption of power . . . [and] will destroy our national existence." Winan craved structure, stability, and order while the Republicans, and eventually the war, represented more threats and potential change to a stable future.[8]

As the war progressed, Winan viewed the conflict through a narrow and unwavering lens that subsequently colored his opinion of the Lincoln administration, soldiers, and emancipation. He was in the political minority on campus and in the Midwest and he consciously avoided military service by spending the war years obtaining a higher education. Winan remained ideologically unaltered throughout the war; as he himself put it in December 1862, "those ideas which are soonest impressed upon the flexible mind of youth, those which awaken the first impulses of the passions, always produce the liveliest sensations, sink the deepest, and are the most difficult to eradicate." It is surprising then that he courted Annie Cox in Madison, whom he once referred to as "my dear little abolitionist." Instead of finding someone whose political views aligned with his, he chose a mate who challenged him and who pushed him to make changes to his life—to be more social, to attend church regularly, and to come around to the Republican view of the war. By the end of their existing correspondence in 1865, Winan had done none of these things but their commitment to each other remained unaltered.[9]

Annie was born in 1840 in Mineral Point, Wisconsin. Her mother sought and won a divorce from her father during Annie's infancy, one of the first such legal successes for a woman in Wisconsin. After remarrying, Annie's mother and stepfather moved to Madison and Annie grew there into a thoughtful, intellectual, and ambitious young woman. Annie desired education but found her ambitions stifled by an overprotective and possessive mother. Before she met Winan in the late 1850s, Annie worried whether she would ever get married. Additionally, her stepfather was struggling to support the family and they began a series of moves from one home to another as their financial position dwindled. Annie's mother's overbearing nature was similar to that of Winan's father and the two commiserated on their frustrating personal situations. Annie's mother refused to allow Annie to visit her birth father, expressed effusive sadness when Annie and Winan decided not to live with her upon marriage, refused to allow her to teach in a nearby community school, and gave her regular guilt trips about any disconnection, whether emotional or physical (distance), that she felt from Annie. Annie yearned for a much different life—one filled with education, art, fine things, and freedom. It was during all of this uncertainty that the war began and Annie coincidentally met Winan, who seemed to promise her a better future. She was thrilled when their courtship began and wrote to him eagerly upon his removal to Ann Arbor for law school.[10]

Annie's main concern regarding Winan was his lack of belief in God. He attended church occasionally only because she asked him to do so, and throughout the letters he challenged her both seriously and playfully regarding her faith and his apparent shortcoming in that department. She included advice in her letters that she expected him to follow, such as "Will you read the bible every day? You will find something . . . there from a higher authority than myself." She wanted him to keep the Sabbath, refrain from swearing, and contemplate the nature of heaven. Part of her sadness about his deficiency in this area stemmed from her pity regarding his upbringing. She felt that he turned from God because he had been raised in an unloving home. Annie believed him "fearfully enslaved by that dark soulless belief"; she wrote once "you have settled yourself to believe that you are forever bound to evil." Annie wanted to be the one to fill this void in Winan.[11]

Her second concern throughout the letters was how soon they could be together. Annie regularly asked Winan for dates of his expected arrival back in Madison on school breaks, and over the years she became increasingly agitated as his graduation day approached with no firm plan in place for when they would get married. Winan had been gone less than two weeks when she asked "when spring spreads her first carpet over the earth shall we not greet you home?" This pleasant image changed into more urgent expressions as the months went on; at the end of his first year of law school, her request became "I wish you had stated definitely when you would be here whether the last of this week or first of next," while when she waited to join him in Sturgeon Bay in 1865, she wrote "my stock of patience was only calculated to last till March." Their negotiations regarding his absence and the timing of their future consumed much of their letters.[12]

The third most frequent point of contention in their relationship was the war and its meaning. When discussions of the war or politics arose, which it did in more than one-third of their letters, they often became agitated in a way that did not characterize any of their other disagreements. Both had succinct positions on loyalty and patriotism that were never altered during the war, positions that could have easily threatened to make their relationship vulnerable. Winan believed that loyalty was adhering to "a union with slavery." "'The Union as it was,'" Winan wrote, "is the only safe, practical, ground for loyal men to occupy." Annie's support of the war and emancipation was based on her belief that God disapproved of slavery. She also empathized with slaves' oppression, their chains, and their desire to be released from captivity—all metaphors to her own underwhelming life. Yet, she regularly stayed within her domestic sphere by reassuring Winan that she would not express her politics in public. When Madison residents formed a Union League society to express their patriotism, Annie felt the participants "carry the matter to ridiculous lengths." "I love the cause of freedom and the country," Annie wrote, "but choose to express it in a different way and am glad there is a higher power to judge me than the [Madison] Union league." Throughout the letters, Annie's arguments returned to her faith in what God wanted for the country; this was her understanding of loyalty—it was more than to a government, it was to God's will. Like Democrats and Republicans in general, Winan and Annie's main disagreement centered on their beliefs about the constitutionality and morality of the institution of slavery.[13]

In 1862, when a disagreement with faculty prompted Winan to leave the University of Wisconsin prior to graduation and head to Ann Arbor to pursue a law degree, these discussions were in their infancy. With his arrival at the University of Michigan, their correspondence commenced, and the two young adults used their letters to develop the bonds that had taken root during months of courting in Madison. The war served as one touch-point for getting to know each other and for understanding how the dynamics of their relationship would be set. Winan and Annie shared a bond based on a lifetime of unhappiness, guilt, and feelings of not having what they deserved, of not being understood, and of somehow being different than their families. Their goal was to create a new family, with their marriage as its foundation, which would be happy, supportive, and fruitful. "If I could give you a home, and make you comfortable and happy, 'sadness' would be a word for which I would have no use," Winan wrote in 1863. Her answer, "It was my high mission to be a home, sister, and counselor to one who had not received their worth for many years," offers an example of the regular instances of kind, generous, and loving exchanges that illustrated their shared goals for the future.[14]

Their letters followed a pattern that demonstrated how they invoked the war's discourse as one method through which they fleshed out the nature of their relationship. The majority of every letter focused on non-war topics: her family's money and housing issues, their various health ailments, fluctuations in their weight, frustration in waiting from each other's letters, and how eternal their love was for each other. When the topic of war, politics, or slavery arose, it was buried in the letters, often in between paragraphs about, for example, how badly she wanted him to return to Madison or a walk he took in the woods. In the midst of these general subjects, a paragraph or two appeared containing a seemingly heated war debate, but then what followed was just as calm, devoted, and loving as before, as though the fiery words had not been written. This configuration of their letters, repeated over time, makes it clear that although their talk of loyalty, patriotism, and Union seemed dangerous enough at times to put their relationship at risk, it was rarely the fulcrum on which their affections depended. As such, it served as one in a series of topics through which they came to know and understand each other, but never overtook their communication to the point where it consumed an entire letter.

From the beginning, Winan welcomed Annie's frank input on his life. He was familiar with Annie's assertiveness from their short time together, evidenced by his November 1862 letter regarding the minister he heard in church on Sunday. The preacher had "come to your aid in teaching me my duty, but he didn't advance anything new, simply stole your 'thunder.'" "I prefer to go to headquarters for my orders," Winan told Annie, "so be sure and have a discourse prepared by next Sunday." Winan was remarkably respectful of Annie's intellectual capacity. Although she at times poked fun at her outspokenness ("Well, I am verifying the saying that a woman's tongue is never still[.] It holds good when she takes the pen as a substitute," she wrote to end one November 1862 letter), he did not use her gender to discount her perspectives or her right to express them. Within their first few letters, they talked openly about how they would communicate. Annie reminded Winan quickly, "Do not think then when I talk plainly that I am scolding. I never scold those I esteem . . . let frankness be our motto then as the true seal of regard." She believed that Winan was "one of the nation's true noble men" and yet it was her duty to make sure he lived up to that billing. Their letters began with an earnestness and a devotion to discussing their compatibility.[15]

Historian Ellen Rothman encountered Winan and Annie's letters in a study she conducted regarding middle-class courtship in the nineteenth century. She points out that during that period, "young middle class men and women possessed a degree of autonomy and privacy that allowed them to develop genuine closeness in their relationships with one another." This pattern in their relationship was set early and confirms that Winan and Annie believed "that candor was both a sign of and a safeguard for intimacy." Historian Amy Murrell Taylor argues that some women in the border states asserted "national loyalty distinct from their husbands or suitors." Many men "had reason to tolerate" these female expressions of political position because, by the mid-nineteenth century, they had begun to desire friendship and intellectual companionship from their wives. Thus, it was not unusual for the era that Winan encouraged and accepted Annie's expressions of intellectual engagement with such topics; in fact, he and she would have viewed it as a method by which they increased the depth of their intimacy.[16]

Among these early discussions of Winan's religious impurity and how he was liking Ann Arbor society, Annie broached the subject of politics. She must have criticized a speech she read by New York Governor Horatio Seymour, a Democrat, because Winan responded in the fall of 1862 with this opening parlay: "I agree with you, however in all except the politics: and as this subject opens a very fruitful field of contention, by your permission, we will not enter it. A lady wanted to hang me once for venturing to disagree with her in politics, and ever since then, I have had a decided aversion to discussing politics with the ladies." Annie remained undeterred, seeking any subject upon which she could shape her suitor's character. Giving in, Winan later wrote, "Select your propositions, make your points, and I'll try to answer them; but remember the terms are, that you will neither hang me, nor threaten to do so." She clearly understood his position at that time, since he had recently described exiled southern pro-Union politician Parson Brownlow as "disgustingly bitter, vindictive, and revengeful . . . coarse and brutish" and believed that the only good thing about Union General George B. McClellan's removal from command that fall was that it might "tend to an honorable conclusion of our difficulties [in the war]." Annie knew that she was going to encounter a position that ran deep in this man.[17]

Through their discussions of the war, it was clear that Winan viewed his university education as a more worthwhile pursuit than serving in the military. Some university students in the Midwest remained in school during the war because they did not receive parental approval to fight, or they wished to enlist after obtaining their degrees, or because eventually they developed an ideology that earning an education was equally as patriotic as serving on the field of battle. However, a small but vocal segment of young men on university campuses identified themselves as Copperheads and remained in school because of their ideological opposition to the Lincoln administration. Copperheads was the nickname given to Peace Democrats, a wing of the Democratic party that sought a negotiated peace with the Confederacy and called for strict adherence to the constitution including its protections of slavery. In characterizing Copperheads, historian Jennifer L. Weber argues that they "were consistent, and constant, in their demand for an immediate peace settlement. At times they were willing to trade victory for peace." While a law student at the University of Michigan, Winan illustrated Weber's description. He embraced the ideology of the Peace Democrat wing of his party and expressed dismay at the increasing criticism of their position.[18]

Winan's persistent disappointment in the continuance of the war combined with his intense disapproval of emancipation colored his perception of the Civil War. Regarding a speech given by the university president in late 1862, Winan complained that it was "all abolition" and "would have been good if he had left out his pet dogmas." Winan grew more frustrated on the eve of the official Emancipation Proclamation that "every body [sic] must talk about the 'nigger' . . . It seems as though folks had forgotten everything else they ever knew." Upon attending a public lecture in January 1863, Winan wrote to Annie that "a man can hardly go to a lecture, or even to church, without being insulted. Every public speaker I have heard this winter has called down the most bitter curses and imperatives of Heaven upon Copperheads. I am disgusted, and sometimes resolve that I will go no more." It must have frustrated him immensely when Annie wrote that she wanted to "call down God's curse upon" the Democrats who had held a "'sesecsh' [sic] meeting" in Madison the previous night. For Winan, the war was a tragic betrayal of the constitution and the goals of the founding fathers; he abhorred abolitionists and all who supported Lincoln's administration.[19]

Soon after the Emancipation Proclamation was official on January 1, 1863, the intensity of political debates between this couple heated up dramatically. In late January, Winan warned Annie against fraternizing with soldiers. Soldiers, in his view, took advantage of the honorable reputation they gained at home when they enlisted but subsequently acted out "evil deeds" while at the front because "the law cannot reach them." His disdain leaped off the page as he tried to convince Annie that socializing with soldiers would stigmatize her. "Your reputation will be none the better for being with them too much," Winan cautioned. He wished that she would keep her distance from them so that she would not be associated with them once the soldiers' true nature was revealed. Perhaps also he did not want to compete with them in her eyes and risk losing her to like-minded antislavery soldiers. This concern about possible competition came out regularly in Annie's letters as well. After one encounter with someone Winan had courted before her, Annie wrote with equal candor, "You won't feel hurt if I speak bluntly 'Tis not to wound dear Winan, Well, I think if you cannot think me better looking than she, I will hereafter wear a veil in your presence. Why Winan she looks like a red poppy worm eaten and surrounded with dead leaves. Her face is fat red and pimply, her eyes have an unpleasant expression and I don't like her altogether." Clearly both Annie and Winan found ways to criticize potential suitors, using war rhetoric or other forms of prose.[20]

Some of Winan's increased excitement in early 1863 spawned from his recognition that Copperhead political candidates were making progress in the political arena and he hoped that those trends would continue. He read McClellan's report from the Peninsula campaign, published after the general's removal in 1862, and called it a "prominent electioneering document." He was eager for McClellan to set the record straight and overturn the "shameless ignorance of his merits, his devotion to the Union and the services which he rendered it." He eagerly anticipated increased support for Democrats in the backlash against the Emancipation Proclamation. In February, he wrote her: "I rejoice in my very soul that the democrats are at last making a stand . . . God grant that the effort be not too late." He told Annie that he had been afraid that his political opinions were so at odds with the majority that "I did not dare to test the matter by giving expression to my sentiments."[21]

Now that he saw an opening, he began to express his position with gusto. His letters celebrated what he perceived to be growing political clout for the Democratic party. Winan proclaimed, "We, the Democratic party, and in this I believe I truly represent a large majority of that party—hate slavery; yet for the sake of union we are willing to let it remain, and leave the government as our fathers made it." So eager was Winan to feel a sense of community with others who shared his political opinions, he jumped at the chance to associate himself with a political ideology that was becoming more coherent in early 1863. "If we will lay aside our prejudices, we cannot doubt that there are men who believe slavery right, and who desire its continuance," he conceded. The problem in his mind was that he did not agree that Americans in 1863 should "determine this question of right and wrong[.] If we were directly, or even remotely, responsible for slavery, it might be a question for us to determine. But such is not the case; we are in nowise responsible for its existence; nor have we any right or power to control it." Winan was of the firm belief that because the founding fathers had allowed slavery, Americans were bound to respect their decision and not question its propriety.[22]

In response to Annie's accusation that his political party withheld civil rights by disapproving of debates about slavery, he argued that individual Northerners had the right to try and engage Southerners in a conversation about emancipation. However, in return, abolitionists had to respect the fact that the right to free speech included the right of Southerners to decline participating in such a conversation. "Well what now?" he asked Annie in early 1863 regarding the impasse of the country. His answer was to "simply mind our own business, and let them alone, and I tell you if we had observed this little piece of advice, we should have avoided all our difficulties, and the peace and prosperity of our nation would have been secure." Surely there was more from Winan's personal experiences that underlies this argument than a belief that continuing to ignore slavery was the right answer. Winan's reaction underscores his sense of constantly being told what to do and what to believe; the oppressive nature of his experience under his father's thumb pushed him to insist that every man had a right to live free from interference from others. His sorrow reverberated from the page when he insisted regarding Southerners that "We must learn to be respectful and tolerant of the opinions of others, if we would enjoy the fruits of wisdom and the blessings of free government." Winan understood that his perspective might raise questions of his loyalty to the country but he did not shy away from taking a hard stance in his letters to Annie; "if this be treason," he wrote, "I can't help it, it is the truth." Winan's understanding of loyalty and patriotism was wrapped up in a belief in individual rights that were protected from the oversight of a meddling government.[23]

Annie was slower to counter Winan on the topic of slavery than on others about politics but when she did so, it reveals her willingness to use political issues to test the fabric of their relationship. On February 1, 1863, Annie sent Winan a very long letter that began with a description of a recent dream that she wished to interpret for him. In the dream, she was held against her will in an asylum "for the crime and insanity of Anti Slaveryism." Annie's interpretation of the dream was that "The insane were the Republicans, the keepers . . . were the democrats." The disagreement over emancipation drove the two sides into these positions, and the Democrats believed Republicans to be insane for their antislavery beliefs. Somehow the prisoners were released after proving they did not intend harm but instead "good will to all men." This was an indirect attempt on Annie's part to express to Winan her concerns regarding the zealousness of Democrats against emancipation.[24]

Then, she addressed him frankly, writing, "Now a word about politics." As she would in several subsequent letters, she began her discussion by explaining that she understood she was stepping outside of the realm of accepted female behavior with what she was about to write. "You know women should be keepers at home," she acknowledged, "darned of stockings with a little womanly indulgence, now and then of scandal or scolding yet . . ." And with that "yet" Annie unleashed on him a tirade regarding the South, slavery, and civil rights that demonstrated her detailed understanding of the issues of the war and her comfort in expressing her opposing viewpoints to Winan. "I cannot help thinking that democrats support or countenance slavery, thereby crush free speech thought and action. We never could express an honest opinion in the south," Annie argued, "if contrary to their peculiar institution." She was frustrated by the ways that Southerners attempted to end debates about slavery; she felt that their protection of slavery inhibited the civil rights of anti-slavery Americans and told Winan that the Democrats should not choose to support slavery at the expense of civil rights. Annie insisted that the proslavery position of the Democrats caused "slavery [to oppress] the white even more than the black."[25]

She spent more time than usual in this particular letter directly criticizing the Democratic party: "Now do not the majority of your party encourage [slavery's] existence and extension? What is the cause of our superiority in intelligence over the South. You must say slavery in one case, and its nonexistence in the other." Annie's strategy of questioning the intelligence of the Democrats continued as she accused the party of attracting the "rabble" whose "ignorance" on the matter of slavery caused her to believe that she "cannot respect their principles as seen in results." True to the pattern, however, Annie asked Winan to correct her if she "speaks in too unqualified a manner," and then moved on to say good night and tell a story about a friend of the family. The war here served again as a medium through which Annie could express the strength of her intellectual capacity and yet defer to Winan regarding his expectations of her behavior.[26]

Winan responded with a long political diatribe to Annie to refute her points. He held up the Democratic, and expressly Copperhead, position regarding his condemnation of the war by arguing that Republicans pushed the country into a war for the incorrect purpose of freeing the slaves. His perspective on the issue clearly rested upon his ideological identification with the Democratic party and disapproval of the Republicans. "There were reasons which lay deeper than those on which Republicans groom their faith," he explained, and those grounds pushed him further in the direction of the opposing party. He feared that the Civil War might achieve the positive goal of ending slavery but that its costs far outweighed those benefits. "It is a false philanthropy," Winan insisted, "which seeks the good of four millions of negroes, at the expense of the peace and happiness of twenty-five millions of white people." He maintained that there was no way that the war guaranteed the end of slavery, and therefore this generation of Americans would fail in their attempt to eradicate the institution, just as had the forefathers of the country. The ongoing efforts of soldiers in this civil war would result in lives lost, both "fruitless" and "in vain." Ultimately, "if slavery be a sin," stated Winan, "[slaveholders] alone are answerable for it." Therefore, he concluded, the North had the responsibility to continue to compromise with slaveholders for the purpose of ensuring the continuance of the Union.[27]

At this point, within the first five months of their long-distance relationship, Annie must have realized that she was confronting an entrenched position. He had already warned her earlier that he believed she took "a decidedly wrong view" on the war; he characterized her perspective as "a superficial one." In response to his emotional invectives, she balanced her letters by talking wistfully about their long walks when they were together and of festivals at Sunday school. She even reminded him that it was her belief that a woman should have "that gentle confiding nature that shrinks from the noise and strife of the world which it seemed to me a woman should do unless driven forth by necessity. I think a woman's place is in home's quiet retreat." This could have been the end of the discussion but Annie chose not to let Winan have the final word. "Your argument was good," Annie conceded in one February 1863 letter, "and if arguments had the power to turn republicans to democrats I should be one, but on this point you and I shall have to agree to disagree. I think slavery incompatible with union freedom or advancement. Therefore should be removed." Annie implicitly reassured Winan that she would not oppose him in public but expected her opinions to be respected and considered in the privacy of their relationship. Between February and June, issues of war came up only a handful of times.[28]

One of the most interesting aspects of Winan and Annie's correspondence about the war was that she never asked him to fight in it. In fact, she steadfastly opposed it. This may have been because his health was questionable, and there is evidence to support her concerns about his health throughout the letters, but it also proves that her arguments with him about the war were not a ploy to convince him to enlist. On this point, they agreed completely—Winan should not fight. In March 1863, after news that Congress passed the first conscription act that would draft men into the military, Annie wrote, "Suppose you should be one of the fated . . . I will not think of it." In addition to her admission that his serving in the war would be too hard on her, Annie also told him she did not believe him to be "strong enough for camp life." "Your lungs have been diseased once and are weak," Annie reminded him, and "our future happiness and prosperity depends greatly upon your health." Annie's decision to put her own future happiness ahead of her country's needs underlines the role of the war in their relationship. It provided a topic of discussion, a point of contention even, but Annie never thought it required her to sacrifice Winan. On this, she stood in opposition to the many women in Madison who "urged and coaxed and persuaded and driven and ridiculed" men to enlist.[29]

Winan took a hard stance toward the draft. After his name was collected during the conscription enrollment process, he wrote to Annie in June 1863, "If I am drafted you may be sure of one thing, there will be a battle soon after." He did not mean though that he would take up arms against the government but instead that the "battle" he intended would be a war of words. "I'll just make a speech denouncing the administration and the war . . . " Winan imagined, after which "I'll be arrested, have a mock trial, make myself notorious, be sent South, refuse to take the oath of allegiance to the Confederacy, and be sent back, à la Vallandigham." It was unsurprising that Winan would put Clement L. Vallandigham, the vocal anti-Lincoln politician, on a pedestal. He found little to criticize in the actions of the Ohio politician and Winan anticipated a course of events in which he could take action in a similar way.[30]

Winan did not support the draft nor sympathize with its intentions. He was content with his political views and did not hesitate to express them. When he was forced to enroll in an Ann Arbor militia in early June, his patience with the war hit a low point. "This much I think I may venture to say," he concluded with vigor, "at all events, that this war is an abomination in sight of God and honest men; and that our government is in the hands of either fools or traitors." Although Annie agreed with his revulsion of the draft, she could not help but to point out to Winan that "if all had been united there had never been a need of draft." Her concern continued through the summer and fall as various conscription acts pulled more young men from the North. Winan assured her that he would obtain the money to pay the $300 commutation fee if drafted, mainly because his feelings were too strong against the war. The draft "is not among my troubles," he promised Annie later that fall, "and I hope you will think of it no more."[31]

Despite Annie's belief that Winan should not enlist, she responded hotly when he called the war an "abomination." Annie contended that the war gave her "liberty to speak her mind" and "has called out many of our bravest and best . . . in the most intense suffering." This was the closest she ever came to implying that he was less manly than those fighting in the war. She also reiterated her belief that the ideals of the Union would someday free her from her oppressive home life. Annie criticized Winan's beloved founding fathers, writing, "If our forefathers had [ended slavery] they would not have forced upon us this dreaded war." And if Winan did not understand yet that Annie felt his perspective was misguided, she ended this portion of the letter in this way: "Well I am getting pretty earnest. But my brother if you don't want me to get earnest don't write any such speech, so unworthy your otherwise noble orations." She reminded Winan that she would defend her beliefs and that he could shape her behavior by controlling his own. Annie's strong positions regarding slavery and the war effort illustrated how she felt that these issues were ones that would gain her credibility in their relationship and that she meant to be heard.[32]

This exchange led to a clarification of the impact of these debates in their relationship. Annie became concerned that she had gone too far with her denunciation of his view and asked Winan to "forgive that which may be ungentle." When the mails were slow to return his response she wrote again and hypothesized "you are either sick or offended. I would rather have you comfortably sick than offended Winan. I say and write so many ungentle things . . . you must tell me of my faults and I'll try and improve." With these letters she was gauging the degree to which she could challenge him about the war. Winan finally wrote, "I was neither sick nor mad. When I get mad, Annie, I'll let you know it." He attempted to reassure her by explaining that their disagreements over the war were "imaginary" troubles that she did not need to be "fretting about" when "there are real troubles enough in this world." As this young couple sought to define boundaries for their relationship, Winan was clear in that he did not feel the questions of the war necessitated reevaluation of their love.[33]

In June 1863, after a separation of nine months, Winan returned to Madison and lived with Annie's family. They became engaged to be married that summer and began a sexual relationship, further deepening their bond and reliance on the success of the relationship. In September, Winan moved in with a friend's family in Waukesha, Wisconsin, to sell sewing machines in order to raise money for his next year of law school. They resumed their correspondence, now as a couple engaged to be married and even more dedicated to creating a future for themselves. Annie scolded both herself and Winan for their escapades over the summer, and the lack of will and restraint the events revealed, and she discreetly began to discuss birth control in her letters. When they returned to the topic of the war that fall, it was within the context of how it might affect their coming nuptials. "One thing I think of is the uncertain affairs of the nation," Annie lamented, "anyone is liable to have his prospects and happiness instantly and effectually crushed out . . . the future looks uncertain to me . . . we do not hold our destiny in our own hands nowadays." Annie and Winan continued to hold different views on the war and its aims but their first priority remained creating a safe environment for their relationship.[34]

Winan's ardent adoption of the Copperhead position became noticeable around campus and Annie grew concerned about its potential damage to his reputation. When Winan returned to Ann Arbor in October 1863, two other law students, both of whom were Union veterans, took issue with Winan's political loyalties. Their disapproval manifested itself in their refusal to assume positions to which they were elected because Winan was also elected to represent the law department as the orator at the next year's graduation ceremony, a prominent role that essentially represented the class. Lieutenant Charles H. Denison and Colonel Halbert B. Case "are particularly fond of exhibiting their soldier trappings," wrote Winan to Annie. What had begun as a heated exchange outside of the classroom carried into department functions and Winan was disappointed that Case and Denison expressed their disapproval of his political position so vocally. "They are fanatical fools," Winan wrote of the two veterans, "making donkeys of themselves, and don't know it." One day, Colonel Case approached Winan and began to talk about politics. When he disliked what Winan had to say, he "was then ungenteel enough to get roiled." "If he didn't want to hear [my opinions], he shouldn't ask for them," Winan wrote to Annie on October 15. "I expect to have to fight a duel someday with him or Denison, perhaps both for they don't dare to fight alone," Winan concluded.[35]

Ultimately, the two Union veterans did not have to fight alone or fight at all. Instead, by November 1, the two students had rallied enough support among the law students that a movement ensued to remove Winan from his position as a class orator. Winan's friends tried to speak up on his behalf but were not allowed to be heard. The debates over his suitability for the responsibility continued for two days and finally Winan spoke in his own defense for an hour. Ultimately, the movement succeeded and Winan was removed from the honorable role, causing a major rift between his classmates and himself. "Not one of the boys has ventured to speak to me yet, nor hardly look at me," Winan wrote subsequently to Annie. "I shall not court their favor . . . and they do not dare to make the first advances . . . a pleasant state of things among class mates, isn't it?" Yet, his tone was not discouraged, insecure or solemn. Winan's letters continued to exude confidence despite the conflicts he encountered due to his political affections.[36]

Although Annie agreed with the principles of his aggressors, she stood by Winan and supported him through the quarrel. However, she urged him to act responsibly and not to bring the anger of others onto himself. Annie warned Winan that despite what he believed, he held "gunpowder principles" and the mere speaking of his ideology would cause "unnecessary provocation." The students that he faced were the "matches" that would ignite the fire when their two opposing viewpoints collided. Annie realized that she could not turn him into a Republican but pressed Winan to understand that his beliefs needed to be held quietly. She sought above all else to reassure him that "I am interested in all that interests you"; her first loyalty was to him in any conflict that pitted her political view against supporting his honor.[37]

Only once did Winan seem to question his political stance. In November 1863, he received a letter from his older sister and the contents provoked him to write an impassioned letter to Annie. "She calls me a traitor, Annie," he wrote despairingly, "and talks hard things about my politics. She wants to know if my love for you is not enough to prevent my adoption of and adherence to such principles." He did not want to be an unprincipled man, and so he asked her, "Which would you rather, Annie, that I be an honest democrat or a dishonest republican?" By the end, without waiting for her answer, he made his own decision. "I have considered; I believe I am right, and the more I investigate, the more firmly I am convinced . . . it is not a matter of faith, but of fact and consequence." Winan took his sister's challenge about his politics much harder than anything Annie had said to this point. "Democrats are <u>not traitors</u>," Winan insisted in his own defense. The old hurt of family ties lingered in Winan's life and made him momentarily question whether Annie felt the same way. However, his last lines regarding this topic epitomize how Winan and Annie were able to utilize these debates of war to articulate the nature of their relationship. "But," Winan concluded, "I even always turn to you, Annie, and find love and peace; my angel, what would I do <u>without you</u>! There would be nothing worth living for."[38]

Although he seemed to have reassured himself in his decision, Annie chimed in with her opinion in her next letter. She accepted that he believed wholeheartedly in his position and did not wish to push him to change his mind, but she was "sad only for [his] own sake . . . I am sorry that my Winan is found on the wrong side." She asked for God to "convince [him] of that wrong," and assured him that changing his position "would be no additional proof of your love to me." Annie tried to explain that even though they disagreed on politics, she still respected him for not wavering on his beliefs. Just as he looked past her political views and made her the exception to his general aggravation with Republicans and abolitionists, she did not intend for their contentious discussions to detract from their commitment to each other. Annie felt that it was "now my duty . . . to stand by his side through good and evil" and she promised that she would never go as far as to call him a traitor in her confrontations with him. While she felt no qualms about chastising him for his views, she also hastened to reassure him when others did so.[39]

Winan did not take Annie's advice to stay out of politics around campus. In late November 1863, about thirty-five students went to Windsor, Canada, to see Vallandigham, the Copperhead politician from Ohio. In May 1863, Vallandigham had been arrested and sent behind Confederate lines. He then escaped to Canada, where the University of Michigan students felt it convenient and exciting to visit the notorious leader of the Copperhead faction. Winan did not attend, but sanctioned the idea fully and, when the participating students returned to much criticism, he led their "defense." Unionist students were aghast that newspapers outside of Ann Arbor picked up and published the story, arguing that the "institution is disgraced." They held a meeting "to counteract [the] impression," at which strong resolutions were passed condemning these actions.[40]

In response, Winan invited his fellow student Democrats to hold their own gathering in order to articulate their position to the public. He was selected chairman of the meeting and issued an invitation to students and the public that read "COPPERHEADS, ATTENTION!!!—On Saturday Dec. 12h. at 9 a.m. there will be a meeting, in the Law Lecture Room, of all Copperheads, Secessionists, and sympathizers with Jeff. Davis & Co. in the University." Winan felt so assured by late 1863 of the propriety and correctness of his ideology that he openly embraced anyone in the North who would support the right to secede or anyone who identified themselves as pro-Confederate. The group had a rousing few hours of speeches, music, and resolutions. The zealous Copperheads, which Winan told Annie numbered around 300, then formed a procession, marched through the town and around the campus chanting and cheering for the Union and Vallandigham. Winan's account of the feats of the Democratic students at the university contradicted that in the local Republican newspaper at the time, which counted participants around 89 and called the venture a "pitiful failure." Annie was not impressed either; she wrote in mid-December, "You know I cannot approve it. The whole affair seems to me too much like a common mob proceeding." Annie feared that her betrothed might move in a direction that would be perceived as treasonous and by December 1863, it looked as though Winan was approaching that line.[41]

Winan's decision to participate in these events hastened the most turbulent moments into his and Annie's long-distance relationship thus far. A heated exchange occurred from December 1863 through January 1864. "Do you still love me?" Winan asked on December 30, 1863. "You must love me because I am a monster," he pleaded, after reading her letter that he believed accused him of supporting "cruelty, oppression, licentiousness, and crime of every nature." He interpreted her words as calling him a traitor and launched into a detailed denunciation of her statements. He reiterated again his belief that his main hope was for an immediate end to the war. "War always ends in treaty . . . sooner or later this war must end in this way. Why not begin at once? Have we not had war enough?" Winan demanded. Winan felt that Annie overlooked the wrongdoings of the Lincoln government and the Union military in her blind faith in the cause, whereas he claimed to see "wrong on both sides." Winan was frustrated that even after more than one full year of explaining his views to her, she continued to be concerned that Winan was supporting the wrong perspective in the war. "Cannot a man be a friend of peace without sympathizing with treason?" Winan challenged. He drew the argument around to their relationship by writing, "It is hard enough, Annie, to listen to such things from those whose business it is to misrepresent. I hope my darling will have too good sense to believe them, and too much respect for my feelings ever to repeat them." His patience and indulgence of her political views seemed to have reached a breaking point.[42]

When he did not receive a response, he wrote another emotional letter on January 3, 1864, in which he continued to express his disappointment in her recent chastisement of him. He told her that he expected her to judge him more "justly" than did others because he did not regard her opinion with "indifference." Winan hammered away at theories about respect and loyalty as they applied to the relationship between himself and Annie and told her that if someone said to him about her those same statements, he would have defended her despite the fact that he "heartily . . . [condemned] the political principles which you believe." He expected her to do the same and not heap more criticism on him when he already received it from so many other sources. "You did not consider what you were saying," he finished sadly, but also sought middle ground by "asking for my little girl's pardon" for how "cross" he had been the previous letter. Winan feared any negative impact on their relationship and aimed to rebalance the role of the war's questions into their rightful place.[43]

As he penned that letter, Annie was also furiously writing to him from Madison, attempting to backtrack and make peace but at the same time hold her ground. She asserted that her description of him as "siding with cruelty, crime and so on I meant your favoring those politics" and she argued that both he and she wanted the same thing: permanent peace. However, Annie did not clarify, apologize, and then meekly retreat. She fired back that "peace cannot be when three millions of <u>human beings</u> are groaning under oppression" and that the war must be fought to a conclusion to save the South from "wallowing in the wine of sin." Demonstrating her continued understanding of the war goals of the Union and the depth of her political loyalties, Annie wrote that she did not believe Winan to be traitorous, but that she would never agree with his wish for a negoti-ated peace that might potentially secure slavery as a permanent institution. These conversations about loyalty shaped the behavior expectations they were setting for each other, as Annie in several letters around this period reiterated her dis-pleasure at reading about his support for slavery and the party that espoused that position. In her mind, his politics were distasteful because they conflicted with the will of God, and she felt it her place to remind him that they still disagreed. "I love you if you are a copperhead," she concluded.[44]

Winan and Annie worked out the miscommunication by the end of Janu-ary. Twice, in December 1863 and January 1864, he wrote to her that "we must not talk politics anymore." After this potentially disastrous exchange, the two young adults curtailed their talk of politics for most of early 1864. They focused instead on contemplating the nature of their upcoming marriage. "O darling," Annie wrote in February 1864, "I want so to be a . . . loving wife different than most I see around me," as Winan reassured her that nothing "shall diminish my love for you, You will always be my wife, my darling angel, first and best. A man shall put away everything for his wife—break every natural tie, but cling to her." Perhaps the intensity of the last month or two convinced them both to stifle their opinions more or, likely, they were distracted by major transitions in their lives—transitions that demanded their attention. Winan graduated from the University of Michigan in the spring of 1864 and left Ann Arbor on the first of April. He accepted a position in Sturgeon Bay, Wisconsin, and waited eagerly for Annie to join him there. Because the issue of politics and the war had not damaged their relationship and its future, it was possible for Winan and Annie to put them on the back-burner when they needed to address more immediate problems.[45]

After getting settled in Sturgeon Bay, Winan joined a literary society in the town and began to participate in political debates. The upcoming presidential election of 1864 inspired him to reengage with politics. With their marriage on the horizon, Annie quickly resumed her admonitions about churchgoing ("So to church every Sabbath will you Winan and study the bible . . . I fear dear one you will feel its judgments") and his politics: "Winan leave politics out of your duties at present . . . you cannot turn the tide of public opinion until you have station reputation and money to assist you but you <u>will</u> turn yourself and my happiness if you persist," Annie wrote following the election. "It matters but little in this short life whether we are republicans or democrats," she reminded him, "but it matters much whether we have a home . . . we should do nothing to hinder us till that is accomplished." She also warned him that she noticed in the newspaper that the county in which Sturgeon Bay was located "cast not a single democratic vote, remember that," as further admonition that he had better be careful how brashly he flourished his political ideals.[46]

It seemed that he managed to make a good first impression despite her concerns because he was named district attorney and opened a busy private practice over the winter. Both Annie and Winan were aware that a draft would be possible in the spring of 1865; she urged him to bring her from Madison to him so that she could have "a taste of joy before that time of suspense." Winan handled this new conscription threat by joining the town's "mutual insurance company against the draft" to pool their money to buy substitutes if drafted. Sturgeon Bay filled its quota in March 1865 and did not have to endure a draft but in telling Annie this good news, he also commented that he "had got so used to thinking of the matter, that personally, I would as soon go as not." This is the first time he ever discussed such a possibility, which raises the question whether he said it sincerely or whether he, as he was prone to do, said it to get a reaction out of her because he was also well aware that the war was nearing an end. She did not find him amusing, hence his later reassurance to her in the quote that opened this essay, that he had only meant he would have gone if he had not known her. Even after the bells pealed across the land in victory and the question was no longer at hand, Annie took Winan to task about why he would ever risk their future; the country's call could not be allowed to jeopardize their marriage or their prospects for a better life.[47]

Gideon Winan Allen and Annie Cox were united in marriage in 1865 and their letters of correspondence came to an end coincidentally in conjunction with the end of the war. Although they were isolated from the battlefield itself, they participated in the discourse and debates about what made someone loyal to the Union and what it meant when someone did not follow the majority line. As such, they participated in the war itself, but the conversations in which they engaged related the war to their own personal goals. Winan was not a politician or a community leader, but a law student, a man of obvious military age whose zeal to remain in school seemed not as much about gaining an education but about withholding his support from the war. Annie pushed him to question his ideals, expressed disappointment and frustration in his positions and actions, but never asked him to fight for her beliefs.

Many Americans made the ultimate sacrifice during the Civil War, giving up their loved ones for the cause. Not all Americans chose that path but even the ones who remained untouched by the war's tragedies learned to incorporate its issues, imperatives, and interrogations into their daily discourse. Winan and Annie, young Americans setting out to overcome rocky childhoods by setting their sights on a bright future, refused to let the war diffuse their happiness or their prospects. They used the war for their own purposes, as rhetoric for negotiation in a budding relationship. Their construction of and debate over notions of loyalty shaped their agreement on the nature of marriage. They spoke frankly of the need to agree on what would make a happy home; in early 1864, Winan wrote that Annie had every "right to know whatever you wish to know about my affairs; and I in turn shall expect an equal indulgence on your part. You see, we are setting the terms now . . . you wear the hoops, with all the rights and privileges . . . and I the trousers with like restrictions and limitations." Their concern was building a future; by March 1865, Annie believed they were well on their way:

> My dear Winan we will find it a matter of disiplin [sic] and time to become in perfect harmony with each other. We will not have as much to do as many for we have talked upon many things and have decided a good many questions . . . We are both rather set in our own way we must therefor [sic] be willing each to yield half. I say these things that we may avoid those unpleasant clashes frequent in the marriage of most people.

The war did not dictate the outcome of this courtship but its circumstances and concerns yielded fruitful matter for their courtship dance. In this manner, we can see that contestations of loyalty during the American Civil War could even help a couple shape the nature of their relationship.[48]

Notes

1. The collection of original letters between Gideon Winan Allen and Annie Cox is held at the Newberry Library in Chicago but for this essay I have used the microfilmed copies from the Wisconsin Historical Society. There are approximately 200 letters extant in the collection. In her book *The Sea Captain's Wife*, historian Martha Hodes explains the process of letter writing in the nineteenth century and the challenges that Americans faced in conducting this type of communication, such as the cost of supplies and the slowness of the mail. She contends that "writing a letter often became the sole means of maintaining intimacy" and yet "as a one-sided conversation, a letter always posed risks." Allen and Cox confirmed these conclusions in their frequent apologies for inferior paper, unattractive envelopes, blotchy ink, and impatience in waiting for letters. "When we

quarrel again, Annie, we must wait till we are together," Winan wrote after a particularly difficult argument in early 1864, "or till the mails go more regularly, so it will not take so long to make up our difficulties." Gideon Winan Allen to Annie Cox, January 17, 1864, Gideon Winan Allen correspondence, 1862–1867, 1872, Wisconsin Historical Society (hereafter, Allen papers); Martha Hodes, *The Sea Captain's Wife: A True Story of Love, Race, and War, in the Nineteenth Century* (New York: Norton, 2006), 22–23, 32–33.

2. Historians can use gender ideology to explore the way power hierarchies are created and legitimated in a relationship such as courtship or marriage. Scholars such as Amy Greenberg have documented the way that the uncertain years of the antebellum period challenged existing notions of masculinity, and those fluid and fluctuating categories of masculine identity continued to be negotiated into the war years, as Lorien Foote, Reid Mitchell, LeeAnn Whites, and Amy Murrell Taylor have discussed. The Allen-Cox letter collection requires interpretation through this lens because gender shaped the very nature of their communication. See Joan Scott, "Gender: A Useful Category of Historical Analysis," *The American Historical Review* 91, no. 5 (December 1986), 1053–75; Amy S. Greenberg, *Manifest Manhood and the Antebellum American Empire* (Cambridge and New York: Cambridge University Press, 2005); Lorien Foote, *The Gentlemen and the Roughs: Manhood, Honor, and Violence in the Union Army* (New York: New York University Press, 2010); Reid Mitchell, "Soldiering, Manhood, and Coming of Age: A Northern Volunteer," in *Divided Houses: Gender and the Civil War*, ed. Catherine Clinton and Nina Silber (New York: Oxford University Press, 1992); LeeAnn Whites, *The Civil War as a Crisis in Gender: Augusta, Georgia, 1860–1890* (Athens: University of Georgia Press, 1995); Amy Murrell Taylor, *The Divided Family in Civil War America* (Chapel Hill: University of North Carolina Press, 2005).

3. Annie Cox to Gideon Winan Allen, November 17, 1863, Allen papers.

4. William C. Davis, "Foreword: Civil War History Plows a New Field," in *Union Heartland: The Midwestern Home Front during the Civil War*, ed. Ginette Aley and J. L. Anderson (Carbondale: Southern Illinois University Press, 2013), xi. In this same volume, Aley and Anderson assert that "multiple Norths existed that were marked by regional differences and distinctiveness on several levels, and each, like the Midwest, asserted its own counternarrative of the larger Northern narrative of the Civil War." Aley and Anderson, "The Great National Struggle in the Heart of the Union: An Introduction," in Aley and Anderson, 2. Frank L. Klement, *The Copperheads in the Middle West* (Chicago: University of Chicago Press, 1960); Jennifer L. Weber, *Copperheads: The Rise and Fall of Lincoln's Opponents in the North* (Oxford, New York: Oxford University Press, 2006); Jon K. Lauck, *The Lost Region: Toward a Revival of Midwestern History* (Iowa City: University of Iowa Press, 2013), 19, 28. See also, R. Douglas Hurt, "The Agricultural Power of the Midwest during the Civil War," in Aley and Anderson; Andrew R. L. Cayton and Susan E. Gray, eds., *The Identity of the American Midwest: Essays on Regional History* (Bloomington, Indiana University Press, 2001), 10; Nicole Etcheson, *The Emerging Midwest: Upland Southerners and the Political Culture of the Old Northwest, 1787–1861* (Bloomington and Indianapolis: Indiana University Press, 1996), 9; Jon Gjerde, *The Minds of the West: Ethnocultural Evolution in the Rural Middle West, 1830–1917* (Chapel Hill and London: University of North Carolina Press, 1997), 5, 7, 28; Susan-Mary Grant,

North Over South: Northern Nationalism and American Identity in the Antebellum Era (Lawrence: University Press of Kansas, 2000), 10; Doug Kiel, "Untaming the Mild Frontier: In Search of New Midwestern Histories," *Middle West Review* 1, no. 1 (Fall 2014), 20; John E. Miller, "Frederick Jackson Turner and the Dream of Regional History," *Middle West Review* 1, no. 1 (Fall 2014), 6; William N. Parker, "From Northwest to Midwest: Social Bases of a Regional History," in *Essays in Nineteenth Century Economic History: The Old Northwest*, ed. David C. Klingaman and Richard K. Vedder (Athens: Ohio University Press, 1975), 28; Matthew E. Stanley, "Between Two Fires: War and Reunion in Middle America, 1860–1899," unpublished dissertation, University of Cincinnati, 2013, 13.

5. Melinda Lawson, *Patriot Fires: Forging a New American Nationalism in the Civil War North* (Lawrence: University Press of Kansas, 2002); William Blair, "We are Coming, Father Abraham—Eventually: The Problem of Northern Nationalism in the Pennsylvania Recruiting Drives of 1862," in *The War Was You and Me*, ed. Cashin, 205. Robert M. Sandow, *Deserter Country: Civil War Opposition in the Pennsylvania Appalachians* (New York: Fordham University Press, 2009). Lawson and others believe that a new nationalism and a new nation emerged from the war, whereas other historians identify more continuity in the period. Don H. Doyle believes that "historians of nationalism often blame nationalism for causing wars but it may be the other way around. The huge citizen armies required for modern warfare demanded a powerful nationalist sense of patriotic loyalty and sacrifice." This concurs with Gary Gallagher, who does not "believe a new nation was born amid military upheaval in 1861–1865," and Lorien Foote, who points out that "antebellum modes of thought remained vital and tenacious well after the Civil War." Historians who study Southern nationalism also disagree on whether the Confederacy ever created a distinct nationalism and to what extent the existence of such sentiment contributed to their loss in the war. These sources are significant to this study because they all highlight the importance of the individual in the creation and development of nationalism. Historians agree that individuals needed to come to some sort of conclusion about the role/significance of the nation in their lives in order to act upon a nationalism, regardless of the nature of its construction. For studies about whether nationalism in the Union and Confederacy existed or was created during the war, see George M. Fredrickson, *The Inner Civil War: Northern Intellectuals and the Crisis of the Union* (New York: Harper and Row, 1965); Richard Bensel, *Yankee Leviathan: The Origins of Central State Authority in America, 1859–1877* (Cambridge and New York: Cambridge University Press, 1990); Gary Gallagher, *The Union War* (Cambridge, Mass.; London: Harvard University Press, 2012), 6; "Interchange: Nationalism and Internationalism in the Era of the Civil War," *Journal of American History* (September 2011), 478; Lorien Foote, "Historians and Intellectual Life in the Civil War Era," in *So Conceived and So Dedicated: Intellectual Life in the Civil War–Era North*, ed. Lorien Foote and Kanisorn Wongsrichanalai (New York: Fordham University Press, 2015), 17; Earl J. Hess, *Liberty, Virtue, and Progress: Northerners and Their War for the Union* (New York: Fordham University Press, 1997, 2nd edition), 56; Drew Gilpin Faust, *The Creation of Confederate Nationalism: Ideology and Identity in the Civil War South* (Baton Rouge and London: Louisiana State University Press, 1988); Gary W. Gallagher, *The Confederate War* (Cambridge and London: Harvard University Press, 1997); Paul Quigley, *Shifting*

Grounds: Nationalism and the American South, 1848–1865 (Oxford: Oxford University Press, 2012; Stephanie McCurry, *Confederate Reckoning: Power and Politics in the Civil War South* (Cambridge: Harvard University Press, 2010); and Anne S. Rubin, *A Shattered Nation: The Rise and Fall of the Confederacy, 1861–1868* (Chapel Hill: University of North Carolina Press, 2005).

6. Whites, 3, 13; Foote, 3–4; Judith A. Giesberg, *Army at Home: Women and the Civil War on the Northern Home Front* (Chapel Hill: University of North Carolina Press, 2009); Mitchell, 44; Taylor, 39. See also Clinton and Silber, 244; Nicole Etcheson, "No Fit Wife: Soldiers' Wives and their In-Laws on the Indiana Home Front," in Aley and Anderson; Ginette Aley, "Inescapable Realities: Rural Midwestern Women and Families during the Civil War," in Aley and Anderson, 133; LeeAnn Whites and Alecia P. Long, eds., *Occupied Women: Gender, Military Occupation, and the American Civil War* (Baton Rouge: Louisiana State University Press, 2012), 2; Kristen L. Streater, "She-Rebels on the Supply Line: Gender Conventions in Civil War Kentucky," in Whites and Long, eds., 89; Cita Cook, "The Practical Ladies of Occupied Natchez," in Whites and Long, eds., 134; Drew Gilpin Faust, *Mothers of Invention: Women of the Slaveholding South in the American Civil War* (Chapel Hill: University of North Carolina Press, 2004), 21, 140. Cox to Allen, November 17, 1863, Allen papers.

7. Mabel L. Ruttle, "Remnants of Pride," Unpublished manuscript, Gideon W. Allen family papers, 1862–1964, Newberry Library, 27–43; Allen to Cox, October 5, 1862, Allen papers. Allen defies historian Joel H. Silbey's generalization that it was normal in the antebellum era for political loyalty to be passed down through generations. Somehow Allen managed to develop fully articulated Democratic party principles, including a proslavery stance, within a family that abhorred those very ideas. Silbey, 6.

8. Allen to Cox, December 30, 1863, Allen papers; October 11, 1860, Wisconsin Republicans Club, University of Wisconsin Archives. Democrats condemned increasingly far-reaching Republican legislation as revolutionary and abhorrent. Heather Cox Richardson, *The Greatest Nation of the Earth: Republican Economic Policies During the Civil War* (Cambridge and London: Harvard University Press, 1997), 3; see also James Oakes's discussion of how the Democrats feared the changes that the Republicans understood to be necessary to save the Union. James Oakes, *Freedom National: The Destruction of Slavery in the United States, 1861–1865* (New York and London: Norton, 2013), xxiii–xxiv.

9. Allen to Cox, December 20, 1862, June 18, 1863, Allen papers. Annie's regular encouragement to Winan that he be more social was illustrated by this portion of a March 1863 letter: "Let me say a word to you Winan. Go into society, into good polished society—gain the customs and etiquette—all you can. It will be of great value to you . . . you cannot learn those in your room, your books, or in the courtroom." Cox to Allen, March 1, 1863, Allen letters.

10. See letters dated October 13, 1862, March 18, 1863, and March 27, 1863 for examples. Newberry Library Manuscript Data Reference Sheet, Inventory of the Allen Family Papers: http://mms.newberry.org/html/Allen.html. Annie discusses how she was not sure whether she would marry in a March 5, 1865 letter. Regarding her family's moving, see February 1, 1863, March 27, 1863, and April 18, 1863.

11. One example of their discussions related to religion is the stern position Winan expressed on October 5, 1863: "The idea of a savior necessarily involves the idea of a hell;

the one is improbable, the other, impossible, hence I reject both. But while I am satisfied with my belief in this matter, I am also satisfied to let you think as you please." Throughout the letter collection, Winan tried teasing, bluntness, serious consideration, and mollification to get Annie to accept his disbelief, but she never did. His soul was a matter of great concern to her. Allen to Cox, October 5, 1863, Allen papers. Cox to Allen, October 1862; December 27, 1862, Allen papers.

12. Cox to Allen, October 13, 1862, June 16, 1863, December 18, 1864, Allen papers.

13. Allen to Cox, February 10, 1863, Allen papers. Cox to Allen, May 3, 1863, Allen papers.

14. Their expectations for each other's behavior outside of the questions of the war fill the pages of these letters. For example, when Annie expressed sorrow at his absence, Winan used notions of gender to encourage her. "You never forget to be a true woman, Annie, but try and be cheerful, it will not be long till I come," he wrote in March 1864, and she teased him about waiting to judge her character until he saw her "kitchen side." They also wrote openly of their quest to create a successful relationship and what it might take to accomplish that goal. When her twenty-third birthday loomed, Annie wrote that she believed they were approaching the future "perfectly united in purpose," and reassured him once that she would avoid sickness because she knew "how much of your happiness I hold in my hands and not one particle shall be destroyed if I can prevent it." Winan also matched Annie's effusive expressions of affections, writing, for example, "remember I love you, that I live for you." Allen to Cox, October 5, 1863, November 22, 1863, March 27, 1864; Cox to Allen, April 9, 1863, September 20, 1863, n.d, October 20, 1863.

15. Allen to Cox, November 11, 1862, Allen papers; Cox to Allen, November 3, 1862, Allen papers. James McPherson notes in his study of soldiers that "duty and honor were closely linked to concepts of masculinity in Victorian America." Annie and Winan discussed both of these concepts in their letters, as they sought to establish gender roles in their relationship. In particular, Annie was sensitive to how Winan protected his honor and executed his duty. On May 16, 1863, she wrote, "I am going to scold a little too because my brother [Winan] expressed an inclination to tardiness of duty [regarding how frequently he wrote to her]." In October, she wanted Winan to come to Madison to begin his law practice instead of finishing his degree but he wanted to graduate. She deferred to him to make the decision, writing, "The point of honor involved I do not understand [but] if your honor is at stake in any degree go at all events." In both cases, she expressed concern about his reputation and character, both traits linked to notions of masculinity at the time. She wanted what was believed best for him at that time, with the assumption that it would later benefit their life together. Cox to Allen, May 16, 1863, October 6, 1863, Allen papers. James McPherson, *For Cause and Comrades: Why Men Fought in the Civil War* (New York: Oxford University Press, 1997), 25.

16. Ellen K. Rothman, *Sex and Self-Control: Middle Class Courtship in America, 1770–1870, Journal of Social History* 15, no. 3 (Spring 1982), 409; Taylor, 36, 43–44.

17. William "Parson" Brownlow had been a politician in Tennessee who was vocally anti-secession, a viewpoint that got him exiled to the North in 1861. When Winan arrived in Ann Arbor in October of 1862, Brownlow was there, as Winan said, "another great natural curiosity . . . on exhibition," revealing his low opinion of the man. Allen to Cox, October 5, 1862, November 24, 1862, February 1, 1863, Allen papers.

18. See Julie A. Mujic, *Between Campus and War: Students, Patriotism, and Education at Midwestern Universities during the American Civil War* (unpublished Ph.D. dissertation, Kent State University, 2012). It is important to distinguish between being "pro-southern" and being an adherent of the conservative wing of the Democratic party, who were labeled Copperheads during the Civil War. Weber, 3.

19. Allen to Cox, December 7, 1862, January 30, 1863, Allen papers; Cox to Allen, January 25, 1863, Allen papers. Winan adhered to the Democratic notion of life being better in the antebellum era in several statements throughout the letters. One such example appeared in a November 1863 letter, in which Winan argued that only through democratic principles could a government be successful, not through war. He asked, "in the name of humanity, when will men be satisfied? What a change from the peaceful happy and prosperous nation of three years ago!" This naïve perspective illustrates how he saw the past through rose-colored glasses. Allen to Cox, November 15, 1863, Allen papers. For more insight on how the Democratic party responded to the war, see Richardson, 3, 5; Sandow, 11, 59; Silbey, ix–xi, 31–32.

20. Allen to Cox, January 30, 1863, Allen papers; Cox to Allen, September 23, 1863, Allen papers.

21. Allen to Cox, January 30, 1863, February 1, 1863, Allen papers.

22. Allen to Cox, February 10, 1863, Allen papers.

23. Ibid.

24. Cox to Allen, February 1, 1863, Allen papers.

25. Ibid.

26. Ibid.

27. Allen to Cox, February 10, 1863, Allen papers.

28. Taylor finds that "the allure of companionship thus helped maintain a space for women's dissenting political expression in marriage"; Annie must have been counting on that. Taylor, 44. Allen to Cox, February 1, 1863, Allen papers; Cox to Allen, February 15, 1863, Allen papers.

29. Cox to Allen, March 1, 1863, Uncertain month, 4, 1863, June 16, 1863, Allen papers. Sabra Warner Lewis Smith, "My Recollections of Civil War Days," *Wisconsin Magazine of History* 2, no. 1 (September 1918), 30. Joan Cashin found that "just as community expectations could encourage men to enlist, they could encourage men to avoid military service." Joan E. Cashin, "Deserters, Civilians, and Draft Resistance in the North," in Cashin, ed., 263.

30. Allen to Cox, June 9, 1863, Allen papers.

31. Allen to Cox, June 9, 1863, September 20, 1863, Allen papers. Cox to Allen, June 16, 1863, Allen papers.

32. Cox to Allen, June 16, 1863, Allen papers.

33. Cox to Allen, June 14, 1863, June 16, 1863, Allen papers; Allen to Cox, June 18, 1863, Allen Papers.

34. Rothman, 418–19; Cox to Allen, September 16, 1863, Allen papers. For examples of letters in which they discuss sex and birth control, see Cox to Allen, October 20, 1863, February 19, 1865, February 28, 1865, Allen papers. Regarding their decision to have sex that summer, Annie wrote, "Winan you must love me with your whole heart now and

always. I do not feel, strange as it may seem, any the less pure <u>now</u>." He felt guilty about it and worried that she would blame him but she spent several letters reassuring him that her love was only deeper. After their engagement, they also began to discuss their upcoming roles as husband and wife. One notable example came from Winan in late 1863 when he told Annie, "Though I <u>may sometimes</u> want a wife for a play thing, I <u>never</u> want a plaything for a wife." She made similar statements about her expectations that he would provide her a nice home, reminding him that "A house and its surroundings have a great deal to do with a woman's health and spirits, for she is confined there most of the time." Allen to Cox, December 3, 1863, Allen papers; Cox to Allen, March 16, 1865, Allen papers.

35. Allen to Cox, March 6, 1863, April 27, 1863, October 15, 1863, Allen papers. For more information about the ways college students "performed intellectual manhood" through debate and other extracurricular activities, see Timothy J. Williams, *Intellectual Manhood: University, Self, and Society in the Antebellum South* (Chapel Hill: University of North Carolina Press, 2015), 171.

36. Allen to Cox, November 1, 1863, n.d., 1863, Allen papers.

37. Cox to Allen, November 7, 1863, Allen papers.

38. Allen to Cox, November 15, 1863, Allen papers. For a detailed study of how Americans perceived treason during the war versus its constitutional definition, see William A. Blair, *With Malice Toward Some: Treason and Loyalty in the Civil War Era* (Chapel Hill: University of North Carolina Press, 2014).

39. Cox to Allen, November 17, 1863, Allen papers.

40. William M. Hayes to Parents, December 6, 1863, William Mordecai Hayes papers, 1862–1864, Bentley Historical Library. Allen to Cox, December 12, 1863, Allen papers. "Aid and Comfort," n.d., Erastus O. Haven papers, 1838–1873, Teal Scrapbook, Bentley Historical Library. Accounts of the protest meeting described the unionist resolutions as having "repudiated Vallandigham and all his works, and his followers." "Michigan University" by C. C. Coffin, n.d., Erastus O. Haven papers, 1838–1873, Teal Scrapbook, Bentley Historical Library. Other accounts expressed a desire to publish the names of those who participated in the visit "for the benefit of their posterity." "Aid and Comfort," n.d., Erastus O. Haven papers, 1838–1873, Teal Scrapbook, Bentley Historical Library.

41. Allen to Cox, December 12, 1863, Allen papers. "The Copperheads in the University," Erastus O. Haven papers, 1838–1873, Teal Scrapbook, Bentley Historical Library. Cox to Allen, December 18, 1863, Allen papers. William M. Hayes to Parents, December 6, 1863, William Mordecai Hayes papers, 1862–1864, Bentley Historical Library. Allen to Cox, December 12, 1863, Allen papers. "The Copperheads in the University," n.d. Erastus O. Haven papers, 1838–1873, Teal Scrapbook, Bentley Historical Library.

42. Allen to Cox, December 30, 1863, Allen papers.

43. Allen to Cox, January 3, 1864, Allen papers.

44. Cox to Allen, December 4, 1863, December 5, 1863, January 4, 1864, Allen papers.

45. Allen to Cox, December 30, 1863, January 12, 1864, February 4, 1864, Allen papers; Cox to Allen February [n.d.], 1864, Allen letters. Interestingly, while Allen rarely mentioned manhood or masculinity directly in his letters, it did appear in relation to his law school graduation. "My diploma does not make me feel any more like a man than I did

before," he reported in April 1864, "though, I imagine, it has a different effect on some of the boys." Just as he often criticized soldiers in an effort to boost his image in Annie's eyes, here he attempts to decrease the impact of his degree in a ways that espoused his masculinity. Allen to Cox, April 1, 1864, Allen papers.

46. Cox to Allen, November 18, 1864, Allen papers.

47. Cox to Allen, December 18, 1864, Allen papers; Allen to Cox, January 1, 1865, March 26, 1865, Allen papers. With regard to the draft, Annie invoked gender ideology about how she should control her reaction. "If the worst is realized, I will try and be a woman but God pity us both," she wrote in December 1864. Even though she drew attention to her female status and its difference to the men who would be drafted, by saying that she would "be a woman," she reminds Winan that she should be strong and in control of her emotions.

48. Allen to Cox, January 10, 1864, Allen papers; Cox to Allen, March 29, 1865, Allen papers.

Loyal to the Union

*College-Educated Soldiers, Military
Leadership, Politics, and the Question
of Loyalty*

Kanisorn Wongsrichanalai

The strongest peace party is the army. If the small fry at Washington want to hear treason talked, let them come to the army," a distraught Henry L. Abbott angrily informed his sister at the end of 1862. His friend Leander Alley had died at the Battle of Fredericksburg on December 13. Abbott, a Harvard graduate and Union officer, declared, "the men who ordered the crossing of the river are responsible to God for murder." His friend Alley "was just as much murdered as if he had been deliberately thrown into the river with a stone tied round his neck." Abbott's frustration at the mismanagement of the Union war effort led him to suggest that the army should march on Washington "& lay our hands on our true enemies, those blood stained scoundrels in the government." "McClellan alone," he concluded, "can save the army."[1] Blaming President Lincoln for reassigning Maj. Gen. George B. McClellan in November, Abbott now had proof—a military disaster—that the general's successor, Maj. Gen. Ambrose E. Burnside, could not lead the Army of the Potomac to victory. In the end, victory is what Abbott wanted and if, by some stroke of fate, Burnside had brought triumph rather than defeat on that cold December battlefield, Lincoln's star would have risen with Abbott in turn.

Neither Henry L. Abbott nor anyone in the Army of the Potomac ever marched on Washington, D.C. to overthrow President Lincoln's administration. Abbott vented his rage on paper, a semi-private setting, while continuing to excel at his army duties. Indeed, Abbott's actions at Fredericksburg and throughout the war made an impression on future Supreme Court Justice Oliver Wendell Holmes, Jr., one of his fellow officers. Abbott moved Holmes because he exposed himself to deadly fire despite disagreeing with the order to advance and opposing the new war aim of emancipation. In the words of one of his biographers, Holmes learned from Abbott's dedication to his duties, "that nobility of character consists in doing one's job with indifference to ends."[2]

An examination of the writings of men such as Abbott—twenty-five college-educated New Englanders who fought in the Civil War, referred to here as *New Brahmins*—reveals an important lesson about the malleability of morale, opinion, and professed support. Additionally, it demonstrates that, at their core, New Brahmins remained loyal to the preservation of the Union above all else. New Brahmins' wartime beliefs reflect the intellectual environment and socialization of their antebellum world. New England, the region most identified with the North because it embodied themes of free labor, business, education, and abolitionism, serves as an excellent backdrop to study individuals who ought to have been fully committed to both the Union and the policies of the first Republican administration. Variations in how some elite New Englanders felt about Lincoln's policies and management, therefore, stand out even more starkly given what one might expect. Readers should bear in mind that this sample depicts only a small and unrepresentative subsection of the Northern populace. Regardless, these individuals' conceptions and perceptions reveal their unique experiences when considering the matter of loyalty in the wartime period.[3]

The socialization and intellectual world that the New Brahmins encountered as college students helps explain their wartime actions and beliefs. In an era when few individuals possessed a college degree, those who had completed their undergraduate education automatically became part of Victorian America's professional classes. These elite youths practiced law and medicine, conducted business, and preached the gospel. Their bachelor's degrees, however, did not prepare them for careers. Colleges in the mid-nineteenth century aimed to build *character* rather than set their pupils on one career path or another. The schools infused young Americans with ideas about how to properly act in the face of crises while professors taught young men to develop leadership traits and see themselves as society's shepherds. The dictates of proper gentlemanly character ultimately helped push many college-educated individuals toward volunteering for the war effort.[4] Like the three individuals Melinda Lawson considers in her essay for this collection, the New Brahmins interpreted their actions by considering their duty.

Trained to become society's leaders, these young men attempted to behave like northern gentlemen. While historians know a great deal about southern gentlemen who based their lives around the system of honor, few scholars have paid attention to the northern counterpart. Those who have attempted to grapple with the contours of northern honor emphasize the importance of restraint and the greater reliance on societal institutions to address grievances. Focusing on one particular group whose members attempted to live by a gentlemanly code reveals the world of northern honor, distinct from the southern version. Where southern honor revolved around reputation and public endorsement, northern honor rejected the need for societal approval. Honorable northern men—they often referred to their version of honor as "character"—based their decisions on informed conscious choices without fear of the consequences. The elitist college men argued that their advanced schooling comprised a critical component of honor and only the people with the highest education could make the best decisions for society. The northern man of honor supposedly pursued a righteous course based on what he judged best for the greater good regardless of popularity. Instead of courting public applause, men of character ignored it. Consistency and unswerving dedication to their course marked a northern man of honor. Indeed, such a rigid belief in one's righteousness portended problems for times when these individuals needed to compromise. Commitment to character and to a single course explains why New Brahmins backed the sectional Republican Party over the Constitutional Union Party in the election of 1860. While the latter offered the moderate leadership of seasoned statesmen, many young Americans blamed the previous generation of political leaders for failing to solve national crises because of their proclivities to compromise. In an era of polarization, more rigid displays of masculinity and character, perhaps even inspired by the commitment of the controversial abolitionist John Brown, came to the fore.[5]

Another component of college classes in the nineteenth century, part of the process of preparing young men to accept societal leadership, included introducing students to the study of the past and the role of the United States in human history. This exercise forced them to think about how they defined the United States. In written compositions, they described their nation as a source for democratic reform, spreading around the world through trade and example. As products of New England education, however, these students also articulated a regional bias based on free labor ideas that they did not even conceive of as skewed. The New England model for national development, to these youngsters, simply represented *the* model for the nation. The South and its dependence on slavery represented an outmoded system destined to wither and die unless infused with new life. The Confederacy provided slavery with that chance for a new life. New Brahmins' inherent conservatism, meanwhile, revealed itself when the goal of restoring the Union merged with the cause of emancipation. Historian Susan-Mary Grant has argued that, midway through the Civil War, in an attempt to develop a new and more robust nationalism, the Lincoln government had to reframe the conflict so that it moved beyond motivations at the local community level. Dedicating the nation to ending slavery satisfied that need.[6] Because college men had already articulated a national vision of the Union, they greeted the president's added justification for the conflict with confusion. The Union that college men wrote about developed *gradually*, hence their belief that slavery would *eventually* die out on its own. A radical and sudden shift, evoking deep passions, appeared unwise and dangerous. Only the military applications of the Union's emancipation policy won them over since their overall goal involved bringing the conflict to a triumphal close.

College-educated New Englanders internalized a New England–centric version of American history, one deliberately crafted by a generation of intellectuals concerned about the region's loss of political and cultural influence. In this vision, New England and the free labor system that underpinned its society represented the true vision of American nationhood. Free labor allowed the democratic institutions set loose by the American Revolution to take hold. New Englanders viewed the system of slavery as aberrant and inconsistent with real American nationalism. When thinking of what defined America, most college men educated in New England thought of the free labor system. Taking in a view of ancient and classical history, New England college students also connected the American experiment with those past civilizations, portraying the United States as the culmination of human development. They brazenly claimed that American-inspired democracy would light a liberating path for the rest of the world to follow. But aside from the Founders of the republic and a sense of America as a force for good, inspiring democratic change in the world, students did not express any concrete attachments to any specific political party or party leader. While their beliefs resembled policies promoted by the Republican Party and they viewed the free labor system as the only legitimate vision for the future, they did not conflate party platforms with their national vision. Nineteenth-century Americans understood the temporary nature of political parties. Ideas rather than political organizations endured. In the case of the Civil War, Northerners' nationalist ideas happened to coincide with the Union cause while most southerners identified their beliefs with a new political entity. Confederate nation-builders faced a challenge that those who fought to restore the Union did not. In fact, the New Brahmins considered here might not have even noticed that their nationalist beliefs, articulated as college students, meshed seamlessly with the Union cause.[7] This understanding of the Union helps explain why their allegiances seemed malleable during the war. New Brahmins evaluated the national leaders and pledged their support to whomever offered the most plausible way to restore the Union in the swiftest fashion.

When New Brahmins marched to war, they expressed two interconnected reasons for doing so. First, they claimed that the dictates of character compelled them to serve the nation in a time of crisis. Second, they declared that they needed to help save the Union. These two motives informed many of their opinions and decisions during the war years, including ones about whose leadership to trust. Many historians have attempted to explain soldiers' motivations. The reigning modern consensus, however, suggests that ideology motivated and influenced Civil War soldiers on both sides. While some scholars propose that Northern soldiers targeted slavery as the cause of the war, Gary W. Gallagher has argued that most Northern soldiers fought to maintain the Union and all it represented: democratic government, opportunities for advancement, and the inheritance from the Founders. As several scholars have pointed out, fearing the loss of the tangible items in life—property and land—provides a more concrete reason for serving. Those who professed to fight for the Union, a nebulous political entity, therefore, required a more complicated ideological conception of their cause. Yet, embodiments of the Union cause abound and contemporaries need only have looked to the armies that formed for the nation's protection as a sure symbol of its strength and struggle for survival.[8]

New Brahmins considered the army the very embodiment of the Union's struggle for survival. Entering the world of the military, they also developed a sort of tunnel vision where military expediency outweighed all other considerations. As a result, they disliked lenient policies aimed at those they believed responsible for prolonging the war or federal initiatives that appeared, to them, to have no bearing on military victory. Having committed themselves to the army, they believed the military alone could succeed in reuniting the nation and crushing the rebellion. President Lincoln and these New Brahmins shared identical goals: Preserve the Union and bring the conflict to a close as soon as possible. But their differing roles also guaranteed that they would have different vantage points. Lincoln, as president, needed to consider political, economic, and diplomatic ramifications of his actions while the New Brahmins could pontificate about the seemingly simple solutions to end the crisis without the full perspective. While they considered themselves in command of all the facts, New Brahmins simply did not have the broad scope or command of the broad set of events pertaining to the war.

While New Brahmins criticized the civilian administration and military commanders from within the ranks, many similar individuals chose not to volunteer. While some aided the war effort in different ways on the home front, others had ambivalent feelings or did not want any part in the war at all.[9] Julie Mujic's essay in this collection, for example, considers the case of one Midwestern college student whose Democratic leanings kept him away from the frontlines. Matthew Warshauer's essay, meanwhile, explains the ideological position of New Englander Copperheads who opposed the war. Whatever their reasons, many of Lincoln's enemies lobbed attacks against his administration from the sidelines and opened the door to a prolonged debate about the nature of loyalty and treason.

Where Lincoln's critics could be labeled as traitors on the home front, such accusations could not be easily applied to men who wore the Union blue and fought in the armies of the United States. Yet Union soldiers certainly expressed opinions that went against the administration's policies. A close examination of gentleman soldiers' writings reveal that, when discussing wartime leadership, they often wrote about two individuals: Abraham Lincoln and George McClellan, one a politician and another a soldier. Their attraction to the latter may have stemmed from their admiration of the general's professional background but also from more cultural prompts. Scholars have explained how antebellum Americans distrusted political parties and politicians, being drawn more to the military figures. In a time of war, New Brahmins sought and found the model of patriotic and non-partisan service in the "Young Napoleon." While they remained weary of politician Lincoln's motives, they trusted soldier McClellan's patriotism. When McClellan shed his uniform, however, he also lost his non-partisan cloak. By election day in 1864, most soldiers rejected McClellan's candidacy because they saw his alliance with Peace Democrats as harmful to the Union cause. Republicans, meanwhile, had successfully fused their party's prospects with diverse patriotic appeals and movements, running under the Union Party banner. With regards to Lincoln, some scholars have observed that he had a close relationship with the men who marched in his armies. However, support for the president did not solidify until it became clear that Lincoln, above all others, was the leader most committed to seeing a restored Union.[10]

As they thought about their own responsibilities as leaders, these college-educated men also assessed military and national leaders using the same rubric. Unswervingly committed to the Union, they hoped that their superiors shared the same goals and fought to achieve the same ends. Most of the New Brahmins considered here identified themselves as Republicans but even they did not always support the Republican president. While some hoped that the conflict would bring an end to slavery, most fought only to restore the Union. They reasoned that slavery would die as a result of the war and saw no reason why the armies should directly target the institution. The War Democrats in this sample also expressed willingness to support whichever political party's candidate offered the best chance of bringing the conflict to a successful close. They, like other Democrats at the time, did not want the war for the Union to turn into a revolutionary one. Despite their claim that they acted in a nonpartisan manner and sought only the restoration of the Union, New Brahmins' debates about the course of the war and specific policies or movements certainly carried political connotations. Political party identification, however, did not always predict whom these young officers' would support.[11] Focusing on soldiers' thoughts about the war effort reveals that their loyalty lay with neither political party but, rather, to the Union cause itself.

For the first few years of the war, the New Brahmins favored the opinion of George B. McClellan, the creator and first commander of the Army of the Potomac, over Abraham Lincoln's. Young and professional, McClellan epitomized the success that these ambitious officers craved for themselves. Taught to rely on professionals and shun politicians, they naturally gravitated to McClellan's point of view and continued to see him as the republic's best hope. These men's social class and education also influenced them to advocate the curtailment of democratic impulses in the volunteer ranks. Appalled by the lack of discipline and demands of common troops, these men sometimes wondered how the Union would ever win the war. Victory required discipline and strict adherence to the orders of professional soldiers. Such beliefs corresponded with these men's low opinion of the masses in general. As George M. Fredrickson has pointed out, northern intellectuals resented losing authority in public discourse as a result of a rising democratic wave ushered in during the Jacksonian Era. Their service in the war, therefore, served the dual purpose of returning professionals to a prominent position as societal leaders, all the while demonstrating the folly of an overly democratic society.[12]

Lincoln's Leadership

Even more than others, New Brahmins viewed the army as the embodiment of the Union. They demanded strong and resolute leadership to command the power of the state, setting a high standard for both the army and its leaders. They lambasted President Lincoln when he seemed unable to articulate a reason for fighting, called him weak when they misunderstood his motives for emancipation, and declared him incompetent when military campaigns ended in failure. Because he lacked military experience, New Brahmins expected that the president would defer to the opinion of the nation's professional soldiers. Lincoln's seeming indecision, when coupled with these men's poor opinion of undisciplined volunteer troops, led some to the conclusion that the United States needed a dictator.

New Brahmins hoped that the war would rally the nation and help unite the citizenry. They particularly detested individuals who appeared more concerned with pursuing partisan ends during the crisis. "When I see the outrageous meanness of the democrats [sic] and the timid and cowardly course of many of the republicans [sic]," James A. Garfield, a Williams College graduate and Republican, wrote his wife, "it makes me long to be in the strife and help fight it out." In the present crisis, Garfield thought the nation needed "men to stand by the country and sustain its authority." "Politics of all kinds are a curse and a sin, and have ruined the country," Franklin A. Haskell, a Dartmouth College graduate and Republican, complained in 1863.[13] Throughout the war, college men hoped that national leaders would set aside their politicking and work toward a swift end to the conflict. They viewed political dialogue as distractions rather than debates about the nature of conflict and the shape of the post-war society.

Like others, New Brahmins gave the new Lincoln administration a grace period, expecting that it would focus its energies on ending the rebellion. Democrats pledged their support but warned the administration not to conflate the goals of Union and emancipation. "The abolitionists are making a great row in Congress," Henry L. Abbott told his aunt in December 1861, "but they will get floored as they deserve, with that miserable old humbug [Sen.] Charley Sumner [of Massachusetts, an outspoken abolitionist] at the head." The staunch Democrat could not imagine that, beyond some groups in Washington and Boston, anyone supported abolitionist ideas. He reported that he hadn't "seen any men or officers in this part of the loyal army who are willing to fight for abolitionists, though I hope we are too good soldiers to disobey if such are the orders." War Democrat Thomas H. Hubbard, a Bowdoin College graduate, uncomfortable with using the conflict as an excuse for interfering with slavery, also hoped that the administration would avoid the issue. He thought the South deserved "a gentul [sic] thrashing" for they stood "in the wrong most plainly in this context." Hubbard believed the war "a very good institution provided it can be conducted by Democratic or Union leaders, and not by abolitionists; provided it continues as the maintenance of a just political right, a fair Election and doesn't degenerate into a war of Emancipation."[14] New Brahmins viewed Union and emancipation as separate issues and considered the latter a distraction from the task of preserving the former.

Two months after the firing on Fort Sumter, the Union war machine still seemed lethargic and even some of the most dedicated men expressed anxiety. In addition, they discerned no consistent statement from the Lincoln administration about the nature of the contest and feared that officials had not done enough to root out disloyal elements in the government. Such fears stemmed from the recognition that, during the Buchanan administration, several cabinet members had aided the nascent Confederacy. Many Northerners also feared that rebel sympathizers still lurked in various government offices. In his essay for this volume, Timothy J. Orr examines how fears about loyalty in one war-related industry continued deep into the conflict. Harvard graduate Charles Russell Lowell, a Republican, complained to his mother in the summer of 1861 that, "the Administration seem to me sadly in want of a policy—the war goes on well, but the country will soon want to know exactly what the war is *for*." After the First Battle of Bull Run, Harvard man Charles P. Bowditch criticized "the people at the head of our Government," specifically calling out Secretary of War Simon Cameron for being an incompetent "old heathenish rascal." A few months later Charles Francis Adams, Jr., a Harvard graduate and Republican, conceded that the government had "done much" but, in that same time, "the rebels have performed miracles." "At the end of six months have we a policy?" he asked, continuing, "Are traitors weeded out of our departments? Is our blockade effective? Is the war prosecuted honestly and vigorously?" Adams thought Lincoln simply "not equal to the crisis" and went on to criticize other members of the administration, declaring Simon Cameron "corrupt" and Gideon Welles, the secretary of the navy, "incompetent." He was "tired of incompetents" and wanted "to see Lincoln forced to adopt a manly line of policy which all men may comprehend. The people here call for energy, not change, and if Lincoln were only a wise man he could unite them in spite of party cries, and with an eye solely to the public good."[15]

New Brahmins who distrusted political leaders thought that civilians ought to give the military a free hand in managing its own affairs and prosecuting the war. Understanding the necessity of discipline in the ranks, they detested when civilians interfered in such proceedings. They especially viewed the actions of their own commander-in-chief (prone to pardon soldiers) as meddlesome. Robert Gould Shaw, who had attended Harvard before the war, criticized Lincoln for interfering in military matters, pointing out, "when it was necessary to shoot some men last winter for desertion, the President pardoned them and every one thought it was too bad to punish our 'brave Volunteers' for just going home to see their families for a little while, without permission." Such actions signaled to deserters that "nothing will be done to them." Henry L. Abbott told his mother, "privately I think Lincoln is responsible to God for the deaths of many poor men, since, until the matter was taken out of his hands entirely by congress [*sic*], he persistently pardoned every case of death for desertion until the crime came to be thought trivial." "The President, in his wisdom or his weakness, has stopped all capital punishment in the army," wrote a disgusted Charles F. Morse, another Harvard man. "Is it humanity for a man virtually to pardon all these deserters, who have committed one of the greatest military crimes, when, by so doing, the life of every soldier who does his duty and goes into battle is endangered to a greater extent?" he asked. All three men believed that the threat of capital punishment effectively deterred disciplinary infractions and, by reducing the penalty for crimes, the president's actions contributed to the corrosion of army discipline.[16]

By 1862, many soldiers had concluded that Lincoln lacked the ability to pursue the war to its end. The president, they thought, could control neither his armies nor the war. Believing the nation needed strong leadership, New Brahmins toyed with the idea of accepting a dictator's temporary rule. In September 1861, Harvard graduate Wilder Dwight complained that Union troops could not become good soldiers because of their strong adherence to democratic citizenship. He could not believe, for example, that some men dared to talk back to their officers. The men in the ranks needed to accept the fact that, in the armed forces, only the opinion of military superiors mattered. Discipline, he believed, had been too lax and no leader had risen to take control. Exactly one year later, Dwight remained dissatisfied with the Union men and commanders. "We want SOLDIERS, SOLDIERS, and a GENERAL IN COMMAND," he insisted. In July 1862, while observing that Congress had adjourned for the session, Robert Gould Shaw commented, "I think we should do better still, if the President and his Cabinet would adjourn too." "Our republican government," Shaw explained, "never managed the country with a very firm hand, even in time of peace, and one year of war has shown pretty clearly that that is not its forte." Shaw called for "some men, any man almost, with a few common-sense military ideas, to manage matters, without being meddled with and badgered by a lot of men who show the greatest ignorance about the commonest things." "If we were sure of having a perfectly disinterested and patriotic man," Shaw concluded, "what a good thing it would be to appoint a dictator in time of war." In August 1862, Uriah N. Parmelee wished "Abe had a little more of old Jackson in him," referring to the brash leadership of Andrew Jackson, which some contemporaries considered tyrannical. He thought Lincoln's advisers, who had "sharp eyes to their own interest and the next president," exercised too much influence and feared "the honesty of the President is far beyond his independence of spirit." A few months later, Parmelee expressed his lack of faith in Lincoln's ability, writing, "God never made . . . Lincoln to rule so big a country in perilous times like these." "I almost think," Charles Russell Lowell wrote in 1863, "we shall need a Cromwell to save us."[17]

Even after the Union victory at Antietam and Lincoln's issuance of the Emancipation Proclamation, the gloomy mood persisted. James A. Garfield told his wife he was "ashamed to be seen on the streets with the U.S. uniform on." From Washington, D.C. to New York City, he noticed "a settled gloom on nearly every face." "A great nation" was simply "groaning in an agony of suspense and anxiety to have something done." "A people that have poured out with a lavish hand their life and treasure to save their government" and had "trusted their Executive head with a constancy and faith" were, he continued, "beginning to feel that their confidence has been betrayed, their treasure squandered and the lives of their children sacrificed in unavailing slaughter."[18]

McClellan's Men

Military stalemate in the fall of 1862 led Harvard graduate John C. Gray to confess, "How the war can be carried to a successful issue under our incompetent administration and generals and against the growing disaffection abroad and at home is, I sometimes fear, an insoluble problem."[19] Gray made these observations after a rollercoaster year for Union hopes and morale. Between the summer of 1861 and the fall of 1862, one man's meteoric rise and fall captivated the army and nation. And even after his removal from command, George McClellan still left a lasting legacy on his soldiers and the war itself.

As a dashing young professional, George Brinton McClellan represented the great hope of the Union cause in the weeks after the defeat at the First Battle of Bull Run. Young, martial, and possessing superb organizational skills, McClellan captured the imagination of his troops. He had attended the University of Pennsylvania before completing his education at West Point, serving in the Mexican War, and becoming a very successful engineer and railroad president. His education, career trajectory, and achievements awed the college-educated young men who had also chosen a professional path. Although McClellan appeared to be every bit the professional soldier who did not dabble in politics, by taking a stand against emancipation and waging a limited war against the Confederates, McClellan clearly betrayed his own political preferences.[20] At the same time, McClellan's actions—or lack of action—along with his political leanings made him one of the most divisive and political figures that New Brahmins discussed.

While Democrats and most Republicans thought that McClellan could initially do no wrong, these men eventually concluded that the general could not win the war. Some continued to trust him, even after his dismissal from command, believing that he offered the Union its best chance for victory.

When he first took command of the Union army, McClellan dazzled the nation. In a successful demonstration of his skills, he whipped the defeated Bull Run army into shape. Charles F. Morse applauded the general's energy. "The people at the north," he wrote, "have no idea what a fine army ours is becoming under McClellan's influence. The men are being thoroughly drilled and they, as well as the officers, are kept under the strictest discipline." The young general had turned a demoralized mob into a confident, professional military force. McClellan's blend of organizational skill and showmanship helped to solidify his support with the men. Henry L. Abbott recalled that the general rode past all the troops one day and "was cheered most lustily by all the regiments." The soldiers, he observed, "don't share the hatred which politicians feel towards him." Abbott admitted to personally liking McClellan's "looks very much. . . . His cap was off all the time as he rode through miles of troops & he looked most smilingly gratified, as he might at the expression of such warm devotion." Charles P. Chandler, a Bowdoin graduate, expressed "great confidence in the Youth and pluck of General McClellan. The army loves him."[21]

McClellan's early popularity rested on the assumption that he would move swiftly to defeat the Confederates after he had reorganized and trained the army. However, as summer turned to fall with no sign of a forward movement, some officers began to complain that the "young Napoleon" did not live up to his moniker. By winter, some had begun to lose confidence in the general. In January 1862, Wilder Dwight lamented that the country was lacking "two things, one is a General, the other a statesman." He doubted that McClellan, "whatever may be the future record of him as a battle-victor, will ever excite the praise of ruling cabinets or statesmen," because he "fails to be master of the whole position." Dwight hoped that the much lauded general would prove his worth once he finally took the field but, until then, "in the organizing and preparatory season, whose opportunity is *now*, his impulse is not as widely or as directly felt as I could wish." That same month, frustrated by delays, abolitionist Uriah Parmelee complained, "Inaction and Pro-Slavery are the watch words. . . . I'd like to wring Gen. McClellan's and Gen. Franklin's necks." In March 1862, Harvard graduate Stephen M. Weld pronounced McClellan "a failure," perhaps due to the general's unwillingness to move forcefully against the rebels.[22]

Grumblings about McClellan's inactivity ceased after he began his advance on Richmond in spring 1862, demonstrating another instance of the malleability of popularity. The general's popularity rose after several successful battles. Thomas W. Hyde, a Bowdoin College graduate, reported from near the Williamsburg battlefield that the men "perfectly idolized" their commander. Hyde's unit, the Seventh Maine, fought a sharp engagement and greatly appreciated McClellan's personal praise. The general "came up at our dress parade, made us a speech, told us that our charge gained the battle and saved the Union, told us how deeply grateful he was to us and gave us permission to have 'Williamsburg' inscribed upon our banners." McClellan called Hyde's unit, "the finest body of men Maine had sent forth." Such rhetoric from a man who was already popular helped strengthen the men's admiration for him. "When he rode away," Hyde recalled, "the cheering was tremendous—officers and men. We threw ourselves into each others arms, embraced and some wept for joy." The Maine officer called McClellan's visit "the proudest event in all our lives and we feel now more than ever, that whoever slanders George B. McClellan, *our second Washington*, does himself shame and his country harm."[23]

In the midst of his first major campaign, McClellan commanded most New Brahmins' loyalties as he slowly approached the gates of Richmond. Well aware that the army commander faced pressure from the capital to achieve a swift victory, New Brahmins sided with their general, believing that he had their best interests at heart with his cautious tactics. They even came to believe the general's accusations that political leaders conspired against him for selfish purposes. As a result, they blamed politicians for holding back troops that McClellan requested. Charles P. Chandler criticized "*members of Congress*" for wanting "a *fight*" and expressed his preference for a more deliberate military approach. "Better to conquer an enemy with picks and shovels than with muskets," Chandler declared, signaling his support for McClellan's often lethargic advances, which involved building entrenchments along the way. "Why don't they send us reinforcements?" Stephen M. Weld, who suspected McClellan's enemies of attempting to undermine the general behind the lines, asked in late June 1862. In the face of a powerful rebel force entrenched around the Confederate capital and "notwithstanding McClellan's frequent and earnest appeals for more troops," Weld declared "the Government at Washington refuses us any reinforcements." He blamed "Abolitionists in Congress" and accused them of "purposely protracting the war in order to render emancipation necessary." This supposed abolitionist strategy threatened "our existence as a nation united and whole." Weld believed that McClellan had been *too successful* and threatened to end the war before radicals could enact their abolitionist schemes.[24]

Some New Brahmins, however, did not disguise their disdain for McClellan's policy toward Confederate civilians and cautious military tactics. "But the thing which we have done which most reflect the spirit of the conservatives (I may say of the McClellan School)," Uriah Parmelee wrote to his mother, "is to guard the property, women and children of the rebels, because their husbands and fathers have left to fight against us." On McClellan, he declared, "A general that coolly allows his enemy to evacuate a position which he has for months been preparing to take, merely to fall back behind stronger intrenchments [sic] is no man for me." Thomas Hyde also criticized the protection of rebel property, writing, "I have seen rebel property protected and our wounded dying near by in a field by scurvy from exposure, while a rank rebel talks his treason in splendid halls in safety." The Maine soldier, however, appears not to have blamed McClellan for the policy he detested.[25]

Following the failure of the Peninsula Campaign, politicians took the blame for supposedly meddling in military affairs. Harvard man Paul J. Revere mentioned to his wife, Lucretia, that the "late experience of the army, with the great loss of life and accompanying suffering, seems to have been necessary to convince the country of the wretched folly of interference with military movements on the part of politicians." New Brahmins, many of whom participated in the campaign, became convinced that the patriotic and noble McClellan faced both Confederate troops in his front and partisan operatives in his rear.[26]

Most New Brahmins found it easier to blame Washington politicians rather than the army commander who led them. So used to viewing politicians negatively, they dared not lay blame with the army, the embodiment of the Union cause. Stephen M. Weld claimed that Edwin Stanton, the secretary of war, had prolonging the conflict "by his meddling and interference." He accused Stanton of having "prevented McClellan from receiving reinforcements, and delayed him in every way possible." Uriah N. Parmelee wanted the war to be "waged in earnest, deadly quick" with assurances that "those who take up arms . . . need not sacrifice their lives to please politicians catering for the next Presidential campaign or to please generals who seek to prolong the war for their own aggrandizement." Although he had enthusiastically supported Abraham Lincoln in 1860, Thomas W. Hyde was "completely disgusted with the whole management of this war and so are we all. The best are losing heart." Henry L. Abbott sympathized with McClellan, calling him "the greatest general the country every produced" and criticized the administration for not fully sustaining his actions.

After the Union defeat at the Second Battle of Bull Run at the end of August 1862, Lincoln called upon McClellan to rally the troops once again. Paul J. Revere recorded that the "enthusiasm in the army . . . was unbounded. Tired as the men were, they fairly howled; and, in the hospitals, the wounded raised a cheer as well as they could." McClellan's subsequent victory at the Battle of Antietam on September 17 confirmed to his admirers that he could win the war. Charles Russell Lowell, serving in the headquarters of the Army of the Potomac, reminded a correspondent that McClellan had "started from Washington with a demoralized army." His victory had, therefore, "been very creditable to him." McClellan, so it seemed, had saved the republic yet again.[27]

After Confederate Gen. Robert E. Lee's badly bruised army escaped back into Virginia following its retreat from Antietam, however, one outraged gentleman officer criticized both McClellan and the Lincoln administration. James A. Garfield, writing to his wife from Washington, D.C. complained about the "weak, timid government, on the one hand, and the deep plottings [sic] of the old Breckenridge wing of the Democratic Party in connection with Gen[.] McClellan" on the other. The general, Garfield gossiped, had not vigorously pursued the retreating Confederates because it was "not the plan to whip the rebels. They are to be kept from invading the north [sic], and the two armies are to be kept in the field till both sections of the country are exhausted, and the[n] the armies and the Democracy will compromise the matter." He also criticized the "criminal vacillation that has marked the course of the Government in its desire to remove him [McClellan] from Command and its cowardly drawing back at the very important moment when hesitation was surrender." The general himself, Garfield observed, had refused to pursue the retreating Confederates "till the river is permanently swelled by rains so that the rebels can't get around behind him into Maryland—at which time of course the roads will be bad and the winter near." "My heart burns with indignation," Garfield wrote a few days later, "when I see these beautiful autumn days pass and McClellan's army idle." Lamenting the waste of good campaign weather, he disgustedly concluded, "Shame! if not treason."[28]

The Lincoln government's "vacillation" came to an end following the 1862 midterm elections when the president relieved McClellan from command of the Army of the Potomac. Many New Brahmins joined in the outpouring of support for their old commander and expressed concern about the management of the war. John C. Gray voiced one "great objection" to McClellan's dismissal: "there is no one to put in his place." Gray, "no idolater of" McClellan's, conceded that the general had used "bad management . . . on the Chickahominy; . . . delayed too long in September and October, and . . . made a great mistake in not following up his victory at Antietam on Thursday following the fight." He accused the general of being "overcautious" and having "a certain mulishness of disposition insisting upon always following out an original plan." But no other general he had yet seen could "plan and execute (slowly, indeed, and clumsily) a campaign for an army of 150,000 men." Gray dismissed rumors that McClellan planned to seize control of the government. There was, he argued, "not an act or word of McClellan's which does not give it the lie." He concluded that the general was well meaning but ineffective. And, ultimately Gray saw no alternatives to the "Little Napoleon."[29]

Abolitionist soldiers who had long harbored concerns about the general, meanwhile, expressed their relief. Yale graduate William Wheeler refused to criticize McClellan directly while he still commanded the army. Once the general had been relieved, however, he no longer felt it necessary to withhold criticism. "I do not wish to triumph over the fallen," he wrote in November 1862, "but I must say that I consider the removal of McClellan as just and necessary." The general had "been tried, and found wanting in those qualities of swiftness, energy, and ready talent which are absolutely needful in a leader who would successfully combat the genius of Lee, the dash of Stuart, the daring rapidity of Jackson."[30] McClellan may have been the darling of his political supporters but others had their reservations about his forcefulness in conducting an aggressive military campaign. And, ultimately, all these men wanted a successful end to the war above all else.

The Controversy of Emancipation

New Brahmins wanted competent professional soldiers rather than political leaders to manage the war. They believed that the civilian administration had a responsibility to fill the military's requests and not involve itself otherwise. This belief rested on the naïve assumption that political and military issues did not affect one another. Lincoln, however, had no intention of resting on the sidelines while the military did its job. The president played a critical role in the war and, in the most dramatic demonstration of his will and authority to shape the course of events, revealed his intention to make emancipation a war aim in September 1862.

New Brahmins considered Lincoln's emancipation policy with the same framework that they considered everything else and asked: How will this help win the war? Most men in this sample, regardless of political affiliation, initially viewed the Emancipation Proclamation as a distraction and detrimental to the war effort. Even Republicans who supported emancipation suspected the timing of the announcement and the effect of the policy. Thomas W. Hyde considered "the Presi-

dent's Proclamation . . . ill-timed and unnecessary." Robert Gould Shaw wrote
that the act "ought to have been done long ago." However, "as a *war-measure*," he
confessed, "I don't see the immediate benefit of it." Stephen M. Weld, who sympathized with the president's stance, noted the "expediency of the proclamation at the
present time is all I doubt." Charles Russell Lowell later admitted that he thought
the Proclamation "ill-timed and idle."[31] Democrats, not surprisingly, reacted with
anger and disapproval. Henry L. Abbott reported, "The president's proclamation
is of course received with universal disgust, particularly the part which enjoins
officers to see that it is carried out." Threatening insubordination, he promised
that the army men "shan't see to any thing of the kind, having decidedly too much
reverence to the constitution [*sic*]." Moderate men responded ambiguously to the
proclamation. Conservative Theodore Lyman willingly supported the president
and his party through the war but this Bell-Everett voter thought the Emancipation Proclamation a misstep that revealed Lincoln's weakness. Lyman did not
think the president had "enough steel in his backbone. He cannot make up his
mind to see with his own eyes & with nobody else's."[32]

For New Brahmins, most of whom held conservative and moderate positions,
the issuance of the Emancipation Proclamation signaled a radical turn. They
feared this new policy confirmed the ascendance of Radical Republicans. The
proclamation's goals remained unclear to them and Lincoln's action appeared to
signal his capitulation to abolitionists' demands. In January 1863, John C. Gray
expressed his dislike of "the 'radicals' policy," which, he explained, had been pursued by "the abolitionists from the beginning and . . . adopted afterwards by the
President." Since the start of the war, Gray suggested, "some men whose number
is now very largely increased made up their minds that here was a chance to abolish slavery and that they would try to do it." Radicals had pursued this approach,
"independently of the endeavor of the government to unite the country." He did
not think that abolitionists necessarily opposed the reunion of the country but
they had "acted without regard to it and thus necessarily often in opposition."
More than a year later, Gray still maintained his opinions about emancipation.
As he explained, his concern had to do with the manner in which the president
arrived at his policy. Gray would have preferred a constitutional amendment to
"those crooked ways by which" Lincoln had sought to use his military power to
justify emancipation.[33]

Democrats charged that, by changing the nature of the war, Lincoln revealed
his greater commitment to enslaved blacks and racial equality. They accused
the president of placing the defeat of the Confederacy second to an abolitionist scheme. Others also questioned the administration's priorities. John C. Gray

accused abolitionists of sending military units to "take possession of distant points and free slaves, instead of concentrating forces to destroy their armies." Such criticisms became even more apparent after black soldiers took their place in the army, a consequence of the Emancipation Proclamation. Since Confederate officials refused to exchange black prisoners of war, the Union government refused to trade prisoners of any race. This move outraged angry Union troops who languished in Southern prisons. Their own government had seemingly forsaken them just to signal that it valued black and white soldiers equally. William F. Bartlett, a Harvard man imprisoned in Richmond after his capture at the Battle of the Crater in 1864, reported that the "suffering among the prisoners here and farther south is *too horrible* to *speak* of." It was, he wrote, "a disgrace to our government that they do not make a general exchange." He claimed that the "rebel government" was "ready and willing to do it, on almost any terms." The blame for Union men's suffering rested with Lincoln who refused to negotiate unless Confederates treated captured black soldiers equally.[34]

For the most part, even those who opposed emancipation early on came around to seeing its usefulness as a war measure. Charles F. Morse did not initially think that any change "would be produced by it" but a short time after Lincoln issued the proclamation, he admitted "its effect will be good." It would not only "set us straight with foreign nations," but also finally provide "a decided policy." And even though Lincoln "carefully calls it nothing but a war measure," Morse saw that it would be "the beginning of a great reform and the first blow struck at the real, original cause of the war." With such a policy, "No foreign nation can now support the South without openly countenancing slavery." In terms of the immediate military prospects of the war, it might "have the effect to cause disturbances among the troops from the extreme Southern States, who will think, perhaps, that their presence is needed more at home than up in Virginia." He also suggested that, once enslaved blacks learned that freedom awaited them behind federal lines, "there will be a much more general movement among them than there has been before." The proclamation also had the benefit of frightening Jefferson Davis, "to judge by the fearful threats of retaliation he is making."[35]

If they disapproved of their political leaders, New Brahmins knew that they could voice their displeasure at the polls. As elections neared, the men naturally considered their options. Some Republicans considered switching parties in order to assure the elevation of more competent administrators. Before the 1862 midterm elections, John C. Gray declared that he had no objection to supporting the Democratic Party. However, he remained concerned that "the people's party" was not sincere "in their declarations about the war" and might turn "into a peace party." Meanwhile, he thought "the present administration has forfeited its claim to the respect and confidence of the nation." "The support of the war is a very distinct thing from the support of the President in theory," Gray wrote, "the only doubt in my mind is whether they are separable in practice." "The more I think of it," he continued, "the more angry I am with the government for placing in such a dilemma good citizens like myself who desire the complete subjugation of the rebels without showing mercy and without sparing man, woman or child, and who do yet desire with equal warmth to preserve intact our constitutional liberty." Gray described the very dilemma that many voters faced as Democrats attempted to distinguish between the Lincoln administration and the Union government. Republicans, on the other hand, tried to make the connection inseparable.[36]

Partisanship, however, could not be fully purged from politically engaged and opinionated young men. Naturally, they preferred to see members of their own political persuasion in power. Democrats blamed Lincoln for both wartime failures and inspiring mob opposition. Henry L. Abbott thought the anti-draft protesters in New York City "the fruit of Lincoln's teachings." Disliking the rioters and calling them the "vilest rowdies," he worried that "if resistance to tyranny" came only through this source, "then despotism will surely triumph as preferable to anarchy." Abbott thought that only the next presidential election could "save the country. I wish to God it could come now." The Lincoln administration, with more than a year to go in its first term, "still have time to destroy us." He expressed his hope that the people would "overthrow these weak, cowardly rulers," a treasonous sentiment. Feeling persecuted, Abbott defended the bravery of Democrats, asking his father to spread the news that a regiment in the army known for having a large number of Copperheads—a term employed by Republicans to compare their political opponents to the venomous snake and embraced with pride by the Democrats—had "lost over one half of the enlisted men, & 10 out of 13 officers. Not an abolitionist in it, with the exception of one officer."[37]

Although they praised non-partisanship, New Brahmins who identified with the Republicans echoed common criticisms of the opposing party. Yale graduate and Republican Joseph H. Twichell sounded a defiant tone in a letter to his brother. Although the "Copperhead virus may poison the loyalty of the Northern voters," he wrote in 1863, "the Northern soldiers are untainted by it." He promised that before long "the sound of loyal cannon will offset the hand-organ din of disloyal croakers. If any man says that the North is divided, let faithful patriots point proudly to the *Arms* of the Republic—remaining unalterably fixed in the purpose to which they were originally sent." The Army of the Potomac had, in its ranks, plenty of men who "hate colored folk with all the intensity of depraved ignorance." Others hated the administration and abolitionists. But, Twichell maintained, "we have not one who [does] not deeply feel that the Copperhead Peace-Democratic party is a mighty mean set of fellows. They are a stench in all our nostrils." "Abolitionist, Republican, Democrat, negro-hater, whatever we may be," he concluded, "despondent, despairing, hopeful, confident, brave, timid—however we may feel, all agree in loathing the persons and principles of those political reptiles who smear the loyal North with the slime of a sneaking secessionism." Yale graduate James C. Rice called Democrats "worse than traitors" and accused them of crying for peace before the "unholy rebellion" had been suppressed. Rice warned that seeking peace, as the Democrats demanded, and "upon any term less than those of an entire submission on the part of the traitors in arms to the government of the United States" would lead to only a temporary halt in military campaigning. At some point, "sooner or later," he predicted, "you will be obliged to send your younger sons and brothers to enrich this soil, already fertile with the dead, younger and fresher blood to re-crimson these streams, already red with slaughter."[38]

The Choice, 1864

The election of 1864 presented American voters with the best opportunity to change the course of the war. The New Brahmins who had long wished for a more vigorous pursuit of the rebels, once again, supported the candidate they believed most committed to winning the war. By Election Day, most young men thought that President Lincoln had proven his dedication to the preserving the Union. "I have not a thought of any one but Abraham Lincoln," Charles H. Howard, a Bowdoin College graduate, wrote to his brother in March 1864. Referring to the attempt to replace Lincoln with Secretary of the Treasury Salmon P. Chase on the Republican ticket, Howard continued, "It would be a fatal mistake in the Republican party to nominate anyone else. . . . It would stand before the South as a repudiation of Pres. Lincoln & all his policy if any other should be elected."[39]

Lincoln's chances for a reelection depended on whom the Democrats chose as their nominee and on the military situation after the summer campaign season. In early September, John C. Gray was "very anxious to hear from the Democratic Convention at Chicago." He heard that the potential nominees included "McClellan, [former President Millard] Fillmore and [former senator and treasury secretary, Gen. John A.] Dix." Gray thought that Lincoln would "try to induce

Grant to make a great effort before the Chicago Convention as the capture of Richmond would seriously damage McClellan's chances of nomination, and he is far more to be feared than any other candidate." As late as the end of August, Democrats seemed poised to win the presidency. "I do not believe Mr. Lincoln can be elected," Yale man Theodore J. Holmes wrote, "there is so strong a party against him even am'g Union men." Lincoln was "very unpopular to a great extent . . . because of certain very unjust legislation in different matters at t. War Dept. w. ref. to officers & men."[40]

New Brahmins observed the military campaigns with a keen eye, knowing full well that the president's approval fluctuated with each victory and defeat. The Union cause, in the spring of 1864, rested on the shoulders of Lt. Gen. Ulysses Grant, promoted to command all American armies. After some of the heaviest fighting of the war, however, some soldiers soured on Grant's leadership and called for their old army commander, McClellan. After the horrific battles of the Wilderness and Spotsylvania, and the death of Thomas W. Hyde's beloved commander, General John Sedgwick, chief of the Sixth Army Corps, the Maine officer expressed his dissatisfaction with Grant. In the past few weeks he had "lost so many friends, and have seen so many sacrifices without adequate result, that I feel very doubtful as to the general result." Hyde claimed that he would "not write so despondingly, did I see any Generalship." "McClellan is the only man to save the country," he insisted. Although he admitted that Grant was "certainly persevering" in the face of strong Confederate opposition during the Overland Campaign, Hyde concluded that the new general-in-chief possessed "no genius." "If McClellan," were in charge, however, "we would be sure to win. Grant will lose 50,000 men and then commence on McClellan's plan." Hyde, as it turned out, underestimated the toll from the Overland Campaign by around 10,000. John C. Gray recorded that Democratic sentiment was "quite strong in the Western Army" and predicted, "if we gain no great military success before November, I think McClellan will give Lincoln a close run."[41]

In late summer, however, the military tide had turned in the Union's favor. "Sherman's guns," Charles Francis Adams, Jr. advanced, "will discuss most eloquent arguments in the Presidential issue, and, as the sound of his cannon advances or recedes, so will the hopes of Lincolnite and McClellanite rise and fall." After the fall of Atlanta in early September, Charles Russell Lowell felt confident in Lincoln's reelection prospects and encouraged everyone to work and fight even harder to ensure the desired outcome. "Every officer," he declared, "ought to show double zeal, and every citizen double interest in recruiting, if any military success is to have an effect on the result." Although it pained him to say so,

Lowell thought "that four years under McClellan would destroy what is left of the Republic."[42]

New Brahmins ultimately supported the candidate most committed to winning the war. John C. Gray viewed both Lincoln and McClellan as "very honest men, both above all things wishing the reunion of the country, both with a singular faculty for taking bad advice and surrounding themselves by bad advisers, both of decided ability." The decision to support one man over the other, however, also required considering "the character of the influences that will be brought to bear upon the men than upon the men themselves, for I believe that neither can stand the outside pressure." Gray concluded that he would cast his ballot for Lincoln, explaining, "I think the great bulk of the republican party [*sic*] sincerely desire first of all things the restoration of the country, and that a very large and influential part of the democratic party [*sic*] do not make it their first object."[43]

As election day approached, McClellan's former soldiers began to question the general's principles. Even long-time admirers began to wonder about his motives. Writing in his journal while a prisoner of war, William F. Bartlett recorded hearing the news that the Democratic Party had nominated McClellan. "I fear," he commented, "there is not much chance of his being elected." Bartlett himself did not "like the names that he is associated with," perhaps referring to Copperhead politicians. Stephen M. Weld, also imprisoned in the Confederacy, wrote that McClellan's "nomination on a peace platform" would "kill him." Charles F. Morse expressed disappointment in the former army commander. His opinion of McClellan changed after the general espoused views that contradicted the Democratic platform. Why had he accepted the nomination if he disagreed with the party's positions? Morse thought this action changed him "from being an honest, straightforward soldier, into a politician seeking office." "He knew," Morse lamented, "that a large part of the Convention was for peace and not for war [yet] carried on in any way, and as an honest man he had no business to say what he did." Charles Russell Lowell sympathized with McClellan. He regretted that the general's name had "to be dragged through the mud" alongside the Democratic Party's "contemptible" platform. He also thought that if McClellan won the election, "the North will split before his four years are passed, and we shall be left in the condition of the South American republics, or worse." The general's election would lead to "either half a dozen little republics, or *one despotism*." Because "success to our arms will further Lincoln's chances," Lowell wrote, "I feel as if each one of us, both in the army and at home, had a tenfold motive for exertion now."[44]

Some men observed the erosion of McClellan's following and doubted that he would even win the army vote. "McClellan's organs count greatly on his popularity in the Army to lessen there the Union majority," Charles Francis Adams, Jr. wrote. He explained that "Soldiers don't vote for individuals" but rather "vote against those who delay the progress of the war at home; they want to vote down the copperheads [sic]." As the election results proved, Lincoln's support trumped McClellan's among the soldiers: The president won 78 percent of soldiers' votes. On November 13, 1864, Thomas H. Hubbard reported to his father the tally from his regiment's election: "For Lincoln Electors 184, for McClellan Electors 26." At the national level, Lincoln bested McClellan 212 to 21 electoral votes.[45]

Abraham Lincoln's supporters celebrated his victory by praising the contest as a divine sign. Charles Francis Adams, Jr. recorded from Boston, "We are very gay over the election." He bragged about "the popular majority, two-thirds and over of Congress, and not one single State Executive, except New Jersey, that is not in harmony with the Administration." "This election," Adams concluded, "has relieved us of the fire in the rear and now we can devote an undivided attention to the remnants of the Confederacy." Additionally, the election had "ratified our course at its most doubtful stage and it has crushed domestic treason as no other power could have." Lincoln's victory gave him "a new and almost unbounded faith in the faculty of a free *and intelligent* people to manage their own affairs." At the end of the contest, Oliver O. Howard pronounced McClellan's defeat the result of his "pro-slavery proclivities . . . for providence had to go on with the great work and leave him behind." Howard doubted that McClellan himself had "a bad heart" but the general had "made a mistake to ally himself with malcontents at such a time as this."[46]

Whatever New Brahmins thought about their military and civilian leaders, they remained committed to the cause of the Union. This dedication explained their impatience at the pace of the war and their willingness, at least in theory, to welcome a dictator. At times, their zeal to protect the Union caused them to forget the more democratic elements they fought to preserve. From the beginning of the conflict they had longed for a swift victory but each passing season brought only delays and missed opportunities. "This golden Indian-summer time is just the season for marching and fighting," William Wheeler wrote in October 1862, "and I chafe at our present inaction." He wanted to know why the government didn't "send us on troops enough to move with, or, if we have troops enough already, why don't we 'pitch in?'" There were, he noted, "mysteries about the conduct of this war that puzzle and almost disgust me." Despite this, he managed to keep his "faith in 'something' alive, although I can hardly say what that 'something' is." He tried to explain his determination as being "mostly confined to the sturdy determination of the people of the North to bring the war to a just and honorable termination." A few weeks later, Wheeler reiterated that he had "great faith in the army which is now coming into the field, and also in the firm determination of the people and the President, to treat the war as a serious matter."[47] Whatever disappointments he felt toward the military or civilian leadership of the country, Wheeler, like other New Brahmins, remained determined to see the war through and the Union preserved.

Having set their own civilian lives aside, New Brahmins hoped that individuals from all political persuasions could learn to work together to preserve the nation. They did not necessarily view the military and civilian leadership as antagonists but wished that both would support the other to achieve victory. In August 1862, Luther C. Howell, an Amherst man and Republican, told his sister, "I am very sorry that you northern folks are losing your confidence in Lincoln & McClellan." He admitted to having "but very little patience with that class of persons who without sufficient data are continually passing judgment upon our leaders." He admitted his willingness to trust the pair because they were "the best we have and if the nation is saved it must be by their leadership."[48]

From the start of the conflict, New Brahmins defined loyalty in terms of preserving their beloved Union. To them, the Union represented a legacy from the Founders and a divinely blessed nation with the potential to lead mankind into a democratic dawn. William Wheeler called the fight for the Union "God's cause" while Charles Francis Adams, Jr. referred to Confederates as "the enemies of morals, of government, and of man."[49] As young professionals raised in a culture that defined commitment to one's conscience and selfless sacrifice as the key components of honor, these men expected their national leaders to demonstrate similar traits. Of course, these political beings often disagreed about the proper course of action. Death and loss prompted some of them to use revolutionary and treasonous language but such words underlie the commitment these men had to winning the war. In the end, these men were too loyal to the cause of the Union to overthrow the incompetent government they perceived. Their shifting views of who commanded their full loyalty suggests that, rather than being dedicated to a person or a party, these young men had committed themselves to the Union itself, above all others.

Notes

1. Henry L. Abbott to Caroline L. Abbott (sister), December 21, 1862, in Robert Garth Scott, ed., *Fallen Leaves: The Civil War Letters of Major Henry Livermore Abbott* (Kent, Ohio: Kent State University Press, 1991), 155. Threats against civilian government officials were not uncommon during the Civil War but most soldiers threatened Democratic legislators and politicians rather than Republican ones. (Adam I. P. Smith, *No Party Now: Politics in the Civil War North* [New York: Oxford University Press, 2006], 94.)

2. Louis Menand, *The Metaphysical Club* (New York: Farrar, Straus and Giroux, 2001), 43–44, 54. Civil War correspondences were not necessarily personal. Family members shared their loved ones' writings with others and the authors themselves expressed awareness of such activities. Henry L. Abbott, for example, asked his father to not share his "that miserable old production of mine" with "strangers" and "distinguished ones." (Henry L. Abbott to Josiah Gardner Abbott, November 23, 1861, in Scott, ed., *Fallen Leaves*, 78.)

3. Nina Silber and Mary Beth Sievens have neatly summarized the reasons why New England offers a useful case study in the Civil War era. Nina Silber and Mary Beth Sievens, *Yankee Correspondence: Civil War Letters between New England Soldiers and the Home Front* (Charlottesville: University Press of Virginia, 1996), 4–7. In studying Union soldiers' attitudes toward the presidential election of 1864, Jonathan W. White also concluded that soldiers cared most about ending the war. Jonathan W. White, "'For My Part I Dont Care Who Is Elected President': The Union Army and the Elections of 1864," in *This Distracted and Anarchical People: New Answers for Old Questions about the Civil War-Era North*, ed. Andrew L. Slap and Michael Thomas Smith (New York: Fordham University Press, 2013), 106–7. These New Brahmins' actions and commitment to the Union support historian Gary W. Gallagher's argument that restoring the Union remained the primary goal of Northern forces throughout the conflict. See Gary W. Gallagher, *The Union War* (Cambridge: Harvard University Press, 2011).

4. For a more comprehensive discussion of the influence of college educations, the development of character, and what motivated educated men to volunteer, see Kanisorn Wongsrichanalai, "Universities and Their Sons: New England College Students and Graduates in the Civil War," *Massachusetts Historical Review* 13 (November, 2011): 69–79.

5. For discussions of Southern honor, see Bertram Wyatt-Brown, *Southern Honor: Ethics and Behavior in the Old South* (New York: Oxford University Press, 1983) and Kenneth S. Greenberg, *Honor & Slavery: Lies, Duels, Noses, Masks, Dressing As a Woman, Gifts, Strangers, Humanitarianism, Death, Slave Rebellions, the Proslavery Argument, Baseball, Hunting, and Gambling in the Old South* (Princeton, N.J.: Princeton University Press, 1996). For works that discuss Northern honor, see Edward L. Ayers, *Vengeance & Justice: Crime and Punishment in the 19th-Century American South* (New York: Oxford University Press, 1984), 19–24; Patrick Rael, *Black Identity & Black Protest in the Antebellum North* (Chapel Hill: University of North Carolina Press, 2002), 130–31; and Bertram Wyatt-Brown, *Yankee Saints and Southern Sinners* (Baton Rouge: Louisiana State University Press, 1985), 189–92. On reasons why the Constitutional Union Party did not seemingly appeal to voters in 1860, see Peter Knupfer, "Aging Statesmen and the Statesmanship of an Earlier Age: The Generational Roots of the Constitutional Union Party," in *Union & Emancipation: Essays on Politics and Race in the Civil War Era*, ed. David W.

Blight and Brooks D. Simpson (Kent, Ohio: Kent State University Press, 1997), 75–77
and A. James Fuller, "The Last True Whig: John Bell and the Politics of Compromise in
1860," in *The Election of 1860 Reconsidered*, ed. A. James Fuller (Kent, Ohio: Kent State
University Press, 2013), 132. On how John Brown "excited Yankee adulation because his
actions were *manly*," see Wyatt-Brown, *Yankee Saints and Southern Sinners*, 124; David S.
Reynolds, *John Brown, Abolitionist* (New York: Knopf, 2005), 333; Greenberg, *Honor and
Slavery*, 91.

6. Susan-Mary Grant, "'How a Free People Conduct a Long War': Sustaining Opposition to Secession in the American Civil War" in *Secession as an International Phenomenon: From America's Civil War to Contemporary Separatist Movements*, ed. Don H. Doyle
(Athens: University of Georgia Press, 2010), 138–43.

7. Wongsrichanalai, "Universities and Their Sons," 75–78; Kanisorn Wongsrichanalai,
"'What Is a Person Worth At Such a Time': New England College Students, Sectionalism,
and Secession," in *Children and Youth During the Civil War Era*, ed. James Marten (New
York: New York University Press, 2012), 47–48, 50–52; Mark E. Neely, Jr., *The Union
Divided: Party Conflict in the Civil War North* (Cambridge: Harvard University Press,
2002), 7; Paul Quigley, *Shifting Grounds: Nationalism and the American South, 1848–1865*
(New York: Oxford University Press, 2012), 9, 13, and Chapter 1.

8. Bell Irvin Wiley, *The Life of Johnny Reb, The Common Soldier of the Confederacy*
(Indianapolis: Bobbs-Merrill, 1943); Bell Irvin Wiley, *The Life of Billy Yank, The Common
Soldier of the Union* (Indianapolis: Bobbs-Merrill, 1952); Gerald F. Linderman, *Embattled
Courage: The Experience of Combat in the American Civil War* (New York: Free Press,
1987); James M. McPherson, *For Cause and Comrades: Why Men Fought in the Civil War*
(New York: Oxford University Press, 1997); Chandra Manning, *What This Cruel War
Was Over: Soldiers, Slavery, and the Civil War* (New York: Vintage Books, 2007); Gal-
lagher, *The Union War*, 2–3, 34, 120. Scholars studying Northerners who fought for the
Confederacy have noted their personal, familial, and economic connections to Southern
society. (Christian B. Keller, "Keystone Confederates: Pennsylvanians Who Fought for
Dixie," in *Making and Remaking Pennsylvania's Civil War*, ed. William Blair and William
Pencak [University Park: Pennsylvania State University Press, 2001], 21–22. See also
David Zimring, *To Live and Die in Dixie: Native Northerners Who Fought for the Confed-
eracy* [University of Tennessee Press, 2014].)

9. Glenn C. Altschuler and Stuart M. Blumin, *Rude Republic: Americans and Their
Politics in the Nineteenth Century* (Princeton, N.J.: Princeton University Press, 2000),
160–61; Robert M. Sandow, *Deserter Country: Civil War Opposition in the Pennsylvania
Appalachians* (New York: Fordham University Press, 2009), 45–46, 55.

10. William A. Blair has pointed out discussions of the war's progress allowed "partisanship the means to cloak itself within the banner of patriotism." Men who marched
in the armies of the United States did not need such cover to vent their anger at the slow
pace of the war. See William A. Blair, *With Malice Toward Some: Treason and Loyalty
in the Civil War* (Chapel Hill: University of North Carolina Press, 2014), 164; Smith, *No
Party Now*, 6–10, 160–61; Altschuler and Blumin, *Rude Republic*, 10–11. For Northern
soldiers' political discussions and beliefs, see Reid Mitchell, *Civil War Soldiers* (New
York: Viking, 1988), 188–89; Paul Cimbala, *Soldiers North and South: The Everyday*

Experiences of the Men Who Fought America's Civil War (New York: Fordham University Press, 2010), 108–109. Frank J. Williams observed an "unusual bond" between President Lincoln and his men. Williams claimed that "soldiers generally respected Lincoln and believed he had their best interests at heart, even when he was appointing inept generals to command them." Chandra Manning pointed out that the commander-in-chief and the soldiers shared a "vision of the war's cause and purpose." The present essay suggests a more complicated relationship. Jennifer L. Weber, meanwhile, has explained how anti-war Democrats' actions pushed Union soldiers into Republican ranks and solidified the men's support for President Lincoln. (Frank J. Williams, "Voting for Uncle Abe," *Civil War Times* 45, no. 9 [2006]: 34–39; Chandra Manning, *What This Cruel War Was Over: Soldiers, Slavery, and the Civil War* [New York: Vintage Books, 2007], 13; Jennifer L. Weber, *Copperheads: The Rise and Fall of Lincoln's Opponents in the North* [New York: Oxford University Press, 2006].)

11. The Republicans in this sample include Charles Francis Adams, Jr. (Harvard 1856), Charles P. Chandler (Bowdoin 1854), Wilder Dwight (Harvard 1853), James A. Garfield (Williams 1856), John C. Gray (Harvard 1859), Franklin Aretas Haskell (Dartmouth, 1854), Charles Henry Howard (Bowdoin 1859), Oliver Otis Howard (Bowdoin 1850), Luther Clark Howell (Amherst 1864), Thomas Worcester Hyde (Bowdoin 1861), Charles Russell Lowell (Harvard 1854), Uriah Nelson Parmelee (Yale 1863), James Clay Rice (Yale 1854), Robert Gould Shaw (Harvard 1860), Joseph Hopkins Twichell (Yale 1859), Stephen Minot Weld (Harvard 1860), and William Wheeler (Yale 1855). The Democrats include Henry Livermore Abbott (Harvard 1860), William Francis Bartlett (Harvard 1862), and Thomas Hamlin Hubbard (Bowdoin 1857). Theodore Lyman (Harvard 1855) supported the Constitutional Union ticket in 1860. Those whose political affiliation is unclear include Charles Bowditch (Harvard 1863), Theodore James Holmes (Yale 1853), Charles Fessenden Morse (Harvard 1858), and Paul Joseph Revere (Harvard 1852). For a discussion of political participation on New England college campuses, see Wongsrichanalai, "'What Is a Person Worth At Such a Time': New England College Students, Sectionalism, and Secession," 53–57. This sample of twenty-five represents a subsection of the individuals that I have examined elsewhere. For additional information, along with an explanation of the term "New Brahmins," see Kanisorn Wongsrichanalai, *Northern Character: College-Educated New Englanders, Honor, Nationalism, and Leadership in the Civil War Era* (New York: Fordham University Press, 2016).

As Frank L. Klement has noted, the war brought change to ideas of equality, transformed "a federal union into an American nation," and helped industrialism gain in the predominantly agricultural American nation. Conservative Democrats, he notes, "thought that the wheel of revolution turned too fast and too far. Their wartime slogan, 'The Constitution as it is, the Union as it was,' proved that they looked toward the past and feared the changes which the war foisted upon the country." Democrats also challenged the idea that they were disloyal, insisting "that they . . . had the right to criticize the Lincoln administration, even in the midst of a fratricidal war." (Frank L. Klement, *The Copperheads in the Middle West* [Chicago: University of Chicago Press, 1960], 1; Frank L. Klement, *Dark Lanterns: Secret Political Societies, Conspiracies, and Treason Trials in the Civil War* [Baton Route: Louisiana State University Press, 1984], 4.)

12. George M. Fredrickson, *The Inner Civil War: Northern Intellectuals and the Crisis of the Union* (1965; New York: Harper & Row, 1968), 9–10, 23.

13. James A. Garfield to Lucretia Garfield, April 14, 1861, in John Shaw, ed., *Crete and James: Personal Letters of Lucretia and James Garfield* (East Lansing: Michigan State University Press, 1994), 113; Frankin A. Haskell to undisclosed recipient, October 31, 1863, in Frank L. Byrne and Andrew T. Weaver, eds., *Haskell of Gettysburg: His Life and Civil War Papers* (Kent, Ohio: Kent State University Press, 1989), 226.

14. Henry L. Abbott to Elizabeth Livermore, December 21, 1861, in Scott, ed., *Fallen Leaves*, 93; Thomas H. Hubbard to Emma G. Hubbard, May 29, 1861, box 5, folder 43, Hubbard Family Papers, George J. Mitchell Department of Special Collections and Archives, Bowdoin College Library, Brunswick, Maine (repository hereafter cited as BCL; collection cited as Hubbard Papers, BCL).

15. Blair, *With Malice Toward Some*, 42, 50; Charles R. Lowell to Anna J. Lowell, June 17, 1861, in Edward Waldo Emerson, ed., *Life and Letters of Charles Russell Lowell* (1907; Columbia: University of South Carolina, 2005), 212; Charles P. Bowditch to Jonathan I. Bowditch, July 28, 1861, in "War Letters of Charles P. Bowditch," *Massachusetts Historical Society Proceedings*, vol. 57 (Boston: Published by the Society, October, 1923–June, 1924), 415; Charles F. Adams, Jr. to Henry Adams, November 5, 1861, in Worthington Chauncey Ford, ed., *A Cycle of Adams Letters 1861–1865*, 2 vols. (Boston: Houghton Mifflin Company, 1920), 1:63–64.

16. Robert G. Shaw to Sarah B. S. Shaw, July 23, 1862, in Russell Duncan, ed., *Blue-Eyed Child of Fortune: The Civil War Letters of Colonel Robert Gould Shaw* (Athens: University of Georgia Press, 1992), 217; Henry L. Abbott to Caroline L. Abbott (mother), September 4, 1863, in Scott, ed., *Fallen Leaves*, 207; Charles F. Morse to unspecified recipient, July 16, 1864, *Letters Written During the Civil War, 1861–1865* (Boston, Mass.: privately printed, 1898), 178–79. For a discussion of class conflict between upperclass officers and men in the ranks as well as disciplinary proceedings against the latter, see Lorien Foote, *The Gentlemen and the Roughs: Violence, Honor, and Manhood in the Union Army* (New York: New York University Press, 2010), Chapters 1 and 5.

17. Wilder Dwight to Elizabeth A. Dwight, September 7, 1861, in Elizabeth A. Dwight, ed., *Life and Letters of Wilder Dwight, Lieut.-Col. Second Mass. Inf. Vols.* (Boston: Ticknor and Fields, 1868), 97–98; Wilder Dwight to Elizabeth A. Dwight, September 7, 1862, folder title "September 1–18, 1862," Dwight Family Papers, Massachusetts Historical Society, Boston, Massachusetts (repository hereafter cited as MaHS; collection hereafter cited as Dwight Papers, MaHS); Robert G. Shaw to Sarah B. S. Shaw, July 23, 1862, in Duncan, ed., *Blue-Eyed Child of Fortune*, 216–17, 219; Uriah N. Parmelee to Sam Parmelee, August 2, 1862, letter 61, folder "Typescript of Letters and Diaries," unpaginated, Parmelee Papers; Parmelee quoted in Norman MacLeod, "Uriah Parmelee's Ordeal: A Connecticut Yankee's Abolitionist Principles and the Reality of the Civil War," in *Annual Proceedings of the Dublin Seminar for New England Folklife (2011)* 36 (2017): 36; Charles R. Lowell to Josephine Shaw, October, 1863, in Emerson, ed., *Life and Letters*, 314. Michael Thomas Smith has demonstrated how Lincoln's critics employed gendered language to challenge his fitness to command. Claiming that he lacked manliness and moral character, these detractors argued that the president was easily manipulated by

others. (Michael Thomas Smith, "Abraham Lincoln, Manhood, and Nineteenth-Century American Political Culture," in *This Distracted and Anarchical People*, ed. Slap and Smith, 29–41.)

18. James A. Garfield to Lucretia Garfield, October 25, 1862, in Shaw, ed., *Crete and James*, 167.

19. John C. Gray to John C. Ropes, November 13, 1862, in *War Letters, 1862–1865* (Boston: Houghton Mifflin Company, 1927), 21–22.

20. For additional information on George B. McClellan, consult Stephen W. Sears, *George B. McClellan: The Young Napoleon* (New York: Ticknor & Fields, 1988). For further information about the education that young cadets received at the United States Military Academy at West Point see James L. Morrison, Jr., *"The Best School in the World": West Point, the Pre-Civil War Years, 1833–1866* (Kent, Ohio: Kent State University Press, 1986). For a discussion of how the national and military leaders professionalized the United States Military Academy at West Point in the decades before the Civil War see Wayne Wei-siang Hsieh, *West Pointers and the Civil War: The Old Army in War and Peace* (Chapel Hill: University of North Carolina Press, 2009), especially Chapters 1–4. For a discussion of what historian Mark Grimsley has termed the "conciliatory policy" during the war's first fifteen months, see Mark Grimsley, *The Hard Hand of War: Union Military Policy Toward Southern Civilians, 1861–1865* (New York: Cambridge University Press, 1995), especially Chapter 2. Ethan S. Rafuse has noted McClellan's "very modern approach to the conduct of war" and his adherence to "the professional model of labor organization associated with modern American society." (Ethan S. Rafuse, *McClellan's War: The Failure of Moderation in the Struggle for the Union* [Bloomington: Indiana University Press, 2005], 3–6.)

21. Charles F. Morse to unspecified recipient, September 1, 1861, *Letters Written During the Civil War*, 22; Henry L. Abbott to Caroline L. Abbott (mother), April 9, 1862, in *Fallen Leaves*, 109; Charles P. Chandler to Sarah W. Chandler, September 7, 1861, box 3, folder 16, Chandler Papers, BCL.

22. Wilder Dwight to Elizabeth A. Dwight, January 10, 1862, folder title "January 1–19, 1862," Dwight Papers, MaHS; quoted in MacLeod, "Uriah Parmelee's Ordeal," *Annual Proceedings of the Dublin Seminar*, 31; Stephen M. Weld, Jr. to Stephen M. Weld, Sr., March 9, 1862, in *War Diary and Letters of Stephen Minot Weld, 1861–1865* (Cambridge, Mass.: Riverside Press, 1912), 68.

23. Thomas W. Hyde to Eleanor D. Hyde, May 7, 1862, in Thomas W. Hyde, *Civil War Letters* (Privately Printed, John H. Hyde, 1933), 3–4.

24. Charles P. Chandler to Sarah W. Chandler, May 4, 1862, box 3, folder 48, Chandler Papers, BCL; Stephen M. Weld, Jr. to Stephen M. Weld, Sr., June 22, 1862, in *War Diary and Letters of Stephen Minot Weld*, 120.

25. Parmelee quoted in MacLeod, "Uriah Parmelee's Ordeal," *Annual Proceedings of the Dublin Seminar*, 32; Thomas W. Hyde to Eleanor D. Hyde, July 6, 1862, in Thomas W. Hyde, *Civil War Letters*, 33.

26. Paul J. Revere to Lucretia Revere, July 7, 1862, *A Memorial of Paul Joseph Revere and Edward H. R. Revere* (1874; Clinton, Mass.: The W. J. Coulter Press, 1913), 133. For a discussion of McClellan's own thoughts about his "enemies" and his tortured relationship

with President Lincoln, see James M. McPherson, "My Enemies Are Crushed: McClellan and Lincoln," in *Wars Within a War: Controversy and Conflict Over the American Civil War*, ed. Joan Waugh and Gary W. Gallagher (Chapel Hill: University of North Carolina Press, 2009), 52–67.

27. Stephen M. Weld, Jr. to Stephen M. Weld, Sr., June 4, 1862, in *War Diary and Letters of Stephen Minot Weld*, 111–12; Uriah N. Parmelee to his mother, July 27, 1862, letter 60 and Uriah N. Parmelee to Sam Parmelee, August 2, 1862, letter 61, folder "Typescript of Letters and Diaries," unpaginated, Parmelee Papers; Thomas W. Hyde to Eleanor D. Hyde, September 3, 1862, in *Civil War Letters*, 44–45; Henry L. Abbott to Josiah G. Abbott, September 3, 1862, in Scott, ed., *Fallen Leaves*, 140; Paul J. Revere to unspecified recipient, September 2, 1862, *A Memorial of Paul Joseph Revere and Edward H. R. Revere*, 145; Charles R. Lowell to John M. Forbes, September 19, 1862, in Emerson, ed., *Life and Letters*, 226.

28. James A. Garfield to Lucretia Garfield, October 3, 1862 and James A. Garfield to Lucretia Garfield, October 8, 1862, in Shaw, ed., *Crete and James*, 161–62, 163.

29. John C. Gray to John C. Ropes, November 13, 1862 and John C. Gray, Jr. to John C. Ropes, January 5, 1863, in *War Letters*, 22, 61–62.

30. William Wheeler to "Aunt E.," November 25, 1862, in *Letters of William Wheeler of the Class of 1855, Y.C.* (Cambridge, Mass.: H. O. Houghton and Company, 1875), 365–66.

31. Thomas W. Hyde to Eleanor D. Hyde and his sister, October 3, 1862, in *Civil War Letters*, 54; Robert G. Shaw to Sarah B. S. Shaw, October 5, 1862, in Duncan, ed., *Blue-Eyed Child of Fortune*, 252; Stephen M. Weld, Jr. to Stephen M. Weld, Sr., October 9, 1862, in *War Diary and Letters of Stephen Minot Weld*, 143; Charles R. Lowell to H. L. Higginson, February 15, 1863, in Emerson, ed., *Life and Letters*, 236.

32. Henry L. Abbott to Elizabeth Livermore, January 10, 1863, in Scott, ed., *Fallen Leaves*, 161; David W. Lowe, ed., *Meade's Army: The Private Notebooks of Lt. Col. Theodore Lyman* (Kent, Ohio: Kent State University Press, 2007), 10–11.

33. John C. Gray, Jr. to John C. Ropes, January 5, 1863 and August 21, 1864, in *War Letters*, 62–63, 377.

34. John C. Gray, Jr. to John C. Ropes, January 5, 1863, in *War Letters*, 62–64; William F. Bartlett to Harriet P. Bartlett, September 11, 1864, in *Memoir of William Francis Bartlett*, ed. Francis Winthrop Palfrey (Boston: Houghton, Osgood and Company, 1879), 136.

35. Charles F. Morse to unspecified recipient, October 6, 1862, *Letters Written During the Civil War*, 98–99.

36. John C. Gray, Jr. to John C. Ropes, October 15–20, 1862, in *War Letters*, 6; Blair, *With Malice Towards Some*, 204; Sandow, *Deserter Country*, 10, 71.

37. Henry L. Abbott to Josiah G. Abbott, July 27, 1863, in Scott, ed., *Fallen Leaves*, 192. Other Democratic soldiers also felt the pressure from those who disagreed with them. See Smith, *No Party Now*, 94–95.

38. Joseph H. Twichell to Edward W. Twichell, March 19, 1863, in Peter Messent and Steve Courtney, eds., *The Civil War Letters of Joseph Hopkins Twichell: A Chaplain's Story* (Athens: University of Georgia Press, 2006), 221–22; John M. Pellicano, *"Well Prepared To Die," The Life of Brigadier General James Clay Rice* (Fredericksburg, Va.: John M. Pellicano, 2007), 164–65.

39. Charles H. Howard to Rodelphus Gilmore, March 20, 1864, box 1, folder 21, Charles Henry Howard Collection, BCL.

40. John C. Gray, Jr. to his mother, September 1, 1864 and John C. Gray, Jr. to his mother, August 26, 1864, in *War Letters*, 393, 391; Theodore J. Holmes to Ellen L. Goldsmith, August 29, 1864, Theodore James Holmes Papers, Manuscripts and Archives, Yale University Library, New Haven, Connecticut.

41. Thomas W. Hyde to Eleanor D. Hyde, May 19, 1864 and Thomas W. Hyde to Eleanor D. Hyde, May 25, 1864, in *Civil War Letters*, 132–33, 136; John C. Gray, Jr. to John C. Ropes, August 21, 1864, in *War Letters*, 376.

42. Charles F. Adams, Jr. to Abigail B. Adams, September 3, 1864, in Ford, ed., *A Cycle of Adams Letters*, 2:190; Charles R. Lowell to Anna J. Lowell, September 4, 1864, in Emerson, ed., *Life and Letters*, 334.

43. John C. Gray, Jr. to John C. Ropes, August 21, 1864, in *War Letters*, 376–77.

44. Quoted in Palfrey, ed., *Memoir of William Francis Bartlett*, 135; Stephen M. Weld, diary [September 2, 1864 entry], in *War Diary and Letters of Stephen Minot Weld*, 368; Charles F. Morse to unspecified recipient, September 18, 1864, *Letters Written During the Civil War*, 191; Charles R. Lowell to Josephine Shaw, September 1, 1864, in Emerson, ed., *Life and Letters*, 332–33.

45. Charles F. Adams, Jr. to Charles F. Adams, Sr., October 15, 1864, in Ford, ed., *A Cycle of Adams Letters*, 2:204; Thomas Hamlin Hubbard to John Hubbard, November 13, 1864, box 7, folder 14, Hubbard Papers, BCL.

Jonathan W. White has argued that soldiers' motivations are more complex than previous studies have suggested. Even though Lincoln won a vast majority of soldiers' votes, White points out that many soldiers did not vote for either candidate because of disillusionment or intimidation. Some cast their votes for the candidate they thought the lesser of two evils while others made a calculation and voted for the person they thought would "end the war quickly and honorable." (White, "'For My Part I Dont Care Who Is Elected President,'" in *This Distracted and Anarchical People*, ed. Slap and Smith, 104–22.)

46. Charles F. Adams, Jr. to Henry Adams, November 14, 1864 and Charles F. Adams, Jr. to Charles F. Adams, Sr., November 18, 1864, in Ford, ed., *A Cycle of Adams Letters*, 2:223, 225; Oliver O. Howard to Elizabeth A. W. Howard, November 11, 1864, Oliver Otis Howard Papers, BCL.

47. William Wheeler to "M.," October 9, 1862 and William Wheeler to unspecified recipient, October 30, 1862, *Letters of William Wheeler*, 362–63, 361.

48. Luther C. Howell to his sister, August 30, 1862, Luther Clark Howell Papers, Amherst College Archives and Special Collections, Amherst College Library, Amherst, Massachusetts.

49. William Wheeler to Theodosia D. Wheeler, May 9, 1861, *Letters of William Wheeler*, 283; Charles F. Adams, Jr. to Henry Adams, December 10, 1861, in Ford, ed., *A Cycle of Adams Letters*, 1:79.

"Patriotism Will Save Neither You Nor Me"

*William S. Plumer's Defense
of an Apolitical Pulpit*

Sean A. Scott

On Sunday, November 17, 1861, the congregation of Central Presbyterian Church dedicated its new building, an unpretentious yet impressive structure furnished with stained glass windows, carpeted floors, and padded pews that could seat five hundred people in the main sanctuary. Only seven years earlier, William S. Plumer had moved from Baltimore to Allegheny City, Pennsylvania, and organized a church with forty-four charter members. Since this modest beginning, nearly 450 people had received membership, one-third of them new converts who had come to faith under Plumer's ministry. From all appearances, the fifty-nine-year-old pastor and his congregation displayed a spirit of unity and brotherly affection as they consecrated their newly completed house of worship.[1]

On this momentous day, Plumer could not have imagined that ten months later he would resign his pastorate and professorship at Western Theological Seminary. A few scholars have briefly outlined his troubles during the Civil War, but none has analyzed his story in the context of perceptions of loyalty in the North. His only crimes, according to patriotic contemporaries, were his failure to pray for Union victories during Sunday worship or forcefully denounce the Southern rebellion. Accused of disloyalty and condemned in the press, he maintained that political matters such as war had no place in the church. He prayed for elected officials, for soldiers' protection in battle, and for national peace, but he refused to supplicate God for specific outcomes of battles. Born in Pennsylvania but primarily educated and employed in the South, he deprecated a war that claimed the lives of loved ones from both sections. He was not a pacifist for its own sake but took an apolitical stand because he believed that it best served the interests and promotion of the gospel.[2]

Plumer's case highlights how some Northern civilians employed the rhetoric of loyalty to compel conduct that a majority required to meet their subjective standards of good citizenship. William Blair has demonstrated that broad, popular notions of disloyalty, rather than a strict, legal definition of treason, functioned as the primary measure of an individual's personal allegiance. To accomplish this, "the northern public and authorities often resorted to excessive means, especially when it came to examining the behavior of neighbors." This certainly was true with Plumer, who constitutionally could never have been found guilty of treason. An Old School Presbyterian, he held conservative principles theologically, politically, and socially, and these views conspicuously set him apart from many Northern clergy who were openly patriotic, Republican, and increasingly antislavery in their public pronouncements.[3] Unfortunately for him, during the Civil War many Northerners demanded more overt displays of patriotism than his conscience would allow him to make. Based on these higher standards, his position of public neutrality seemed to be nothing less than outright disloyalty.

The study of religion during the war has come into its own over the last twenty years. Timothy L. Wesley recently has examined how ministers' opinions on politics and the war oftentimes brought them into conflict with civil and military authorities, newspaper editors, or their own coreligionists. He notes that clergymen who adopted an apolitical posture might have done so for several reasons. Some feigned neutrality in hopes of hiding their partisan views; others, such as Catholics, respected their denomination's traditional silence on political matters; another segment feared that the politicization of the church would hasten the secularization of society; and a certain number believed that commenting on secular affairs demeaned their holy calling to preach the gospel message of Christ crucified and resurrected to save sinners.[4]

Plumer invoked the latter explanation, yet because he had lived in the South and maintained close friendships with many Southern families, several antagonists suspected him of harboring Southern sympathies. Some of these detractors likely knew that a quarter century earlier he had defended slavery on biblical grounds during the Presbyterian schism that produced separate Old and New School bodies, and his wide-ranging conservatism marked him as out of touch with the times. Nevertheless, during the war he affirmed his devotion to the U.S. government and never expressed sympathy for the Confederacy. He saw his multiple loyalties as completely congruous, a hierarchy where his allegiance to God and Scripture superseded but did not conflict with commitments to country, community, and friends. However, the public instead detected divided sympathies and consequently accused him of disloyalty. He simply deprecated war and emphasized spiritual over political matters. For example, in mid-March 1861 he hoped that Virginia would stay in the Union but concluded, "We need nothing so much as a revival of pure religion. We might have national unity & peace, & yet be sinking deeper & deeper in corruption & be treasuring up wrath against the day of wrath. But if God's Spirit be poured out on the land, all that is really good will be . . . preserved to us."[5] Considering the nation's political precipice, these views seem absurd to many people today, yet they clearly demonstrate that Plumer placed eternal concerns above the country's temporal troubles and foreshadow his steadfast determination to keep the war from entering his church.

This account is one facet of a broader narrative of ministers forced into uncomfortable positions because of the war. Clergymen in the border states often faced divided congregations or risked intervention by civil or military authorities when questions arose regarding their political sympathies.[6] For instance, the Union military removed Samuel B. McPheeters from Pine Street Presbyterian in St. Louis for nothing more than suspected disloyal sentiments, and this well-known incident prompted Abraham Lincoln to underscore that the federal government had no business trying "to run the churches."[7] Claims of disloyalty in the North typically stemmed from politically partisan disputes between Democrats and Republicans within the church. When cooler heads prevailed, the parties might resolve their differences and preserve congregational unity, but in several instances in Ohio and Illinois, Republican members brought allegedly traitorous Democratic clerics before an ecclesiastical court.[8] In order to avoid the likelihood of being defrocked, a pastor under these circumstances had little choice but to tender his resignation.[9] In at least one highly exceptional case, the reverend Alvah R. Rutan of Luzerne County, Pennsylvania was arrested three times by Union soldiers and eventually tried before a military commission for disloyalty and conspiring to resist the draft.[10]

These examples demonstrate that average civilians and laypersons closely monitored the actions and words of Northern ministers to find evidence of loyalty, and historians have paid little attention to pastors whose political opinions led to their imprisonment or removal from ministry. It is impossible to know or even estimate how many Northern ministers faced opposition from within their churches, denominations, or communities because of their known political beliefs or perceived disloyalty. Extant information about a clergyman's difficulties may be as little as one newspaper article, but Plumer's prominence within the Presbyterian church generated a rich documentary record from which to reconstruct this narrative. This microhistory illuminates better than most other known incidents of alleged clerical disloyalty what George Rable has called "the politics of loyalty," further confirming the war's pervasive politicization of religion and highlighting the public expectation that the church should unambiguously support the Republican party's war aims.[11]

Four days before the church dedication, Plumer learned that some members of his flock had begun to question his loyalty to the U.S. government. Nine leading members of the congregation urged him to silence this public rumor and follow the Presbyterian General Assembly and most other Northern Presbyterian churches by condemning rebellion and forcefully sustaining the government. In particular, they implored him to pray publicly for God to bless and preserve the Union and give victory to its armies. Most members of Central Presbyterian, they insisted, attended Sunday worship with the war weighing heavily on their minds and causing their emotions to be "imbued with high and holy patriotism." They truly appreciated his "heart-searching expositions of God's word" but claimed that his failure to pray in accordance with their deepest desires "distracts our councils, paralyses our efforts[,] closes our purses, and prevents a proper devotional feeling in church."[12]

Despite his busy schedule, on the following day Plumer crafted a carefully worded nine-page rejoinder. To prove his allegiance to the government, he outlined five biblical principles of Christian citizenship that he had scrupulously followed. He had honored rulers, prayed for them in private and public devotions, paid taxes, obeyed all laws, and always regarded the decisions of fallible elected officials with the best intentions. In fact, he was so careful to avoid giving offense that he had abstained from voting since moving to Allegheny. Numerous people had complimented his apolitical stance "because they hear from me no prayer or sentiment in which they cannot heartily unite."[13]

His response failed to convince these apprehensive church members, who found his definition of loyalty deficient. The nation's future hung in the balance, yet he conducted services as if the Union remained intact and the land unstained by blood. They reiterated their demand for a conspicuous display of patriotism, particularly public prayer "asking God's blessing upon *our Armies*" and entreating him to preserve "the best Government which God has ever given to man." The trustees did not directly allege that Plumer's neutrality was a cloak for harboring traitorous sympathies, but they implied that it could be the case and that many local residents and some church members had construed it as such. "He that is not for the Government is against it," they insisted in no uncertain terms. "There is no middle ground in the church or outside the church." If this warning did not stir him to action, they hoped that a less than veiled economic threat would. They initially had planned to solicit subscriptions toward the debt of the new building the Sunday following the dedication but decided to postpone this endeavor to give him another opportunity to demonstrate his loyalty openly and thereby avert "the danger of a dissolution of your congregation."[14]

These ominous words reached him the evening before the Sunday dedication, but he seemingly took them in stride. Within the next forty-eight hours he spoke directly with one of the signatories who expressed complete satisfaction with his answer, and a third party informed him that his response had assured all the trustees.[15] Undoubtedly encouraged by these positive interviews, Plumer may have regarded the matter settled. The lack of any immediate action by the trustees suggests that they determined either to defer to their pastor's prerogative to lead worship according to his conscience, to place the unity of the church above their particular preferences, or to wait until a more opportune time to press the issue.

The war dragged on through winter, and Plumer continued to ignore it in church. During this time anxious civilians rarely received encouraging news from the front, but a successful Union counterattack on the second day of brutal fighting at Pittsburg Landing, Tennessee, and the capture of the Confederate garrison on Island No. 10 boosted Northern morale. On April 10, 1862, Abraham Lincoln issued a proclamation attributing these "signal victories" to "Almighty God" and urged citizens to thank him for his aid, to supplicate him to comfort the grieving, and to pray for the nation's leaders during public worship. Seizing this opportunity, one church member entreated Plumer to comply with this decree. The resolute clergyman declined to commit himself and vaguely replied, "'I will do the best I can.'"[16] When Sunday came and he failed to read the proclamation, mention the recent battles in prayer, or invoke blessings on the Union army, his critics had what they considered to be conclusive evidence of his inadequate loyalty.

In a last-ditch effort to persuade him to adopt their position, the concerned faction again beseeched him to pray in accordance with their patriotic feelings. They had considered it "a *religious duty*" to give their sons to fight for the Union's preservation, and having their pastor supplicate God to bless the army and vindicate its cause seemed a requisite obligation. But instead of offering inspiring prayers with "warm, glowing sentiment[s] of patriotism in sympathy with our loved & suffering Country," Plumer had offered what appeared to be formal, perfunctory petitions that "manifested but the stern demands of Christianity as they rest upon the conscience of every professor of Christ's religion under whatever government he may live—Christian or Pagan." Furthermore, his utter disregard for Lincoln's proclamation when he knew their specific wishes confirmed that his opinions conflicted with those of most of the congregation. While they claimed to have no desire to harm "the cause of Christ in our own church," they nevertheless held out the possibility of calling a congregational meeting to resolve their differences.[17]

By threatening formal action, these influential members hoped to pressure Plumer to capitulate. His twenty-two page response, a wide-ranging epistle containing a fiery defense of his convictions juxtaposed with tender appeals for compassion, attests to the gravity of the situation. As an accomplished Bible expositor, Plumer defended himself from Scripture. In response to his critics' appropriation of the verse, "'He that is not with me is against me,'" an aphorism he called "a favorite text of persecutors of opinion's sake in all ages," he pointed out the converse from Luke 9:50, "He that is not against me is for me." He reminded them of the biblical precept to exercise Christian charity in all things and further rebuked them by listing examples of false accusations of "sedition [and] conspiracy" made with the intention of silencing God's representatives. Elijah, Mordecai, Jeremiah, and ultimately Jesus were all charged with defying or undermining civil authorities, and by identifying with them he cast his opponents as furthering the evil designs of "the adversary" by "cover[ing] with suspicion & odium" a faithful minister.

Having placed himself in the ranks of those persecuted for the sake of righteousness, Plumer directly addressed the subject of his patriotism. "Patriotism is a good thing," he acknowledged, "but patriotism will save neither you nor me." As a minister his chief objective in life was to convince people to turn to Christ, not to make them patriotic. Nevertheless, he loved his country intensely and maintained that loyal citizens displayed their patriotism differently. Naturally unassuming, he had attempted to keep his personal life private, but their allegations of disloyalty left him no alternative but to boast about his patriotic deeds. He had stayed awake entire nights praying for the nation and wounded soldiers. Numerous religious tracts he had written reached countless soldiers and sailors, and he had received letters testifying to spiritual awakenings stimulated by these leaflets.[18] Furthermore, his loyalty encompassed more than spiritual devotion, for prior to war he had published his views opposing the Union's breakup. Over the last year he had generously given money to meet the temporal needs of soldiers and their families. As a loyal citizen he had performed these patriotic actions without compulsion; but as a clergyman he refused to tolerate anyone "to prescribe to me what I shall say in prayer or in preaching." His leading of public worship was not haphazard; he carefully chose or wrote his prayers, conversed with ministerial friends about the style and substance of their prayers, and used many historic liturgical forms. While he supplicated God on behalf of "'the country, its rulers[, and] its people,'" his purposeful exclusion of any reference to the war or politics allowed him to minister to all people regardless of party affiliation, drew commendation from several congregants, and enabled him to speak for "him whose Kingdom is not of this world." Indeed, he considered it "a great compliment" when they depicted his ministrations as nothing more or less than the fundamentals of Christianity taught the world over irrespective of forms of government.

If this vindication of his loyalty failed to win over his critics, Plumer hoped that an earnest appeal to any remaining personal affection for him might convince them to let matters be. He would not resign, for he believed that God had called him to preach there and had blessed the ministry bountifully. Leaving under a cloud of alleged disloyalty would likely result in his forced separation from the seminary, where enrollment had grown from fifty-six his first semester on faculty to 157,[19] and he could never surrender "such a field of usefulness." Finally, he feared for his personal safety if driven from the church, for as a defrocked minister he might be vulnerable to "some of the worst forms of persecution & outrage." He did not seek martyrdom but would accept "expatriation or a violent death" if God willed it. Plumer knew that none of them sought to bring such an ignoble end upon him, but their dogged determination to make him pray for the success of Union arms and his equally steadfast resolve to keep the war out of public worship had brought them to this impasse. "I honestly believe the course I pursue," he maintained, "is, in the main, most for God's glory & the salvation of men." If none of these pleas aroused their sympathy, he hoped to soften their hearts by recalling that several of them had come to faith in Christ through his ministry. In fact, one of the signatories, William H. Forsyth, had already expressed sorrow that the rift had occurred.[20]

Plumer did not mail the letter immediately, and any compassionate feelings he might have evoked were likely stifled as a result of a postscript he added two days later. In the interim he learned that some people had criticized him for neglecting to read Lincoln's proclamation the preceding Sunday. Clearly irritated, he appended several reasons for doing so. In the past he had never recited from the pulpit decrees by elected officials, and he failed to see why he should treat this announcement any differently. In his opinion, "Jesus Christ & Jesus Christ alone, not the Governor of the commonwealth, nor the President of a nation, has a right to be heard in the house of God." In addition, Christians gathered on Sunday to celebrate Christ's resurrection from the dead, and he maintained that the day should be wholly devoted to religious matters rather than "celebrating victories that have filled ten thousand habitations with wailings." This rationale for separating the sacred from the secular would have surprised no one who knew him, but the dissatisfied members might have been taken aback when he added, "Sometimes, in civil wars, when the liberties of a people are leaving them, & the government of a country is rapidly assuming the form of a despotism, proclamations are issued as tests of loyalty."[21]

This statement offers a rare glimpse into Plumer's personal political views, and his critics likely interpreted it as a stab at the Lincoln administration. In fact, if they could have read some of his private correspondence, they would have discovered additional evidence to satisfy their desire to remove him from the church. Shortly before South Carolina's secession, Plumer had revealed his belief that "the South has been very badly treated" and was beset by unnamed Northern "aggressions." Although he considered secession illegitimate, after the war's commencement his willingness to end it by nearly any means—either letting the South separate through an "honorable settlement" or holding a constitutional convention to address their interests—would have stigmatized him in their minds as an antiwar Democrat, doughface, and traitor. Plumer most likely considered Lincoln's proclamation to be little more than a public loyalty test and recognized that passing it would violate his conscientious scruples against mixing religion and politics. Failing it, however, might prove his undoing.[22]

His twenty-two–page letter neither persuaded his discontented church members nor cowed them into silent submission. Indeed, they continued to insist that the war was spiritual in nature. God had allowed it to purge the nation of its sins before restoring the newly sanctified government. Praying for Union victory during Sunday worship was therefore essential for them to cultivate proper "*religious* feelings." Just as Plumer had wielded Scripture to support his position, they turned to the Old Testament and compiled several examples of religious leaders supporting combat, supplicating God before or during battle, and thanking God after Israel's military triumphs. If only he could adopt their position and ask God to bless the Union army, then the church could once again enjoy spiritual unity; but if his conscience would not allow this, then they would bring the matter before the congregation.[23]

As they probably anticipated, Plumer again held his ground and asserted that the war was a political matter. Battles would continue, prove indecisive, and ultimately fail to end hostilities between North and South. President Lincoln had said as much in his inaugural address,[24] and in his mind his agreement with the president's prewar remarks further bolstered his conviction that "no number of victories, however great, will bring us peace." Their continual harping about their "*religious* feelings" being stifled because of his refusal to pray for Union victories demonstrated that they had placed their subjective, personal desires over "the Holy Scriptures[, which] alone determine all right *religious* belief." The Bible, of course, never spoke directly of "this war" in America, so no one should claim to know God's intentions by it. Far from condoning war, Jesus had warned that anyone who took up the sword would die by it. Plumer's antiwar stance was far from a justification of pacifism for its own sake; he opposed the sectional conflict because he considered it antithetical to the gospel. "I believe the general spirit of the Gospel is peace," he insisted, and "Christianity will yet abolish all war by the power of the very precepts it now inculcates." Furthermore, the Old Testament examples of Israel praying for victory in battle occurred under a theocracy, and their triumph accorded with God's revealed will. The book of Judges recorded a more appropriate comparison when it described a "dreadful civil war" between the men of Benjamin and the other tribes of Israel. After three days of fighting and 65,000 casualties, the victorious Israelites "'came to the house of God, & lifted up their voices, & wept'" because of their slaughtered kindred. Unable to pray for Union victory in a war between brothers in the flesh and in Christ, Plumer contended that every battle, regardless of its outcome, should elicit weeping rather than thanksgiving. If his disgruntled church members could not accept these views as scriptural and loyal, then their actions, humanly speaking, would likely determine his future status with the church and seminary.[25]

Nearly six months after the initial exchange of letters, no amount of arguments, explanations, or appeals contained in sixty-five pages of correspondence altered either Plumer's or the dissatisfied church members' opinions about the proper content of public prayer during services at Central Presbyterian Church. On the evenings of May 12 and 13, the session of the church held a congregational meeting, and the disaffected party presented nine patriotic resolutions supporting the government and the war and calling for Plumer to pray publicly for the success of Union arms. Before discussing the motions, the pastor's supporters put forward two substitute resolutions, which asserted that no grounds existed for considering his removal. Plumer then held the floor for nearly two hours, condemning the proceedings as "unpresbyterial" and a display of "'congregationalism of the worst sort.'" According to his detractors, he preempted a vote on the resolutions by bringing up tangential issues and pleading for sympathy. The congregation instead adopted the substitute measure by an overwhelming vote of those members present, 111 to 24, thereby nullifying the need to deliberate over the first set of resolutions.[26]

Foiled in this attempt to prove that the majority of the congregation shared a desire for Plumer to deliver patriotic prayers in church, approximately sixty members, led by ruling elder Richard Bard, withdrew from Central Church and on June 5 presented a memorial of their grievances to Allegheny Presbytery. After hearing all the written evidence when it convened on June 10, the following day the presbytery heard testimony from both camps. The newspaper reported that Plumer "ably defend[ed]" his loyalty to the Union and denounced the "wicked" whispering campaign that he believed had created the unrest. A committee of five individuals ultimately decided in favor of the memorialists, concluding that secular appeals for prayer for the government and its armies should be followed in public worship. Although the committee deplored bringing into church mundane political questions over which citizens might disagree, they regarded the present war to preserve the Union and the Constitution as possessing "sacred character." Finally, they recommended appointing another committee to mediate between the offended parties to restore congregational unity.

The committee's vindication of the memorialists prompted some presbyters to rail against Plumer. William Annan questioned the validity of Central Presbyterian's vote to adopt the second set of resolutions, for less than half of the voting members had approved the measure. Furthermore, he alleged that ministers who opposed the so-called politicization of the pulpit by ignoring issues of national import had traditionally done so to defend slavery. John F. McLaren denounced Plumer's views on political preaching and remarked that any man ought to be able to defend his loyalty, "*if he has any*," in two minutes. These less than implicit allegations that he at least sympathized with the South, if not being utterly disloyal, provoked Plumer, who stood and denounced them as utterly fallacious. Annan and McLaren then asked their affronted colleague to identify the insulting portions of their comments, but he declined. After the tension died down, the presbytery unanimously endorsed the committee's recommendations. Plumer commented that he sided with the majority "*because he approved of the resolutions*."[27]

The congregation of Central Presbyterian took the presbytery's decision in stride and on June 18 resolved to retain him as minister. In their opinion, his public prayers for the country and its rulers had completely complied with all biblical guidelines and "expressed comprehensively the wants of a Christian and patriotic people." The congregation truly hoped that the memorialists would return to the church but held no ill feelings if they wished to withdraw permanently.[28]

Because the local press published detailed reports of the controversy, it became difficult for citizens to avoid forming an opinion about Plumer. Most letter writers and editors denounced him, with one particularly harsh critic referring to him euphemistically as a clergyman "of *Southern* habits and proclivities" who attempted to hide his disloyalty behind the cloak of "piety, usefulness, . . . [and] exclusive devotion to what [he] call[s] 'the gospel' [and] 'preaching the cross.'" Even if he ignored the newspapers, on June 22 Plumer witnessed firsthand the depth of his unpopularity. While attending Sunday evening services at Christ Methodist Episcopal Church in Pittsburgh, the officiating pastor summoned him to the pulpit to pray. The presiding minister may have hoped to show support by extending the hand of fellowship, but his ill-advised gesture flopped. Before Plumer could begin, "a considerable number of people skedaddled from the church" in protest over his position on the war.[29]

He had little time to ponder this public repudiation, for two days later the committee appointed by the presbytery met at Central Church with the hope of reconciling the divided parties. The memorialists, who now numbered ninety-one and comprised one third of the congregation, insisted that he either pray for Union victory or resign. If the majority sustained him as pastor, they demanded that their financial contributions toward the new building, which amounted to $4,927, be reimbursed. His supporters, who totaled 174 members and pewholders but had contributed only $3,465 to the church's construction, contended that the memorialists had forfeited their financial stake by withdrawing. After much discussion, neither side acceded to the other's demands.[30] However, ten days later the congregation offered to refund the nearly five thousand dollars on condition that the memorialists surrender all claims to the property, building, name, and charter of Central Presbyterian Church. Both sides unanimously approved this agreement, thereby effecting, from the congregation's standpoint, a mutually satisfactory split.[31]

Allegheny Presbytery, however, still had to officially sanction the division. At its meeting on July 8, Dr. Elisha P. Swift, head of the committee assigned to resolve the dispute, blamed Plumer for the schism and recommended that the presbytery either call for his resignation or accept the congregation's amicable separation. Lengthy debate revealed that several men clearly favored his removal. One minister claimed that the public derided Central Presbyterian "as the 'Secession Church,'" and neither it nor the seminary would thrive by employing a disloyal clergyman. Another preacher alleged that Southerners praised Plumer as a Northern supporter of the Confederacy. A few men disapproved his course but accepted the congregation's decision based on majority rule. On several occasions, Plumer interjected to explain his actions and defend his loyalty, but he could not sway some men's opinions. John F. McLaren remarked that the sample prayer Plumer had submitted for examination was "a beautiful composition" but "*evasive*," and Dr. Aaron Williams added that his omitting a specific petition for the Union army's success fell short of the patriotic standard that "the circumstances of the time require." After this extended discussion, six presbyters voted for Plumer's resignation and six opposed it. Placed in the unenviable position of breaking the tie, moderator David A. Cunningham sided with the nays. There is no record of Plumer's immediate reaction, but he assuredly took some comfort that the presbytery had allowed him to remain as pastor of Central Presbyterian. If such a narrow vote could be considered a victory, it was a pyrrhic one indeed.

After a recess, presbyters discussed the church's division and financial settlement. Several men feared that allowing Plumer to remain as pastor and sanctioning the separation would give a public impression that the presbytery had endorsed his apolitical position. To offset this misperception, they proposed patriotic resolutions to demonstrate their unquestionable loyalty. McLaren desired a resolution denouncing Plumer's stance as unbiblical and "subversive" to government. But instead of singling him out by name, the presbytery unanimously (excepting Plumer, who received permission to abstain from voting) adopted three resolutions that denounced the rebellion as "desperately wicked," maintained that all Christians had a responsibility "to seek its overthrow," and asserted that all ministers must pray for God to uphold the government and to "give success to our armies." As one unnamed member later explained, the resolutions made it clear that the presbytery, far from sustaining Plumer as pastor of Central Church, wholly repudiated his position on the war. Furthermore, the last resolution in particular "was intended directly to condemn Dr. Plumer's course" in failing to pray for Union victories. However, because he technically was not "*on trial*" for his views and no person had formally sought to have him removed from his office, the presbytery could merely recommend his resignation. Failing to do this, the patriotic members wished to avoid the least hint of having "*any sympathy with secession, or with Dr. Plumer's neutrality.*"[32]

Plumer may not have been formally tried by Allegheny Presbytery, but for all practical purposes he was being examined in the court of public opinion. A verdict of insufficient loyalty there might shut the door to future ministry opportunities, and one man in particular determined to sway popular opinion against him. David McKinney, editor of Pittsburgh's *Presbyterian Banner*, thoroughly doubted Plumer's loyalty and emphatically insisted that he should not teach seminarians. His sullied reputation would hinder Western Theological Seminary's ability to raise money and attract students, and his "defective or erroneous" interpretation of biblical passages on government and citizenship would lead astray the church's future leaders. If this biting editorial did not ruin completely Plumer's already tarnished reputation among readers of his paper, McKinney also printed a nearly month-old letter by "New Jersey" in which the author reviled Plumer as a traitor whose refusal to pray for the Union army had done "more to strengthen the hands of the rebellion" than if twelve of Pittsburgh's leading politicians had defected to the Confederacy. The unnamed writer noted that Union officers and provost marshals in occupied Southern cities had closed churches and arrested preachers for inadequate loyalty, and he urged civil authorities to silence Plumer if the Presbyterian church declined to do so.[33]

The personal hostility evident in these attacks left Plumer little choice but to defend himself publicly. He approached James Allison, pastor of the Presbyterian church in Sewickley and former editor and proprietor of the Banner, about rebutting McKinney in print. Allison admitted that McKinney's methods were insensitive and offensive, but he nevertheless gave several legitimate reasons—most notably that the editor rented a pew at his church—for steering clear of the controversy. Likely disappointed that he could not enlist Allison's aid, Plumer instead sent for publication a brief "card" affirming his loyalty. He attempted to silence all rumors that he supported the Confederacy by praising the "noble Constitution" and affirming his desire to live out his days on Union soil. As a Christian citizen, he regarded the U.S. government and the president as God's ordained authorities over him. In addition, he pledged to defend this government "against any and every attempt to destroy it," specifically promising to uphold it with his words, actions, prayers, possessions, and even his own life. In fact, he always had believed secession to be illegitimate and nothing short of "revolution." These views had been known "for many years," and he repeated them again publicly to clear up any "misunderstanding of my true positions." Plumer considered himself to be a model citizen of indisputable loyalty, and under normal circumstances he may have been right. The war, however, raised the stakes for what passed as loyalty, and as a prominent figure under public scrutiny he fell short of the expectations of the times. Perhaps nothing drove this home more pointedly than when he awoke on July 22 and saw a twenty-five foot Confederate flag hanging from a tree outside his door.[34]

Plumer's statement received mixed responses. One local critic complained that he had yet to condemn the rebellion as treasonous but instead labeled it a "revolution," which could be construed positively by comparing it to the War for Independence. James G. Monfort, editor of Cincinnati's Presbyter, was simply bewildered, uncertain whether or not to believe the damaging reports from the Banner or take the apology at face value, which appeared to exonerate Plumer of all charges of disloyalty. The New York Evangelist described him as "loyal at last" but alleged that he had delivered this "rather grandiloquent exposition" out of desperation to preserve his pastorate and future influence. In Richmond, the *Central Presbyterian* considered his card "*a lamentable failure.*" Ambiguous enough to appease his Northern opponents, the statement instead pleased almost no one, infuriated many Southerners who felt betrayed by their presumed supporter, and caused editor William Brown to rebuke Plumer for "'paltering in a double sense.'"[35] While public reaction was either ambivalent or unfavorable, in private he received encouraging words from ministerial colleagues and friends who deplored "the crusade" against him. These supporters denounced his critics as "extreme abolitionists," especially singling out McKinney, and they encouraged him to stand firm against attacks printed in the *Banner* and "every other slanderous and dirty abolition sheet." Some disagreed with his reasons for not praying for Union victories, but they "never doubted" his loyalty and reckoned that his card "should satisfy every reasonable man" of his personal devotion to the country.[36]

The *Banner* certainly had handled Plumer severely, particularly in publishing the letter by "New Jersey." After Charles Hodge learned of it, he assured his former pupil that no one affiliated with or even sympathetic to Princeton Seminary had composed it. Nevertheless, he could not divulge the writer's identity. Signing his brief letter "very truly your friend," Hodge's more than perfunctory endearment surely encouraged Plumer. Armed with this small token of support from the distinguished professor, Plumer asked McKinney to publish the epistle. Unwilling to accommodate this request, the editor instead disclosed in the *Banner* that no person with ties to any seminary had penned the letter. Two days later, he implored Plumer "not to involve Dr. Hodge in your troubles. He would be injured, and the Redeemer's cause wounded, by the publication of the note." Hodge had written "some able articles against the rebellion" for the *Biblical Repertory and Princeton Review*, and McKinney seemed flummoxed by his apparent willingness to stand by Plumer. "I trust that he is *sound*, and . . . I would be sorry, on account of his obstinacy in maintaining a *crotchet*, to help to bring him under suspicion. If once generally suspected, he must retire, or do injury to the ministry & the church."[37] McKinney's forthright acknowledgement must have deeply troubled Plumer. According to the editor's skewed thinking, it would be tragic if Hodge became tainted with disloyalty, for he would be ruined and the church would suffer. Plumer, in contrast, was evidently expendable, and the church could sacrifice him to satisfy some people's demands for conspicuous patriotism.

Still unconvinced of his loyalty and unrelenting in their pursuit, some critics attempted to raise a groundswell of public opposition by agitating for his removal from Western Theological Seminary. McKinney called for his resignation, and another opponent urged the directors and trustees to suspend the seminary's "leading" professor so that it did not become "a nest where traitors are to be hatched to scatter treason broadcast from all the Old School Presbyterian pulpits of the land." In mid-August, seven members of the seminary's board of directors, including forty-two-year-old Robert McKnight, who represented Pennsylvania's 22nd district in Congress, requested a meeting to discuss Plumer's status at the seminary, and a date was set for September 18.[38] When not in Washington, McKnight served as an elder of Central Presbyterian, and he had not joined the memorialists' camp. With the Republican convention less than two weeks away, one unnamed constituent alleged that the second term congressman sanctioned Plumer's course by worshiping at Central Presbyterian, and this dubious association called into question his discretion and, implicitly, his suitableness to return to Congress. McKnight bristled at this accusation and publicly declared that he in no way endorsed Plumer's apolitical stance. He desired unity and remained optimistic that "sound judgment" would still prevail and reunite the congregation. However, if the church offered no "clear and distinct" support for the Union, then he would part ways. This attempt to distance himself from his pastor evidently came too late, and his relationship with Plumer proved to be a millstone that sunk his political career. Shortly before the convention on September 1, he withdrew his name from consideration, choosing "to decline a contest which, in the heated state of the public mind, could only result to his injury."[39]

McKnight's inability to satisfy the patriotic demands of the public simply because of his church membership did not bode well for Plumer. Frequently maligned in the press, he attempted to carry on his ministerial duties amid the intensifying storm. However, his Presbyterian colleagues in western Pennsylvania had determined to purge him from their ranks. With Plumer conveniently absent because of a speaking engagement in Ohio, at the September 2 meeting of Allegheny Presbytery Dr. L. H. McAboy recommended that the presbytery reconsider its decision regarding Plumer's status as pastor of Central Church on the basis of his refusal to approve the patriotic resolutions passed at the previous gathering. After John F. McLaren, the resolution's author, contended for the propriety of the action, the presbyters determined that someone who had voted with the majority the previous meeting must second the motion. Because of absences of several members,[40] John Launitz quickly realized that he alone could move the initiative forward, and he "kept quiet." In a less than veiled threat, elder Thomas Nevin hinted that the matter might come up in a different and "*worse*" form, likely alluding to the possibility of pressing official charges against Plumer in a church court if Launitz obstructed the motion. Assured that his assent to the proposal would only open the floor for debate, he "reluctantly yielded" and seconded the motion. Once it carried, with only Launitz opposing, several presbyters vehemently condemned the absent pastor as indisputably disloyal because he had not supported that body's patriotic resolutions. The actual wording of the resolution, in contrast, only accused him of "reputed disloyalty" and blamed him for dividing his church, damaging the presbytery's reputation, and "encourag[ing] the public and armed enemies of our Government." One man thought a final decision should be postponed to a subsequent meeting, and Launitz pointed out that the nonattendance of many leading members, as Plumer's opponents had argued in an attempt to cast doubt on the verdict reached at the previous meeting,[41] would again give the impression that any decision was neither conclusive nor reflected the will of the entire presbytery. This reasoning swayed no one, and more presbyters again denounced Plumer. The vote was taken, and only Launitz opposed the resolution to recommend that Plumer resign from Central Church. The presbyters then passed additional measures entreating the memorialists to rejoin the congregation and urging the seminary's directors to suspend Plumer until the General Assembly's meeting in 1863. When the minutes were read, Launitz was aghast that the clerk had recorded all resolutions as having passed unanimously. He later regretted his timidity to correct the record and confessed to Plumer, "I felt the wrong which was done you & I could have wept aloud. Ever since I was troubled in mind & even sick in body."[42]

Forsaken by nearly every member of his presbytery, Plumer returned from Ohio to find a copy of the resolutions at his house. There is conflicting evidence as to whether or not he had been forewarned that the presbytery might act against him.[43] If he had advance knowledge, then he had simply resigned himself to the probability of an unfavorable decision. But if this news was completely unexpected, he gave no sign of astonishment or anger. Unquestionably grieved, on September 5 he notified his elders of the presbytery's action, instructed them to find replacements to fill the pulpit, and directed them to explain to the congregation "why I do not continue to preach to them & do other parts of the pastor's work." The following day he met with some elders, who requested the presbytery to convene at Central Presbyterian on September 19 to determine his status. The congregation gathered a few days later, expressed astonishment and dissatisfaction at the presbytery's decision, and resolved to retain Plumer as pastor. His future uncertain, he did not bemoan his trials but focused on his duties, inquiring of the other faculty members of the seminary if they wished him to begin teaching when the fall session opened on September 8 or wait for the result of the meeting of the directors on September 18. They replied in the affirmative, and for the next week and a half he quietly went about his work, likely praying for strength to survive the impending tempest which he must have known would soon engulf him. After family friend Samuel Irenæus Prime, a regular contributor to the Presbyterian *New-York Observer*, learned of Allegheny Presbytery's action, he felt "grief and indignation" over that body's "persecution" of Plumer. In his estimation, the self-effacing minister would "be the first martyr in the North to the accursed spirit of abolition fanaticism. I do not know a man in all the earth more entitled to the honor of dying for the truth."[44]

Knowing the intense opposition he faced, Plumer determined to bow out on his own terms rather than give his critics another opportunity to flay him publicly. On September 17, which coincidentally proved to be the bloodiest single day of the fratricidal war that he deplored, Plumer wrote his resignation letter from the seminary. After reading it aloud in his study at home, "he bowed his head on the table & wept bitterly, saying '[I]t is all dark to me. I have more lectures prepared than I can deliver. I love the young men & feel that I can do more good among them than any where else.'"[45]

When the board of directors convened the following day at 2 p.m., from all rumors intent on forcing his resignation, Plumer unexpectedly arose immediately after the meeting came to order, pulled a sheet of paper from his pocket, and declared, "I hereby resign my professorship in this institution. I take the step not because I do not love my work here. On the contrary, it is truly pleasant to me. But my peace is destroyed, my life is embittered, & my health is suffering from cruel calumnies, which I have borne silently & as patiently as I could, & from the line of conduct pursued towards me by some of the Directors, & approved, as I fear, by others of your number." After this unanticipated announcement he returned home. Now needing only to approve the resignation, a seemingly easy procedural matter, the twenty-one directors nevertheless spent five hours discussing Plumer's lack of loyalty and the necessity of combining "the interests of our country and our religion." According to a secondhand report two professors, Drs. Melancthon W. Jacobus and William M. Paxton, each spoke for five minutes, ostensibly defending Plumer to some degree but ultimately being forced to yield the floor. A local newspaper reporter recounted that Samuel Galloway, former U.S. congressman from Ohio, subsequently gave a "soul inspiring" speech portraying Plumer as a Southern sympathizer, and in his mind any "sympathy with rebellion may be proved to be as much a sin against true morality, as a little drunkenness or shuffling a few cards." The directors did not "authoritatively" condemn Plumer as disloyal, according to one member of the board, but they concluded that numerous Presbyterian churches connected with the seminary disapproved of his views and desired his removal. Finally voting at 7 p.m., the directors "unanimously accepted" his resignation.[46]

Still waiting at home, Plumer evidently expected to be summoned back for further explanation after the board discussed his resignation; instead, he learned of the decision from a passerby. As word spread many students dropped in, some weeping openly and others relating how they had been converted under his preaching. In fact, thirty-four students, likely all seniors, had sent resolutions to the board of directors defending their mentor and avowing that they had never detected "any sentiment in the slightest degree indicating disloyalty in himself, or in the slightest degree tending to encourage disloyalty in others." The board, however, disregarded the students' resolutions until after officially approving Plumer's departure. (Four disgruntled students protested by transferring to other seminaries.) On September 18, 1862, Western Theological Seminary lost arguably its greatest asset, a seasoned minister who for more than seven years had devoted himself to training students and who, according to one estimation, had traveled over thirty thousand miles at his own expense to promote the seminary and self-lessly spent between six and nine thousand dollars of his own money to assist needy students. Because he already had determined to submit to the presbytery's decision and leave his congregation, despite the majority's support, he resigned his professorship to make a clean break from Allegheny, escape his dogged pursuers, and look for a fresh start elsewhere.[47]

At 2 p.m. the following day Allegheny Presbytery met at Central Church. Only a bare outline of what transpired there has survived. From the perspective of his supporters, it was the shameful culmination of a months' long witch-hunt. "Satan seemed to have been let loose," a family friend recounted. "To tell anything would require sheets. Dear Uncle Sam says his prayer is to be able to forget the wickedness seen there." The newspaper simply reported that Plumer sought a discharge from his pastorate, but his church members submitted a formal remonstrance against this separation. After much discussion among the presbyters, Plumer delivered an emotional speech, perhaps defending himself one last time, forgiving his enemies, or even claiming the mantle of martyrdom. After his address, the presbyters formally accepted his resignation and dismissed him in good standing to the Presbytery of Burlington, New Jersey, although William Annan and James Park, Jr., who evidently wanted to destroy him completely, opposed releasing him with a clean slate. (During the meeting, Park Jr. allegedly threatened to "head a mob to hang" the sixty-year-old minister before he could leave town.) From all appearances, it seems the presbytery attempted to conceal from the public specific details of the meeting and muzzle dissent, for upon motion it elected to exclude the remonstrance from the official record of the proceedings.[48]

After several nerve-racking hours, the presbytery adjourned and Plumer returned to his Allegheny home for the last time. He packed some clothes, ate something, gave instructions about selling the furniture and storing his books, and left in a carriage. Heavy-hearted friends bid him farewell, and several students ran beside the carriage on its way to the train depot. The next day more friends streamed into the house, consoling his wife and daughters and asking for mementos of their beloved pastor. On Sunday at Central Presbyterian many church members wept openly. Others stayed away, protesting the presbytery's action and fearing that it might again intrude and force a reunion with the memorialists. After witnessing firsthand the congregation's affection for her husband, Plumer's wife Eliza encouraged him to reciprocate his love for them. On September 28, the congregation listened to a heartfelt farewell letter that betrayed no signs of bitterness or enmity. Always a staunch believer in God's sovereignty, Plumer emphasized the supremacy of Christ, the importance of trusting and obeying God, the futility and sinfulness of holding grudges, and the necessity of maintaining unity. He thanked them for their unswerving support and admonished them not to fret over his hardships, for he remained content in the Lord despite losing home and employment.[49]

If he ever entertained second thoughts about giving up the fight in Allegheny, they were likely fleeting. His foes had relentlessly pursued him and shattered his tranquility, dragging into the public limelight a naturally private man who wanted nothing more than to preach the gospel and avoid making "any noise in the world." His immediate future looked uncertain, but he did not complain of mistreatment. "I have no grudges, no hatred, no resentments," he wrote to a close pastoral friend. Ever mindful to view his circumstances through a theological grid, he added, "We are not hurt till our souls are hurt; & our souls are not hurt till sin defiles them."[50]

Supportive friends offered needed comfort and helped lift his spirits. David A. Cunningham, who had cast the deciding vote to sustain him at the July meeting of presbytery, explained that he had accepted the resignation for Plumer's own good because so many presbyters "seemed determined to get you away at all risks" and to "destroy your usefulness." Cunningham's defense of Plumer had even motivated a few members of his church to question his loyalty and unsuccessfully attempt to raise a public ruckus against him. Brooklyn's staunch conservative Henry Van Dyke never doubted his counterpart's loyalty and related "how much I love and honour you for not sacrificing your own conscience to the demands of popular passion." George H. Fullerton, a former member of Allegheny Presbytery who had recently resigned as chaplain of the 1st Ohio Volunteers after one year's service, likewise affirmed Plumer's loyalty. In his opinion, the minister's demise stemmed from "the frothy zeal of some w[ou]ld-be patriots who, because they cant or wont go abroad to fight, must hunt up some enemy at home who is more convenient." Remembering how in 1860 many of these same men had opposed his entry into the presbytery for no apparent reason, he concluded that they were "the most narrowminded, bigoted set of men I ever saw." Samuel Irenæus Prime hoped someday to vindicate Plumer by publishing an account of "one of the most remarkable cases of irreligious persecution in the annals of the church." Extremely incensed by the whole affair, he confessed, "Nothing would now more gratify the old Adam in me than to gibbet those ministerial dragons on the gallows of public & righteous indignation. But it is more Christlike to pray 'Father forgive them' though we cannot add 'they know not what they do.' They do know & this is their sin & shame."[51]

Plumer's friends in Allegheny did not sit idly after their pastor left town. Thus far, his opponents had effectively used the press to arouse public hostility against him, but his supporters hoped to rehabilitate his image by publishing their remonstrance against the presbytery's action. They claimed that by pressuring Plumer to resign, the presbytery had blatantly disregarded the congregation's majority and their settlement with the memorialists. This needless interference had damaged the "good name" and patriotic record of Central Presbyterian, which according to one report had furnished eighteen volunteers to the Union army.[52] Furthermore, the presbytery had punished Plumer for not endorsing resolutions which one presbyter later admitted had been passed in order to censure him. Surely it was the height of folly to expect a man to approve measures condemning himself, and by resisting this "test" Plumer had demonstrated "manly firmness" against "tyranny" rather than "disloyalty" as they had alleged.[53]

Allegheny Presbytery, of course, disputed this interpretation and attempted to "vindicate" its handling of the Plumer imbroglio. Presbyters rationalized their vote to omit the remonstrance from the official records, claiming that it was too lengthy and that its absence saved the signers' reputations. Rather than stifling dissent, they had shown "generosity and forbearance." This absurd explanation set the tone for a belabored rejoinder in which the presbytery denied any wrongdoing and refused to accept the majority's desire to retain Plumer as pastor. It alleged that the reputations of Western Theological Seminary, Central Church, and Allegheny Presbytery had all been damaged in the community; indeed "the whole Presbyterian Church was suffering in public estimation" because one man declined to pray for Union victories during Sunday services. Public opinion certainly had turned against Plumer, but the presbytery had engendered and intentionally encouraged much of it by broadcasting the affair in the secular and religious press. By deliberately fueling the fire of zealous patriotism, it ensured that the public would endorse its decision to eliminate Plumer in accordance with the will of the outspoken and more affluent minority. The presbytery recognized that once it hung the albatross of disloyalty around Plumer's neck, no prominent figure would stand by him for fear of being discredited by association. As one of his sympathizers accurately perceived, "When a public hue & cry is raised against a man, even those who do not join in it are too apt silently to acquiesce."[54]

After fleeing Allegheny and finding lodging in New Jersey, Plumer began searching for work. He did not lack invitations for temporary engagements. Prime offered him fifty dollars to write twelve "religious, practical and anecdotal articles" for the *New-York Observer*. James M. Macdonald, pastor of First Presbyterian in Princeton, requested him to preach and assist with communion on October 12. First Presbyterian of New Brunswick made a more permanent offer, and after a few Sundays the session was prepared to invite him to stay the winter or longer if he desired. However, "a busy-body" began circulating damaging articles from the Pittsburgh papers, one of the elders "became alarmed," and church leaders postponed the vote. In the meantime, his supporters, who purportedly represented about 90 percent of the congregation, cautiously "advised further delay or an abandonment of the whole matter."[55] He subsequently received an invitation to Philadelphia's Arch Street Presbyterian, likely aided by complimentary endorsements. Former colleague William M. Paxton assured him, "If any one should attempt to follow you with persecution let us know and we will block the game."[56] After preaching to an "overflowing audience" in mid-November, Plumer cheerfully accepted an offer to officiate at Arch Street for three months beginning the last day of November. "I love to preach," he asserted transparently, and "I am determined to preach as much as I can." Obviously encouraged by the offer of stable employment, he even joked about his earlier trials. "Patriotism & loyalty are sunk, or sinking so low in New York, that I went . . . there & preached a Thanksgiving Sermon. It takes an ex-professor to stir up the people rightly on such matters." In reality, he showed his true colors, passing over texts dealing with thankfulness and instead preaching from Isaiah 60:12 on "the ways in which nations may refuse to serve Christ in the Gospel" and "the perils of so doing."[57]

Once branded as disloyal, Plumer could not easily cast off such a debilitating reputation, and evidently some members of Arch Street Presbyterian objected to his preaching there. After making known his intention to part ways at the end of February, he traveled to Long Island and Boston for other engagements. An elder at Arch Street implored him to return to Philadelphia and preach the fourth Sunday of March, affirming that "very many of the congregation wish to hear you again." Seeking to avoid stirring up conflict or division, Plumer doubted the propriety of returning, but he deferred to the judgment of the elders.[58] It seems he preached a few more Sundays, but at some point in 1863 the church hired a full-time pastor. During the next eighteen months he resided in Philadelphia and, as many people desired to hear him, preached to "very large" audiences in public venues such as the concert hall.[59] In late September 1864, he began filling in at a church in Norwalk, Connecticut, and continued there through the first Sunday of 1865 when the congregation voted to look for a permanent minister. As in Philadelphia, many church members sincerely appreciated his preaching and lamented that the "little millen[n]ium" they enjoyed under him was interrupted by "the canker of *party* politics . . . entering into the house of God" because a few malcontents objected to him.[60] Although no one had ever produced tangible evidence of his disloyalty, he was tainted in many people's minds, even among conservative Old School Presbyterians. At the General Assembly of 1863, he lost his seat on the Board of Publication, primarily because one man pushed for his removal. Even the federal government treated him with suspicion, for the War Department refused to grant him permission to visit the son of a family friend imprisoned at Fort Lafayette. Not until the summer of 1865 and the war's end did Plumer finally emerge from the shadow of disloyalty and obtain a permanent position at Second Presbyterian Church in Pottsville, Pennsylvania.[61]

While Plumer's reputation of disloyalty followed him for the war's duration, forcing him to lead an almost nomadic existence and cutting short promising engagements, his departure from Allegheny left a considerable void in the community and cast a pall over many people's spirits. Seminary students whom he had mentored took his absence especially hard. One senior who withdrew informed him, "I hear frequently from Allegheny. The students seem restless. Many are discontented and would like to be away." One who stayed sadly confessed, "We miss you very much—in the lecture room, . . . in the prayer meeting[,] . . . & in the church. . . . I speak not of myself [alone] but for my class." William Paxton also struggled to move forward without his friend and admitted, "I lecture now as a mere formality. I cannot feel the same interest in the seminary." Whenever he walked by Plumer's empty house he felt his "indignation stirred at that savage spirit of persecution which drove you away." He hoped that Plumer would be vindicated someday and that his adversaries would repent of their wrongdoing and "invite you back."[62]

The memorialists, who began meeting in the seminary's chapel, were unable to find affordable land to purchase despite the nearly five thousand dollar settlement from Central Church. With attendance less than "encouraging," they even considered disbanding, but a philanthropic citizen donated a lot for a new building. In mid-April 1863 between fifty and sixty charter members formed the North Presbyterian Church of Allegheny, and in January 1866 they hired as pastor Archibald Alexander Hodge, son of Plumer's distinguished teacher.[63]

The members of Central Presbyterian, obliged to replace a beloved pastor, had difficulty finding a suitable successor.[64] Not until July 1863 did the church finally settle on Plumer's former student Thomas X. Orr, who as a senior the previous fall had signed the resolutions sustaining his teacher.[65] Although Orr and the men who followed him may have been entirely capable ministers in their own right, they likely were compared to Plumer. While visiting his daughter and son-in-law in Allegheny in May 1878, the venerable minister, now nearly seventy-six and comfortably situated as professor at Columbia Theological Seminary in South Carolina for almost twelve years, learned that the church was preparing to call him back as pastor. He attempted to head off this action and petitioned to have his name removed from consideration. Nevertheless, the congregation, "by a unanimous rising vote," offered him the pastorate of Central Church for the princely salary of ten thousand dollars per year. Without enumerating particular reasons, he declined the invitation.[66] Two years later he died.

William S. Plumer, according to one of his friends, was "crotchety and obstinate" in his views against praying for Union victories. At the same time, he was highly principled in adhering to his "conscientious opinions" and refusing to let anyone usurp his pastoral prerogative by dictating the substance of public worship. He accepted ostracism rather than cave in to the ultimatums of "some brethren [who] make too much of what the outside world clamors [for] and demands." Having met and in some ways exceeded the biblical requirements of good citizenship, Plumer considered himself to be loyal to the U.S. government. Doing more than what he already did, he believed, would hinder his ability to reach people of all political persuasions with the gospel. Although he may have been mistaken in this thinking, he professed, "I had rather suffer wrong than do wrong." Indeed, even after being forced to leave his home and the people he loved so dearly, he continued to fulfill his calling in life. "I am still allowed to preach his Gospel to the poor," he observed, "& that is a privilege never accorded to angels."[67]

Plumer's narrative highlights the difficulties of reaching a consensus definition of loyalty during the war. Nevertheless, his noted contemporary Horace Bushnell attempted to find one. In 1863, the New England Congregationalist asserted that loyalty lay in the realm of morality and religion rather than law. He maintained that "genuine loyalty" went beyond "fidelity to the Constitution" and consisted of voluntarily performing certain tasks, some of which—praying through the night and helping orphans and widows—Plumer had done. But Bushnell ultimately would have judged Plumer's loyalty to be deficient, for he concluded that loyalty was nothing less than "a political worship," the fusing of allegiances to God and state. Three weeks after Fort Sumter fell, Attorney General Edward Bates, a devout layman who considered Plumer "one of the brightest lights" of the Presbyterian church, pleaded, "I pray you [to] exert your influence to save the Church from the convulsions which now distract the Nation." Plumer consistently resisted blending the sacred and secular, but this mindset became increasingly rare as war progressed, to the point that in 1864 even Old School Presbyterians officially endorsed the Republican party's objectives. Most Northern Protestants seemingly prioritized their loyalty to a temporal Union, but Plumer "refused to make the kingdom that shall never end a mere appendage to political strifes." He paid a high price for his multiple loyalties.[68]

Notes

I thank Ken Hinkle and the staff of Princeton Theological Seminary's Special Collections for answering questions and photocopying letters from the Plumer Collection. Elizabeth M. Scott generously scanned the faculty minutes from the archives at Pittsburgh Theological Seminary. Sandra Bossert gained approval from Don Skemer, curator of manuscripts at Princeton's Firestone Library, to provide a digital copy of a vital letter before a looming editorial deadline. Jesse Spencer repeatedly secured microfilmed newspapers through interlibrary loan. All quotes are verbatim except a few cases where I removed superfluous commas to smooth sentence flow.

1. *Pittsburgh Gazette*, November 14, 1861; *Presbyterian Banner (Pittsburgh)*, November 23, 1861. Born in Beaver County, Pennsylvania, in 1802, Plumer grew up on the border between freedom and slavery. Because his merchant father plied his wares along the Ohio River, as a child Plumer lived near the river in Pennsylvania, Kentucky, and Ohio. As a teenager, he went to western Virginia and taught school near Charleston before embarking on his own studies at Lewisburg Academy. In 1825 he graduated from Washington College in Lexington, Virginia, and received additional training at Princeton Seminary. After being licensed to preach in New Jersey, for several years he paid his dues organizing churches in North Carolina and leading small assemblies in Virginia. Recognized as a powerful preacher, in 1834 he began a twelve-year pastorate at Richmond's First Presbyterian. During the General Assembly of 1837, he employed his persuasive oratory in favor of separation, and the following year he was elected moderator of the first Old School Presbyterian General Assembly. Leaving Richmond in 1846, he went to Baltimore for eight years, and as sectional tensions mounted in the early 1850s,

he clearly supported the Union and cautioned his Southern friends against secession. See William Henry Ruffner, *The History of Washington College, Now Washington and Lee University, during the First Half of the Nineteenth Century* (Baltimore: John Murphy & Co., 1893–1904), in Washington and Lee University Historical Papers, no. 5 (1895), 26–29.

2. Lewis G. Vander Velde depicted Plumer as the closest example of a pacifist minister in Old School Presbyterianism in *The Presbyterian Churches and the Federal Union 1861–1869* (Cambridge: Harvard University Press, 1932), 295–99. A student of local Pennsylvania Presbyterianism implied that Plumer's Southern ties caused him to be suspected of misplaced sympathies, and he faced additional difficulties because he resided in a section of Pittsburgh known for intense antislavery views. See George F. Swetnam, "The Growing Edge of Conscience," in *The Presbyterian Valley*, ed. William Wilson McKinney (Pittsburgh: Davis & Warde, 1958), 288–90. Edward J. Blum saw in Plumer's life a prime example of how popular sentiment had changed by the mid-1870s to embrace national reunion and white reconciliation at the expense of blacks. Spurned by patriotic Northerners and condemned in the public press during the war, in 1867 Plumer took refuge in the South to teach at Columbia Theological Seminary and in 1871 served as moderator of the southern Presbyterian General Assembly. Five years after the reunion of the Old and New School wings of northern Presbyterianism in 1869, he urged Southerners to renew fellowship with northern Presbyterians. His transformation complete, he received a standing ovation from Northerners at the General Assembly in Chicago in 1877. See *Reforging the White Republic: Race, Religion, and American Nationalism, 1865–1898* (Baton Rouge: Louisiana State University Press, 2005), 137–40.

3. William A. Blair, *With Malice Toward Some: Treason and Loyalty in the Civil War Era* (Chapel Hill: University of North Carolina Press, 2014), 36–37. For a synopsis of the differences between Old and New School Presbyterians and the reasons for their split, see Sydney E. Ahlstrom, *A Religious History of the American People* (New Haven: Yale University Press, 1972), 464–68.

4. For the best general introductions to this subject, see Randall M. Miller, Harry S. Stout, and Charles Reagan Wilson, ed., *Religion and the American Civil War* (New York: Oxford University Press, 1998), and George C. Rable, *God's Almost Chosen Peoples: A Religious History of the American Civil War* (Chapel Hill: University of North Carolina Press, 2010); Timothy L. Wesley, *The Politics of Faith During the Civil War* (Baton Rouge: Louisiana State University Press, 2013), 9.

5. C. C. Goen, *Broken Churches, Broken Nation: Denominational Schisms and the Coming of the Civil War* (Macon, Ga.: Mercer University Press, 1985), 70, 74; William S. Plumer (hereafter WSP), "My Fidelity to the Government," undated draft, William Swan Plumer Manuscript Collection, Special Collections, Princeton Theological Seminary Library (hereafter PTS; unless otherwise noted, all citations from this collection are from box 3); WSP to R. L. Dabney, March 13, 1861, R. L. Dabney Papers, Special Collections, Union Theological Seminary, Richmond, Virginia.

6. Rable, 197–200; Marcus J. McArthur, "Treason in the Pulpit: The Problem of Apolitical Preaching in Civil War Missouri," *Journal of Church and State* 53:4 (2011): 545–66; Dennis K. Boman, *Lincoln and Citizens' Rights in Civil War Missouri: Balancing Freedom and Security* (Baton Rouge: Louisiana State University Press, 2011), 104–6, 158–68.

7. For McPheeters, see Vander Velde, 305–25; Rable, 319–22; Marcus J. McArthur, "'There Can Be No Neutral Ground': Samuel B. McPheeters and the Collision of Church and State in St. Louis, 1860–1864," *Journal of Presbyterian History* 89, no. 1 (Spring/ Summer 2011): 17–26.

8. Bryon C. Andreasen, "Civil War Church Trials: Repressing Dissent on the Northern Home Front," in *An Uncommon Time: The Civil War and the Northern Home Front*, ed. Paul A. Cimbala and Randall M. Miller (New York: Fordham University Press, 2002), 214–42.

9. In 1863, Theodore P. Bucher resigned from Gettysburg's German Reformed Church because of insufficient patriotism, but a board composed of members of nearby sister churches exonerated him of all charges of disloyalty and instead reprimanded his accuser. See Wesley, 86–87.

10. Convicted of the latter charge and imprisoned in Fort Mifflin, Rutan received a presidential pardon. See Richard A. Sauers and Peter Tomasak, *The Fishing Creek Confederacy: A Story of Civil War Draft Resistance* (Columbia: University of Missouri Press, 2013), 109–10, 121–22.

11. Rable, 322. For the politicization of religion, see Richard J. Carwardine, *Evangelicals and Politics in Antebellum America* (New Haven: Yale University Press, 1993); Harry S. Stout, *Upon the Altar of the Nation* (New York: Viking, 2006); Sean A. Scott, *A Visitation of God: Northern Civilians Interpret the Civil War* (New York: Oxford University Press, 2011).

12. Richard Bard, T. F. Dale, John Patterson, Henry P. Schwartz, Samuel Riddle, William H. Forsyth, B. H. Painter, J. G. Coffin, and J. Painter to WSP, November 12, 1861, PTS. Bard was a ruling elder of Central Church, and five signatories served as trustees.

13. WSP to Richard Bard et al., November 14, 1861, PTS.

14. Richard Bard et al. to WSP, November 16, 1861, PTS.

15. WSP to Richard Bard et al., November 18, 1861, PTS.

16. *The Collected Works of Abraham Lincoln*, ed. Roy Basler et al. (9 vols.; New Brunswick, N.J.: Rutgers University Press, 1953–55), 5:185–86; WSP to T. F. Dale, Henry P. Schwartz, Hugh McIlhenny, J. G. Coffin, William H. Forsyth, Jacob Forsyth, J. Painter, Richard Bard, A. H. Dumont, John B. Sheriff, and William Kirkpatrick, April 17, 1862, PTS.

17. T. F. Dale et al. to WSP, April 16, 1862, PTS.

18. A soldier in the 52nd Pennsylvania testified that he had been converted after reading Plumer's tract "A Friendly Letter to a Young Man." Jerome T. Furman to WSP, November 28, 1861, PTS.

19. Princeton Seminary, by comparison, enrolled 170 students. See Vander Velde, 295.

20. WSP to T. F. Dale et al., April 17, 1862, PTS. Forsyth thenceforth left the ranks of the dissatisfied and stuck by Plumer to the bitter end.

21. *Pittsburgh Gazette*, April 19, 1862; Postscript (April 19, 1862) to WSP to T. F. Dale et al., April 17, 1862, PTS.

22. WSP to Phineas D. Gurley, December 1, 1860, William Swan Plumer Papers, David M. Rubenstein Rare Book & Manuscript Library, Duke University; WSP to "Hon. & Dear Sir," October 7, 1861, PTS, box 11.

23. T. F. Dale, Henry P. Schwartz, Richard Bard, John B. Sheriff, J. G. Coffin, William Kirkpatrick, A. H. Dumont, Hugh McIlhenny, and J. Painter to WSP, April 22, 1862, PTS.

24. Plumer's nearly verbatim quote from the inaugural read: "'Suppose you go to war, you cannot fight always; & when after much loss on both sides, & no gain on either, you cease fighting, the identical questions, as to terms of intercourse, are again upon you.'"

25. WSP to T. F. Dale et al., April 28, 1862, PTS.

26. *Presbyterian Banner*, July 26, 1862; *Pittsburgh Gazette*, June 12, July 26, 1862; *Pittsburgh Post*, September 27, 1862.

27. *Pittsburgh Gazette*, June 12, 1862.

28. *Presbyterian Banner*, July 26, 1862.

29. *Pittsburgh Gazette*, June 17, 25, 1862; *Pittsburgh Dispatch*, June 23, 1862.

30. *Pittsburgh Dispatch*, June 25, 1862; *Pittsburgh Gazette*, July 12, 1862.

31. *Pittsburgh Gazette*, July 4, 12, 1862; *Presbyterian Banner*, July 26, 1862.

32. *Pittsburgh Gazette*, July 10, 12, 1862.

33. *Presbyterian Banner*, July 19, 1862. See also *Philadelphia Press*, July 22, 1862.

34. James Allison to WSP, July 21, 1862, PTS; *Pittsburgh Gazette*, July 23, 1862; *Pittsburgh Dispatch*, July 23, 1862.

35. *Pittsburgh Gazette*, July 26, August 6, 1862; *Presbyter*, July 31, 1862; *New York Evangelist*, August 7, 1862; *Central Presbyterian*, July 31, 1862. In response to a reporter's claim that Plumer held "a snug professorship in an abolition college," Southern Presbyterians defended him as exerting a conservative influence in the seminary by "restrain[ing] the [abolition] fanaticism." See *Richmond Dispatch*, October 19, 1861; *Central Presbyterian*, January 11, 23, 1862.

36. E. P. Humphrey to WSP, August 18, 1862; W. W. Ferguson to WSP, July 23, 1862; J. M. Jones to WSP, August 6, 16, 1862; G. W. Uhler to WSP, August 20, 1862, PTS.

37. Charles Hodge to WSP, July 25, 1862, PTS; *Presbyterian Banner*, August 2, 1862; David McKinney to WSP, August 4, 1862, PTS. Unlike Plumer, Hodge maintained that the church should not take a completely neutral position on important political questions. However, his protest against the unambiguously pro-Union Spring resolutions at the Presbyterian General Assembly in 1861 caused some to question his loyalty. Despite writing several able articles upholding the U.S. government, he continued to receive criticism throughout the war "for being too lukewarm in his Northern loyalties." See Paul C. Gutjahr, *Charles Hodge: Guardian of American Orthodoxy* (New York: Oxford University Press, 2011), 312, 317, 334.

38. *Pittsburgh Gazette*, August 7, 1862; *Presbyterian Banner*, August 9, 30, September 6, 1862.

39. *Pittsburgh Gazette*, August 20, 21, September 2, 1862. Even without the Plumer imbroglio, McKnight may not have secured renomination. Because of redistricting, he was competing against his House colleague James K. Moorhead, who similarly had first won election to the 36th Congress four years previously.

40. Two other men who had voted in the majority were present. Daniel E. Nevin was elected moderator and thus could not second the motion. McAboy, who had joined the ranks of those wanting to be rid of Plumer, introduced the resolution, leaving Launitz the sole person able to stall the proceedings.

41. After the results of the July meeting when only thirteen men had voted, John F. McLaren attempted to defend the loyalty of Allegheny Presbytery by publicly explaining that the body had thirty-four members, twenty ministers, and fourteen elders. One of the ministers was a foreign missionary and never attended meetings. Excluding him and Plumer, thirty-two men could have voted on the resolution to recommend Plumer's resignation. Because only seven voted to take no action, McLaren pointed out that less than one-quarter of the members had supported Plumer, and two or three of them had qualified their votes by declaring that they personally did not endorse his views on the war. In reality, although only thirteen presbyters voted, four others, including Plumer, had been present and abstained from voting for various reasons. See *Pittsburgh Gazette*, July 12, 1862. Launitz contended that since Plumer's detractors did not consider the verdict reached by seventeen members as representative of the entire presbytery, then neither should the outcome of the September meeting, which numbered eighteen participants, be regarded as "a fair expression of the mind of Presbytery." See John Launitz to WSP, September 5, 1862, PTS. However, because only six men attended both meetings, then 29 of 32 had had the opportunity to weigh in on Plumer. Because two of those who had voted in his favor changed sides at the second meeting, at best he could have had only eight men who supported him—Launitz, the four who upheld him at the July meeting, and the three no-shows.

42. Launitz to WSP, September 5, 1862, PTS; *Pittsburgh Gazette*, September 4, 1862.

43. During the meeting, an opponent claimed that Plumer had been informed in advance that the presbytery intended to take up his case, but afterward Launitz could not recall who had declared this. See Launitz to WSP, September 5, 1862, PTS. In their remonstrance the members of Central Presbyterian complained that the presbytery had acted "without notice" to Plumer and without a representative of the church in attendance. See *Pittsburgh Post*, September 27, 1862.

44. WSP to Session of Central Presbyterian Church, September 5, 1862, PTS; *Presbyterian Banner*, September 13, 1862; *Pittsburgh Post*, September 27, 1862; WSP to David Elliott, September 6, 1862; Elliott to WSP, September 8, 1862, PTS; S. I. Prime to "My Dear Friend" [Kate Bryan], September 17, 1862, PTS, box 1.

45. Annie [Kennedy] to "Dear Aunt Margy," September n.d., 1862, PTS.

46. WSP to Board of Directors of Western Theological Seminary, September 18, 1862, PTS; Annie [Kennedy] to "Dear Aunt Margy," September n.d., 1862, PTS; *Pittsburgh Gazette*, September 19, 1862; *Presbyter*, September 25, 1862.

47. Annie [Kennedy] to "Dear Aunt Margy," September n.d., 1862, PTS; WSP to Thomas S. Childs, October 6, 1862, PTS, box 2; Resolutions of Western Theological Seminary Students to Board of Directors, n.d., PTS; Western Theological Seminary Faculty Minutes, September 18, 1862, Pittsburgh Theological Seminary Archives.

48. Annie [Kennedy] to "Dear Aunt Margy," September n.d., 1862, PTS; *Pittsburgh Gazette*, September 20, 1862. In his address to the presbytery it seems that Plumer at least complained about the unfavorable press coverage he had received, specifically indicting the *Presbyterian Banner* and McKinney for refusing to publish the letter from Hodge. McKinney assumed as much, for he defended his rebuffing Plumer's request and maintained that Hodge had not written "one word" supporting Plumer. See *Banner*, September 27, 1862.

49. Annie [Kennedy] to "Dear Aunt Margy," September n.d., 1862; Eliza Plumer to WSP, September 18 [misdated, likely between 20-25], 1862; George W. Patterson to WSP, September 22, 1862; Samuel S. Bryan to WSP, September 22, 1862; Eliza Plumer to WSP, September 21, 1862, PTS; *Farewell Letter of Rev. Wm. S. Plumer, D.D. to the Central Presbyterian Church, Allegheny, Pa. Read September 28, 1862* (Pittsburgh: Barr & Myers, 1862).

50. WSP to Thomas S. Childs, October 6, 1862, PTS, box 2; WSP to Henry Van Dyke, October 6, 1862, Henry Van Dyke Family Papers, box 27, Manuscripts Division, Department of Rare Books and Special Collections, Princeton University Library.

51. David A. Cunningham to WSP, September 22, 1862; Henry Van Dyke to WSP, September 27, 1862; George H. Fullerton to WSP, October 8, 1862, PTS; S. I. Prime to Kate Bryan, October 3, 1862, PTS, box 1.

52. Annie [Kennedy] to "Dear Aunt Margy," September n.d., 1862, PTS). The congregation's most notable soldier was Samuel W. Black, colonel of the 62nd Pennsylvania and former governor of Nebraska Territory. He was shot in the head leading his troops into battle at Gaines' Mill during the Seven Days' Campaign. For his death, see *Pittsburgh Post*, June 30, July 4, 1862. Plumer conducted his fallen friend's funeral, and one editor complained that he never once spoke highly of the Union or lauded Black for giving his life for the country. See *Pittsburgh Gazette*, July 26, 1862. William M. Semple, a signer of the remonstrance and one of two men who came up with the lion's share of the nearly five thousand dollars needed to pay the memorialists for the church property, gave $1,500 to raise three companies of soldiers. See *Pittsburgh Post*, August 11, 1862; *Pittsburgh Gazette*, August 12, 1862. It seems clear that some overtly patriotic members of Central Presbyterian took no issue with Plumer's public prayers.

53. Kate Bryan to WSP, August [September] 20, 1862; Samuel S. Bryan to WSP, September 22, 24, 1862, PTS; *Presbyterian Post*, September 27, 1862.

54. *Presbyterian Banner*, October 25, 1862; Charles C. Beatty to Henry A. Boardman, November 20, 1862, PTS. Probably the best example of the general public's perception of Plumer is an advertisement for cartes de visites of several clergymen, including "Rev. Dr. Plummer (Secesh), of Pittsburg." See *Philadelphia Press*, August 20, 1862.

55. S. I. Prime to WSP, September 30, 1862; James M. Macdonald to WSP, October 6, 1862; John Terhune to WSP, November 19, 1862, PTS.

56. William M. Paxton to WSP, October 31, December 2, 1862, PTS. See also Charles C. Beatty to Henry A. Boardman, November 20, 1862, PTS, for assistance in Philadelphia.

57. *Philadelphia Inquirer*, November 18, 1862; WSP to Phineas D. Gurley, November 21, 29, 1862, Plumer Papers, Duke University. Isaiah 60:12 reads, "For the nation and kingdom that will not serve thee shall perish; yea, those nations shall be utterly wasted." Plumer may have regarded the war as a fulfillment of this warning.

58. WSP to Howell Evans, February 17, March 6, 9, 12, 1863; Evans to WSP, February 27, March 4, 7, 10, 25, 1863, PTS.

59. *Philadelphia Inquirer*, January 9, 1864. Although he spent much of 1863–65 without a permanent position, he consistently found pulpits to fill and reportedly only missed one Sunday of preaching from the time he left Allegheny until the war's

termination. See *Necrological Reports and Annual Proceedings of the Alumni Association of Princeton Theological Seminary*, vol. 1, *1875–1889* (Princeton: C. S. Robinson & Co., 1891), 21.

60. F. S. John Lockwood to WSP, December 26, 1864; Thomas B. Butler to WSP, January 1, 1865; Mary E. S. Chichester to WSP, January 20, 1865; Henry I. Holt to WSP, January 31, 1865; Julia A. Lockwood to WSP, February 6, 1865, PTS.

61. William E. Schenck to WSP, June 1, 1863, PTS; WSP to Phineas D. Gurley, January 12, 1865, Plumer Papers, Duke University; Second Presbyterian Church Pottsville to WSP, July 19, 1865, PTS. Because of the relative paucity of information on Plumer from mid-1863 to mid-1865, rumors and anecdotes sometimes masqueraded as facts, such as this one repeated by a mid-twentieth-century Presbyterian historian. "So bitter was popular sentiment against him that when he removed to the South to accept a church at Pottsville, Virginia, he had to leave at night taking his goods out in a wheelbarrow because no one would haul them for him." See Swetnam, 290.

62. John W. Allen to WSP, October 22, 1862; I. H. Donaldson to WSP, November 26, 1862; William M. Paxton to WSP, October 13, 1862, PTS.

63. *Pittsburgh Gazette*, March 20, April 18, 1863; *Presbyterian Banner*, April 22, 1863; *History of Allegheny Co., Pennsylvania* (Philadelphia: L. H. Everts & Co., 1876), 83.

64. At one point Plumer evidently recommended a man named McLaren, who was not related to the John F. McLaren who had relentlessly sought his removal. Plumer's son-in-law nevertheless averred that the introduction of any person with that cognomen "would produce a demoralization in our little band equal to that which seized our forces at Bull Run." See Samuel S. Bryan to WSP, January 23, 1863, PTS.

65. *History of Allegheny Co., Pennsylvania*, 83; Resolutions of Western Theological Seminary Students to Board of Directors, n.d., PTS.

66. WSP to William H. Hornblower, May 29, 1878; Hornblower to WSP, June 5, 1878; Elders, Trustees, and Deacons of Central Presbyterian to WSP, June 5, 1878; WSP to "Friends of the Central Presbyterian Church," June 13, 1878, PTS.

67. Charles C. Beatty to WSP, September 15, 1862, PTS; WSP to Thomas S. Childs, October 6, 1862, PTS, box 2.

68. Horace Bushnell, "The Doctrine of Loyalty," in *Work and Play: or Literary Varieties* (New York: Charles Scribner, 1864), 339–40, 344–46, 355–58; Edward Bates to WSP, May 7, 1861, PTS; Stout, 388–89; S. J. P. Anderson to WSP, July 27, 1862, PTS.

"American Matrons and Daughters"

Sewing Women and Loyalty in Civil War Philadelphia

Judith Giesberg

When *Harper's Weekly* published the illustration, "Service and Shoddy," the Northern public was in the midst of an ambitious campaign to promote national loyalty—and women were caught in the middle of it (see Figure 1). With morale in the North flagging and the Democratic political opposition emboldened, pro-war pundits took to the press, pamphlet, and the pulpit in 1863 to label the war's critics as disloyal and unpatriotic and to tie national fidelity to Republican Party loyalty. Sanitary Fairs began that year, as did the Union League Clubs, both intent on encouraging support for the war by providing models of loyalty and self-sacrifice; toward that end, the elite Sanitary Fair women modeled self-sacrificing domesticity and Union Leaguers recruited and outfitted United States Colored Troops. In 1863, too, Susan B. Anthony and Elizabeth Cady Stanton organized the Woman's Loyal National League to encourage women to identify with and support the abolitionist aims of the nation.[1] Together, these agents of a new American nationalism, according to historian Melinda Lawson "helped shape the cultural and ideological American nation-state."[2] Positioned in the center of the sketch is the soldier, standing alone on a deserted landscape. Directly below him is a well-dressed wartime contractor, enjoying a drink and a smoke at a comfortable and well-stocked saloon. The juxtaposition of a man serving his country and another one serving himself captures some of the spirit of the nationalists' campaign and serves as evidence of the cacophony of voices that Lawson brought together in *Patriot Fires*.

Women figure prominently in the *Harper's Weekly* sketch, the visual opposition of the soldier's wife and the contractor's offering clues about the lessons readers were supposed to take away from the sketch. Without voting rights and denied access to military service, a woman's war service was defined as sacrifice of son or husband. By 1863, invoking the term "soldier's wife" offered pundits a way of calming class tensions that stood, unacknowledged, at the center of the

Figure 1. "Service and Shoddy: A Picture of the Times," *Harper's Weekly*, October 24, 1863, 677.

nationalist project—tensions that might potentially disrupt it. As historian Nina Silber has argued, attacks on Mrs. Shoddy served as a way to disarm critics who complained that the war was lining the pockets of the rich while it took the lives and sacrificed the health of the working class. Attacking fictional contractors' wives, or "'Miss Shoddies,'" was intended to appeal to "the struggling soldiers and soldiers' wives (or potential soldiers and soldiers' wives), whose own patriotism was wavering . . . and whose commitment to the Union cause . . . was critical to Union success."[3] The plump contractor's wife, dressed in silks and white gloves while she shops, was an easy target, and papers delighted in telling stories about the frivolous spending habits of elite women, in general—particularly if they got their just desserts.[4] Concerns to retain the loyalties of the working-class were at the heart of the campaign against Mrs. Shoddy. The frivolousness of Mrs. Shoddy stands in contrast to the stern face and clenched fists of the soldier's wife pictured in the left frame. Here the young mother stands in her home with only her child as company, confronting a man who does not have her best interests in mind. The man has come either to collect on a debt or, more likely given the theme of the other frames, to pay her for sewing the shirts lying on the table, under her left hand. Whatever the man's purpose, the reader's sympathies are with the woman for having sacrificed her husband to the war.

In the campaign to retain the loyalties of the working class, a woman's *service* was complete when she became a "soldier's wife," but for hundreds of thousands of women who washed clothes or sewed U.S. Army uniforms—many of them the wives, mothers, and daughters of soldiers—their *work* was also service. Among them, sewing women engaged the swirling rhetoric about loyalty, at times embracing and at other times rejecting the label of "soldiers' wives." Although useful in enlisting the state's occasional sympathies, the label proved a mixed blessing for working class women who depended on work more than sympathy. When they petitioned and demanded higher wages, sewing women fit uncomfortably into the nationalist project that relied on a careful evasion of class tensions and that saw women either as loyal soldiers' wives or as self-serving Mrs. Shoddies. Calling themselves "American matrons and daughters," seamstresses working at Philadelphia's Schuylkill Arsenal and others like it throughout the North, launched a petition campaign, seeking higher wages and job security. Pushed to identify themselves and their relation to the nation, petitioners stressed their loyalty to the nation as skilled workers supporting families. Drawing up resolutions and affixing their names to a stream of petitions, hundreds of working class women drew on traditions of women's labor activism that historians thought were long gone before the war began. Focusing on their work instead of their matrimony, women shifted the terms of the loyalty debate to their advantage, implicating government officials in the tawdry business of contracting and insisting that their *own* work, as wives (and mothers, daughters, and sisters) and skilled craftswomen, stood as proof of their loyalty.

Scholarship on women's war work builds on a base of labor history that argues that wartime capitalists enlisted the aid of the state in an effort to discipline workers and derail unionization efforts. Refusing to recognize the difference between worker dissent and Copperheadism, employers nurtured the growth of a wartime state that served their interests and protected them from the demands of their workers. Although paused for the first year and a half of the war, unions reemerged in 1863, at the same time as the Peace Democrats unleashed a full-throated criticism of emancipation and the draft and the unchecked power of the wartime state.[5] Despite their deep loyalty to the state, workers were betrayed by it as it aligned its own interests with men who financed the war against those who fought it. An essential part of capitalists' strategy was to drive would-be labor allies against one another, by playing the nineteenth century's equivalent of a race card—holding up free blacks and former slaves as "loyal" against the bad example set by non-blacks who might demand a living wage or organize. When unions reemerged in the postwar era, workers mobilized entire towns and paralyzed whole industries, ushering in a new era of labor relations and shattering the Civil War–era political party alignment. Labor organizing entered its most radical phase in the decades following the Civil War, after having been abandoned by the "liberal" wing of the Republican Party. "Class conflict," as David Montgomery put it, "was the submerged shoal on which Radical dreams foundered."[6]

Long before that happened, though, women's independent labor activism had died a quiet death, Christine Stansell has argued, sacrificed to the imperatives of "a language of women's sphere—working class version."[7] In the 1820s and 1830s, women organized as shoe binders, tailoresses, and seamstresses and, of course, New England mill operatives organized and struck in opposition to wage cuts made by the big cotton textile corporations.[8] In each case, women drew from a long tradition of trade unionism, insisting on their rights and often refusing to ally with men. But by the 1850s, working-class women's autonomy was sacrificed both to organized labor's paternalism and to middle class reformers' sympathy. This latter threat came in the form of the "solitary seamstress," whose sad silhouette, Christine Stansell explained, signaled the triumph of "[a] 'true womanhood' for the working class." "[C]lothed in meekness and fragility," the solitary seamstress stood waiting to be defended, her links to the spirited and independent women's trade unionism of the 1820s–1830s severed, her defeat complete.[9]

The solitary seamstress is the poster child, too, for manufacturers' heavy reliance on outwork, or the putting out system, which provided critical support to industrial capitalism, in particular in trades in which women predominated, such as the garment industry. Buried unacknowledged in the history of labor during the Civil War are the origins of the sweatshop, made possible when industrial clothing manufacturers hired contractors to manage outworkers. Contractors quickly got the reputation for unscrupulousness and for squeezing, or sweating, labor out of sewing women—even more so with the wartime proliferation of the sewing machine, which women could not afford to own but contractors could. Only one generation separates the seamstress in "Service and Shoddy" from the one pictured working at her sewing machine in "The female slaves of New York: 'Sweaters' and Their Victims" an 1888 *Frank Leslie's* critique of sweatshops (see Figure 2).[10] Separated from one another (or the large shops) and invisible to male workers, outworkers had little chance for organizing and no knowledge of their "rights." In both, the solitary seamstress cowers before the "figure of the villainous employer," alone and defenseless and in need of protection.[11]

Figure 2. "The female slaves of New York: 'Sweaters' and Their Victims 1. Scene in a 'Sweaters' Factory, 2. The End," *Frank Leslie's Illustrated*, November 3, 1888, 189.

If we focus on the two images of the "solitary seamstress," it is tempting to draw a straight line from the declared denouement of women's independent trade unionism in the 1850s to the sweatshop of the 1880s. This would mean, too, that women's labor organizing caved to the prerogatives of male labor and the demands of industrial capitalists decades before men settled for a ten-hour day. If we do, though, we will miss the small window that opened during the

Civil War, when women outworkers engaged in manufacturing military clothing resurrected the traditions and tactics of trade unionism to ward off charges of disloyalty and to engage in a public debate about the sweating system. Ensconced in her "women's sphere, working class version," the sewing woman's thoughts about the war and the changing nature of her work, we assume, must have been an extension of man's.[12] But during the war, Philadelphia's sewing women charted a separate path, one that was reflected in the nature of their work and the daily realities of the wartime North. Though they were unable to slow the growth of sweated labor, they managed to have their demands taken seriously by local and federal officials at a time when men's labor disputes were achieving little.

Late in July 1863, Philadelphia's newspapers carried the news that the Schuylkill Arsenal—the largest employer of women in the city—would no longer employ women who could not prove their fidelity to the Union. The news appeared under the headline "Commendable Movement," on the front page of the *North American and U.S. Gazette*, announcing that women who could not provide written evidence of their relationship to U.S. Army soldiers—or those who "belong to families opposed to the war"—would be "discharge(ed) from the rolls immediately."[13] Newspapers, sanitary fairs, and political pundits might entreat women and men to greater loyalty, but federal employers could enforce it with a heavy hand. Within two days, at least 145 women were let go.

One week later, 200 women—employed and newly unemployed—met in Philadelphia to draft an official set of resolutions, identifying contracting as the chief threat to sewing women, not loyalty.[14] Under the subcontracting system, private firms employed their own seamstresses, creating middle-men (and women) and lowering the per-piece price paid to women employed by private firms. *Fincher's Trades' Review* reported, for example, that whereas the Schuylkill Arsenal paid twelve and a half cents for a haversack, a subcontractor paid women only five cents. The contractor, presumably, made a profit of 7 cents.[15] U.S. Army jackets sewed for the arsenal fetched a seamstress $1.12, when a contractor paid his own employee only 80 cents.[16] By one estimate, sewing women earned as little as $1.50 a week at a time when inflation and shortages raised the price of all necessities.[17]

That the laid-off women did not hurl bricks at the Schuylkill Arsenal buildings or take to the streets to protest—like women and men had in New York two weeks earlier—was the great good fortune of Philadelphia's large black population, who would have been the crowd's likely targets, or the women who took their jobs. But their restraint is not surprising. Since the beginning of the war, sewing women had articulated a clear and consistent agenda that kept them focused on the legitimate enemies of working women—private clothing contractors—and not on scapegoats. To ensure fair wages and high quality, the women insisted, the U.S. Army should employ and pay women directly, instead of turning over half of their wages to contractors as profit. Seamstresses insisted that the contracting system enriched private investors—often the friends and family of U.S. Army officers—at the expense of experienced seamstresses, many of them the wives and mothers of soldiers. Wives, mothers, and daughters of common soldiers in Philadelphia fought a protracted battle against contracting, one that started before the 1863 loyalty order and that informed the women's response to that order. By 1863, surrounded by heightened rhetoric linking dissent with disloyalty, women sought to define loyalty for themselves

In September 1861, Philadelphia sewing women held the first of a number of meetings demanding that the army hire more seamstresses rather than outsourcing the work, condemning contracting in strong words. "[W]e do most emphatically and earnestly protest against, and vigorously and righteously denounce the infamous contract system, by which we are robbed of more than half our wages, and our government not benefited," the women explained.[18] The women called on the government to put an immediate stop to contracting. City newspapers condemned the meeting's leaders—Anna Long and Martha Yeager—for stirring up the women with "their clamor, [that] did more to demoralize our three months volunteers than half a dozen defeats would have done" and assumed that the women were put up to it by "ignorant or malicious men, who imposed upon their fears or credulity."[19] Though quick to dismiss their claims, Philadelphia papers believed seamstresses' demands were negatively affecting military enrollment and the morale of soldiers camped in and around the city. The war had rapidly increased the number of sewing women in the city, and now the demands of a few of them threatened to unsettle the rest. Accustomed to working in their homes, women who attended wartime meetings learned about others facing similar situations in their own communities and about seamstresses in other cities waging similar battles.

In April 1862, Philadelphia's sewing women met again, this time to prepare a petition to Congress demanding an end to contracting. At the meeting, seamstresses considered enlisting the support of Assistant Quartermaster Colonel George H. Crosman in charge of the Schuylkill Arsenal. Mary Pratt entreated the sewing women to look not for male protection but respect and fair remuneration for their work. "We have not met to ask Uncle Abraham to send back our husbands to rock the cradle while we go to combat with traitors and man our national ships," Pratt insisted, calling on her fellow seamstresses to stand together against a threat closer to home. "The only way to save ourselves," Pratt entreated, "is to stand erect and maintain our rights."[20] Mary Pratt's words must have spoken to women who, like her, had small children, husbands away at the war, and who looked to the government to pay them fair wages. Pratt's reference to traitors and husbands away at the war reflected the growing popular critique of corrupt contractors taking advantage of poor and naïve soldiers' wives—and rejecting Crosman's help in effect implicated him in their scheme. In rousing words, Pratt encouraged women to rely on each other, not on army men whose own loyalties might be suspect.

By 1863, dissenting groups had become more plentiful and their complaints louder throughout the wartime North—a standoff was brewing particularly in Pennsylvania as sewing women began to find their voice. Although not always affiliated with the Democratic Party and not necessarily opposed to the war, workers and others were often confused for Copperheads when they levied criticism against how the war was being administered. Bosses readily blurred the lines between dissent and disloyalty, particularly in industries related to the administration of the war. Following the national pattern, miners in Pennsylvania's coal fields restarted their organizing efforts early in 1863, when workers in several northeastern counties struck and shut down the mines, seeking union recognition, wage relief, and a hearing of their safety concerns. Though none of these demands were new—indeed, they reflected workers' long-standing vision of economic equality and republicanism—employers found new recourse in the national government's willingness to defend employers' rights over those of employees. As historian Grace Palladino argued, when the feds endorsed mine operators' "'right' to pay the lowest wages possible and their 'right' to discharge" unionizing miners, they helped to establish "a political and economic structure antithetical to long-cherished notions of a republican social order."[21] Workers who attended meetings or assigned their names to petitions increasingly came up against employers emboldened by the willingness of the state to ignore their demands or to take punitive actions against them.

On July 29, 1863, two days after Colonel Crosman laid-off seamstresses who could not prove their relation to a soldier or whose patriotism was suspect, 145 women met and signed a petition to Edwin Stanton demanding their jobs back and strongly refuting the army's spurious linking of the layoffs with a lack of patriotism.[22] At an even larger meeting held a few days later, seamstresses drafted a series of resolutions demanding Crosman's removal and an immediate end to the new policy that they described as "oppressive and prejudicial." Further, the petitioners insisted, if the work was reserved for "loyal" women and loyalty was defined by one's relationship to a U.S. Army soldier, then Crosman had been "both inconsistent and tyrannical" in enforcing the policy, for "there are at present employed in the arsenal many men who have neither friends nor relatives in the service."[23] If the army was worried about enforcing loyalty among its employees, then the women would offer their own suggestions.

Although there was always a good deal of jockeying among women for positions sewing uniforms at the arsenal, the petitioning seamstresses saw Crosman's order as a thinly disguised attempt to divide them against one another—to distract them from their real enemy, contracting. Some women who signed these early petitions included a brief account of their claim on the work. Of thirty-seven names affixed to one section of an extensive August 1861 petition, eight women identified themselves as widows, and five were related to enlisted men—one of the latter, Eliza Hooper, had already been widowed in the war.[24] One hundred and seven signatures could be identified on the July 1863 petition. Thirty-one women identified themselves as "widows," and twenty described relationships to soldiers. The lines between the two designations often blurred: Ann Nugent, "widow, two sons at the war"; Maria Hale, "Three children, husband killed at war"; Margaret Jackson, "Two children, son killed at war"; and Mary M. Kelley, "lost husban and son at war."[25] At least two women who signed the July 1863 petition—including Martha Yeager, "brother at war" and Anna Long, "Widow, 5 children"—were vocal critics of contracting who had addressed a meeting of seamstresses the previous fall. Yeager and Long likely weren't the only ones who believed their dismissal was linked to their activism.

The attempt to enforce home-front loyalty did not dissuade seamstresses from organizing to protect their work. In the ensuing months, the petition campaign picked up momentum, expanding well beyond the city and the state, even as, elsewhere in Pennsylvania, officials cracked down on workers with an increasingly heavy hand.[26] Affixing their signatures to these petitions, seamstresses declared themselves united behind a growing critique of U.S. Army policy, which they characterized as "oppressive" and "tyrannical," words borrowed from the political critique of the revolutionary generation and that allowed the women to defend their own loyalties while impugning those of their army superiors. These were fighting words delivered at a time when there were heightened concerns about the loyalties of the Northern working class.

Employing words such as "tyranny" and "rights," sewing women laid claim to the same vision of republicanism and egalitarianism that motivated male trade unionists and tapped into a long history of working-class women's traditions. In their earliest expressions of trade consciousness, women laid claim to natural rights that they had inherited from their revolutionary ancestors. "We remain

in possession of our unquestionable rights," Lowell mill operatives insisted in
an 1834 petition, and "[w]e circulate this paper wishing to obtain the names of
all who imbibe the spirit of our Patriotic Ancestors, who preferred privation to
bondage." "[A]nd as we are free," the operatives continued, "we would remain in
possession of what kind Providence has bestowed upon us, and remain daughters of freemen still."[27] What historian Thomas Dublin found to be true among
Lowell's operatives in the 1830s, Christine Stansell reported was alive and well
among the women of New York City's Ladies' Industrial Association (LIA) in
1845. LIA leaders rebuked male leadership, vowing "'to take upon themselves the
task of asserting their rights against the unjust and mercenary conduct of their
employers'" and characterizing their wage demand as "founded upon RIGHT
alone."[28] The language of rights and republican traditions was invoked again
in the 1860 shoemakers' strike in Lynn, where a banner read "American Ladies
Will Not Be Slaves: Give Us Fair Compensation, And We Labour Cheerfully."[29]
Appropriating the republican language of rights, Dublin argued, was evidence
that the women "felt no deference to their employers; they would certainly *not*
call them their masters."[30] Nonetheless, when LIA leaders settled for garnering
middle-class sympathies, Stansell suspected that the women obscured by image
of the "solitary seamstress" had given up on their rights.

Yet women sewing army uniforms seem to have revived these traditions—or
perhaps it was the Civil War's highly charged political environment that encouraged them to speak again in the language of rights. Through their sewing work,
women found a political voice with which to engage the rhetoric about loyalty.
They laid claim to rights that inhered from the work they did—and that their
ancestors had done. Heterogenous and mobile, Philadelphia's Civil War–era sewing women had weaker claims to a revolutionary heritage, perhaps, than Lowell's
Yankee spinners, but that did not stop movement leaders from claiming a patriotic
lineage.[31] Three women who spoke at meetings and whose names figured prominently in petitions—Anna Long, Martha Yeager, and Mary Pratt—were supporting themselves and their families when they first addressed crowds of women,
often with children in tow, and evoked images of their sewing ancestors. In one
of her first speeches made in 1861, Anna Long spoke eloquently of three generations of women who had made uniforms in Philadelphia—grandmothers who
sewed during the American Revolution, mothers in the war of 1812, and current
"old hands" who "have made the army clothing for the soldiers in the Florida war,
the war with Mexico, and some of the loyal soldiers now enlisted."[32] Twenty-nine
in 1861, and with four children ranging in age from nine years old to two, Long's
husband had been a shoemaker before the war. By the time she was laid-off in

1863, Long was a widowed mother of five. Her circumstances had changed, but she expected her work to remain the same. Women had always sewed for the army in the city, for every war, and therein lay their "right" to the work.

With its mix of private and public manufacturing, though, this war was different. Historian Mark Wilson has called the U.S. Army's vast procurement system in the Civil War a "mixed military economy," for quartermasters and other army supply officers created and expanded "wartime public enterprises," such as arsenals and navy yards, even as they purchased more and more goods from private producers, small and large.[33] Whereas the Schuylkill Arsenal and others like it may have been able to meet the demands of these earlier emergencies, they could not during the Civil War. Seamstresses like Anna Long, Martha Yeager, and Mary Pratt were not alone in their preference for public enterprises overseen directly by army officers; army supply officers were suspicious of the imperatives of industrial capitalism and resisted the military's reliance on contractors, particularly the larger private suppliers. Quartermaster General Montgomery Meigs, for instance, worried that army contracting was concentrating wealth in the hands of big contractors calling it an "evil."[34] The solution, he thought, was expanding the network of army depots, a sentiment he shared with disgruntled seamstresses. Army men's suspicion of contracting reflected the public's growing resentment for Mr. and Mrs. Shoddy and helps to explain why sewing women were able to evade the loyalty mandate and get some traction when workers in other industries were not.

Just as hundreds of laid-off seamstresses were holding meetings and signing petitions in Philadelphia, city officials were preparing to send troops out of the city to deal with another labor crisis brewing to the North. Striking miners shut down coal production in mines in Schuylkill, Carbon, and Luzerne counties in the northeast part of the state that summer; by August, the U.S. Army occupied the region. Local and federal officials were determined to enforce "a proper public sentiment" among the miners and devised a number of strategies to enforce loyalty at the end of a bayonet. Soldiers drove striking miners back into the mines, and a small army of U.S. Provost Marshals drafted the strike's "ring leaders."[35] As officials in Philadelphia looked on, they must have wondered about the wisdom of sending troops out of town at the very moment when workers in their own city seemed poised to cause trouble. On the other hand, local officials would never authorize the use of bayonets on unarmed seamstresses; if they could have drafted the "ring leaders," they might have started with Mary Pratt.

Late in April 1864, the Schuylkill seamstresses held the first meeting of the Working Women's Relief Association; at the head of the association was the indefatigable Mary Pratt.[36] While the Relief Association petitioned Congress to raise wages, another group of Philadelphia sewing women formed Sewing Women's Union No. 1, following the lead of women and labor leaders in New York, who earlier in the year began their own union.[37] With two different organizations representing their interests, by June 1864, Philadelphia's sewing women were in the middle of a growing movement applying pressure on local and federal officials on multiple fronts simultaneously. Philadelphia seamstresses drafted a new petition to Secretary of War Edwin Stanton asking for wage increases and an expansion of arsenal production. The petition showed convincingly that contracting was depressing wages for all sewing women in the city—whether they worked for the U.S. Army or for private employers—and that wages were not keeping up with the cost of living. But the women went further.

Speaking on behalf of "Twenty Thousand Working Women of Philadelphia," the petitioners demanded that the government expand public manufacturing and set wages for seamstresses working in the private and public sectors. This petition evidenced sewing women's growing consciousness of themselves as part of a larger movement of women "who have given *their all* to their country; and who now come to that country, not as beggars, asking alms, but as American matrons and daughters, asking an equitable price for their labor."[38] As Mary Pratt had charged, they were women willing "to stand erect" and together for they sought not only to raise their own wages at the arsenal but to set a living wage for all seamstresses engaged in sewing army uniforms.

Facing a growing and organized movement, Colonel Crosman endorsed the women's demands, rather than replace them with women who could "prove their loyalty," as he had done the previous summer. Crosman sent the petition of "Twenty Thousand" on to Meigs, recommending a per-piece wage adjustment and characterizing the current rate as "entirely too low."[39] Meigs, who had expressed his own misgivings about contracting, inquired about the piece-rates paid at clothing arsenals in Cincinnati and St. Louis and surveyed those paid by private contractors in several other cities, including New York. To a one, the heads of the major clothing depots agreed with the Philadelphia petitioners—as a result of private contracting, seamstresses throughout the North received wages that were "quite inadequate," as one put it.[40] In his endorsement of the women's demands, Crosman assured Meigs that a wage adjustment at the Schuylkill Arsenal would "end all cause of complaint," but he failed to acknowledge that the seamstresses' demands ran deeper than a conflict over wages at one facility.[41] Contracting lay at the heart of the problem, they had always insisted, as it allowed unscrupulous businessmen to earn huge profits from the government while denying seamstresses a government wage. Enforcing a minimum wage for all sewing work, the petitioners insisted, "would remedy the evil effectually." Doing so was not a matter of charity but "justice."[42]

By 1864, the sewing women had also caught the attention of local labor leaders, men who aspired to lead a renewed labor movement but who shared with nationalists a vision of women workers that was distinctly at odds with that of the seamstresses. Jonathan Fincher covered the seamstresses' campaign in his labor newspaper, *Fincher's Trades' Review*, and he and William Sylvis, both union men, encouraged the women to unionize.[43] Although he characterized himself as a "friend of working women," readers would have been hard-pressed to find evidence of this claim in his paper. In a June 1863 article, Fincher lamented the growing numbers of women involved in industrial labor, occupations that drew them out of their "more appropriate sphere." Working women were "driving from employment their natural protectors," doing the work of men at lower wages, and dooming returning soldiers to unemployment. Fincher called male readers to action, promising that "we shall spare no effort to check this most unnatural invasion of our firesides by whom the order of nature is reversed, and woman, the loveliest of God's creation, reduced to the menial condition of savage life."[44] Like other male labor leaders, Fincher at times liked to imagine an ideal working-class true womanhood.

Though he remained convinced that working women needed male protection, Fincher applauded the seamstresses' response to the July 1863 layoffs and joined them in condemning contractors in strong terms in the pages of *Fincher's Trades' Review*. Fincher eagerly encouraged the women to unionize, insisting that "working women must follow in the wake of working men."[45] Seamstresses moved cautiously in response to the advice of labor leaders like Fincher and Sylvis, for in the end they thought the solution would come with higher wages for men. Buying into a "women's sphere—working class version," Fincher's views were not unlike nationalists' who viewed women as soldiers' wives. At meetings that Fincher and William Sylvis attended, seamstresses insisted that their work was not temporary and connected only to the needs of the current war, they should not be held to an invasive loyalty test, and that the federal government should not cooperate with industrialists who sought to profit from the enlistment or drafting of working-class soldiers. In his postwar leadership of the National Labor Union, the precursor to the Knights of Labor, Sylvis was a consistent champion of women workers and became a confidante of prominent middle-class suffragists, Susan B. Anthony and Elizabeth Cady Stanton, reflecting, perhaps, the influence of the seamstresses earlier in his career.[46]

Armed with the petition on behalf of "Twenty Thousand Working Women" and 800 signatures, a group of seamstresses went to Washington where they met with President Lincoln, Secretary of War Stanton, and Pennsylvania Congressman William Kelley.[47] After two hours of talks, Stanton agreed to hire 1,000 to 2,000 more women at the Schuylkill—on top of the nearly 5,000 who already worked there—and ordered a 25 percent raise for government seamstresses.[48] This was a significant expansion of government work in the city and was a clear victory for the women who had insisted that the work was their right. The seamstresses could not convince Stanton, however, to set a minimum wage. Doing so, Stanton insisted would be "an unauthorized exercise" of federal power over private employers. Surely the women were disappointed with the outcome, as they well knew, as long as the wages paid by contractors were lower than those paid by the government, the position of all seamstresses was insecure. Stanton must have anticipated the women's disaffection, for he asked Kelley to "please communicate" his good intentions to the sewing women, and Kelley published Stanton's letter offering this piecemeal solution in the papers.[49] Kelley, who had been behind the 1863 layoffs that had fueled the women's movement, also got something that he wanted. A little over a month before the Pennsylvania state election, his name appeared in the announcement of good news for thousands of working-class Philadelphians—even if they could not vote for him.

Although disfranchised by sex and marginalized by class, sewing women found a political voice that allowed them to be heard not only in Washington and Philadelphia, but also in Cincinnati where the army produced uniforms and in New York where the army contracted with private producers. As in Philadelphia, sewing women in New York formed two organizations during the war, a Working Women's Union and a Sewing Women's Protective Union, to petition for wage increases and to lobby politicians to "make it obligatory upon all contractors to pay Government prices." In September, members of the Working Women's Union held the first of a number of large and raucous meetings to draft a response to Stanton's offer to raise the per piece price paid at government arsenals. "We do not ask charity," the New York seamstresses who worked only for contractors explained to the Secretary, echoing the words of Philadelphia's seamstresses, "we come to you as American women, many of whom have sacrificed the dearest treasures of their hearts on the altar of freedom."[50] Without recourse to government pay, New York seamstresses had little leverage with army officials, yet they, too, appealed to officials as "American women" for whom government work was a right. Male union leaders did take notice of the movement in New York, and they invited seamstresses to join the Journeymen Tailors' Union.[51] In

Cincinnati, where thousands of women were employed in government shops that produced tents and army uniforms, local politicians once again joined sewing women in a successful fight to retain government work threatened with privatization. Smaller halls employed a few hundred women in St. Louis, where Charles Thomas advised Quartermaster Meigs that "people here claim a portion of the work as a right and probably they are correct in it." When local residents pushed the army to reopen shops in St. Louis after they were shut down, Congressman Frank Blair successfully took up their cause.[52] In nearly every case, the organizational efforts of disfranchised sewing women yielded some relief, and although at times sewing women were portrayed as "poor soldiers' wives" worthy of the government's sympathy, they insisted that the work was their right—and army officials and politicians agreed.

Still unsatisfied with the progress they achieved the previous summer, Philadelphia seamstresses appointed a new delegation to take their demands directly to the president.[53] On January 26, 1865, President Lincoln met for a second time with Philadelphia seamstresses—this time with Martha Yeager and three other women leaders—who arrived unaccompanied by local congressmen and without the invitation of the Secretary of War. But the President offered the seamstresses the same solution as had Stanton—more government work and a raise in the per piece rate.[54] No sooner had Lincoln met with the women when seamstresses in Cincinnati sent a petition, reiterating the demands of women in New York and Philadelphia.[55] "Women can meet the wants of the Government in this department, without the aid of the opposite sex," an article in Fincher's declared after the seamstresses returned from Washington the second time, "whether they appear as popularity-hunters, Shylock contractors, or Mawworm-philanthropists."[56]

In the end, the seamstresses' campaign yielded mixed results. On the one hand, neither Stanton nor Lincoln was willing to tip the balance of the mixed military economy in favor of more public production of military clothing. With no wage guarantees and no protection from contractors, seamstresses repeatedly had to demand to have their jobs reinstated and their piece-rate wages raised. They remained vulnerable to the whims of private employers and the inevitable contraction of army work. Industrial clothing manufacturing had always relied on women's outwork, which was grossly underpaid, largely invisible, and ripe for abuse. Organizing was difficult because seamstresses worked at home or in cramped shops filled with loud machines. The solitary seamstress raised the ire of male labor leaders and perhaps helped to deflect criticism away from government policies that allowed some to profit while others served. Local politicians' willingness to work on behalf of sewing women may be read as evidence of the failure of a more robust and organized movement during the war, another example of the divide and conquer tactics used by industrialists.

On the other hand, organizing seamstresses helped to initiate and engaged in a conversation about the mixed military economy. Sewing women from Philadelphia met with federal lawmakers twice—at least once with women who had been dismissed under suspicions of disloyalty—and at both meetings members of the Lincoln administration interceded on their behalf. Local authorities often took their side, lobbying to reopen public works and endorsing their demands for an end to contracting. In Philadelphia, a year after local officials tried unsuccessfully to rid themselves of the problem of dissenting seamstresses, the same women were sewing once more for the army, assigning their names to petitions, and bending politicians' ears about the wrongs of sweated labor. Because they sewed in their own homes, gathering hundreds of signatures for each petition required movement leaders to become effective canvassers, calling on lone seamstresses in their homes, discussing the issues, and convincing them to sign a document that might be politically consequential.[57] Facing a growing movement, local officials in Philadelphia thought it important to publish assurances in the papers, suggesting that they had come to accept that the movement was bigger than a few women disturbing the good order of the city. Joining in the critique of the "shoddy aristocracy," the women had managed to keep the public concerns about contracting alive, linking it to corruption and an absence of patriotism. Using words like "oppressive" and "tyrannical" to describe army contracting policy allowed the women to tap into what historian Thomas Smith has described as Americans' deeply held fears about centralization and abuse of power.[58] Working-class women activists expressed a vision of republicanism and egalitarianism that they shared with men; their actions as sewing women and soldiers' wives complicated the popular image of them as the corrupt contractor's hapless victims. Indeed, the petitioners insisted on their identity as loyal workers—American women—doing meaningful and important work for the nation. Seamstresses believed their "rights" were based on the legacy of women's needlework and insisted that their work be evaluated on the basis of its quality and economy—not on their relationships with soldiers. Accordingly, they actively subverted the order requiring them to prove they were married to or had sons who were soldiers when they demanded that men employed at the arsenal prove *their* relation to soldiers and when they shared their work with others. And, in their speeches and petitions, seamstresses demanded that the army conceive of women's service to the country in broad terms, not limiting it to male enlistment.

After taking leave of President Lincoln's company for a second time, Philadelphia seamstresses resolved that, while they did not disagree that women with soldier-relations were deserving of well-paid work, so too were women "who have done the country service in other ways and therefore are entitled to a share of the work."[59] As long as arsenal work was conceived as temporary relief for soldiers' wives, it could disappear once the emergency of the war was over, even though sewing women would continue to rely on the income after the men returned—and even more so when men did not return. Women with children to feed could not afford to have the work defined as welfare for soldier wives and mothers. "Old hands" saw the work as their right—just as their foremothers had sewn uniforms for the nation before them, so did this generation of "American women." Resisting this identification, too, seamstresses rejected a divide and conquer approach to keeping their dissent in check—a tactic that was used to great effect in controlling men's labor demands.

Thanks to the work of Melinda Lawson and others, historians have begun to explore the process of building American national identity during the Civil War. Through the papers and pamphlets, a group of "self-elected apostles" of American nationalism offered models of female patriotism—the Sanitary Commission women who modeled a self-sacrificing elite when they gave generously of their time and shopped at Sanitary Fairs, for instance, and the "soldier's wife" who sacrificed her husband to the cause. Susan B. Anthony and Elizabeth Cady Stanton's Woman's Loyal National League sought to offer a third model for middle class women, political insiders interested in advancing abolition by supporting the Republican Party.[60] At their organizational meeting in May 1863, Anthony offered a series of resolutions endorsing civil and political rights for former slaves and women and defending all Northern women from claims that they, in comparison to their Southern counterparts, lacked enthusiasm. "[T]he women of the Revolution were not wanting in heroism and self-sacrifice," League women resolved, "and we, their daughters, are ready in this war."[61] The seamstresses' campaign against contracting made women's work visible, challenging the image of the lone sewing woman fending off creditors and the desperate young mother who needed man's protection. Their claims to be inheritors of a long line of patriotic workers echoed those of other groups who vied for the rights to define women's loyalty, Anthony and Stanton's and their Woman's Loyal National League, for instance. A history of women's labor during the Civil War is yet to be written, but when it is, the sewing women's movement that took hold in Philadelphia and other Northern cities will warrant a chapter, as seamstresses sought to navigate an intense campaign to define women's loyal behavior and through them to retain the loyalties of the working class.

Notes

1. Nina Silber, *Gender and the Sectional Conflict* (Chapel Hill: University of North Carolina Press, 2009), 63–66.

2. Melinda Lawson, *Patriot Fires: Forging a New American Nationalism in the Civil War North* (Lawrence: University Press of Kansas, 2004), 13.

3. Silber, *Gender and Conflict*, 50.

4. Philadelphia's *Finchers' Trades' Review*, for instance, told of a Mrs. Burgett, "one of the most fashionable ladies of Chicago" arrested for shoplifting and sentenced to a year in the penitentiary. "Shoplifting—An Extraordinary Case," FTR, July 18, 1863, 26. Another Philadelphia paper chastised elite women shoppers who demanded seats from returning veterans and other men returning from a hard day's work. "Right vs. Politeness," Philadelphia *Sunday Dispatch*, August 27, 1865.

5. David Montgomery, *Beyond Equality: Labor and the Radical Republicans, 1862–1872* (New York: Knopf, 1967), 90–114.

6. Montgomery, *Beyond Equality*, x.

7. Christine Stansell, *City of Women: Sex and Class in New York, 1789–1860* (Chicago and Urbana: University of Illinois Press, 1987), 119.

8. Thomas Dublin, *Women at Work: The Transformation of Work and Community in Lowell, Massachusetts, 1826–1860*, New York: Columbia University Press, 1979. Mary H. Blewett, *Men, Women, and Work: Class, Gender, and Protest in the New England Shoe Industry, 1780–1910* (Chicago and Urbana: University of Illinois Press), 1988. Alan Dawley, *Class and Community: The Industrial Revolution in Lynn* (Cambridge: Harvard University Press, 1976).

9. Stansell, *City of Women*, 153

10. "The Female Slaves of New York, Sweaters and Their Victims: 1. Scene in a Sweater's Factory, 2. The End, and 3. Scene at the Grand Street Ferry," *Frank Leslie's Illustrated*, November 3, 1888, 189. In the lower-left frame, "2. The End," an emaciated and ill woman lies alone in a dilapidated hovel. The lower-right frame shows immigrant women and men arriving in the city.

The accompanying article implicated sweaters and immigrants who depress the wages for "our people." "It is no wonder . . . that they go mad when they have to provide food and shelter and raiment for two or three besides themselves and have only $4.50 a week." "Victims of the Sweaters," *Frank Leslie's Illustrated*, November 3, 1888, 191.

11. Stansell, *City of Women*, 112.

12. Stansell, *City of Women*, 119.

13. "Commendable Movement," *North American and U.S. Gazette*, July 27, 1863, 1. The original order came from Pennsylvania Congressman William D. Kelley to Colonel G. H. Crosman, Assistant Quartermaster, in charge of the Schuylkill Arsenal. In the end, this was largely irrelevant to the seamstresses, as they held Crosman responsible. Colonel G. H. Crosman to Captain George Martine [*sic?*], July 20, 1863, National Archives and

Records Administration (hereafter: NARA), Old Military Records, Washington, D.C., Record Group (RG) 92, Box 1004.

14. Elizabeth Steinmeyer and Maggie Murphy, et al., to E. M. Stanton (August 4, 1863), NARA, RG 92, Box 1004, No. 105, 2.

15. "A Word for Our Starving Seamstresses," *Fincher's Trades' Review* (December 12, 1863), 6.

16. "Who Pockets the Difference?" *Fincher's Trades' Review* (September 5, 1863).

17. Rachel Seidman, "Beyond Sacrifice: Women and Politics on the Pennsylvania Homefront during the Civil War," Ph.D. diss., Yale University, 1995, 133.

18. "A Meeting of Female Operatives in the Arsenal," *North American and U.S. Gazette*, September 4, 1861, 1.

19. "The Schuylkill Arsenal," *North American and U.S. Gazette*, September 5, 1861, 1. The paper referred to Yeager as "Yeaker," but a Martha Yeager is listed on the 1861 and 1863 petitions. The paper refers to "Mrs. A. Long," which is presumably Anna Long appearing on the 1863 petition as "widow with 5 children."

20. "The Wrongs of the Sewing Women," *North American and U.S. Gazette*, April 27, 1862, 1.

21. Grace Palladino, *Another Civil War: Labor, Capital, and the State in the Anthracite Regions of Pennsylvania, 1840–68* (Chicago: University of Illinois Press, 1990), 172–73.

22. Although this petition is dated 1862, the grievances described in the petition indicate that the petition was signed in response to the 1863 layoffs. "Petition," Anna Long et al. to Edwin Stanton, July 29, 1863, NARA, RG 92, Box 798 (old), e. 225.

23. Elizabeth Steinmeyer and Maggie Murphy, et al., to E. M. Stanton, August 4, 1863, NARA, RG 92, Box 1004, No. 105, 2. "Philadelphia Seamstresses: Meeting of Women Employed in the U.S. Arsenal," *Fincher's Trades' Review*, August 8, 1863, 38.

24. August 1, 1861, Petition, Box 789, Old, NARA, RG 92, e. 225.

25. "Petition," Anna Long et al. to Edwin Stanton, July 29, 1863, NARA, RG 92, Box 798 (old), e. 225

26. For Brooklyn, see "The Sewing Women," *Finchers' Trades' Review*, December 12, 1863, 7. For New York, see "Spasmodic Sympathy for Working Women" *Finchers' Trades' Review*, April 2, 1864, 70. For Detroit, see "The Sewing Women," [Reprinted from *The (Detroit) Mechanic and Workingmen's Advocate*], *Finchers' Trades' Review*, March 18, 1865, 62. For Cincinnati, see "Wrongs of Sewing Women," *Finchers' Trades' Review*, March 18, 1865, 62.

Yeager seems to have gotten her job back, for her name appears again on the June 13, 1864 petition from 800 "female employees" of the arsenal. Anna Brooks et al. to Colonel G. H. Crosman, June 13, 1864, NARA, RG 92, Box 1004.

27. Quoted in Dublin, *Women at Work*, 93.

28. Quoted in Stansell, *City of Women*, 146.

29. Dawley, *Class and Community*, 82.

30. Dublin, *Women at Work*, 94.

31. Anna Long's household in 1860 included Patrick Long, 31 years; Mary Long, 8 years; John Long, 5 years; Anna E Long, 3 years; and Charles Long, 1 year. Whether Patrick died in the war or from another cause could not be determined. Anna Long,

Philadelphia Ward 5 Southern Division, Philadelphia, *1860 United States Federal Census*, www.Ancestry.com.

Census records suggest that Mary Pratt, organizer of the Working Women's Relief Association, was likely thirty-six with three children (twelve, nine, and three years old) when she attended the 1862 meeting, condemned Colonel Crosman as no friend of the seamstresses and encouraged women to stand together. There were two potential candidates. The latter seems likely for if her husband was serving in the U.S. Army, as she suggested in her 1862 speech, this might explain his absence from the 1870 census. (1) Mary Pratt, b. @ 1832, Philadelphia Ward 21 Dist 70, Philadelphia, *1870 United States Federal Census*, Ancestry.com. (2) Mary Pratt, b. @ 1826, Philadelphia Ward 19 District 60, Philadelphia, *1870 United States Federal Census*, www.Ancestry.com.

In January 1865, Martha Yeager was likely thirty-five years old and a veteran of the petition campaign when she met with President Lincoln to discuss the needs of sewing women. When Yeager lost her Schuylkill job due to the 1863 order, she indicated that she had a brother in the war. Only one Martha Yeager could be identified in Philadelphia in the 1870 census—none in 1860. The other members of her household were forty-five year old William and twenty year old Anna. Martha Yeager, b.@1830, Philadelphia Ward 2 Dist 5, Philadelphia, Pennsylvania, *1870 United States Federal Census*, Ancestry.com.

32. "A Meeting of Female Operatives," *North American and U.S. Gazette*, September 4, 1861, 1.

The editor of the *North American and U.S. Gazette* published an editorial the next day in which he carefully corrected Long's claims, pointing out that some of the uniforms used in the Mexican war were made in New York. "The Schuylkill Arsenal," *North American and U.S. Gazette*, September 5, 1861, 1.

33. Mark R. Wilson, *The Business of Civil War: Military Mobilization and the State, 1861–1865* (Baltimore: Johns Hopkins University Press, 2006), 2–3.

34. Meigs quoted in Wilson, *Business of War*, 142.

35. Palladino, *Another Civil War*, 144–45.

36. Philip S. Foner, *Women and the American Labor Movement, From Colonial Times to the Eve of World War I*, New York: The Free Press, 1979, 114.

Early in 1864, Moses Beach, editor of the *New York Sun*, called a meeting of the Working Women's Protective Union. Foner, *Women and Labor*, 119–20.

"Another Meeting of the Sewing," *Philadelphia Inquirer*, April 27, 1864, 8.

37. A "Mrs. Miller" led the May 18, 1864 unionization meeting, with help from local male labor leaders, including William Sylvis, leader of the Iron Molder's Union, and Jonathan Fincher, editor of *Fincher's Trades' Review* who were also in attendance. "The Sewing Women Again," *North American and U.S. Gazette*, May 19, 1864, 1. "Working-Women's Meeting, *Fincher's Trades' Review*, May 28, 1864, 108. For New York seamstresses' Working Women's Protective Union, see: "Spasmodic Sympathy for Working-women," *Fincher's Trades' Review*, April 2, 1864, 70. Seidman, *Beyond Sacrifice*, 152.

38. "Twenty-Thousand Working Women" to Edwin M. Stanton, June 1864, RG 92, Box 439, NM 81, e. 225, NARA.

39. G. H. Crosman to Brig. Genl. Meigs, June 6, 1864, RG 92, Box 439, NM 81, e. 225, NARA.

40. Lt. Col. Vinton (New York) to Meigs, June 20, 1864, Box 439, e. 225, RG 92, NARA. Although the New York City depot produced none of their own clothing, army supply officers there contracted with the city's private manufacturers.

41. G. H. Crosman to Brig. Genl. Meigs, June 6, 1864, RG 92, Box 439, NM 81, e. 225, NARA.

42. "Twenty-Thousand Working Women" to Edwin M. Stanton, June 1864, RG 92, Box 439, NM 81, e. 225, NARA.

43. Seidman, *Beyond Sacrifice*, 160.

44. "Working Women," *Fincher's Trades' Review*, June 6, 1863, 2.
Fincher was right in noting the increase in female industrial labor during the war. James McPherson estimates there was a 40 percent increase in the number of women involved in industrial work during the war. James McPherson, *Ordeal by Fire: The Civil War*, vol. 2, 3rd ed., New York: McGraw Hill, 2001, 406.

45. "The Workingwomen's Movement," *Fincher's Trades' Review*, April 30, 1864, 86.

46. David Montgomery, "William Sylvis and the Search for Working-Class Citizenship," in Melvyn Dubofksy and Warren Van Tine, *Labor Leaders in America* (Urbana: University of Illinois Press), 1987. 24–28.

47. Anna Brooks et al. to Colonel G. H. Crosman, June 13, 1864, Box 1004, RG 92, NARA.

48. The numbers of women sewing for the arsenal fluctuated throughout the war, and with nearly all of them sewing on an outwork basis, exact numbers are hard to come by. Mark Wilson estimated that by the summer of 1861, there were 5,000 women employed at the arsenal. Wilson, *Business of War*, 86.

49. "The Wages of Sewing Women—A Letter from Secretary Stanton, 18 August 1864," *New York Times*, August 26, 1864, 1.

50. The New York petition was reprinted in *Fincher's Trades' Review* on September 17, 1864. Foner, *Women and Labor*, 115.

51. Foner, *Women and Labor*, 116. It is not clear if the sewing women accepted the offer to join the men or if they preferred to retain their own organization.

52. Wilson, *Business of War*, 87–89.

53. "Indignation Meeting of Working Women," January 20, 1865, *Philadelphia Inquirer*, 8. The women who accompanied Yeager were Mrs. Brooks, Mrs. Davison, and Mrs. Alexander.

54. "The Sewing Women on Arsenal Work," February 11, 1865, *Fincher's Trades' Review*, 42.

55. "Sewing Women of Cincinnati to Abraham Lincoln," February 20, 1865, reprinted in *Fincher's Trades' Review*, March 18, 1865, 2.

56. "The President and the Arsenal Women," *Fincher's Trades Reviews*, February 4, 1865, 38

57. In *Signatures of Citizenship*, Susan Zaeske traces the progress of self-realization underway in the antislavery petition campaign, in which women first signed their names with a "Mrs." but then dropped the title. Susan Zaeske, *Signatures of Citizenship: Petitioning, Antislavery, and Women's Political Identity* (Chapel Hill.: University of North Carolina Press, 2003), 109.

58. Michael Thomas Smith, *The Enemy Within: Fears of Corruption in the Civil War North* (Charlottesville: University of Virginia Press, 2011), 2.

59. "The Sewing Women on Arsenal Work," *Fincher's Trades' Review*, February 11, 1865, 42.

60. Silber, *Gender and Conflict*, 63–66.

61. "The Ladies' League: Meetings at Dr. Cheever's Church and Cooper Institute," *New York Times*, May 15, 1863, 8. The resolution about women's equality raised at least one dissenting voice, a Mrs. Hoyt claiming that "[t]he women of the Revolution did not ask for equal political privileged and rights with men."

"A Source of Mortification to All Truly Loyal Men"

Allegheny Arsenal's Disloyal Worker Purge of 1863

Timothy J. Orr

On May 13, 1863, the commander of Pittsburgh's Allegheny Arsenal fired fifteen skilled workers, citing disloyalty as cause for their dismissal. For several weeks, the city's partisan newspapers erupted into fiery dialogue, turning all eyes onto this controversial U.S. Army facility, an installation accustomed to negative attention. The editors attempted to judge a critical question: Was it wise to rid one of the nation's leading ammunition-production centers of workers who possessed undeniably skilled hands, but who also possessed potentially treasonous minds? In answering this question, the rival political parties took starkly oppositional postures. Pittsburgh's Republicans defended the decision to purge the arsenal's skilled workers, pointing out the necessity of removing possible sources of sabotage. Further, or so noted one editor, it seemed a great indignity—"a source of mortification to all truly loyal men," as he put it—for the federal government to provide wartime occupations for disloyal workingmen. Factory work allowed workingmen an opportunity to avoid military service, and while hidden under this veil of protection, these same individuals derided the government that shielded them. Meanwhile, the Democrats defended the shop workers, painting the purge as a simple case of partisan hatred. In the end, Pittsburgh's Democrats succeeded in reinstating the fired workers. Those who wanted to return to work did so, but in the aftermath, the wartime factory operatives lost a larger prize. In 1864, the U.S. Army clarified its relationship with wartime workers. For male workers, industrial service no longer served as an able substitute for taking up a rifle. If a local draft commissioner pulled their names, factory work could not serve as a form of exemption.

On its own, the story of the fifteen fired arsenal workers at Allegheny Arsenal might rate nothing more than an insignificant footnote with the larger tale of America's Civil War, but when cast as part of the greater debate to define the meaning of loyalty in Pennsylvania, it emerges as an important incident illuminating the contours of the North's turbulent labor history. In short, this particular incident—the Allegheny Arsenal purge—reveals the volatility that attended accusations of disloyalty among men who handled the nation's ammunition. The mass firing underscored the importance that arsenal commanders placed upon the loyalty of factory operatives. It was not enough that workers merely labored for the cause; they had to exhibit loyal sentiments as well. Arsenal chiefs refused to risk the production of vital military equipage to potentially treasonous hands. In an environment where sabotage could endanger workers' lives and imperil the Union war effort, the Allegheny Arsenal's commander— and the Republican newspaper editor who encouraged him—considered it best to remove questionable hands and deal with the consequences later. The incident reminded everyone—all across the North, and most especially in Western Pennsylvania—that workers needed to mind their tongues when they served on the shop floor.

Chronology played a role in the dispute. Not only had the Allegheny Arsenal faced two years of public criticism, but Pennsylvania's third year of the war, 1863, was rife with debate about the meaning of loyalty. In March, more than two dozen Pennsylvania regiments published anti-Copperhead resolutions, defining peace activism as evidence of disloyalty.[1] That same month, Congress passed the first federal conscription law, sparking a debate about draft resistance. In November, this dispute culminated in an important state-level case, *Kneedler v. Lane*, in which the Commonwealth's Supreme Court ruled that the federal draft law was unconstitutional.[2] Finally in May, in neighboring Ohio, Union forces arrested Clement Vallandigham, the nation's most well-known Copperhead, banishing him to the Confederacy.[3] Almost to a person, Pennsylvania Republicans supported the banishment as a political victory in the name of national security. One newspaper editorialized, "The rebel on the battlefield is shot down constitutionally with due process of (military) law, very summary though it be; so the spy is constitutionally hung by drum-head court-martial; and so, too, may he who gives aid and comfort to the enemy be constitutionally imprisoned by military authority."[4] Democrats, meanwhile, lamented the Vallandigham arrest and banishment as an unspeakable violation of civil liberty. One editor explained, "It is not a question as to what party he [Vallandigham] may have belonged[,]. . . nor whether he has been for the war or opposed to the war. It is a question of *public right*, violated and outraged through an individual. [It is] a constitutional right, *trodden down* and trampled underfoot in order to vent the spleen of the administration."[5] More than a dozen Pennsylvania counties held mass meetings protesting Vallandigham's arrest, prompting equally dyspeptic replies from vocal

Republican opponents.[6] No period in Pennsylvania's turbulent Civil War history tested the boundaries of loyalty more acutely than the spring of 1863.

When the debate over loyalty spilled onto the floors of Allegheny Arsenal, it must have come as no surprise to party leaders. It was an election year for Pennsylvania. For weeks, partisan stalwarts mobilized their presses for battle. Loyalty—and its meaning—served as a primary bone of contention. As Melinda Lawson has astutely argued, "Given the centrality of parties to nineteenth-century political culture, it is not surprising to find that, for many Americans, definitions of loyalty and national identity during the Civil War revolved around party."[7]

Still, the fact that parties and partisan definitions of loyalty seeped into Allegheny Arsenal underscores the anomalous place occupied by the Union's wartime workers. The U.S. Army required a surge of wartime workers to complete its mammoth task of materiel mobilization—a fact that cannot be doubted. Yet, the Allegheny Arsenal purge—and other purges that followed it—proved the willingness of Army officers to discard their manufactory's skilled hands, particularly when they had no assurance that the Republican Party had decisively won the war for their employees' hearts and minds.

In a comparative sense, the Allegheny Arsenal purge is instructive. Other American wars required an up-swell in industrialism as a precondition for victory. In those wars, too—the Great War and the Second World War, especially—the U.S. Army battled to win the loyalty of its arsenal employees. Of course, America's wartime workers in the World Wars were not free from abuse. Accusations of sabotage abounded, unionization met with discouragement, and propaganda infested every element of wartime production. Throughout the total wars of the twentieth century, public disdain handicapped the nation's essential factory operatives. However, in some ways, the Civil War experience stood in contrast to the World Wars of the twentieth century. When the clarion trumpet of total mobilization beckoned, officers of the twentieth-century Army could not flagrantly dismiss industrial labor as inconsequential, that is, as something unequal to military service. Those who wanted wartime work found it. Industrial workers received praise for their efforts, particularly if they avoided unionization or pledged to work overtime. Partisanship rarely shaped their day-to-day lives. In the Civil War, by contrast, wartime workers expected political discrimination as part of their working conditions.[8]

What caused the wartime workers of the Civil War to lack protection for their political beliefs? The answer lay in the fact that the United States had not passed through the industrial revolution, not in a complete sense, anyway. The economic distinctions of the working class did not always become apparent, largely due to the Republican Party's efforts to emphasize unity among free laborers and obscured all evidence that revealed the yawning disparities of wealth. In 1988, in his history of the Union home front, A People's Contest, Phillip Shaw Paludan explained how this phenomenon worked. Paludan pointed out that economic hardship served the dual purpose of pushing the plight of the industrial working class to the forefront of public discourse, but at the same time, it provided the Army with the ideological rationale for stamping out working-class protest. As Paludan explained it, a major element in the free labor ideology "served to diffuse the claim of workers for special attention." He continued, "Since all of society was linked in the free labor struggle, owners, industrialists, capitalists, might equally assert their devotion to free labor goals, thus weakening the special force of labor's claim to the idea." In short, it was easy for factory managers to mark unionization and union activities as conspiracies to limit the Union's industrial production. When workers asserted their rights or stretched the limits of free speech, the paranoia of the North's two-party system reared its head. Republicans, then, saw work stoppages as treason designed to overturn the nation's mobilization.[9]

In Allegheny County, the region that surrounded the arsenal, the two-party system was especially vibrant. Early on, the Republican Party dominated at elections. In the Election of 1860, Abraham Lincoln won the county with a 10,000 vote plurality, one of the highest pluralities anywhere in the country. Over the course of the war, Republican supremacy dwindled, but only slightly. During the gubernatorial election of 1863, Allegheny County counted only 17,700 Republican voters and 10,000 Democratic voters, and during the presidential election of 1864, the county polled 21,500 Republican votes and 12,400 Democratic votes.[10] Of course, this did not mean that Democratic dissidents were drowned by a sea of Republicans. As the war progressed, wartime workers found themselves aligning with the antiwar faction of the Democratic Party. Decades ago, David Montgomery convincingly argued that wartime workers across the country did not remain Copperheads for long, shedding their peace activism by the summer of 1864; however, he noted that, during the high point of Copperhead popularity—the spring and summer of 1863—antiwar Democrats enjoyed heavy support from working-class voters. As Montgomery stated, "the major grievances which sparked labor protest were all related to the growing power and centralization of government, and opposition to that tendency was the very essence of old-line democracy." Of course, wartime workers focused on near-term, local issues, not broad attacks against centralization. But when they felt exploited, workers in Pittsburgh and elsewhere found it easy to ally with the Democratic Party, the organization that blamed the administration, or even the war itself, for the troubles that vexed the urban poor.[11]

With the exception of Judith Giesberg's *Army at Home*, the tribulations of Pennsylvania's wartime workers are fairly unknown.[12] Historians have seldom described the process of constructing ammunition and weaponry, and neither have they delineated the conditions of life on the factory floor, the pace of work, nor the safety concerns that hovered over employees on each and every arduous work day.[13] What is certain is that the North's materiel mobilization could not have been achieved without these arsenals and the hard-working crews who managed them and toiled within. At the beginning of the war, the Commonwealth of Pennsylvania possessed only three United States arsenals.[14] At forty-seven-years, Allegheny Arsenal was one of the oldest in the nation. By 1861 it consisted of a thirty-one-acre plot. Several structures existed, but the arsenal's primary edifice was its ammunition manufactory. Like the other major arsenals along the East Coast, it underwent a surge of hiring. Allegheny Arsenal began the war with 304 employees, but by the end, its roster contained more than 950 names.[15] Working at full blast, its employees assembled 128,000 cartridges per day, or more than 46,000,000 rounds per year. This constituted about 17 percent of all small arms ammunition expended by Union soldiers. All day long, employees rolled paper cartridges, cleaned and stored small arms, or assembled artillery fuses and leather harnesses.[16]

No one in Pennsylvania doubted Allegheny Arsenal's importance for maintaining the logistical mobilization of the Union's army and navy, but the facility struggled to achieve positive relations with citizens of Lawrenceville, the community on the south bank of the Allegheny River that surrounded the arsenal's grounds. The rush in ammunition production caused residents to wonder if their lives might be in danger. The arsenal was only seventy miles north of the border with Virginia (and forty miles east of it), and the threat of bushwhackers, real or imagined, filled the nightmares of Western Pennsylvania's citizens. Newspapers openly criticized the army officers who commanded at Allegheny, complaining that they did too little to prevent the possibility of sabotage. An explosion might, after all, spread fire, both wide and hot, consuming the entire neighborhood. Three times in October 1861, workers found stray matches strewn about the yard. The arsenal's officers believed (probably correctly) that the teenage boys hired to serve as wagon drivers smoked pipes, carelessly flinging their matches onto the ground. This was a dangerous habit to be sure, but not at all indicative of sabotage. The citizens of Lawrenceville were less dismissive. Pittsburgh's newspapers indulged the paranoia, calling these matches evidence of purposeful "attempts to blow up the magazine." One newspaper explained, "Some of the people residing near the Arsenal were so apprehensive under the excitement of these rumors that they feared to lie down at night, lest they be blown to fragments before morning."[17]

To quell these fears, the arsenal commander, Colonel John Symington, fired most of his boys, hiring girls instead. Women would not smoke; hence, there would be no more matches. Over the winter of 1861–62, women began filling vacant positions at the arsenal. According to Judith Giesberg, "Response to his [Symington's] call for female applicants was brisk, and Symington quickly filled cartridge-former positions with women and girls living in the neighborhood just west of Pittsburgh. Once women were employed in the powder rooms, Colonel Symington reported no additional problems with discipline."[18] The women who went to work at the arsenal tended to perform the ammunition factory's unskilled or semi-skilled tasks: cartridge rolling, cartridge measuring, cartridge pinching, cartridge bundling, percussion cap making, and cannon cartridge bag making. By April 1862, women constituted 92 percent of the workforce. Meanwhile, the minority of men who remained employed at the arsenal continued to fill the skilled or semi-skilled positions. They worked on the precision-based tasks such as bullet trimming, bullet gauging, and bullet encasing. Others worked in the saddlery building, assembling halters, bridles, girths, saddles, and plates.[19]

The arrival of female workers pleased a few troubled minds, but the Arsenal continued to draw criticism. By 1862, it ran seven days a week, drawing the ire of concerned religious leaders. Ministers complained that the army made its new female employees work too much. One newspaper lamented, "It is impossible to estimate the sinister influence this must exert on public morals. . . . The nation is the transgressor. And when a nation violates the law, what prohibitions can be placed upon its subjects?"[20] But if church-going moralism had little effect on slowing down the arsenal's rapid production schedule, a disastrous explosion in 1862 surely gave officials reason to pause. On September 17, a massive detonation rocked Allegheny Arsenal, shattering the edifice of one of its cartridge-rolling establishments, killing seventy-eight workers—nearly all women—literally splattering the victims' innards against the sides of adjacent buildings. After bucket brigades quenched the fire, fragments of skulls and scorched bones marred the burnt landscape. The shocking scene led to an investigation by the War Department, which, frustratingly, never fully identified the cause of the catastrophe. Several theories surfaced, but all of them pointed to different culprits. All agreed that barrels of unrolled powder stored on a wagon had exploded. At 2 o'clock, that vehicle had just rolled up to the door to unload, and some people believed that a young boy had jumped up and down on one of the barrels, causing the conflagration. Others believed that the iron-rimmed wheels of the wagon had created a spark in the wrong place at the wrong time. Still others contended that a few of the women entering the building had refused to wear their leather moccasins, allowing a dangerous build-up of static electricity, thus sparking the detonation. Consequently, in the aftermath, no one was quite sure who should bear the burden of culpability.[21]

Most Pittsburghers knew that, at some level, unsafe working conditions had caused this accident. A coroner's jury placed the blame on the arsenal commander, Colonel Symington, castigating him for failing to notice and correct the hazardous working environment. Meanwhile, a military investigation exonerated him, claiming that the private business that had stored the powder and sold it to him must be at fault. In the tribunal's opinion, no officer, no matter how clairvoyant, could have prevented an explosion, given the inferior condition of the powder. The Army's "not guilty" verdict did little to assuage the feelings of citizens who lost loved ones in the explosion. The tortured relationship between citizens and the staff only worsened when a junior officer at the factory, John R. Edie, publicly blamed the female workers for failing to do their job in a safe manner. (Later on, his harsh treatment of grieving families led a religious committee to call for Edie's banishment from Pittsburgh.) In any event, Symington—who had requested retirement back in August—left the arsenal at the beginning of 1863, as did other officers, who now bore the guilt of losing so many of Pittsburgh's patriotic daughters.[22]

The resignation of Colonel Symington brought a new commander to Allegheny, Major Robert Henry Kirkwood Whiteley, a fifty-four-year-old Delaware native and West Point graduate, Class of 1830. Whiteley had commanded U.S. arsenals for more than twenty years, having directed the facilities at Baton Rouge, St. Louis, San Antonio, and New York. The War Department's Chief of Ordnance, James Wolfe Ripley, transferred Whiteley to Lawrenceville with hopes that his expertise would improve its safety. Upon arrival, Whiteley suspended production of small arms cartridges, complaining that the arsenal had more than 8,000,000 rounds in storage, "in a leaky frame shed," which was, as he said, "by no means safe from accident by fire."[23] The suspension of cartridge rolling mollified critical citizens, but Whiteley's subsequent firing of fifteen skilled employees for charges of treason captured Pittsburgh's headlines.

The firings occurred because a few of the skilled employees loved to talk politics on the shop floor. One of these men was John Beck, a Democrat who brought newspapers to work. When not busily assembling harnesses at the saddlery building, he read through the columns and then spoke critically of Abraham Lincoln and his administration. Particularly, the results of the 1862 elections elated him. In November 1862, when the state of New York elected Horatio Seymour as its governor, Beck could not refrain from gloating. In January 1863, he endorsed Seymour's inaugural address, declaring, "Thank God[!] New York has now a Gov. that will see to the poor mans rights and there will be no more arbitrary arrests there." Beck, it seemed, lacked the ability to judge how much his smirking upset his Republican coworkers. They quietly bore their party's defeat and Beck's mockery with grace—that is, until March 1863, when Congress passed its controversial Conscription Bill. Given a new issue upon which to hammer, Beck lambasted the Republicans for concocting iniquitous legislation. Specifically, Beck considered the $300 commutation clause a travesty of justice. He ridiculed anyone who endorsed it, including Pennsylvania's Republican governor, Andrew Gregg Curtin.[24]

At some point, in March 1863, Beck brought to work a Democratic newspaper, the *New York World*, and he read aloud two scathing articles that criticized Lincoln and the draft law. In April, another arsenal worker, one who shared the same boarding house as Beck, reported these incidents to Allegheny County's Republican "Union League Club," a private association of gentlemen who meant to spread nationalist literature throughout the state. One member of the club, a carpet dealer named James W. McFarland, collected a lengthy list of accusations. By April, he had testimony to incriminate fifteen workers, charging them with the crime of uttering disloyal affirmations.[25] On April 8, 1863, McFarland took his notes to Samuel Riddle, editor of the Republican *Pittsburgh Gazette*. Unnerved by what McFarland presented to him, Riddle contacted Major Whiteley and insisted that he launch an investigation of his own, and if satisfied with the results, fire the accused workers. Riddle forwarded McFarland's list of charges to Whiteley, announcing, "I have faith in my informant and hope to see the U.S. Arsenal purged of disloyalty."[26]

McFarland's list identified the specific workers by name and linked them to treasonous expressions delivered on the shop floor. However, none of the accusations linked the accused workers to quoted material; instead, McFarland's blacklist offered vague descriptions of political dissent based on second-hand knowledge. For instance, McFarland accused one worker, James Morris, of denouncing "the administration as dam'd abolitionist[s]"; he accused another worker of damning the federal Oath of Allegiance, even though that worker had willingly taken the Oath in 1861; and he accused mechanic John Jeffrey of being "disloyal, from general conversation among his fellow workmen."[27]

McFarland's accusations oscillated between vague disparagement and improbable hearsay, but editor Riddle considered the evidence unimpeachable. Writing to Major Whiteley, Riddle alleged:

> I am not the prosecutor of these persons; as a public journalist, *known to hate disloyalty*, I was requested to direct your attention to a fact which, for two years past has been a source of mortification to all truly loyal men, viz: That within the walls of the U.S. Arsenal at Lawrenceville there were persons in the employ of the Government who habitually, in the workshops, in the village— amongst fellow-workmen and amongst fellow-citizens—had only words of ignominy and reproach when alluding to the government of the United States and its friends, and who, by common consent, amongst the loyal and patriotic workmen in the arsenal shops, and the citizens with whom they associated, were ever considered sympathizers with, if not guilty of, *treason*.[28]

Spurred by Riddle's demands for an inquiry, Major Whiteley confronted each of the accused workers one by one. Predictably, each accused person denied the allegations. Whiteley briefly considered a trial by jury to allow his employees a chance to defend themselves, but editor Riddle rejected this suggestion, telling Whiteley that, "it seems strange that a soldier of the United States, . . . entrusted with command of one of her arsenals," should satisfy himself with a trial by jury to validate the truth of the charges.[29] After receiving Riddle's rebuke, Whiteley appointed an internal investigatory committee consisting of five men chosen by Riddle and five men chosen by the fifteen workers. The accused workers chose not to participate in this internal investigation. Instead, one of them—Master Machinist Thomas K. Laley—attempted to bring charges of libel against the *Pittsburgh Gazette*. Unfortunately for Laley, no lawyer took the case. On May 13, after waiting for weeks, the five-person committee established by Riddle rendered its verdict, and because the accused had sent no persons to represent them, Riddle's committeemen confirmed the workers' guilt. Dutifully, Whiteley fired them all.[30]

Why did Whiteley eventually believe these charges of treason? Or, more to the point, why did he allow a hostile newspaper editor sufficient latitude to dictate the prosecution of his fifteen employees? Unfortunately, insufficient evidence exists to answer these questions. No known document explains Whiteley's relationship with Samuel Riddle. Consequently, his reasons for taking the accusations of disloyalty seriously can only be derived through context. Quite possibly, in the wake of the September 1862 explosion, Whiteley could not afford to discount any rumors that might connect disloyalty to potential acts of sabotage. Since the beginning of the war, Pittsburgh's citizens had expressed fears of a city-wide conflagration, and in 1862, an accidental detonation upheld those fears. The subsequent investigation led to the dismissal of Allegheny Arsenal's previous commander. The April 1863 disloyalty accusations, despite their flimsiness, probably accelerated Whiteley's own pre-existing fears—fear of sabotage and fear for his reputation. Once he encountered pressure from an aggressive Republican newspaper editor, Whiteley made a move to placate his critics. In so doing, he cast his Democratic workers as traitors.

Pittsburgh Republicans applauded Whiteley on a job well done, but Democrats complained that he had overreacted to slanderous allegations originating from a party press. For the next two months, the Pittsburgh newspapers debated endlessly the "Arsenal Question." A Democratic newspaper, the *Pittsburgh Post*, called Whiteley's decision a "shock to the moral sense of every law-abiding and good citizen." The *Post* condemned Riddle, Whiteley, and the five-man committee for "illegally and unrighteously" driving the fifteen workmen "from their places," and ruining the lives and reputations of their "friends, wives, and children." The *Post* covered the affair in detail thanks to the aid of Major John B. Butler, the arsenal's paymaster, who happened to contribute to the Democratic newspaper. Butler censured the proceedings, declaring that:

> 1st. They [the accused] had no knowledge of any charge against them. 2d They had no notice of the trial. 3d They had no counsel nor witnesses. 4th. They had no chance to make a defence. 5th. They had no jury. 6th. They had no judge in the case. 7th. They were tried before a secret and packed enclave. 8th. And by that cabal, they were convicted and sentenced. 9th. They were called up and told (mark the conclusion!) 'If you can *prove* your innocence, you shall be restored to labor, and *permitted* to associate again with your fellow workmen!'[31]

When Butler published his rejoinders in early June, Pittsburgh's Republicans responded with their own censures, demanding that the *Post* release the name of its secret correspondent, so they could sue him for libel. Luckily, Butler had saved himself the inconvenience of litigation by publishing his letters under a pseudonym, "Wayne." When the *Pittsburgh Gazette* learned that Major Butler probably authored these articles, its writers accused him—although not by name, specifically—of being out-of-touch with the situation, calling him a "feeble-minded old dotard." The writers insisted that Whiteley relieve him of his duties at the arsenal.[32] The *Gazette's* attacks on Butler became so spiteful that seven of the fired arsenal workers wrote him an apologetic letter. "We are sorry," they wrote, "very sorry, that men who have persecuted us are trying to injure you. This is what we most grieve about, that you have stood by us while others whom we least expected looked on us with suspicion, and that you are to be injured and abused on our account."[33]

Butler's reply exhibited an awkward mix of hopefulness and despair. He demurred from blaming his accusers, claiming that they simply assimilated too much hysteria—a forgivable error, given the times. He wrote, "Do you know that many good and ordinarily just men reproach and vilify me for this effort? But I excuse them, on the ground that *they* do not know you and your *assailants* as well as I do." However, Butler argued for less clemency when dealing with the Republican arsenal workers who, he argued, falsely indicted their Democratic shop-mates. He continued, "I have been informed that several who appeared against you, refused to *swear* to their statements; and that others who did take the oath, have expressed regret and great contrition that they consented to do so! In charity and mercy to them, let us hope it was not from a want of moral courage, that they took the oath; or that in the excess of their allegiance to their party, they forgot their allegiance to God, by ignoring the solemn injunction contained in the ninth command of the Decalogue! Justice is slow, but it will *surely* overwhelm the guilty, as it will console and sustain the innocent!" Although he did not want to believe it, Butler had identified the primary source of the problem, as he put it, "excess[ive] . . . allegiance to . . . party." Idle political talk on the shop floor had angered fellow workers, who in turn retaliated with charges of disloyalty. In a time and place where the fabric of Union mobilization hinged on the efficiency and loyalty of shop-hands, endorsements of the opposition party could easily be seen as treason.[34]

In late June, while the war between the *Gazette* and *Post* focused on the credibility of Butler, the fifteen accused arsenal workers contacted friends and neighbors, asking them to sign statements that testified to their loyalty. By July, each of the fifteen had collected about a dozen references apiece. One of the accused, Thomas H. Rowland, collected twenty-five witnesses. John Beck received the support of seven, including the President of Denison University in Ohio and a federal provost marshal from Ohio's Thirteenth District. Each witness offered evidence to restore the besmirched reputations of the accused. For instance, George Rundels stated that he "never heard [accused worker] George Beissenger say anything disrespectful of the constitution or the war. He never interfered with his son to prevent him from going into the army." Alderman Philip Kincaid confirmed that accused worker Walter T. Hill "has often called in my office and conversed with me, and since the war and on the war, and in all of which I have received him as a sober, steady and industrious man, and never do I recollect of hearing him say anything that might be considered disloyal to the government of the United States."[35]

In late July, Major Whiteley reconsidered the arsenal terminations. With the Confederate Army of Northern Virginia now in retreat after its defeat at Gettysburg and with the first federal draft proceeding peacefully in Pennsylvania, Whiteley decided that perhaps he had followed too much hysteria. Quietly, he reinstated the fifteen arsenal workers to their former positions. Most took Whiteley's offer, but not all of them. Thomas K. Laley, the former master machinist, had already found a better position as inspector of arms at Washington, D.C.'s arsenal.[36] John Beck, angered at his mistreatment, simply refused to return to work.

The *Pittsburgh Post* did not let the story die. After Whiteley announced the reinstatement, the *Post* published several editorials intended to make the Republicans squirm. "We almost pity the slanderers," wrote one editor, "who possessed with malice and uncharitable-ness, constituted themselves a mock tribunal, to pass upon the honesty and fealty of industrious, worthy men. . . . It is high time that this sort of persecution should cease—it only engenders strife and ill-will, and aggravates the public in these disjointed times." Nevertheless, the same writer advised caution, warning fellow Democrats and friends of the accused workers to refrain from retaliation. Perhaps fearing that retribution would cause additional Republican recriminations, or perhaps desiring to restore dignity to Pittsburgh's political dialectic, the *Post* opined, "If we might advise, we would earnestly counsel forbearance and moderation on the part of the artisans who suffered such abominable injustice. Let them teach their persecutors a lesson of magnanimity that shall sink deep in the heart of the editor of *Gazette*."

The Allegheny Arsenal purge offers historians a crucial window into the world of the Civil War factory worker, showing how arsenal workers faced dangers beyond the combustible materials with which they worked. They also faced troublesome questions pertaining to the definition of loyalty. Unlike America's other wars—where factory work served as a substitute for military service—Civil War factory labor did not protect arsenal workers from suspicion of treason. In an environment where loyalty to the government and to the nation became mutable constructs, Pennsylvania factory workers found it hard to insulate their reputations from the political paranoia. Laboring with their hands, making the Union's necessary weapons of war, was not enough to prove loyalty. Further, Major Whiteley's response to the accusations of disloyalty reflected the federal government's ambivalent tone toward factory work. Rather than see it as an essential component of wartime mobilization, he viewed it as a benevolent gift, bestowed upon America's non-military working class, or perhaps as a potential liability, a place for enemy saboteurs to wreak havoc.

Several other examples in Pennsylvania substantiate this conclusion. Allegheny Arsenal was not the only federal facility to experience a controversial purge in 1863. During the last week of July, Schuylkill Arsenal—a federal clothing manufactory in Philadelphia—fired 200 female workers when Republican Congressman William D. Kelley complained that too many of the seamstresses employed there were not near relatives of soldiers, or were "opposed to the war." Kelley considered military tailoring to be a temporary privilege granted by the federal government to patriotic families in order to supplement incomes when male relatives fought on the battlefield. In consequence, Colonel George H. Crosman, the federal commander of the Army Clothing and Equipage Office posted at Philadelphia, directed the superintendent of Schuylkill Arsenal's clothing manufactory, Charles Thomas, to provide satisfactory evidence, in writing, of each female employee's military relatives. Only those who were "wives, mothers, and sisters, or near relatives" of soldiers or sailors could be retained.[37] Thus, more than 200 workers found themselves unemployed at the end of the month. The fired seamstresses organized a mass protest in August, carrying their public outcry into 1864, but even an appeal to Secretary of War Edwin Stanton failed to reinstate them.[38]

By comparison, the Allegheny Arsenal workers faced a better fate than the women fired from Schuylkill Arsenal. The Allegheny employees lost their jobs, but only momentarily. Of his own volition, Whiteley reinstated the fifteen fired workers. More to the point, the workers escaped physical harm, incarceration, and banishment, measures often contemplated or executed by legal or extralegal parties when punishing cases of treason. The rhetoric of the debate at Allegheny arose to polemical heights—that much is certain—but in the end, the episode did not restructure daily life at the factory. Excepting a few disgruntled workers who left in disgust, in the end, nearly all of the accused workers stayed put.

However, in the aftermath of the Allegheny purge, no one at the factory could say that day-to-day activities carried on as if nothing had happened. The scuffle had imparted an important message, that wartime laborers lacked the protected status to which they believed they were entitled. More than likely, the accused arsenal workers might even have expected rough treatment, but due to the substandard nature of the evidence mounted against them, they were spared the grim political beheadings and public ostracism that happened to accused Copperheads elsewhere. The other employees had to have gleaned the meaning, that being a factory worker—by choosing to labor for the Union cause rather than fight in its ranks—their loyalty would always be called into question. Routinely, wartime factory managers insisted that their businesses came second to soldiering. To them, taking up arms—not making them—was the true barometer of loyalty. For instance, on July 29, 1863, Philadelphia held a grand dedication for the opening of Bridesburg Armory, a new weapons manufactory administrated by Barton Jenks and Company, which expected to employ 1,700 workers by the end of the year. Two thousand spectators gathered to hear J. Price Wetherill explain how the "machine shops" of Philadelphia would furnish the material to "dethrone the tyrannical monarch" of "King Cotton." However, Wetherill paused to say that all of Bridesburg's employees must aspire to do more than produce firearms. He said that gun manufacturers should not sit idly, because "any man who could make a gun could [also] shoulder a musket."[39]

The War Department upheld this notion, too, making it clear that no one at Allegheny Arsenal could use factory employment as a substitute for military service. In July 1864, a few days after the War Department called for its third draft of the war, it issued a circular—Number 39—which clarified the Allegheny Arsenal workers' relationship with the army. The circular explained that arsenal work did not exempt them from the draft—not in the same way a physical deformity or alienage might—but instead, arsenal work merely excused employees from active military duty as if they were on an extended furlough. This meant that if the assistant provost marshal pulled a Lawrenceville employee's name from the draft wheel, he officially went "in service," but with an immediate temporary reassignment to the factory. To get this reassignment validated, each drafted employee had to receive a letter from the commander at Allegheny Arsenal—Whiteley— one that stated the worker's name, length of contract, and the value of his work. Theoretically, if Whiteley disliked any employee, he could refuse to sign the reassignment form, requiring the worker to go into the army. If any drafted arsenal worker found himself out of his job at any point during the war, he could not avoid military service.[40]

The Allegheny Arsenal example contrasts sharply when it is cast against the experience of workers during the World Wars. During the World Wars, the U.S. government viewed factory work as an acceptable substitute for military service. Beginning in 1916, the government created a sequence of agencies designed to balance the surge of wartime labor alongside the necessity of filling the manpower quota for the U.S. armed services. New agencies such as the Council of National Defense, the War Labor Conference Board, the National War Labor Board, and the War Industries Board protected wartime workers, allowing them to advocate for labor rights without fear of federal harassment. As a form of compromise, the agencies vowed to prohibit strikes, but in return, they claimed concessions from the government, protecting workers' right to unionize, to bargain collectively, to regulate factory safety standards, and to demand equal pay for equal work.[41]

Of course, the Great War was not without its messiness. Americans adhered to a strict code of conduct, one that left wartime workers with little room to negotiate the acceptable definition of patriotism. For instance, the U.S. Selective Service Act compelled Americans to adopt a "Work or Fight" policy, a blunt message spread by propaganda agencies that, as historian Gerald Shenk has revealed, prompted vigilantism as a means of regulating popular perceptions of manhood and whiteness. In 1917 and 1918, gangs went door-to-door hunting down delinquents and deserters, pressuring men to purchase liberty bonds. Although the Selective Service Act contained a host of exclusions that allowed fencible men an opportunity to defer their draft notice for familial reasons or religious scruples, in the popular mind, every able-bodied American had to either work or fight.[42] Collusion between business owners and army depot commanders formed another kind of restriction. The United States witnessed many high-profile army-suppressed worker strikes—particularly in the oil, lumber, and coal businesses—with Regular Army and National Guard commanders intervening in instances where labor radicalism had supposedly tainted the factories' unions. During the nineteen months of U.S. participation in the Great War, fifty-three cities and towns witnessed federal intervention to subdue labor disputes. In many of those instances, so argued one study, the Army "acted as a strikebreaking force." Generals ignored injunctions, overlooked statutes that restricted state control of federal forces, and operated with a consciously anti-labor bias. Altogether, wartime workers during the Great War faced obstacles that Civil War arsenal workers could never imagine.[43]

During the Second World War, the U.S. Army and National Guard operated with greater swiftness, halting labor protests that might unravel wartime production. Between 1941 and 1945, federal forces seized sixty-four privately owned industrial plants, railroads, and municipal systems. Although civil rights abuses spurred some of these interventions, disputes between labor and management accounted for the majority of the seizures. Federal troops seized only four plants during the first two years (all authorized by executive order), but during the last three months, the Regular Army and National Guard seized approximately one defense industry per week. The massive strike by the United Mine Workers in May 1943 in which some 530,000 coal workers walked off the job, closing

4,000 mines, resulted in tide-turning Congressional legislation, the War Labor Disputes Act—passed over Franklin Roosevelt's veto—which declared that in cases of labor disputes, the federal government could automatically seize a private business, and that it became a criminal offense to interfere with labor at an occupied plant.[44]

In some ways, the examples from the World Wars suggest that wartime workers in the twentieth century faced greater threats to their collective bargaining posture than those who worked during the Civil War. Although wars are, by nature, fought according to the unique generational outlook of its participants, it is tempting to view the Civil War as the beginning of Americans' broader quest to question the loyalty of their wartime workers, wondering aloud why men who made weapons so often refused to fight. This process of questioning the manhood of factory laborers found its birth in 1863, and it reached a culminating point during the World Wars, when army take-overs of businesses became a common response to deal with a stuttering mobilization.[45]

However, Civil War arsenal workers faced problems exclusive to their conflict. For instance, during the World Wars, the selective service act exempted workers in industries deemed essential for the war effort, a generosity not afforded to Civil War workers in the North. Without an overarching concept to connect factory work to loyalty, Civil War workers fell prey to political extremism. Despite the fact that the Allegheny Arsenal workers regained their employment, the Allegheny Arsenal purge of 1863 offered a sobering reminder that loyalty was a shapeless concept. Making weapons of war for the Union cause could not save a factory worker tainted by suspicion. Harnessmaker John Beck's case illustrated the point. After issuing his reinstatement proclamation, Major Whiteley asked Beck if he would reconsider his decision to leave Pennsylvania. Beck told him that he would remain only if Whiteley fired his accuser, the only way to restore his besmirched reputation. Whiteley tried to mediate the dispute between the two men; he held a conference that ended badly, with Whiteley telling each person that they should simply quit their employment and enlist in a Union regiment. At first, Beck was too angry to contemplate the possibility of donning a suit of blue, but the arrival of the draft changed his mind. The first federal draft missed him, but in mid-October, Lincoln called for a second draft. By December 1863, as the date of the drawing neared, Beck wrote to Governor Horatio Seymour—the same politician he had supported while boasting on the factory floor—requesting an opportunity to join a New York regiment. Beck wrote, "I have been employed at this Arsenal since May 1861, and although a citizen of Ohio, I am enrolled and liable to be drafted here [in Pennsylvania]. I prefer to enlist under a Democratic

Gov. to being drafted in a place like this and being under the so called soldiers friend Gov. Curtin, or enlisting in Ohio under [John] Brough. I am by occupation a Harnessmaker and would prefer an Artillery Co. with the position of Saddler in the same to anything else."[46] Beck relayed the tale of his firing to the governor, explaining everything from the accusation, to his reinstatement by Major White-ley, to his decision to quit the arsenal. Beck pointed out that he was no shirker. He wanted to go to New York and become a soldier, while his accuser, who remained in the arsenal, had "refused to do so."[47] At this point, even Beck had come to real-ize an important truth. He wanted to be remembered for his deeds, not his words. So long as he worked in an arsenal, his deeds meant nothing.

Notes

1. Timothy J. Orr, "A Viler Enemy in Our Rear: Pennsylvania Soldiers Confront the North's Antiwar Movement," in *The View From the Ground: Experiences of Civil War Sol-diers*, ed. Aaron Sheehan-Dean (Lexington: University Press of Kentucky, 2007), 171–98.

2. Arnold Shankman, *The Pennsylvania Antiwar Movement, 1861–1865* (Cranbury, N.J.: Farleigh Dickinson University Press, 1980), 151–52.

3. Scholars universally agree on the details of Vallandigham's arrest, trial, and banish-ment, but quarrel over its significance. For a sympathetic portrait of Vallandigham, see Frank L. Klement, *The Limits of Dissent: Clement L. Vallandigham in the Civil War* (New York: Fordham University Press, 1998). For a critical depiction of Vallandigham, see Jen-nifer L. Weber, *Copperheads: The Rise and Fall of Lincoln's Opponents in the North* (New York: Oxford University Press, 2006).

4. *Huntingdon Globe*, June 10, 1863.

5. *Harrisburg Patriot and Union*, May 30, 1863.

6. Shankman, *The Pennsylvania Antiwar Movement*, 123.

7. Melinda Lawson, *Patriot Fires: Forging a New American Nationalism in the Civil War North* (Lawrence: University Press of Kansas, 2002), 67.

8. The historiography of wartime labor in World War 2 is rich with analysis. Histo-rian Allan Winkler summed up the consensus by saying, "Most historians studying labor trends have acknowledged that industrial union activity came of age during the war. Labor and management, committed to a common goal, learned to talk together and, un-der government direction, bargained collectively." Allan M. Winkler, *Home Front U.S.A.: America during World War II*, 3rd ed. (Wheeling, Ill.: Harlan-Davidson, 2012), 22–23. See also, Andrew E. Kersten, *Labor's Home Front: The American Federation of Labor During World War II* (New York: New York University Press, 2006), Nelson Lichtenstein, *Labor's War at Home: The CIO in World War II* (Cambridge: Cambridge University Press, 1982).

9. Phillip S. Paludan, *A People's Contest: The Union and Civil War, 1861–1865* (Law-rence, KS: University Press of Kansas, 1988), 195–97.

10. Shankman, *The Pennsylvania Antiwar Movement*, 134, 199. The presidential elec-tion of 1864 included votes cast by soldiers in the field. The gubernatorial election of 1863 did not.

11. David Montgomery, *Beyond Equality: Labor and the Radical Republicans, 1862–1872* (New York: Alfred Knopf, 1967), 102.

12. Judith Giesberg, *Army at Home: Women and the Civil War on the Northern Home Front* (Chapel Hill: University of North Carolina Press, 2009).

13. In addition to Giesberg's *Army at Home*, a few additional books describe Allegheny Arsenal during the Civil War. See James Wudarczyk, *Pittsburgh's Forgotten Allegheny Arsenal* (Apollo, Pa.: Closson Press, 1999), and Arthur B. Fox, *Pittsburgh During the American Civil War, 1860–1865* (Chicora, Pa.: Mechling Bookbindery, 2002).

14. These were Frankford Arsenal (ordnance), Schuylkill Arsenal (uniforms), and Allegheny Arsenal (ammunition).

15. Arthur B. Fox, *Our Honored Dead: Allegheny County, Pennsylvania in the American Civil War* (Chicora, Pa.: Mechling Bindery, 2008), 377–96.

16. Ibid., 29.

17. *Pittsburgh Daily Gazette and Advertiser*, October 3, 1861.

18. Giesberg, *Army at Home*, 78.

19. Fox, *Our Honored Dead*, 377–96.

20. The newspaper was the *Christian Advocate*, n.d., reprinted *Pittsburgh Daily Gazette and Advertiser*, November 12, 1862.

21. *Pittsburgh Daily Gazette and Advertiser*, September 23 and November 11, 1862. The exact cause of the explosion remains unknown, but investigators speculated that workers unsafely carried fresh powder to the rollery inside open wheelbarrows. Inside the rollery, workers were required to wear moccasins, not shoes. Some workers may have disregarded this safety protocol and built up static electrical charges and thus sparked the conflagration. Another theory was that the explosion occurred outside the building because the flanged wheels of transport vehicles produced sparks when they hit the iron roadway. Initially, the explosion might have occurred outside the building, causing hot shrapnel to fly into the building, producing a larger secondary eruption.

22. Theresa R. McDevitt, "Explosion at Allegheny Arsenal," in *Women in the American Civil War*, vol. 1, ed., Lisa Tendrich Frank (Santa Barbara, Calif.: ABC-Clio, 2008), 99–100.

23. James Wudarczyk, "By Valor and Arms," n.p., Lawrenceville Historical Society, http://www.lhs15201.org/articles_b.asp?ID=16.

24. John Beck to Horatio Seymour, December 21, 1863, in Adjutant General's papers, New York State Archives, Albany, N.Y. [hereafter, NYSA].

25. The fifteen fired workers included John Beck, Thomas H. Rowland, Robert Duff, James Essler, George Beissenger, Tilly Potter, Walter T. Hill, Thomas K. Laley, James Morris, Joseph Lemmon, and John Jeffrey. The remaining four names are unknown.

26. *Pittsburgh Post*, July 18, 1863.

27. Ibid.

28. Samuel Riddle to R. H. K. Whiteley, April 9, 1863, NYSA.

29. Ibid.

30. Samuel F. Barr to R. H. K. Whiteley, May 13, 1863, NYSA.

31. "Wayne," in *Pittsburgh Daily Post*, July 10, 1863.

32. Quoted from *Pittsburgh Post*, June 30, 1863.

33. John Beck, et al., to John B. Butler, June 26, 1863, NYSA.

34. John B. Butler to John Beck, et al., July 4, 1863, NYSA.

35. "The U.S. Allegheny Arsenal Question!" A Circular, n.d., n.p., NYSA.

36. *Pittsburgh Daily Gazette and Advertiser*, November 28, 1863.

37. *Philadelphia Inquirer*, July 27, 1863.

38. *Fincher's Trades' Review*, August 8, 1863 and April 23, 1864; Rachael Filene Seidman, "A Monstrous Doctrine? Northern Women on Dependency during the Civil War," in *An Uncommon Time: The Civil War and the Northern Home Front*, ed. Paul Cimbala and Randall M. Miller, 180–82 (New York, Fordham University Press, 2002); see also, J. Matthew Gallman, *Mastering Wartime: A Social History of Philadelphia during the Civil War* (Cambridge: Cambridge University Press, 1990), 245; Mark R. Wilson, *The Business of Civil War: Military Mobilization and the State, 1861–1865* (Baltimore: Johns Hopkins University Press, 2006), 97.

39. *Philadelphia Inquirer*, July 30, 1863.

40. *Pittsburgh Daily Gazette and Advertiser*, September 19, 1864.

41. Clayton D. Laurie and Ronald H. Cole, *The Role of Federal Military Forces in Domestic Disorders, 1877–1945* (Washington, D.C.: Center of Military History, 1997), 225.

42. Gerald Shenk, *Work or Fight!: Race, Gender, and the Draft in World War One* (New York: Palgrave Macmillan, 2005), 2–7.

43. Laurie and Cole, *The Role of Federal Military Forces in Domestic Disorders*, 252–53.

44. Laurie and Cole, *The Role of Federal Military Forces in Domestic Disorders*, 392–96.

45. The historiography of American manhood at war is too large to survey here. For pertinent works, see Kristin L. Hoganson, *Fighting for American Manhood: How Gender Politics Provoked the Spanish-American and Philippine-American Wars* (New Haven, Conn.: Yale University Press, 1998); Christian G. Samito, *Becoming American Under Fire: Irish Americans, African Americans, and the Politics of Citizenship During the Civil War Era* (Ithaca, N.Y.: Cornell University Press, 2009). Christina S. Jarvis, *The Male Body at War: American Masculinity during World War II* (DeKalb, Ill.: Northern Illinois University Press, 2004); Herman Graham III, *The Brothers' Vietnam War: Black Power, Manhood, and the Military Experience* (Gainesville: University Press of Florida, 2003).

46. John Beck to Horatio Seymour, December 21, 1863, NYSA.

47. Ibid.

"All of That Class That Infest N.Y."

*Perspectives on Irish American
Loyalty and Patriotism in the Wake
of the New York City Draft Riots*

Ryan W. Keating

L oyalty during the Civil War is a complex issue, as a number of historians have recently shown, and as the broader scope of this collection seeks to illustrate, such ideologies cannot be adequately defined through any singular narrative. Men and women, north and south, east and west, responded to pressing war-time issues in a variety of ways and, often, proclamations of loyalty and disloyalty reflected local concerns as much as, if not more so, national ones. Consequently, in order to truly understand the ideological nuances that drove men and women to act in support of, or in reaction to, federal policies, we must understand not only how citizens understood their actions but also how their local communities responded to shifting circumstances and national rhetoric.[1] Because of the similarly varied experiences of immigrant communities scattered throughout the North during the nineteenth century, this same methodological framework must be applied to analysis of Irish American patriotism and loyalty during the Civil War. For years, the narrative of Irish participation in the Union war effort has focused upon the rise and fall of Irish American loyalty, with the New York City Draft Riots in the summer of 1863 as the proverbial hinge upon which this immigrant group's popular support for the war effort swung shut. As we begin to deconstruct broader questions surrounding patriotism and loyalty in the Civil War North, so too must we revisit the way that Irish, Irish Americans, and their friends and neighbors understood their own place in Northern society and as part of the Union war effort.[2]

The discord inherent in the New York City Draft Riots, because of the unsettling and very public nature of the events that July, can mask the ways that immigrants in other areas contended with changing federal policies and the ways local observers responded to, and understood, immigrant place in smaller locales. Nativist backlash that portrayed the Irish as unfit and unworthy of citizenship (in part because of its disquieting commentary on these immigrants—to both contemporary and historical observers) has tended to overshadow the outspoken support professed for these adopted citizens by men and women in their communities. This was as much a factor of the time as it has become in the historical literature. It is tempting to understand these national reactions to the riots in New York as simply another expression of apathy toward the Irish immigrants who had flooded America's cities in the decades before the war. This narrative provides important insight into public debates surrounding the ability of immigrants to assimilate into their adopted home, but such a perspective can serve to distort the reality of this event for immigrants outside of Manhattan. Consequently, the melding of the local and national narratives becomes all the more important to deepening our understanding of the complex nature of Irish loyalty and patriotism, self-professed as well as publicly assigned, during the American Civil War. From this perspective, we find that Irishmen and their local communities were much more likely to reject the means and motives of the rioters in New York while simultaneously espousing the individual loyalty and patriotism of immigrants in smaller communities in the North.

In the second year of the war, Irish apathy for Lincoln's war effort was placed on display for all the world to see. In July 1863, New York City erupted in flames as men and women poured into the streets in protest of the draft and the shifting federal policies on emancipation. The mob that descended upon the city was unparalleled in size and scope and was composed of the "lowest and most ruffian . . . [sort] . . . which ever disgraced" New York City.[3] It was a "formidable riot," that took some two weeks to completely quell and was notable in part for overt violence directed toward the African American population of Manhattan—acts that fundamentally altered the popular conceptions of the riots from simple draft resistance to outright rejection of federal policies and war aims.[4] More importantly, the rioters were predominately Irish and their acts clouded the memory of Irish American patriotism and loyalty to the Union for decades. Etched into the popular memory of the war as the most visible display of the decline of Irish American support for the Union war effort, almost immediately, this event was appropriated and misconstrued by some of the largest newspapers in the country to reflect a simplistic and overtly anti-Irish, anti-Democrat, narrative.[5]

Within the context of nineteenth-century political and social ideologies, especially those driven by the outspoken xenophobia of the antebellum period, the riots and rioters represented not only Irish American wartime disloyalty, but also evidence that Irish Catholics could never truly assimilate themselves into American society. While this trend continued in the postwar years, it emerged as part of the popular rhetoric almost immediately after the riots were quelled.

The riots that the editors of the German language paper *Abendzeitung* foreshadowed in late July 1863 would spring "up a sentiment of deep-rooted hostility against Irish Catholics. No one, it says, can have been an eyewitness of the unparalleled, fiendish outrages which were committed by a mob, almost exclusively consisting of Irish Catholic, without coming to the conclusion that such beings will never be fit to be citizens of a republic."[6] Political cartoons published in *Harper's Weekly* further espoused the anti-Irish sentiment by portraying stereotypical Irish caricatures engaged in brutal acts. Images of the physical act of rioting played well to nativist perceptions of Irish poverty and tendency toward violence while depictions of anti-black sentiment and such commentary were designed to connect these acts to national questions of immigrant loyalty and continued antebellum trends of portraying Irish Americans as disorderly, rebellious, and unstable, stereotypes that would continue to define the relationship between these immigrants and American society well into the twentieth century.[7]

Outspoken critics of Irish immigration ruled the antebellum landscape, and their voices rose with renewed vigor in the wake of the Draft Riots as they linked the violence in Manhattan to larger issues of immigrant place and community instability. This xenophobic backlash, however, distorted the riots, painting them simply as expressions of Irish-Catholic disloyalty. Interestingly, Irish Americans across the nation immediately recognized that the heinous acts of their countrymen in Manhattan would be cited as evidence of broader ethnic disloyalty and actively sought to counter those accusations.[8] The timing of the riots was problematic for Democrats, who had fought off Republican accusations of disloyalty since the early weeks of the war. Already embattled in their opposition to the Emancipation Proclamation, the riots only further alienated Democrats and their stance of loyal dissent.

In the spring and summer of 1861, Irish Americans silenced critics and naysayers, rushing to enlist in the Union war effort and prove their loyalty to their adopted nation. Putting aside antebellum animosities, communities across the nation gave enthusiastic send-offs to their immigrant sons as they marched to war. By 1863, however, support for these immigrant soldiers appeared to shift as "the riots [in New York] had renewed or reinforced nearly every negative stereotype about the Irish in America."[9] Despite the loyalty and sacrifices of Irish soldiers on battlefields across the nation, in the wake of the war "American elites belittled Irish war contributions, excluded or minimized Irish participation in victory celebrations, and cited the New York draft riots of 1863 as continued proof of Irish disloyalty and barbarity."[10] This response was in direct contrast to the early actions and experiences of Irish Americans as vital contributors to the Northern war effort.

In the wake of the attack on Fort Sumter in 1861, Irish America rose up in defense of their adopted nation. The flurry of patriotic activity that these immigrants displayed was encouraging evidence that political and religious allegiances would not determine or influence loyalty to the federal government during the war. Yet this initial enthusiasm appeared to quickly dissipate. As Susannah Ural Bruce notes, "as the nation moved unknowingly towards the horrific losses of Antietam and Fredericksburg and the controversial Emancipation Proclamation, opposition to the war escalated, especially in Irish American communities. They would be among the first to begin a vigorous questioning of the war's direction by the following year and to initiate demands for a peaceful resolution."[11] Following the Draft Riots and "outspoken [Irish American] criticism of a victorious administration, and unfailing support of the opposition party . . . A shadow of disloyalty would darken the Irish for years to come, and the history of Irish bravery, loyalty, and devotion to the Union would remain buried for decades."[12] After July of 1863, the "Irish again were [viewed as] violent hoodlums unfit for civilization."[13] Despite outspoken insistence by Democrats and their Catholic allies that their "defense of the constitution made them, not Republicans, the true patriots of the conflict," the New York City Draft Riots left an "indelible impression on their [the Irish Catholic's] fellow northerners . . . [and] served to symbolize all that was wrong with Catholicism and its influence on American society."[14] Seemingly no other group experienced as clear and rapid a shift in support during the Civil War—from patriots to enemies of the Republic in a matter of weeks—than did the Irish.

Irish immigrants across the United States were loosely linked through a shared ethnic heritage, religion, and (oftentimes) a hatred of England, which, periodically bled over into Irish nationalist political activity. These diasporic links, however, should not be taken to imply that these immigrants chose to isolate themselves from their adopted communities. It is increasingly clear that Irish Americans were active participants in the social, political, and economic spheres of their adopted towns and cities and saw themselves as much a part of those communities as they did the broader the Irish American Diaspora. Important, as well, to the narrative of wartime patriotism is that many local commentators (at least in the public forum) saw their Irish neighbors as full-fledged members of their local communities rather than a disconnected group of "others." Incorporating these perspectives into discussions of loyalty and disloyalty provides a more comprehensive understanding of the ways that immigrants responded to major social and political changes during the Civil War and, in particular, illustrates far-reaching historical consequences that the New York City Draft Riots have had on defining (and misrepresenting) issues of Irish American wartime loyalty.

As historian Christian Samito has shown, resistance to the war "comprises a major part of the legacy of Irish Americans." But there were those who continued to support the war through devotion to soldiers and to the government. On numerous occasions, he argues, "individual citizens joined to pay tribute to universal sacrifice in the name of the United States, further cementing in the process Irish Americans as part of the American people."[15] While these professions of loyalty appear as anomalies within Samito's work, his observations nevertheless suggest that analysis of local responses to the war can provide a much more comprehensive narrative of Irish American loyalty and disloyalty during this period and perceptions thereof. This methodological approach to the study of loyalty and patriotism—analyzing the experiences and responses to national issues from the local perspective—continues the precedent set by historians of the immigrant experience who have argued against the tendency to paint the immigrant experience in broad terms as well as the work of historians of the ethnic experience in the Civil War who, through their rich narratives, have hinted at just how diverse the experiences of immigrant soldiers and their communities were. While Irish American newspapers, published in major eastern cities and distributed nationally, suggest that the defeatist attitude seen in New York and other major cities was an integral part of immigrant society after 1863, the incorporation of the experiences of immigrants living in smaller, less visible ethnic enclaves, allows us to better understand the ways in which the Draft Riots reflected (or did not reflect) the attitudes of immigrants and impacted impressions of ethnic inclusion, patriotism, and loyalty, across the nation.

Connecticut and Wisconsin provide excellent points of comparison for analyzing Irish American loyalty during the Civil War. Both states contained politically active Irish populations that organized Irish American regiments, the 9th Connecticut and 17th Wisconsin. Neither of these units served in the Irish Brigade in the Army of the Potomac and although casualty rates were high, the soldiers and families were shielded, to a degree, from the bloodshed in battles along the Washington-Richmond front. While New Yorkers and Bostonians lamented the misuse of Irish troops at Fredericksburg, smaller communities were able to relish in their men's service and sacrifice in defense of the Union. The Irish communities in these states were diverse both in terms of settlement patterns and with regards to socio-economic place. The major cities in both states lacked the visible ethnic enclaves such as Five Points in New York. For example, while New York City was a quarter Irish, the Irish made up less than 20 percent of New Haven's population, and less than 10 percent of Milwaukee's population in 1860. Equally important, the most "Irish" neighborhood in both states, the 5th Ward of New Haven, was only one-quarter Irish-born, a high concentration, but certainly not overwhelming.[16]

In both cities, too, Irish-born men had access to employment and socio-economic mobility that far outpaced their countrymen in New York. In New York, more than 70 percent of the Irish worked in low-paying, unskilled positions, and their visibility in those jobs likely contributed to the nativist backlash that emerged in the decades before the war. In New Haven, which lay in close proximity to New York, less than half—40 percent—of men working in 1860 identified as unskilled laborers. Nearly 45 percent of Irish men in New Haven worked as skilled workers or artisans many in the carriage-making industry, though Irishmen worked in a surprising array of skilled professions in that city. Milwaukee was a port of landing for settlers arriving in Wisconsin and attracted a relatively small but vibrant Irish community. Employment statistics for Irish born men in this city were similar to those in New Haven. Less than half of the working-age men toiled as unskilled laborers while approximately 35 percent of Irishmen worked in skilled professions. Importantly, though, nearly 11 percent of the men in that city were employed in white-collar professions, working, for example, as clerks, grocers, and police officers. This was double the presence of this class of immigrants in New Haven, and while employment statistics from both states suggest a far different experience for immigrants in smaller cities and states, the data from Wisconsin suggests that socio-economic opportunities only increased with westward migration. The growing influence of the Catholic Church and the emergence of prolific and vocal Irish American community organizations in both states further attested to the arrival and success of these men and woman in these areas.[17]

This is not to say that the Irish were necessarily welcomed with open arms. While local histories that appeared in the late nineteenth century tended to laud the contributions of these Irishmen, not all contemporaries were thrilled with their arrival. The rapid growth of the immigrant population in Wisconsin in the fifteen years before the war caused some concern among nativist groups who feared being left a "minority in their own land." The influence of this party, one Democratic editor lamented, would ultimately "*enslave* the religious sentiments of a large portion of our people."[18] In Connecticut, things were a bit more acrimonious as nativist politicians wrestled control of the state legislature in 1855 and immediately began disbanding militia units composed predominately of foreign-born volunteers. Foreigners, opponents argued, "are subjects of foreign governments and are under the protection of, and owe their obedience to foreign powers. Such men ought not to be in our military companies."[19] Although supporters of the Irish pointed to the character of these men as proof of their broader loyalty to the state, proponents of the nativist platform ultimately won the day and ethnic units were disbanded. Although the law was reversed the following year, it nevertheless stood as a stark reminder of the antebellum tensions undercutting the "land of steady habits."[20]

The secession of the Southern states in the winter of 1860–61 revitalized questions of immigrant place in these two states as some pondered whether their adopted citizens would join a Republican-backed venture to save the Union. For an immigrant group that had faced degrees of nativist animosity during the antebellum period, though, the outbreak of war offered the ideal platform for public displays of loyalty to the United States. The enthusiasm with which Irish Americans responded to the war seemed to undermine nativist arguments regarding the place of these immigrants in American society. Newspapers in Connecticut and Wisconsin reported, encouragingly, the speed with which the Irish rushed to the defense of the flag and Unionism became the rallying cry in communities in both states. In Connecticut, one news outlet proclaimed that "The Irish population are unanimous in their wish and determination to support the Government. In spite of the prophecies of many to the contrary, we have not heard of a single Irishman who has shown a disposition to prove false to the stars and stripes."[21] When New Haven's Irish militia volunteered their services to the state in late April 1861, some saw in this act deeper ties of fealty. Many of these men were victims of the nativist militia purge of 1855, their arms taken "under a boldly imputed doubt of their loyalty . . . Let justice be done them, by a generous acknowledgement of their loyalty and the restoration of their character. Such Soldiers cannot be spared."[22] Another editor reminded his readers that "in the days of Know Nothingism, when adopted citizens were under the ban, and Gov. Minor revoked the charters of military companies on the plea that people of the Catholic persuasion owed a political allegiance to the Pope of Rome, above their oath to support the Constitution of the United States, we remonstrated against the ostracism, and contended that they were as loyal as native born citizens—We had no doubt of it then—we have none now."[23]

In Hartford soon after the war began, a Catholic priest called for "every man who can leave his family to enlist. This is the first country the Irishman ever had that he could call his own . . . The flag of the stars and stripes is the only flag he can fight under and defend as his own . . . there are two classes who I most despise—cowards and traitors—and those who can enlist and do not are either one or the other."[24] Another pointed out that few in Connecticut "hasten[s] to don the armor of his country and to strike in her defense as the much-maligned and proscribed Irish Catholic." "I will not say that all other classes do not arm for conflict in defense of the Union," noted another observer, "but none with greater alacrity or fight more bravely than this very class, which has been so often pronounced by these falsehearted politicians as faithless to freedom and insensible to its many blessings. Let Irishmen . . . demand the respect their devotion and truth to freedom and Union deserves."[25] "Look in our Army," the editors of the *Hartford Daily Connecticut Courant* claimed, "in the front ranks we find Irish, Germans, Scotch, all clinging to this government as to the horns of the altar for protection."[26] The response of the Irish in Connecticut to the war was important. For years their proclamations of loyalty to the United States were questioned by men wary of the growing influence of this immigrant population. The Civil War offered the Irish the opportunity to back these assertions with physical proof.

Wisconsin's Democrats were equally vocal in their proclamations of loyalty. As Southern states seceded, Democrats disavowed this act in language that clearly linked their party and their immigrant constituents to the plight of the nation and the Union. "Our Republic would cease to be a refuge for the oppressed of all nations if broken in twain," one editor claimed. "Under such circumstances of peril, it behooves every good citizen to stand firmly by the Union."[27] As news reached Milwaukee of the fall of Fort Sumter, an American flag was raised above a cathedral there. "We happen to know the bishop," reported the editors of the *Milwaukee Sentinel*, and he "like all other good Catholics, is a Union man."[28] Swiss born Bishop Martin Henni would become one of the first highly placed Catholic Americans to openly support emancipation.[29] Throughout the state, "strong resolutions passed without reference to party to sustain the Union at all hazards," and Irish volunteers flocked to the flag.[30]

Wisconsin's newspapers reported with enthusiasm the earnest response of Irish Americans in other cities, and the loyalty of this immigrant group became proof that "this class of citizens would be true to their allegiance."[31] Speaking for their countrymen scattered across the continent, Boston's Irish asked that "every adopted citizen remember the oath which he has taken to support the constitution and no people pay greater reverence to the sanctity of an oath than those of Irish birth." Disloyal Irish were "a few designing traitorous demagogues," and "the Irish people on this continent are loyal to the Union, the Constitution and

the Government, and will support them by every means in their power."[32] Such
was the response that by 1862, the editors of the *Wisconsin Patriot* noted satis-
factorily that

> a few years ago the greater part of the political party now styled Republican,
> and professing to be *par excellence* the guardians of the government, were
> the *know-nothing party*, and were carrying on a crusade against the Roman
> Catholic people of the country on the alleged score that they were not loyal
> to the government and should not be trusted in any of its offices . . . We can
> speak for this section, that the Catholics have shown their loyalty to our Gov-
> ernment, without flinching. They are ready to fight for the Government and
> its institutions and laws, as established by our forefathers—He who seeks for
> toryism among the Catholics will seek in vain, for a more chivalrous, patriotic
> class cannot be found on this or any other continent.[33]

Time and again, the overt Irish support for the war effort was used as proof that
questions surrounding immigrant loyalty had been greatly exaggerated.

Neither Connecticut nor Wisconsin fielded Irish regiments during the first
months of the war. In both states many Irish chose to enlist in mixed regiments
rather than wait for larger Irish units to form, in large part because they hoped
to get to the battlefield more quickly. Nevertheless, there was a flurry of ethnic
organization led by Irish militia units and largely in response to the success of
other Irish regiments during the early months of the war, and in particular of the
69th New York at First Bull Run in July of 1861 and the 23rd Illinois (Mulligan's
Irish Brigade) at the siege of Lexington, Missouri that September. This organization reinforced that any lingering fears of Irish allegiances were misplaced.[34] In
Connecticut, "the departure for war of the sixty-ninth regiment . . . [of] New
York, is an indication that the Irishmen who have always been famed as soldiers,
are not the boys to flinch at this time of trial."[35] In Wisconsin, the stand of James
Mulligan and the 23rd Illinois at Lexington, Missouri in September 1861 proved
to many that the men who newspapers "used civilly to style 'voting cattle' have
covered themselves with glory in the cause of the Union. Mulligan's Irish Brigade
justify the reputation which their native countrymen have won in every civilized
nation for loyalty and higher military courage . . . [and] . . . deserve to be ranked
[in gallantry] with the gallant New York Sixty-ninth . . . *the naturalized citizens of
this country have been as patriotic and self sacrificing in war as the native born*."[36]

Lincoln's call for volunteers after the defeat at First Bull Run gave Irishmen
in Connecticut and Wisconsin the opportunity to put their patriotic words into

action. The rhetoric and publicity that accompanied the organization of Irish regiments in these states reinforced professions of loyalty, and these units served as a physical reminder of Irish American support for the war effort. The 9th Connecticut began its initial organization in late April 1861 after William Buckingham promised that "officers chosen by that company [would] be fully commissioned immediately upon being reported by the Adjutant-General, without the usual formalities attending the organization of a military company."[37] Although the Irishmen from New Haven were not accepted for service that spring (due simply to the fact that the state quickly reached its initial quota of troops), enthusiasm for the war nevertheless remained high. "Our adopted fellow citizens mean to send a regiment worthy of a place in the Irish brigade," wrote the editors of the *New London Chronicle* in September 1861. "In other parts of the State they have taken hold of the matter in earnest . . . [and] we doubt not that their response will be prompt, and such as will do no dishonor to their patriotism."[38] "I do not say that all other classes do not arm themselves for the conflict in defense of the union," observed another, "but none go with greater alacrity or fight more bravely than this very class . . . when peace and unity again dawn upon us as a people, let them [the Irish of the state] demand the respect their devotion and truth to freedom and Union deserves."[39] Joining the call, the *Hartford Daily Courant* claimed "there is no reason why Hartford should not be represented by a full company of Irishmen in the 9th, under Col. Cahill; They *can* be raised."[40] They were, and the men from Connecticut went on to distinguish themselves time and again over the course of the war.

Although the Irish in Wisconsin were equally vocal in their support for the Union in 1861, there was significantly less enthusiasm for the formation of an independent Irish unit than in Connecticut. This was not a consequence of a lack of support for the war but, rather, reflective of two factors. First, that early in the war many Irishmen chose to enlist in mixed regiments—suggesting a degree of inclusion that many of these men felt within their local communities and the lack of any significant ethnic enclave in the state.[41] Second, that the leadership of the Irish community was culled in September 1860 when the steamship *Lady Elgin* sank while returning from a Stephen Douglas campaign speech in Chicago. Among the more than 300 dead were a large number of Wisconsin's prominent Irish politicians and militia leaders.[42] The push for an independent Irish unit in the state came only after the success of other Irish regiments during the first six months of the war. "Irishmen! Rally to the Rescue," a recruiting advertisement noted in the *Watertown Democrat*. "Hurrah for the GALLANT 69th . . . Cannot the Irishmen of Wisconsin do as well as her sister state?" Speaking on the recent action in Missouri that fall, one newspaper noted, "Illinois has won for herself fame by the heroic conduct of her brave Col. Mulligan and his Brigade on the bloody field of Lexington. Let the Irishmen of Watertown and surrounding country not be the hindhand."[43]In late November, Napoleon Mignault, the chaplain of the 17th Wisconsin, stood before a large crowd in the village of Watertown. Mignault called for his audience to "fill up the ranks of the Irish Brigade, take their fortunes on the field of battle, in defense of the starry flag that had always protected them—in support of the constitution that secured them equal rights—in the maintenance of that Union they had hoped would be perpetual—and against the traitors who were trying to dismember a Republic that had brought to all nothing but blessings, prosperity and honor."[44]

As men rushed to the join the war effort, their organization came to symbolize the broader patriotism and loyalty of the immigrant communities living in the two states and their service throughout the war reinforced this perception. Although not all of the soldiers who enlisted in the 9th Connecticut and 17th Wisconsin were Irish-born (61 and 31 percent of the soldiers respectively were born in Ireland before immigrating to the United States), the ethnic identity espoused during the early months of organization nevertheless came to define both units throughout the war. Perhaps equally important was the geographical and socio-economic diversity reflected by the immigrant volunteers. Most of the Irish volunteers were members of the working class, but neither regiment had any single identifiable urban recruiting base and volunteers often enlisted with their friends, neighbors, and colleagues—Irish-born or otherwise—and ethnic connections may have been only one of many reasons for choosing to volunteer in their respective units. As these men united in defense of the Union, they did so surrounded by visible and vocal displays of patriotism—expressions of dual loyalties directed toward both Ireland and the United States. Such rhetoric continued throughout the war and was bolstered by an equally boisterous chorus of support from men and women at home who, through a local lens, saw these soldiers, their regiments, and their sacrifices as continued proof of Irish loyalty—this in spite of larger national trends calling into question immigrant loyalty.

In both states, public expressions of loyalty among Irish citizens ultimately shifted away from the exclusivity of antebellum politics and towards that of the inclusive nature of the republican citizen-soldier. Through public proclamations of loyalty, Irish Americans exhibited an inclusive understanding of their place in American society. Irish by birth or descent, proud of their ethnic heritage, and staunch Democrats, these men were loyal American citizens pledged to defend the Union against all enemies, foreign and domestic and despite clear links to the ethnic communities in these states, there was a public willingness to accept volunteers as, first and foremost, American soldiers. Over the course of the war, the valor, patriotism, and loyalty of men from both the 9th Connecticut and 17th Wisconsin were portrayed time and again on the home front as meaningful and representative of the struggle against rebellion in the South.

By late 1862, many Irishmen, especially those with connections to the Irish Brigade then serving in the Army of the Potomac (with regiments from New York City, Boston, and Pennsylvania) began to question what seemed to be the needless sacrifice of the Irish American soldiers in battles such as Antietam and Fredericksburg where Irish volunteers were "slaughtered like sheep, and no result but defeat."[45] The next summer "the draft riots . . . [driven by the exemption fee were] worse in New York City than anywhere else, [and] marked the climax of Irish alienation from the Union war effort."[46] But the visibility of New York City within the historical memory of the Irish American experience does not mean that the Irish in Connecticut and Wisconsin experienced or exhibited similar emotional responses to the losses from an "Irish Brigade" that contained no regiments from their states. Although recruiters did capitalize on ethnic links during the early phases of regimental organization, men and women in these communities largely focused their attention away from the Irish regiments in the Army of the Potomac and toward units their sons, brothers, friends, and neighbors served.

In this context, the heroic action of the 9th Connecticut under fire at battles such as Pass Christian and Baton Rouge in the spring and fall of 1862 and the tenacity of the 17th Wisconsin at the major engagements that took place in Mississippi such as Corinth and Vicksburg were more important to those at home than the losses of ethnic regiments on the eastern front. In the weeks before the invasion of New Orleans, for example, the 9th came under fire for the first time. At Pass Christian, on April 4, 1862, the Irishmen from the Nutmeg State succeeded in routing Confederate forces, distinguishing themselves by becoming the first Union regiment to capture a Confederate battle flag, lost when the Third Mississippi retreated from the city. "Ship Island letters speak in high terms of the conduct of the Ninth Connecticut," the *Hartford Courant* noted in the aftermath of the battle.[47] "It is hardly necessary for me to say that the conduct of your men meets my cordial approval," Governor Buckingham wrote to Thomas Cahill, "and I am proud of both officers and their command."[48] The following August, the *Hartford Courant* proclaimed with enthusiasm "Victory at Baton Rouge" in the wake of the 9th's performance on the battlefield in Louisiana. Colonel Thomas Cahill wrote home that "we have always been in the advance but I rather expected that as it deems to be expected by the people of every thing that has the name of being Irish in the fighting line; well we have not suffered more than Others and we have a good name, wherever we are known at home or here."[49] As the war dragged on, those on the home front could take comfort in the fact that their men were proving an honor to their state and serving with valor in the face of the enemy.[50]

The men from Wisconsin were equal to the task. At the Battle of Corinth (Mississippi), on October 3, 1862, the men of the 17th Wisconsin rushed into the fray, halting a Confederate advance threatening the army's right flank. Observers writing home noted that it was "an Irish charge, with its accompaniments, [and] rather astonished the enemy."[51] "The soldiers of the Seventeenth distinguished themselves all through the fight, particularly in a bayonet charge," another recounted.[52] That evening the Irishmen were "loudly cheered by the other regiments in the division" for their decisive role in single-handedly driving the Mississippi brigade from the field, a further testament to those back home of the heroic conduct of the Irish brigade.[53]

Six months later, in the trenches outside the Confederate stronghold at Vicksburg, the men from Wisconsin again surged forward with fixed bayonets and "charged through an abattis of felled trees, which severed [their] ranks [and] exposed [the men] to a crossfire of shot and shell" from the Confederate positions on their right and left.[54] "No regiment could stand such a tempest of lead and iron," wrote one soldier. The men from Wisconsin did, for a while.[55] When the attack stalled on the afternoon of May 22, General Thomas Ransom allegedly lamented, after ordering a retreat, that "if I had put the 17th ahead, we should have been inside [the city] now."[56] The disillusionment that emerged among ethnic groups in larger east coast cities as a consequence of the stagnant Washington-Richmond front and the continued call for volunteers in the wake of devastating casualties at Antietam and Fredericksburg seemed to be of little concern to men and women in Connecticut and Wisconsin, who saw the war locally, through the experiences of their men-in-arms. In these states, the fate of the Irish Brigade does not appear to have impacted the Irish and their supporters in any substantial way. Thus, the war-weariness that bred resistance in New York City did not spread to communities in Connecticut and Wisconsin in large part because the Irish regiments from these two states encouraged positive morale among the citizens at home and shaped encouraging images of Irish American patriotism, loyalty, and sacrifice for the Union cause.

War and politics collided in spectacular fashion in the summer of 1863 as the Draft Riots publicly exposed the apparent deep-seated animosities that the Irish held for African Americans. While Irish and African American laborers clashed on numerous occasions in cities such as Toledo, Ohio and Brooklyn, Newburgh, and Buffalo, New York, in the months preceding the riots in New York the events that July appeared to be more symbolic of the growing disaffection of this immigrant group for the war effort than did the more simplistic issues of wages that drove the battles in other areas.[57] In spite of the outspoken support for the Union and the enthusiasm surrounding Irish organization and service, dissent did emerge in both states with Irish American leaders often identified as among the most vocal opponents of Lincoln's policies. This does not mean that all Irish were radical, and there emerged a very clear link between the rhetoric of moderate, or War Democrats, and their Irish constituents not only through the political alliance of these immigrants to that party, but also because these men all believed they held a vested interest in preserving the legacy of the American republican experiment.[58]

Irish Americans had a vested interest in the survival of the Union. Although the Potato Famine (1845–50) drove hundreds of thousands to the shores of North America, many immigrants recognized that in their journey across the Atlantic they "left their land to enjoy in this the liberty of speech and conscience denied them under the crown of England."[59] America was "the country where the broken heart of Ireland is bound for, her daughters protected, her sons adopted: where conscience is free, where religion is not hypocrisy, where liberty is a reality, and where the Gospel is a holy profession of Divine love, and not a profligate trade of national vengeance."[60] Furthermore, there was a close relationship between Ireland and the United States which revolved around the Irish Republican (Irish nationalist) belief that the preservation of the American union was necessary for Irish independence because America's survival justified self-determination at home in Ireland.

Men in these communities understood loyalty to be not only the continued support for the restoration of the Union at all costs, but also the continued commitment to the practice of democracy. Consequently, in public forums, the Irish in Connecticut and Wisconsin remained steadfast in their support of the war and their rejection of the means of the New York rioters. But they also continued to vocally oppose shifting federal policies. These were not contradictory positions, although there was some concern, rightly so, that such attitudes would be misinterpreted or misconstrued to reflect broader disloyalty to the Union cause. The changing nature of the war, however, forced these issues to the surface.

Despite early war efforts to set aside political allegiances in Connecticut, there was the belief after 1862 that "Democrats were to be stigmatized as 'traitors' for adhering to their own party organization," and in Wisconsin editors noted that "well meaning men have serious apprehensions that an attempt will be made to stifle the freedom of political expression at the ballot box in the coming election. It is feared that the signs of the times predict the prohibition of Democrats the exercise of the elective franchise unless they vote the Abolition ticket."[61] Irish Americans in these communities understood loyalty as the continued support for the restoration of the Union at all costs, and although political ideologies would be tested as the war progressed, there is no indication that these men and women perceived their political stances to reflect disloyal sentiment. Publicly, Irishmen in Connecticut and Wisconsin remained steadfast in their support of the war, and their rejection of the means of the New York rioters despite continued questions surrounding shifting federal policies illustrates the nuanced ways that these men and women understood their place in their communities and as part of the broader war effort and, in particular, the fact that they did not see debate over federal policy and broader issues of loyalty as contradictory.

When riots erupted in New York City, men and women in both Connecticut and Wisconsin immediately moved to distance themselves from the dubious acts of their countrymen and rhetoric that emerged from these communities illustrates the duality of political identity and allegiance that existed among this group. In both states, too, local news outlets, both Democrat and Republican, spoke out in defense of their adopted citizens in ways that contradicted broader nativist efforts aimed at painting the acts of New Yorkers as reflective of the inability of these immigrants to fully assimilate into American society. The rioters, claimed newspapers in Wisconsin, were encouraged by men for whom "robbing and plunder was the main object." New York was a city of "thieves, gamblers, garroters, shoulder hitters, thugs, and scoundrels of every conceivable hue and grade. Most of this class are never at ease unless they are in a fight."[62] "We hope," the editors of the Wisconsin *Daily Patriot* noted, "that no resistance will disgrace the West, but that if any think they have cause, to resort to the courts."[63] Matthew Hart, a Catholic priest from New Haven, wrote "that from being organized to resist the draft, the mob turned out to be one of the most heinous, murdering, robbing, burning crowds that ever cursed any city in the world, it was made up of pick-pockets, thieves, robbers, blackslegs, gerotters and all of that class that infest N.Y."[64] Many saw the riots in New York as "a scheme for plunder—opposition to the draft being made the pretext. But the leaders only desire plunder and pillage."[65] "I read all about the Riot in New York," private Thomas Knablin of the 9th Connecticut noted in a letter to his wife. "It was a Pitty that one of those Murderers Should escape I hope the Police will furit every one of them out and hang them. You will find that if they Soldiers are Called on they will do their Duty. Those Simpitizers of the North has done more to Injure the Cause than a hundred thousand Rebels in Arms. I hope the whole of them will be hanged."[66]

In the face of accusations of disloyalty, many Irish Americans and their Democratic supporters were quick to reassert their loyalty to the Union, illustrating the important, if at times contradictory, nuances surrounding ethnic support for the war. In New Haven, for example, Republican mayor Samuel Walker fervently denied the existence of a Democratic plot for insurrection in a speech that concluded with an apology to the Irish of that city. "I feel it due to many of our Irish citizens," he wrote, "to inform the public that, in the face of many cruel suspicions against them, I have had kind offers of their assistance in case of any disturbance and I caution the public against an indiscriminant condemnation of a sect of race for the indiscretion of some. I have not learned of but two threats made by this class of our citizens, and those too insignificant to be noticed, which is more than I can say for our native born."[67]

In Milwaukee, the *Sentinel* noted that "Irish Americans, even of the humblest class, bring with them to this country not one particle of prejudice against the colored race. They acquire it here under the debasing influence of . . . demagogues . . . No practical Catholic has ever violated law or order in this country . . . the so-called Catholics who disturb the public peace, are Catholics only in name." True Catholics were "ever unswervingly loyal and ever obedient to authority."[68] Since the war began, the *Chicago Times* noted, "the Roman Catholics have been among the most steady and faithful adherents and supporters of the Union cause . . . None of our people have volunteered more freely or fought more bravely than Catholics." The editors of the *Wisconsin Patriot* agreed. "We can speak for this section," they wrote in response to the editorial in the *Times* "that the Catholics have shown their loyalty to our Government without flinching. They are ready to fight for the Government and its institutions and laws . . . a more chivalrous, patriotic class cannot be found on this or any other continent."[69]

Certainly, the rejection of the means and motives of the New York rioters should not be taken to imply that debate over federal policy did not rage in both states. Yet, for the most part, such discussions lack the inflammatory rhetoric and broader war weariness that appears to have incited the violence in Manhattan. Equally important was that although there was a shift in acceptance of federal policy over time, rhetorical arguments did not drastically change after the Draft Riots, suggesting that accusations of disloyalty were not strong enough to encourage outright rejection of pre-riot political platforms. Emancipation was a hotly debated subject in both states and was an important topic for all Northerners during the time.[70] Democrats in Connecticut worried that, with freedom, "the emancipated negroes [would] come in swarms to New England, as the two races, black and white, are not found anywhere working together in harmony, our working men will very naturally turn their attention to the west," leaving New England industry at the mercy of these black migrants.[71]

In Wisconsin, men proclaimed their loyalty and support under the "sole condition . . . that the war should be conducted to the end, as it have been professedly undertaken, for the preservation of the Constitution and the restoration of the union, with all the rights of the states unimpaired." A shift in those goals toward that of abolition would "make it a war not only for the subversion of the political Constitution of the country, but of sudden, radical and inevitably ruinous revolution in the social and industrial relations of the people."[72] "I was disappointed," wrote one soldier of the 17th Wisconsin, "[that] he [Lincoln] yielded to the clamor of the radicals, and issued the emancipation proclamation . . . Yet I hope the people of the north will give their support in prosecuting the war, by obeying the call of the President, in giving men and money . . . however much they may be opposed to the President's war policy, they will submit with patriotic forbearance until it can be replaced by a better through the ballot box."[73] Nevertheless, the preservation of the Republican process was paramount, and dictated local Democratic responses.

The ensuing discussion naturally carried over to that of arming freedmen. "We think it is high time that the Government should look into this absurd and dangerous matter," the editors of the Patriot wrote in response to news that the government had authorized raising African American regiments. "It is nothing but an absolute waste of time and money . . . in the first place there is no necessity whatever for such auxiliaries; and in the next, the idea can never be carried out to any practical result." They believed it was a "foolish illusion" that these regiments could play an integral part in the war effort, the editorial continued, had preoccupied Generals throughout the country. Had these men "continued themselves to the care and discipline of the regular white army . . . we should certainly have had fewer reverses and more victories to record."[74] When Brigadier General Lorenzo Thomas arrived at Lake Providence, tasked with recruiting black regiments for the Union war effort, the Seventeenth Corps (of which the 17th Wisconsin was a part) held a dress parade for Thomas, and was presented "in one solid mass in front of headquarters, drawn up by regiments, battalions, and batteries." The 17th, however, "had been put away back in the rear [due to the fact that] there are many men in that regiment who do not believe in arming the black man."[75] But, public charges of disloyalty did not ensue.

This rhetoric was not ubiquitous among Irish, illustrating the potential difficulties that come with defining the anti-black acts of the New York mob as reflective of Irish American attitudes broadly. Rhetorical shifts often coincided with
lengthy service in the Deep South and the recognition of the potential benefits
of African American service. "The negro is not that animal he has been represented; far from it . . . he has tasted of that fruit of American culture, *Liberty*, and
he is willing to fight for it. *The negro will fight*," reported one officer in the 9th.[76]
Another noted in August 1863 that "the regiment to which I belong came South
Democrats—that you know—and on my honor as a man, they are this day abolitionists, almost every one of them, and why? Because they have seen slavery
in its naked deformity, in its every guise . . . We shall have gained everything in
this context if we gain a free country."[77] In the wake of state elections in 1864, it
was reported that "in answer to this slanderous intimation that the 'Old Ninth'
would vote the copperhead ticket, we state on authority of a Democratic officer . . . that there is not a good soldier in the Regiment who would not vote
the Union ticket."[78] As part of the larger war effort, one Wisconsin editor finally
noted, "every negro [who] enlisted saves a white man from the draft, and the
white men—even the copperest of them—are beginning to realize this."[79]

The draft was an equally contentious issue. The New York Riots were aptly
termed the "Draft Riots" for they emerged in the wake of the draft in the city and
conscription was a hotly debated topic throughout the North. Yet as early as August 1862, the editors of Irish newspapers spoke out against violent resistance to
the implementation of the Draft and this continued in earnest in the wake of the
July 1863 riots. Early in the war, the *Wisconsin Patriot* rebuked Republican editors of the Milwaukee *Sentinel* and Chicago *Tribune* who claimed the existence of
considerable "apathy or hostility" amongst the German and Irish residents of the
state.[80] A month later, a speech to the Catholics of Cincinnati given by Irish-born
Archbishop John Purcell was reprinted in Connecticut. "If you are drafted, go
you must," the article noted. "We have heard of some foolish, some very foolish
men, protesting that they would resist the draft. Let them try that game, and they
will soon be brought to their proper senses. The man who talks of resisting the
draft deserves scant mercy. It is the same as if your house was on fire, and your
neighbor would cut the hose so that the water could not reach the burning building. Our whole country is in danger . . . Are you better than other men that you
assume the right to oppose the draft?"[81]

Arguments surrounding substitutes, exemptions, and the bounty marked
components of the ideological shift toward a "rich man's war and a poor man's
fight" that allegedly motivated New Yorkers to the streets also appeared in Con-

necticut and Wisconsin, though in less inflammatory terms. The editors of the
Patriot suggested that the government simply "'ignore' substitutes, and make *all*
go who are drafted. This would put each man on level."[82] The draft was portrayed
as "a summons to join, not a discomfited and broken-spirited soldiery, but a
band of heroes, the monument of many a well-fought field."[83] In the wake of the
growing need for soldiers and an impending draft, the Irish citizens of Hartford
resolved that "as our proportion of the men who will inevitably be obliged to go
the war will more than fill a complete regiment, it is a duty to ourselves—our
children and to history—to form an [a second] Irish Regiment in Connecticut."
Furthermore, they desired that "we will each and all use our utmost influence to
render a draft unnecessary by filling up at once the companies forming for this
our own special organization."[84] The *Palladium*, the voice of the New Haven volunteers in the 9th Connecticut, called attention to those "skedaddling" to avoid
the draft and reminded those at home "that everyone who leaves makes the obligation resting upon those who remain so much greater."[85]

Ultimately, with "assurances of the fairness with which the draft is to be conducted," Democrats publicly stated that "there will be few who dream of creating
any disturbance or difficulty."[86] Opponents in Wisconsin conceded to the draft
so long as it was "properly enforced, and under such circumstances as to give
no just grounds for offense and suspicion of trickery."[87] The riots in New York,
some argued, were "a scheme for plunder—opposition to the draft being made
the pretext. But the leaders only desire plunder and pillage."[88] In Connecticut, the
editors of the *Hartford Daily Courant* claimed "a suspension of the draft now [in
the wake of the Draft Riots]—we mean anything more than a temporary suspension which the circumstances of the moment render inevitable—will be simply
a surrender to the basest mob that ever aspired to rule and ruin a great city."[89]
While animosity surrounding the draft existed, and there was an undeniable
Copperhead presence in both these states, the Democratic press was consistent
throughout the war in contextualizing loyalty while preserving political dissent.
Mob violence was not a legitimate means of enacting change.

Editors and local citizens in both states offered alternative methods for
avoiding the draft. The three hundred dollar commutation, out of reach for
many immigrant laborers, was seen by some in Wisconsin as necessary to keep
the price of substitutes within the reach of the average draftee.[90] "A new and
good way is suggested for those who wish to escape the draft," the *Daily Patriot*
noted in June of 1863. "Not more than one in six will be taken, and six persons
can make up a fund among themselves, by contributing $50 each, to pay for
a substitute if any one of them is drafted."[91] Contributions were taken in New

Haven to help pay the commutation fee for the draftees and Ward Associations organized in many cities to provide a means of collectively providing commutation fees. The Irish in that city were lucky. Parish priest, Matthew Hart noted, that "Only 136 of [our people] were drafted out of our aggrigate [sic] of 804," He wrote to Cahill on July 25, 1863. "Of these 136, more than half were legally exempt and at a town meeting held on last Thursday the Town voted to pay three Hundred Dollars for every Drafted man who was not able to pay it for himself: So you See, the teeth are pulled out of the Draft in this part of the World."[92] In Connecticut, then, the realities of the draft were hardly as dramatic as they appeared to be in Manhattan. In Wisconsin, 300 draftees and 99 substitutes joined the ranks of the state's Irish regiment between 1863 and 1865, and most loyally served their time.[93]

Implicit here, with the exception of "skedaddling," is the legal rather than militant means of subverting authority. Men had options, and were supported, to a degree, by their party and their communities. Though opinions regarding the draft and emancipation inherently criticized federal policy, loyal dissent was an option through participation in the democratic process and aversion to violence. Men struggled to deal with the shifting realities of a nation at war and the continuation of normal elections in Connecticut and Wisconsin throughout the war—in so far as free elections occurred in spite of the war itself—was a testament to importance that both Republicans and Democrats placed upon the Democratic principles of the United States. But a vital component of the rejection of the Draft Riots in these states was the continual public pressure to address grievances through loyal dissent rather than to the streets.

"Loyalty," noted one Connecticut newspaper October 1864, "means, in its true sense, a firm and faithful adherence to the law and the Constitution of the community of which we are members . . . [this] will accurately characterize the party that is rallying for the UNION, the CONSTITUTION, and the LAWS."[94] Disloyalty, the editors of the *Patriot* added, was not synonymous with disagreeing with Republican ideology.[95] This succinct definition, a response to questions surrounding wartime support and the place of political dissent during a period of rebellion, perfectly contextualizes the efforts made after 1863 in Connecticut and Wisconsin to defend opponents of the Republican agenda in the face of growing criticism. The same news outlets that worked so diligently to portray Irish loyalty and patriotism in the face of nativist backlash and questions of Irish American support for the Union in 1860–61 renewed their efforts to illuminate the continued support of this group and of the Democratic process in the wake of the Draft Riots and questions of Democratic and ethnic commitment to the cause.

This was continually reinforced by the service of the soldiers in the state's Irish regiments. The push for reenlistments began in the later winter of 1863 and carried through the spring of 1864 with furlough to take place before the start of the summer campaign season. The campaign for reenlistments was relatively successful. Approximately 263 men reenlisted in the 17th Wisconsin and 367 soldiers rejoined the 9th Connecticut.[96] Reenlistment came with a veteran furlough, and the men returned home to great fanfare. The men of the 17th had a "first rate time" as they prepared for their journey home to Wisconsin.[97] The trip home was an exciting one as "everybody [in the regiment was] drunk fighting sweating &c." The excitement escalated as they traveled through Illinois, met in every town by "very patriotic [folks'] waving hand kerchiefs table cloths and every thing to be got a hold of."[98] When the returning veterans of 9th Connecticut landed in New York, they were met by "an immense crowd of friends and citizens . . . present to extend to them a hearty welcome home . . . the street was crowded with the friends of the returning soldiers, while flags were flying and fire-works exploding. The men cheered and the women pressed forward to greet their husbands and brothers."[99] Hardly the response expected from a war-weary and disillusioned citizenry, this response was equally important to the morale of the veteran volunteers, who returned from furlough and fought until the fall of the Confederacy.

To ignore the importance of the Copperhead movement and the growth of political tensions over the draft and emancipation would be to downplay a vital part of wartime politics in both states during this period. But the issues were not black and white and, more importantly, the acts of the mob in New York cannot be used to accurately gauge the sentiment of Irish Americans in communities throughout the North. It is clear that the New York City Draft Riots themselves only peripherally impacted the wartime experiences of the Irish in Connecticut and Wisconsin. Although men and women followed the events in New York in July in 1863 with interest, the riots were not barometers of public opinion or Irish American support for the war, broadly. Certainly, there were Irish Americans in Connecticut and Wisconsin who were disloyal, men who joined the anti-war movement, and who violently or through other means rejected Lincoln's policies. But these men were not alone. They joined the ranks of dissenters from all ethnic backgrounds. Publicly, most Irish ardently rejected radical dissent.

Although portrayed as Copperheads by their political opponents, Irish Americans strove to distance themselves from these accusations. Time and again they rejected this designation and their language and acts throughout the war illuminate their self-identification as War Democrats who continued to support the war effort while offering loyal political opposition to the federal policies. Ultimately, and unfortunately, the charges of Copperheadism that emerged in the wake of the Draft Riots became synonymous with the Irish American experience in the Civil War and charges of disloyalty followed these adopted citizens into the twentieth century.

Disloyalty, in this context, was not an ethnic trait. Rather, ethnicity and political party often appeared as a descriptive tool used to identify perceptions of disloyalty which subsequently makes Irish dissent appear more widespread and radical than it actually was. Nationally, the Draft Riots were appropriated to signify dissatisfaction amongst the immigrant population, sentiment that was cultivated by vocal opposition to Lincoln's war measures by many prominent Irishmen. This was compounded by Republican tendencies to portray all political opponents as Copperheads. These issues served to revitalize questions of immigrant place that had proliferated across the antebellum landscape. Yet, the narrative of the Irish American experience during the Civil War is incredibly nuanced. Publicly, most Irish Americans in Connecticut and Wisconsin rejected the Draft Riots as a spontaneous manifestation of a certain class that lived in New York City and sought to challenge federal policy legally rather than violently.

But this issue is not cut and dried, and ideologies and actions must be understood as part of a broad spectrum of political acts undertaken by men who were active participants in local, state, and national affairs. Professions of loyalty occurred hand in hand with accusations of disloyalty and men often took conflicting ideological stances on important issues of the day, illuminating the agency of a group who were so often described as "voting cattle" for the Democratic Party machines or blind followers of dissenting parties. In order to fully understand the Irish experience during the Civil War, we must understand the subtle differences in responses among smaller immigrant communities, for these were as important to defining the political and social lives of Irishmen in Wisconsin and Connecticut as the New York City Draft Riots were to defining broader issues of Irish American dissent during the latter part of the nineteenth century.

Notes

1. The existence of vocal and visible dissent in the form of the politicization of the Copperhead movement in the North and resistance to authority in communities North and South are the predominant themes in Robert Sandow, *Deserter Country: Civil War Opposition in the Pennsylvania Appalachians* (New York: Fordham University Press, 2009); Jennifer L. Weber, *Copperheads: The Rise and Fall of Lincoln's Opponents in the North* (New York: Oxford University Press, 2006); David Williams, *Bitterly Divided: The South's Inner Civil War* (New York: The New Press, 2008); Margaret M. Storey, *Loyalty*

and Loss: Alabama's Unionist in Civil War and Reconstruction (Baton Rouge: Louisiana State University Press, 2004); Frank Klement, "Catholics as Copperheads during the Civil War," *Catholic Historical Review* 8, no 1 (1994); Matthew Warshauer, *Connecticut in the Civil War: Slavery, Sacrifice, and Survival* (Middletown, Conn.: Wesleyan University Press, 2011); Mark V. Wetherington, *Plain Folk's Fight: The Civil War and Reconstruction in Piney Woods Georgia* (Chapel Hill: University of North Carolina Press, 2005); David William, Theresa C. Williams, and R. David Carlson, *Plain Folk in a Rich Man's War; Class and Dissent in Confederate Georgia* (Gainesville: University Press of Florida 2002). These studies illustrate the necessity of redirecting analysis of dissent toward local perspectives. One of the primary problems that comes from attempts to create a national narrative of political opposition is that this methodological framework forces certain concessions. For example, opposition to issues such as emancipation and the draft can certainly be fit within a broad narrative of Democratic ideologies but, as Sandow illustrates in his study on the Pennsylvania Appalachian region, citizens often understood these issues as they pertained to local experiences that can be oversimplified when contextualized as part of nation-wide dissent. In order to truly understand the far-reaching implications of political opposition during the Civil War, we must understand it, to the best of our ability, as it pertained to individuals in disparate communities throughout the North during this period. The same applies to the Irish experience during the Civil War. Questions surrounding wartime measures were not necessarily black and white. Rather, they were part of a complex set of relationships with local, state, and national communities. Dissenting ideologies often appeared side by side with public proclamations of loyalty and rejections of more violent means of protest. Thus, the rise and fall of Irish support of the war must be analyzed through the lens of local experiences in order to better understand responses to the war and shifting federal policies.

2. Parts of this chapter appear in my book *Shades of Green: Irish Regiments, American Soldiers, and Local Communities in the Civil War Era* (New York: Fordham University Press, 2017).

3. "Shall Ruffians Rule Us?" *New York Times*, July 14, 1863.

4. "General News," *New York Times*, July 15, 1863; "The Riot," *New York Tribune*, July 16, 1863; Susannah Ural Bruce, *The Harp and the Eagle: Irish American Volunteers and the Union Army, 1861–1865* (New York: New York University Press, 2006), 179–85.

5. Iver Bernstein, *The New York City Draft Riots; Their Significance for American Society and Politics in the Age of the Civil War* (Lincoln: University of Nebraska Press, 1990), 23–38. Bernstein's argument is not one of loyalty or disloyalty, but rather, the nuances that existed in regards to the relationships among working class in New York City. Intrinsic to the riots was the fear of competition that existed among Irish circles, especially among men and women who understood their place at the bottom of the socio-economic ladder, and saw African Americans as potentially undermining their tenuous hold on those jobs. Christian Samito, *Becoming American Under Fire: Irish Americans, African Americans, and the Politics of Citizenship during the Civil War Era* (Ithaca, N.Y.: Cornell University Press, 2009), 128–33. Susannah Ural Bruce, *The Harp and the Eagle: Irish American Volunteers and the Union Army, 1861–1865* (New York: New York University Press, 2005), 180–90. Samito and Bruce illustrate Republican

attempts to link the Draft Riots to larger issues of Irish disloyalty over the course of the war.

6. "The German and French Press of New York on the Riot," *New York Tribune*, July 23, 1863. Spelling in all quotations appears exactly as it did in the original documents.

7. Nativism has played a major role in American history and was an important component of the Irish American experience. Although it differed by locale, there were broader themes that linked nativist ideology from the 1850s through the 1930s, which included a fear of the Catholic Church, issues over naturalization, stereotypical assessments of ethnic behavior including a focus on violence, alcoholism, and cleanliness, and questions of assimilation. The literature on the subject is extensive, but see, for example: Kerby A. Miller, *Emigrants and Exiles: Ireland and the Irish Exodus to North America* (New York: Oxford University Press, 1985); Noel Igantive, *How the Irish Became White* (New York: Routledge, 1995); Kevin Kenny, *Making Sense of the Molly Maguires* (New York: Oxford University Press, 1998); John Higham, *Strangers in the Land: Patterns of American Nativism, 1860–1925* (New Brunswick, N.J.: Rutgers University Press, 2002); David Noel Doyle, "The Remaking of Irish America, 1845–1880," in *Making the Irish American: History and Heritage of the Irish in the United States*, ed. Joseph J. Lee and Marion R. Casey (New York: New York University Press, 2006), 213–55.

8. Bernstein, *The New York City Draft Riots*, 6.

9. Bruce, *The Harp and the Eagle*, 181.

10. Kerby A. Miller, *Emigrants and Exiles*, 324.

11. Bruce, *The Harp and the Eagle*, 112.

12. Ibid., 232.

13. Martin W. Öfele, *True Sons of the Republic: European Immigrants in the Union Army* (Westport, Conn.: Praeger, 2008), 135.

14. William B. Kurtz, *Excommunicated From the Union: How the Civil War Created a Separate Catholic America* (New York: Fordham University Press, 2016), 4, 109.

15. In spite of sacrifice in defense of the Union, Irish Americans were forced to continually justify and validate their service during the later half of the nineteenth century as their loyalty was replaced by negative memories of disloyal conduct that was intrinsically linked to the Draft Riots. Furthermore, the decline of support during the winter and spring of 1863 is fascinating because the sentiment, especially in New York, was so at odds with the enthusiasm exhibited by immigrants in 1861 and early 1862. In spite of the very visible decline of Irish American support for the war effort in New York City, ethnic heritage did not necessarily yield similar experiences among local communities and although ethnic associations can be derived from regimental designations, local relationships and associations often contributed as much, if not more, to the identity and experiences of soldiers in these units than national ones. Similarities existed among Irish immigrants, but Irish Americans outside of large urban areas experienced a significantly different relationship with their adopted communities as a consequence of more liberal notions of acceptance and assimilation. To define Irish loyalty through the experiences of the New York Irish would be to overlook the nuanced responses of Irish in other areas of the country to shifting war measures. For evidence of this tendency see, for example,

William Corby, *Memoirs of a Chaplain Life: Three Years with the Irish Brigade*, Lawrence Frederick Kohl, ed. (New York: Fordham University Press, 1992); David Power Conyngham, *The Irish Brigade and Its Campaigns* (London: F. Pitman, 1866); Thomas Hamilton Murray, *The History of the Ninth Regiment Connecticut Volunteer Infantry, "The Irish Regiment" in the War of the Rebellion, 1861–1865* (New Haven: The Price, Lee and Adkins Co. 1908); *The Story of the 116th Regiment, Pennsylvania Volunteers in the War of Rebellion*, Lawrence Frederick Kohl, ed. (New York: Fordham University Press, 1996); William Burton, *Melting Pot Soldiers: The Union's Ethnic Regiments* (New York: Fordham University Press, 1988), 14, 17; John Gjedge, *The Minds of the West: Ethnocultural Evolution in the Rural Middle West 1830–1917* (Chapel Hill: University of North Carolina Press, 1997); Christian Samito, *Becoming American Under Fire*, 126.

16. Database of soldiers of the 9th Connecticut Volunteer Infantry and 17th Wisconsin Volunteer Infantry compiled from the Descriptive and Muster Rolls of Civil War Regiments, RG 949, National Archives and Record Office, Washington D.C.; Wisconsin Adjutant General's Regimental Muster and Descriptive Rolls, Wisconsin State Archives, Madison, Wisconsin; Eighth Census of the United States, *Population of the United States in 1860*.

17. Database of Irish-born men of Military Age in Connecticut and Wisconsin. This database was constructed from a 20 percent sample of men between the ages of 13 and 50 living in eight cities in these two states. From Connecticut: Bridgeport, Hartford, New Haven, and Waterbury. From Wisconsin: Beloit, Fond Du Lac, Madison, and Milwaukee. These were the cities that sent the largest numbers of Irish soldiers to serve in their respective regiments *and* also contained the largest concentration of Irish-born citizens in their states. This database was derived from the Eighth Census of the United States, completed in 1860.

18. Joseph Schafer, "Know-Nothingism in Wisconsin," *The Wisconsin Magazine of History* 8 no. 1 (September 1924), 9; "Black Republicans and Know Nothings Melted Together," *Weekly Wisconsin Patriot*, June 28, 1856.

19. "Untitled," *The Constitution* (Middletown, Conn.), February 14, 1855.

20. "The Militia Disbandment," *Columbian Register*, October 6, 1855.

21. "Irish Volunteers," *The Constitution* (Middletown, Conn.), April 24, 1861.

22. "Untitled," *Columbian Register* (New Haven, Conn.), May 11, 1861.

23. "In the Days of Know-Nothingism," *Columbian Register* (New Haven, Conn.) May 11, 1861.

24. "A Priest's War Speech," *Hartford Daily Courant*, June 25, 1861.

25. "Connecticut Correspondence," *Irish American Weekly*, October 12, 1861.

26. "Grand Union Meeting on the Park," *Connecticut Courant* (Hartford, Conn.), September 21, 1861.

27. "The Adopted Citizens of the Union," *Weekly Wisconsin Patriot*, January 5, 1861.

28. "The American Flag on the Cathedral," *Milwaukee Sentinel*, April 26, 1861.

29. Kurtz, *Excommunicated from the Union*, 97–98.

30. "From Fond du Lac," *Wisconsin Daily Patriot*, April 19, 1861.

31. "Irish True to the Union," *Wisconsin Daily Patriot*, April 17, 1861; "Latest News. Military Spirit Thoroughly Aroused!" *Milwaukee Daily Sentinel*, April 14, 1861; "The

Foreign Element in the Federal Army," *The Albany Evening Journal* (Albany, N.Y.),
reprinted in the *Milwaukee Morning Sentinel*, June 20, 1861.

32. "The Irish and the War," *Weekly Wisconsin Patriot* (Madison, Wisc.), April 27, 1861.

33. Untitled, *Weekly Wisconsin Patriot*, August 23, 1862.

34. For discussion of the place of immigrant soldiers in American armies and
national perceptions of ethnic soldiers in the antebellum period, see James Callaghan,
"The San Patricios," *The American Heritage* 46, no. 7 (November 1995), 73–81; Tyler V.
Johnson, "Punishing the Lies on the Rio Grande: Catholic Immigrant Volunteers in
Zachary Taylor's Army and the Fight against Nativism," *Journal of the Early Republic* 30,
no. 1 (Spring 2010), 66–84.

35. "The Departure for the War of the Sixty-Ninth," *Hartford Daily Courant*, April 25,
1861.

36. "Our Noble 69th (Irish) Regiment," *Wisconsin Daily Patriot*, July 27, 1861. Italics in
original.

37. "The War Feeling in the State," *Hartford Daily Courant*, April 23, 1861.

38. "Recruiting Office for the Irish Regiment," *New London Daily Chronicle*, September 17, 1861.

39. "Connecticut Correspondence," *Irish America Weekly*, October 12, 1861.

40. Untitled," *Hartford Daily Courant*, September 12, 1861. Italics in original.

41. Carolyn J. Mattern, *Soldiers When They Go: The Story of Camp Randall* (Madison:
State Historical Society of Wisconsin, 1981), 57.

42. Terrible Catastrophie!" *Wisconsin Daily Patriot*, September 10, 1860; "The Calamity on the Lady Elgin—Is Gov. Randall Responsible," *Wisconsin Daily Patriot*, Septem-
ber 14, 1860; William George, *The History of Milwaukee, City and County* (Chicago: S. J.
Clarke Publishing Company, 1922), 128–29; Charles Martin Scanlan, *The Lady Elgin Di-
saster, September 8, 1860* (Canon Printing Co., 1928); Brian A. Kangas, *Tragedy, Myth and
Memory: The Sinking of the Lady Elgin and Its Impact on Irish American Nationalism in
Milwaukee 1850–1870* (Ph.D. diss.) University of Wisconsin, Milwaukee, 2011; M. Justille
McDonald, *History of the Irish in Wisconsin in the Nineteenth Century* (Washington D.C:
Catholic University of America Press, 1954), 55. McDonald notes that Charles Martin
Scanlan in *The Lady Elgin Disaster, September 8, 1860* (Cannon Printing Co., 1928) sug-
gested that the Lady Elgin disaster pushed Milwaukee back at least twenty years, while
allowing the Irish community in Chicago to thrive; William George Bruce, *The History
of Milwaukee, City and County* (Chicago: S. J. Clark Publishing Company, 1922), 128–29;
"Terrible Catastrophie!" *Wisconsin Daily Patriot*, September 10, 1860; "The Calamity on
the Lady Elgin—Is Gov. Randall Responsible," *Wisconsin Daily Patriot*, September 14,
1860.

43. "Irishmen! Rally to the Rescue," *Watertown Democrat* (Watertown, Wisc.), November 7, 1861.

44. "Irishmen at Home and in America," *Watertown Democrat* (Watertown, Wisc.),
November 21, 1861.

45. Bruce, *The Harp and the Eagle*, 130–35.

46. Burton, *Melting Pot Soldiers*, 127.

47. "News," *Hartford Daily Courant*, April 30, 1862. Ship Island was the staging point

for the invasion of New Orleans. The 9th Connecticut was stationed there from December 1861 through April 1862 before moving to garrison duty in New Orleans.

48. Thomas Hamilton Murray, *The History of the Ninth Regiment, Connecticut Volunteer Infantry, "The Irish Regiment" in the War of the Rebellion, 1861–65* (New Haven: The Price, Lee & Adkins Co., 1903), 85.

49. Thomas Cahill to Sister, October 20, 1862, Cahill Collection.

50. "Victory at Baton Rouge," *Hartford Daily Courant*, August 19, 1862; Thomas Cahill to Sister, October 20, 1862, Cahill Collection.

51. "From the Seventeenth Regiment," October 19, 1862, Quiner Scrapbooks, Correspondence of Wisconsin Volunteers, Volume 6, 16th–29th Regiment, MS 600, State Historical Society of Wisconsin, Madison, Wisc. (hereafter cited as "Quiner"), 34.

52. "From the 16th and 17th regiments," Quiner, 34.

53. "From the Seventeenth Regiment," October 19, 1862, Quiner, 35. The author of this letter is adamant about the fact that the 17th Wisconsin acted alone in their charge. He noted that "I see it stated in the Chicago journals that Baldwin's brigade assisted, or made the charge. Such is not the case; the 17th *alone made it*."; "The Battle Near Corinth," *Watertown Democrat*, October 16, 1862. The *Democrat* noted that "the Seventeenth Wisconsin made a charge through the lines of the enemy, wheeled and charged back again."

54. "'Parvus' to 'Friend Ballou,'" *Watertown Democrat*, June 11, 1863.

55. Ibid.

56. Ibid.

57. "Bloody Riot Among the Stevedores at Toledo," *Wisconsin Daily Patriot* (Madison, Wisc.), July 7, 1862; "Bloody Riot Among the Stevedores at Toledo," *Wisconsin Daily Patriot*, July 7, 1862; "Untitled," *Macon Telegraph* (Macon, Ga.), July 25, 1862; "The Hiberno-African Riots in the West," *New York Tribune*, August 1, 1862; "Rioting Among Laborers," *Chicago Tribune*, August 10, 1862; "Riot in South Brooklyn," *New York Tribune*, August 5, 1862; "Riot at a Tobacco Factory," *Wisconsin Daily Patriot*, August 6, 1862; "Serious Riot in Brooklyn," *The Crisis*, August 13, 1862; "Riot in Buffalo," *New York Tribune*, August 13, 1862; "Another Riot Between Irish and Negroes," *Philadelphia Inquirer*, August 27, 1862; "Riot in Detroit," *The Liberator*, March 9, 1863; "Riot in New York," *Hartford Daily Courant*, April 14, 1863; "Riot in New York," *New York Tribune*, April 14, 1863; "Riot at Newburgh, N.Y.," *New York Tribune*, June 24, 1863; "Disgraceful Riot and Murder," *Albany Evening Journal*, June 23, 1863; "Riot in Buffalo," *Milwaukee Daily Sentinel*, July 7, 1863.

58. One cannot ignore the existence of political dissenters in both states, and to do so would be to overlook a critical component of the home front experience. See Matt Warshauer, "Copperheads in Connecticut: A Peace Movement That Imperiled the Union" in *This Distracted and Anarchical People: New Answers for Old Questions About the Civil War Era North*, ed. Andrew Slap and Michael Thomas Smith (New York: Fordham University Press, 2013); La Vern J. Rippley, *The Immigrant Experience in Wisconsin* (Boston: Twayne Publishers, 1985), 38–40; Lynn Ira Schoonover, *The History of the Draft in Wisconsin* (Madison: MA Thesis, University of Wisconsin, unpublished), 1915; and Klement, "Catholics as Copperheads." While we should acknowledge the pervasive nature of dissent in these communities, which undoubtedly included immigrants, we should also not

overlook the fact that publicly, Irish Americans attempted to negotiate and balance this loyalty with loyal, legal opposition.

59. "Eloquent Speech of the Irish Patriot, Meagher," *Weekly Wisconsin Patriot*, September 7, 1861.

60. Cahill, "Anniversary Dinner in Honor of Saint Patrick's Day: Address at Glasgow," in *The Works of the Rev. D. W. Cahill, D.D.* (Boston: Patrick Donahoe, 1855), 54.

61. "Shame on Them," *Columbian Register*, October 18, 1862; "Freedom of Political Expression," *Wisconsin Patriot*, October 11, 1862.

62. "The Great Riot in New York," *Wisconsin Daily Patriot*, July 18, 1863.

63. "The Draft and Riots," *Wisconsin Daily Patriot*, July 18, 1863.

64. Matthew Hart to Thomas Cahill, July 25, 1863, Cahill Collection, held by Charles Sibley, Cheshire, Conn..

65. "Untitled," *Wisconsin Daily Patriot*, July 17, 1863.

66. Thomas Knablin to Mary Knablin, August 2, 1863, Thomas Knablin (Co D, 9th CT Vol. Inf., Civil War), pension application no. 429,164, certificate no. 399,850, Case of Files of Approved Pension Applications, 1861–1934; Civil War and Later Pension Files; Department of Veteran Affairs, Record Group 15; National Archives, Washington, D.C.

67. "To the Public," *Connecticut Constitution* (New Haven, Conn.), July 22, 1863.

68. "How Catholics Regard the Late Riot," *Milwaukee Sentinel*, July 25, 1863.

69. "Untitled," *Weekly Wisconsin Patriot*, August 23, 1863.

70. For an excellent overview of the political and social issues surrounding emancipation, see James Oakes, *Freedom National: The Destruction of Slavery in the United States, 1861–1865* (New York: Norton, 2013).

71. "The Negro Question," *The Columbian Register*, May 5, 1862.

72. "The Democratic Party and the War," *Wisconsin Patriot*, December 27, 1862.

73. "From the 17th Regiment," *Wisconsin Daily Patriot*, October 13, 1863.

74. "The Enrollment of Negro Regiments—Utter Futility of the Idea," *Wisconsin Daily Patriot*, April 29, 1863.

75. Thomas Christie to James Christie in Hampton Smith, ed. *Brother of Mine: The Civil War Letters of Thomas and William Christie* (St. Paul: Minnesota Historical Society, 2010), 120.

76. "Extract from a letter written by a well known officer of the 9th C.V., and an Irishman, who was a strong Democrat when he left Connecticut, to a friend in this city," *Connecticut Courant*, August 28, 1863.

77. Ibid.

78. "Now the election is over, it is deemed safe to let the old Ninth visit home," *Hartford Daily Courant*, April 12, 1864.

79. "The Coming Draft," *Wisconsin Daily Sentinel*, June 13, 1863.

80. "Who's Hit?" *Weekly Wisconsin Patriot*, August 2, 1862.

81. "Irishmen and the Draft," *Connecticut Courant*, September 6, 1862.

82. "Secretary Stanton; Madison; Mr. Copperhead," *Wisconsin Patriot*, May 30, 1863.

83. "The Draft in this State," *Milwaukee Daily Sentinel*, July 18, 1863; "How A Democratic Paper Talked About the Draft," *Milwaukee Sentinel*, July 18, 1863.

84. *The Hartford Daily Courant*, "City Intelligence: Adopted Citizens Meeting," August 27, 1862.

85. "Untitled," *New Haven Palladium*, June 9, 1863.

86. "The Draft in this State," *Milwaukee Daily Sentinel*, July 18, 1863.

87. Ibid.

88. "Untitled," *Wisconsin Daily Patriot*, July 17, 1863.

89. *Hartford Daily Courant*, "Suspension of the Draft," July 18, 1863.

90. "Secretary Stanton; Madison; Mr. Copperhead," *Wisconsin Patriot*, May 30, 1863.

91. "Untitled," *Wisconsin Daily Patriot*, June 8, 1863.

92. Matthew Hart to Thomas Cahill, July 25, 1863, Cahill Collection.

93. Lorien Foote, *The Gentlemen and the Roughs; Violence, Honor, and Manhood in the Union Army* (New York: New York University Press, 2010), 129. Foote contends that there was a growing trend of stringent army discipline after 1863 when the Northern recruits were disproportionately immigrant or poor, native-born Americans who were coerced into fighting. In the case of this study, of the 290 men who joined the 17th Wisconsin as draftees in the fall and winter of 1864, only four deserted, suggesting that the draftees who served in this unit were not necessarily more prone to this type of behavior because of the fact that they were conscripted into service. Descriptive and Muster Rolls of Civil War Regiments, RG 949, National Archives and Record Office, Washington D.C.;

94. "Loyalty Means," *Republican Farmer*, October 18, 1864.

95. "Lying vs. Copperheads," *Wisconsin Daily Patriot*, February 23, 1864.

96. "Return of the Ninth C.V.: Grand Reception and Immense Turn Out of Citizens," *Columbian Register* (New Haven, Conn.), April 23, 1864; Database of Volunteers to Irish Regiments.

97. Diary of James B. Fowler, January 5, 1864, MSS 119S, Wisconsin Historical Society, Madison, Wisc. Diary of James B. Fowler, "Memoranda," February 18, 1864.

98. Diary of Orin Jameson, March 15–16, 1864, MSS 118S, Wisconsin Historical Society, Madison, Wisc. Diary of James B. Fowler, March 16, 1864.

99. "Grand Reception and Immense Turn Out of Citizens," *Columbian Register* (New Haven, Conn.), April 23, 1864.

"Deeds of Our Own"

Loyalty, Soldier Rights, and Protest in Northern Regiments of the United States Colored Troops

Thaddeus M. Romansky

On an April night in 1864 several dozen soldiers of the 55th Massachusetts Infantry Regiment (Colored) mutinied aboard the transport steamer *Sentinel* to free Sergeant Sampson Goliah from what they believed to be an improper arrest. Colonel Alfred S. Hartwell had ordered the civilian captain of the steamer to tie Goliah to the rigging. The mutineers saw this as a violation of the rights and protections that belonged to them as members of their regiment. After a brief struggle with officers and fellow soldiers on guard detail, they spirited him below decks. The mutinous soldiers only savored a brief moment of triumph before more officers and soldiers confronted them. Even as Goliah bellowed in defiance, he was rearrested and the mutiny collapsed less than an hour after it erupted. After the steamer disembarked on Folly Island, South Carolina the next day, the colonel ordered courts-martial to try Goliah and four ringleaders for mutiny.[1]

Military protest actions, like the Goliah incident, in African-American regiments raised in the North reveal free Northern black soldiers and emancipated slave soldiers articulating a body of soldier rights that they claimed as loyal members of the federal army pledged to defend the Union. Defining and defending these rights during military protest actions, however, put them in a position of ostensible disloyalty against the Army; the very vehicle of their drive for freedom. Northern and Southern black soldiers in the 55th Massachusetts Infantry and the 14th Rhode Island Colored Heavy Artillery (RICHA) located these rights in their own experience with Northern antebellum political culture and the enslaved's patterns of confrontation and resistance, respectively.[2]

Free Northern blacks and freedmen from the South brought different antebellum understandings of rights and self-government to their Civil War military service. These distinctive conceptions became the basis for their definition of soldier rights while serving in the army. Furthermore, these regional traditions came together in black regiments raised in the loyal states. When black soldiers thought these rights were being abridged, then it was their duty to resist. Resistance was complicated for Northern blacks because of an antebellum protest culture enriched by the nation's founding ideals and its culture of associationalism. Soldiers' defense of their rights, therefore, rested on the nation's ideals and its civic culture at the same time it challenged a military authority guilty of unjust discipline and discriminatory policies. This showed the complicated nature and meaning of loyalty during the Civil War. In addition, Northern black soldiers' resistance was a crucial part of the fight for full citizenship during Reconstruction and beyond.

While the focus of these protest actions is on how Northern free blacks used them to define their soldier rights, Southern blacks played important roles as comrades in arms. These military protest actions were yet another example of how the Civil War intensified African-American political cooperation across sectional boundaries in the pursuit of freedom. In this way, it links the black soldiering experience more firmly to the larger trends of nationalization unleashed by the Civil War and Reconstruction.

Although the two regiments that I focus on in this essay were part of the United States Colored Troops (USCT), they contained Northern free black men in a far greater proportion than the typical African-American regiment. Defined as a person of African descent not in a state of bondage at the war's outbreak and resident in the states loyal to the Union, these Northern blacks were a divergent collection of volunteers from the Northeast as well as the Middle West and the border states. Of the roughly 2.8 million men who served for some length of time in the Union forces, only 33,364 "colored troops" were officially credited to the enlistment quotas of the northern and western states. The slaveholding border states and the seceded states contributed 139,715 such men, the vast majority of whom who were emancipated slaves. Nevertheless, several regiments beyond the 54th Massachusetts Infantry immortalized in the film *Glory* contained not only freedmen but Northern free blacks as well. Pennsylvania sponsored eleven USCT regiments, New York three. Other states such as Illinois, Connecticut, and Iowa each raised a single regiment.[3] Although by the beginning of 1864 these units accounted for 18 percent of all blacks under arms, probably only one in every one hundred Union soldiers could be considered a Northern free black.[4] Despite the numbers, regiments raised in the loyal states had a distinctive role as places of cultural encounter between free and freed African Americans.

A minority in the larger USCT, Northern blacks made up the majority inside regiments like the 55th Massachusetts and the 14th Rhode Island. Sixty-two percent of the 55th Massachusetts's soldiers had been born in non-slave, North-ern states. Nearly 56 percent had been born in the Ohio Valley states of Ohio, Pennsylvania, Kentucky, and Indiana. Furthermore, in the 55th Massachusetts nearly 45 percent had been artisans, skilled workers, or unskilled laborers before the war compared to the entire Army where that number was around 10 percent. Company A of the 14th RICHA, the locus of the protest actions discussed in the text that follows, was almost entirely Northeastern drawing over 80 percent of its soldiers from New York City, Pennsylvania, or New England. An urban company as well, only a little more than 15 percent of its members claimed prewar occupa-tions as farmers. The percentage of soldiers in the 55th Massachusetts and the 14th Rhode Island whose state of origin allowed slavery was 36 and 13, respec-tively. Judging the proportion of freedmen-soldiers in both regiments is compli-cated by the reality that some recruits born in the South resided in free states by the war's outbreak.[5] An escapee could have been living in freedom for many years before he enlisted. Take Private William H. Smith in the 14th Rhode Island, for example. A twenty-five-year-old born in Richmond, he had lived with his family in Ohio since about 1844.[6] Even with their component of emancipated slaves, these particular black regiments reflected the urban, working-class makeup of the Northern, free African-American community.[7]

Antebellum escapees from slavery or freedmen within these Northern regi-ments contributed a voice of protest distinct from their Northern comrades. They negotiated a place for themselves in the Army structured by the institution of slavery. Masters treated the enslaved as second-class children of an imagined household who received sustenance, but owed obedience and labor. Enslaved African Americans never completely accepted this arrangement. Degrees of confrontation gained the enslaved capricious protections and privileges. While the most dramatic were slave revolts and maroon communities, they achieved more permanent gains by turning slavery's labor arrangements to their ad-vantage. Historians have found a precarious system of customary obligations, privileges, and even rights vis-à-vis the master within the institution's internal economy, which the enslaved used to protect their fledgling dreams of freedom. Often over a span of decades a neighborhood of slaves won concessions from their master through confrontations over kin-based work parties, free time on weekends, and routines of paid labor. While these reciprocities rested on slaves' membership in the fictive household, one scholar has argued such con-frontations constituted nothing less than a "politics of slaves." The freedman-soldier, therefore, knew something of institutions structured by the rights of its members.[8]

Serving alongside their comrades who had slipped loose from bondage were the Northern blacks who contributed the bulk of the rank and file to the 55th Massachusetts and the 14th RICHA. These soldiers also had a particular culture of protest born of African Americans' longstanding, broadly based participation in Northern public culture. Scholars have uncovered ample evidence that despite exclusion from the statehouse and the polls, Northern blacks formed civic organizations to press for suffrage, conducted parades to mark the anniversaries of state emancipation laws, and inaugurated a national convention movement to articulate a vision of full citizenship. Through a network of black newspapers they interjected their collective voice into contemporary print culture while rallying their churches to shape the era's wave of moral reforms, most notably through abolitionism. In the view of one historian, "antebellum black protest" gained "power from precisely the factors that rendered northern free blacks *less* culturally and intellectually autonomous of the white world than their enslaved brethren."[9] As the 1853 Colored National Convention proclaimed: "We are Americans" who "address you as American citizens asserting their rights on their own native soil."[10]

As the sectional crisis of the 1850s intensified, Northern blacks remained loyal to their race and to the principles of the Revolution. The free blacks of Boston and other Northern cities publicly interfered with federal officials' arrest and remanding of escaped slaves under the Fugitive Slave Law of 1850.[11] In response to news of the Harper's Ferry raid, African Americans convened a Providence, Rhode Island public meeting in November 1859 to express they "fully sympathize with our friend Capt. John Brown."[12]

The soldier status that both groups of African Americans gained inside regiments of the USCT opened up a conventional realm of American civic action: the self-governing association. Understanding why requires an explanation of the antebellum tradition of citizen self-government within a volunteer military company. The national government's call for volunteers in 1861 to suppress the rebellion inaugurated a "national war fought by local communities" in the words of Matthew Gallman. Gallman and Reid Mitchell point to antebellum America's fundamental localism as a source of the citizen rights that Union volunteers believed they retained. William Novak's definition of the "political-legal" construct of "associationalism" offers a concrete mechanism to explain why. Reid Mitchell likewise contends that "localism aided rather than hindered national patriotism."[13] Members of a voluntary association—a business, church, or fraternal order—accrued specific rights, privileges, and obligations via a charter of incorporation from the state granting them legal power to make bylaws for the good governance of their affairs.[14] For example, New York's 1854 Militia Law used this mechanism to "entitle" members "of any uniformed company to the privileges and exemptions allowed by law" if they "complied with the by-laws of his particular company or troop." At the war's outbreak, associational concepts shaped how Northern white volunteers filtered their interpretations of the Articles of War and the military's published regulations in light of their society's associational way of life.

Northern blacks had their own citizen-soldiering tradition that attuned them to notions of self-government and soldier rights. Black abolitionists such as William C. Nell recovered black military service in the War for Independence and the War of 1812. Memories of the promises of freedom to slaves who served during the Revolution and with Andrew Jackson at New Orleans served as reminders that soldier status could confer rights.[15] African Americans also participated in antebellum military associational culture by forming their own volunteer companies. In 1855, Providence's blacks organized a volunteer rifle company and Cincinnati's African Americans formed a "well drilled, well uniformed, and well officered" unit called the "Attucks Blues."[16] Although officially excluded from military service in 1861, African Americans in New York City, Providence, and Boston continued to form their own drill squads and militia companies during the war's first two years.[17] Following the advice of black abolitionist Alfred M. Green, these Northern blacks prepared themselves to "be armed" and "schooled in military service" with sufficient "manhood to defend the right and the sagacity to detect the wrong."[18]

The Northern USCT regiments, therefore, became fora where two distinct strains of black dissent joined the potent claim that American soldiers possessed specific rights derived from their membership in a military association. The status of soldiers depended on a voluntary pledge of allegiance—loyalty to the nation—yet it also conferred a degree of sovereign power to define what rights the pledge of loyalty should entail. According to such logic, confronting the arbitrary orders of officers, writing letters in the black press, and even taking up mutiny did not compromise a soldier's loyalty to the state.[19] Rather, these forms of protest displayed self-government in the ranks. Once placed in the broader contexts discussed previously, military protest actions in Northern black regiments emerge as moments when African Americans in uniform resolved a loyalty to the nation and its ideals, which they had found in conflict thus far. By drawing in black soldiers from both regions, protest actions also encouraged a freedom struggle that was national in breadth. All of these experiences contributed to Northern African Americans' calls during the war for the legal definition of their civil and political rights that intensified during Reconstruction.

Setting Northern black regiments in the context of antebellum associational culture lends greater nuance to the complaints that African Americans eventually voiced about their military service. Northern blacks claimed individual and corporate rights as a consequence of their soldier status. These "soldier rights" flowed from their membership in a particular regiment. Soldiers mutinied when they found membership in the Army at odds with membership in their regiment. Although soldier rights were not identical even from regiment to regiment, free blacks' soldier rights incorporated the associational tradition as well as elements of their antebellum protest movement. Rather, they arose from the localism of American life before the Civil War.[20] That said, some rights such as state affiliation, organizational integrity, and respect for soldiers' exact muster in and out dates, protected the regiment itself. Others covered rights to petition, to protest government policy, to be free from unjust discipline, and to expect fair pay.[21]

Three violations of their soldier rights—unequal pay, discrimination in officer commissions, and abusive treatment—populate the record left behind by Northern black soldiers. Any one of these complaints could evoke claims that "we should be treated in all respects like white soldiers" or that "we have not been treated like men and soldiers belonging to the army of the United States." In both phrasings there was a sense they had been robbed of the dignity due to citizens in uniform. The sense of solidarity created through corporate self-government underlay convictions that black officers "would inspire . . . confidence" because they would be "men from their own ranks." As a mark of soldier status under the wartime recruiting calls, Northern African-American soldiers' uncertainty that they would be able to "claim equal pay with other volunteers" placed "our military and civil equality at issue."[22]

Scholars have been at work since the close of the Civil War centennial telling the political story of black recruitment and those soldiers' performance on the battlefield. What began as an effort to recover the memory of African Americans' role in the destruction of slavery has itself helped to transform Civil War historiography. Several generations of historians have demonstrated two fundamental truths. The 180,000 African-American soldiers were crucial to Union victory, and black enlistment contributed mightily to the destruction of slavery. Along the way, scholars have delved into the relationship of blacks to their white officers, their efforts to secure equal treatment, their medical care and everyday lives, and how they made meaning out of their experience in uniform. Donning Union blue became the ultimate act of self-emancipation for the formerly enslaved. Northern blacks believed their participation in the struggle against slavery would "reward their sacrifices with full freedom, equality, and citizenship."[23]

Military protest actions by Northern black soldiers reveal crucial connections between military service, prewar protest culture, and the definition of soldier rights, which in turn shaped the national African-American struggle for freedom initiated by the war.

Black military service began in 1862, immediately dogged by inequalities of pay, officer commissions, and treatment. Without the blows to the North's battlefield fortunes at the Seven Days Battle and the Second Battle of Bull Run in mid-1862, the piecemeal recruitment of blacks (without federal sanction) in Kansas, Louisiana, and South Carolina might not have continued. These defeats ushered in the bitter reality of a long war against a Confederacy with reenergized morale.[24] In response, the Republican Congress passed the Second Confiscation Act (July 17, 1862) to extend freedom to escaped slaves working within Union lines if their former masters were Confederates. The Confiscation Act remained silent on the pay of blacks in the service of the Army, but the Militia Act of the same date authorized their enlistment for the trifle of $7 per month. These conflicting stipulations eventually created a national controversy over the pay of African-American troops.[25] This story has been well chronicled by historians and cannot be recounted here due to space limitations.

Suffice it to say that the reduced pay rate alongside racial violence during the New York City Draft Riots (July 13–16, 1863), for example, renewed serious questions for Northern blacks about loyalty to country and loyalty to family and community. Unequal pay stung Northern blacks who had absorbed antebellum market values that linked wages to manliness and social status.[26] A soldier in the 55th asked, "Are our parents, wives, children and sisters to suffer, while we, *their natural protectors*, are fighting the battles of the nation?"[27] His question exposed how the pay discrepancy undermined soldiers' manly ability to provide for their dependent wives and children. Acquiescing to unequal military wages threatened to halt the revolutionary consequences of black enlistment. As the Reverend J. P. Campbell explained, "If we go in equal in pay, we hope to come out equal in enfranchisement."[28] Demanding a just wage as one of their rights as soldiers represented a step toward true self-government within the nation.

The War Department promulgated a policy of unequal pay as recruiting came to an end for the two Massachusetts regiments. Ordered to join Union forces occupying the Sea Islands, the 54th Massachusetts arrived first and made its ill-fated assault before the 55th disembarked at Folly Island on August 3.[29] The soldiers responded to news of the pay policy with a boycott in which their officers initially acquiesced. Despite the Articles of War equating refusal of pay with mutiny it continued into the next year. Tensions steadily rose between officers and men.[30]

Meanwhile, Massachusetts's tiny neighbor, Rhode Island, finally began recruiting its first black unit, a heavy artillery company, on July 29, 1863. The governor's initial attempt to raise a regiment in August 1862 under the Confiscation and Militia Acts had prompted the public meeting of Providence's blacks discussed above.[31] Their response had been enthusiastic, but at that time Washington was less sanguine. When the War Department finally sanctioned black enlistment in Rhode Island, it promised to count those recruits toward the state's 1863 enlistment quota. Because that meant fewer white men might face conscription, public opinion encouraged the move. Bolstered by a $300 state enlistment bounty, news of an artillery company drew interest not only from blacks in Rhode Island but surrounding states also. Over several months the steady black response led to the formation of additional companies until the War Department had authorized a complete regiment of almost 1700 men. Despite the fact that blacks were a tiny minority of the state's total population, recruits from the Ohio Valley flocked to Company A along with a handful of former slaves.[32] The recruits who organized the 55th Massachusetts and the first companies of the 14th RICHA "had reason to believe that they were entering a new world of racial equality, or at least equal compensation and treatment."[33] That their hopes were ultimately misplaced does not obviate their clear loyalty to both the cause of Union and the civic advancement of their people. If anything, it marks their later military protests as the efforts of loyal citizens exercising their corporate right to alter or abolish their local government rather than subversives aiming to undermine the national war effort.

African-American military service occurred within a political whirlwind in which African-American soldiers' loyalty to nation was publicly celebrated but defense of their soldier rights was readily squelched. On the one hand, recruits to Company A of the 14th RICHA could parade through Providence to the cheers of its white inhabitants and receive their regimental and national colors from Rhode Island's highest political officials in a public, biracial ceremony.[34] Yet on that same day, November 19, 1863, nine hundred miles to the south emancipated slaves in the 3rd South Carolina Native Volunteers mutinied. Led by Sergeant William Walker, they refused to "'do duty any longer for seven dollars per month.'"[35] Walker's execution on February 29, 1864 after a general court-martial sent shockwaves through Northern black communities. Little wonder that one writer to *The Liberator* grasped that because black soldiers had "no rights which Congress or any other white man is bound to respect," the military's attitude would be simply, "'O if they mutiny, they can be put down with an 'iron hand.'"[36] The protest actions of Northern black soldiers were, in fact, attempts to make the ceremonial trappings of citizenship real through self-government within the ranks.

In this charged atmosphere at the end of December, the First Battalion of the 14th Rhode Island Heavy Artillery departed on January 8, 1864 for the Gulf Coast to garrison Fort Esperanza on Matagorda Island, Texas. The black soldiers had orders to rebuild the large earthen fort after the retreating Confederate garrison placed booby traps and then demolished it.[37] This work quickly turned into the thankless, stultifying, and arduous fatigue and garrison duty performed by Union soldiers elsewhere. The malarial conditions and rising humidity made it worse—no salve to the substandard medical care African-American troops shouldered.[38] Atop it all remained the insult of unequal pay.

The second-class status they had lived as Northern civilians, heightened by unequal pay, made these black soldiers alive to additional threats to the citizenship rights which they believed their Army service should be advancing. The protest actions in the regiments surveyed here divided the men. A majority committed themselves to the boycott campaign and within that group literate soldiers leveraged Northern and African-American print culture to publicize the plight of black soldiers. Most soldiers also believed that alongside the boycott and publicity efforts, loyal service was critical to establishing the moral authority of the soldiers in the eyes of the public and the government. Yet in select moments, a smaller number believed particular violations of their soldier rights required protest actions such as insubordination or mutiny in order to advance the claim to self-government.

The night of the Goliah mutiny, April 19, 1864, marked more than seven months of the pay boycott. The regimental surgeon believed "the non-payment of the men produces in some a marked feeling of insubordination, and exerts on all a depressing influence."[39] This night also came at the end of the inconclusive, three-month Florida Campaign.[40] Transports like the *Sentinel* ferried both Massachusetts regiments back to the Union garrisons in the South Carolina Sea Islands. The soldiers of the 55th had been spared any combat and were temporarily relieved of the enervating "picket, provost, and fatigue duty" at Jacksonville, Florida. It had frayed the nerves of both soldiers and officers. Enjoying a sort of homecoming, they caroused below decks late into the night.[41]

Second Lieutenant Josiah A. Bean, who had only joined the regiment ten days before, ordered Sergeant Sampson Goliah on deck for "talking loud and hollering and using some profane language."[42] Goliah, a twenty-eight-year-old farmer from Kentucky, had served without incident in the 55th Massachusetts since its organization at Readville, Massachusetts in June 1863.[43] As Bean forced Goliah topside, the sergeant objected: "I don't allow any white man to collar me."[44] When Goliah emerged on deck he threatened, "We have been humbugged long enough. You Massachusetts men have been humbugging us long enough. We are going to do as we please after this."[45] Goliah's condemnations echo those of a Northern black comrade's written only days before: "We, by God's help, will settle it for ourselves before this war is over, *and settle it right too, or die in the attempt.*"[46]

The "humbug" Goliah cited encompassed both general and particular violations of their soldier rights. The grievances of unequal pay, dependents' destitution, respectability, and officer commissions loomed large, of course. The denial of black commissions specifically touched on three Northern comrades in Goliah's regiment—John F. Shorter, James M. Trotter, and William H. Dupree—who became second lieutenants on paper between March and May. Barred from assuming their new positions within the regiment they remained de facto noncommissioned officers.[47] In the meantime, new white officers like Bean had begun issuing orders and commanding companies. When some openly boast of having been active participants in the New York riots of last summer, black soldiers like the correspondent "Bay State" naturally asked, "Why is not justice done?"[48] The executions in February 1864 of three comrades also led Corporal Nelson Browning, one of the convicted mutineers, to plead during the mutiny, "We have had enough of our men killed already."[49]

Thus, the open air illuminated only by the moonlight and a few candle lamps contained a highly volatile atmosphere. A veteran Vermonter with a positive reputation in the men's eyes, Captain William Nutt, received Bean's prisoner. Nutt ordered Goliah cuffed and threatened the gag if he continued speaking out.[50] Nutt's mere reputation might have contained the brewing protest. But it was the inexperienced Bean's report to his approaching Colonel Alfred S. Hartwell that shaped what happened next. Hartwell's presence should have alleviated his men's disgust. He had so far proved to be a conscientious commander by recommending men for officer candidacy and acquiescing in the pay boycott.[51] But on that night, Hartwell inexplicably ordered the boat captain, a white civilian, to securely tie Goliah to the rigging for two hours or until he "suffered to [*sic*] much."[52] According to the mutineers' words at the time, and at the subsequent court-martial, the colonel's rash decision inflamed the situation.[53]

Many of his comrades who witnessed the event below decks reacted in "sympathy" to his predicament.[54] Ninety minutes after Goliah's arrest more than a dozen men appeared on deck and ruptured the recent quiet. Two men shouted, "Let's cut him down."[55] He "had been tied there long enough" and they demanded Goliah's release or they would do it themselves. According to Browning, even though they knew freeing Goliah was "wrong," his fetters represented a greater wrong.[56] "There are other ways of punishing a man without having him tied up," they asserted. "It is a shame" and they "would not allow one of their men tied by a citizen."[57]

Browning, a twenty-year-old farmer from St. Louis, encouraged the mutiny (though he did not join) because he "could not stand it to see one of our men tied up." An officer called Browning a "moving spirit," who reminded his comrades gathered below deck, "The man ought not to have been tied up there." He urged them to, "Untie this man and take him down from there."[58] Browning admitted when questioned by Hartwell the next day after coming ashore that he had been "angry" over the treatment of Goliah.[59]

Bean stood between the prisoner and a group of soldiers who steadily advanced and asserted the entire boat supported them.[60] The mutineers overwhelmed Lieutenant Bean and his guard, freed Goliah of the rigging, and broke his handcuffs. Goliah drove Bean to the deck, snatched the .45-caliber Colt revolver from his hands, and cocked it. Almost immediately the scuffle of mutinous and loyal soldiers engulfed them. In the midst of the struggle other soldiers tried to corral members of the crowd, but especially Browning refused to relent.[61] Bean got free as Goliah slipped below.[62]

The mutiny finally came to an end below decks where it had started. Colonel Hartwell, Captain Nutt, and three noncommissioned officers entered the men's quarters where soldiers—both mutinous and loyal—debated one another.[63] Hartwell demanded silence, then Nutt convinced most of the men to quickly return to their bunks. A handful remained including Goliah, one of the loudest disputants, whom Nutt insisted bring himself to order. Although it remains unclear exactly what happened next, the sergeant attempted to strike the captain and Nutt retaliated with the flat of his sword. Goliah urged the soldiers to retaliate, then tackled Nutt when they failed to act. The point of Nutt's sword pierced him in the altercation, which brought several of the remaining soldiers to his aid. In the commotion he slipped away once again. But at this point, with calm mostly restored, guards were able to apprehend him about thirty minutes later. They returned him to the deck and placed new irons on his wrists.[64]

For Northern free blacks, the intervention of a white civilian embodied the racial injustice they knew from civilian life, but more importantly, a violation of their rights as soldiers. What the colonel determined to be a practical matter—relying on the boat captain's expertise in lashing to the rigging—had enormous consequences. More importantly, according to Private Young Gouch, "It would not do for a citizen to tie up one of our soldiers. If one of our own officers had tied him up they never would have said a word."[65] To their minds, the affair had been started by an officer barely removed from civilian life who had not yet earned their trust and respect. The intervention of a civilian outsider in an internal disciplinary matter further transgressed the soldiers' self-government of their volunteer regiment. By taking the oath of allegiance and signing their muster rolls, all the Union's volunteers had freely consented to be bound by the Articles of War and the Army regulations. Nothing within them condoned the colonel's course of action. These soldiers in the 55th Massachusetts mutinied to ensure that the rights they wanted their military service to secure would not be jeopardized.

Goliah and four other soldiers—Privates Nathan Lane, John Lewis, Nelson Browning, and Young Gouch—faced trial as ringleaders. Convened May 7, 1864 at Folly Island, South Carolina, the testimony from these trials is often contradictory and imprecise. The transcripts are full of hearsay testimony mistakenly (perhaps maliciously) admitted into evidence. Although not in law proper for the determination of guilt they, nevertheless, convey the chaotic nature of soldier mutinies. The acceptance of hearsay was one of many flaws in military tribunals of many kinds. Less rigorous standards for admissible evidence was but one aspect of the legal distinctions between civilian and military proceedings. Men knew the risks of dissent. For instance, private John Lewis, previously a waiter from Indianapolis, had spoken out against Goliah's arrest and restraint, but ultimately did not join the mutiny because he believed that the participants would surely suffer execution.[66]

In his closing remarks to the court before it determined guilt and pronounced sentence, the judge advocate quoted from Articles Seven and Nine of the Articles of War, and from Stephen V. Benét's treatise on military justice, which was widely employed as a handbook for officers serving on courts-martial. The articles mandated a maximum penalty of death. Walton reminded the court that the evidence clearly indicated Goliah had been defiant and threatened violence, but asked his fellow officers whether "the acts of the prisoner are of that aggravated [sic] nature called mutiny." He urged the court (only one of whom came from a black regiment) to give weight to Hartwell's and Nutt's testimony of the soldiers' collective grievances regarding their pay, which had created "extraordinary circumstances, which by no means excuse, yet mitigate the offense."[67]

Given that the Articles of War stipulated capital punishment for mutiny or an appropriate sentence determined by the court, perhaps the judge advocate's words worked some small benefit for the defendants. Goliah, Lewis, Browning, and Gouch all received a sentence of confinement at hard labor at Fort Clinch, Florida for the remainder of their enlistments—nearly two years—and the loss of all pay. When their term of confinement concluded, they were to be dishonorably discharged. The department commander approved the sentence without revision.

If there was one short-term victory for the mutineers of April 19, it came through an evolution in their commanding officer's attitude. Hartwell appears to have grown more, not less, sympathetic with his soldiers' predicament. On April 23, he wrote that unequal pay was nothing less than "non-fulfillment of contract" by the government.[68] On May 13, in a concrete act of solidarity with two soldiers who returned late from furlough due to illness, he strongly recommended they be returned to duty without general court-martial.[69] Finally, in the wake of the Goliah mutiny and later acts of insubordination, on June 12, he argued to Governor John A. Andrew that the soldiers' sense of broken "trust"[70] in white authority evidenced in the mutiny had seriously jeopardized the regiment's "proper efficiency and military pride."[71] Hartwell contended "it is difficult to make them endure longer" and wondered how he and his officers could possibly "exercise further military authority."[72]

White officers who testified in the courts-martial viewed the character of black soldiers' service through their own understanding of the soldier rights belonging to citizens in uniform. Colonel Hartwell explained that, "Because the Regiment had not been paid at all—nor offered pay according to terms of enlistment," dissatisfaction had gradually increased to a crisis point. Captain William H. Nutt likewise believed his soldiers' "grumbling" stemmed from their pay diverging from "the *terms* of their enlistment" assured by the state.[73] The Army's unilateral reduction in pay had violated the principles of self-government. The volunteer soldier—black or white—freely offered his loyal service to the nation as member of a corporate body according to specific terms of enlistment.

Only ten days after the Goliah mutiny, another episode of unjust discipline sparked several more mutinies over the men's soldier rights. A camp life of drill and fatigue had, by then, again become routine for the 55th Massachusetts. Second Lieutenant Thomas F. Ellsworth ordered the men of Company I onto the parade ground for afternoon inspection. As his comrades hurried into formation, Private Richard Morrison arrived late and unprepared. Thirty minutes earlier, the orderly sergeant had instructed him to clean a rifle that was not his. The task that usually took a couple of hours remained unfinished.

Like Josiah Bean, Ellsworth was a replacement officer for Company I who arrived in February 1864. Ellsworth went on to be a gallant soldier and a Medal of Honor recipient, but all of that lay ahead. In the spring of 1864, he had been an officer in the company for only a few months. Northern citizen-soldiers—black or white—would have instinctively understood their company and the regiment as more theirs than his. More importantly for blacks, whether Northern freemen or emancipated slaves, Ellsworth's sympathy to their racial cause remained unknown.[74]

A regimental camp's regulation layout structured the place, timing, and nature of officer-soldier interaction. Tents arrayed in company blocks had streets running between to direct the flow of movement and information. The guard house held prisoners awaiting trial or serving short sentences for violating lesser portions of the Army regulations. It represented a site of sanctioned military discipline in the eyes of soldiers as opposed to the capricious punishments meted out by officers in the moment. The open space of the parade ground formed the public square for the regiment to assemble for the reading of orders, inspections, and the recognition of meritorious conduct. But it, too, could be a place of punishment. Drunks would be publicly shamed and insubordinate soldiers might march a seemingly interminable route with full pack or be tied up for the entire regiment to witness. At its most grave, the parade ground could serve as the site of public execution for soldiers convicted of capital crimes in the sight of all officers and men.[75]

In these respects, camps had many functional similarities to America's antebellum cities. Thus, like the urban centers, regimental camps became stages on which citizens (in uniform) defined the boundaries of military self-government. It is no coincidence that Northern black citizen-soldiers performed military protest actions in defense of their right to self-government in the public spaces of their camps. The physical structure of camps made even individual confrontations into public events as bystanders became participants or turned into witnesses for later court-martial proceedings. Because citizenship had such a public dimension in the antebellum era, military dissent also unfolded out-of-doors. It was also done in association with fellow soldiers. Mutinies reveal these mentalities and habits of self-government at work in the Army during wartime.[76]

The April 29th confrontation on the regiment's parade ground unfolded almost identically to the Goliah mutiny. Keen to prove his fitness for command, Ellsworth confronted Private Morrison for violating regulations in this instance about maintaining his government-issued weapon. The private tried to explain he was not at fault; the rifle was not his. Ellsworth balked at the story and ordered that Morrison would stand at attention for two hours with a full pack if the rifle was not cleaned. Rather than speaking out publicly like Goliah, however, Morrison maintained his rectitude by refusing to obey. After company inspection, he walked up the company street to the lieutenant's tent to plead his case again.

Although Morrison insisted later that he remained calm, according to Ellsworth and other witnesses he eventually unleashed a tirade, brought to frustration like Goliah: "The damned old gun is not mine and I won't clean it. . . . I'll have my supper first. Damned if I won't." Ellsworth ordered him to the guardhouse, but Morrison stalked off in the direction of the cookhouse yelling, "I tell you, Lieut., I won't go until I get my supper" and "will swear as much as I damn well please."[77] Ellsworth ordered a detail of two soldiers with a sergeant to arrest him.

Unlike Goliah constrained aboard ship, Morrison used his intervening walk to poise himself and had instead gone to the guardhouse as ordered. By the time Ellsworth and his detail arrived there thirty minutes later, Morrison had requested that the officer of the guard, Captain John Gordon, send for Colonel Hartwell. Under the Articles of War, the Civil War's approximation of today's Uniform Code of Military Justice, a soldier could appeal to his colonel if he believed "himself wronged by his Captain or other officer." The soldier could lodge a formal complaint, which would initiate a regimental court-martial.[78] "I will report you to the Colonel tomorrow, [even] if I have to run the guard," Morrison threatened. When Hartwell did not appear, Ellsworth had the private confined until further orders. The general court-martial convened in May found Morrison guilty of disobedience of orders and disrespect to a superior officer. Less serious than a charge of mutiny, he was sentenced to hard labor at Fort Clinch, Florida for three months and the loss of all pay, but was spared a dishonorable discharge.[79]

While waiting at the guard house, Morrison explained to Captain Gordon that he would heed "no white officer," but obey "only as far as he was mustered."[80] Morrison was a nineteen-year-old waiter from Hamilton, Ohio, and his statement spoke directly to Northern black soldiers' sense of their rights drawn from their participation as citizens in the antebellum political culture of self-government.[81] Morrison was merely echoing the same argument as other Northern black soldiers in the Massachusetts regiments about unequal pay: It violated the promise extended to them at muster-in that they would be granted the same privileges and rights as other soldiers mustered by the state into United States service. And like the Northern black protest tradition generally, it is framed both in terms of race and within the broad political culture of the antebellum North. Furthermore, he laid claim to a legal right of interposition from his colonel specifically his by virtue of his soldier status. Anglo citizen-soldiers during the Civil War did the same, sometimes going so far as appealing to their civil magistrates for relief.[82] Historians who have seen the equal pay crisis only from the perspective of race must also recognize its rootedness in Northern black soldiers' sense of themselves as loyal citizens fully competent in the habits of self-government. Their military protest actions such as mutinies and insubordination during this critical period in turn reflect the pay crisis as a key wartime expression of antebellum Northern political culture.

More conflict over the extent and application of officers' authority over citizen-soldiers erupted two days later between Lieutenant Ellsworth and Private Wallace Baker. The action unfolded on the public space of the parade ground. The Baker incident began like Goliah's and Morrison's over the violation of camp regulations, this time tardiness to inspection without his equipment in proper order. Ellsworth also ordered Baker back to his quarters until called to perform his punishment of a knapsack drill supervised by the orderly sergeant.

If there had been such a thing in the 55th Massachusetts, Baker might have been a candidate for the company's "awkward" squad, a practice used in some regiments to assign additional instruction and drills to men who literally could not stand straight in line, march, or perform the manual of arms properly. One comrade found him not "very rational" and another admitted "he was thought simple in the company." He also had a reputation for talking back after the orders of sergeants "because he thought he ought not to be ruled by another man."[83]

Baker said he would not hurry to comply and, when ordered to his quarters, he took a far different tack from Morrison two days earlier. Baker removed all of his equipment and reappeared in the ranks for inspection. His comrades burst into laughter. His return to inspection with no equipment ridiculed Ellsworth's authority through his own ridiculous response. But his protest of mockery also had rational underpinnings. It occurred publicly on the parade ground. Baker took an unreasonable step to shed light on the unreasonableness of the lieutenant's treatment of the men. It occurred only two days after the disgust recently engendered within I Company by Lieutenant Ellsworth's unreasonable treatment of Morrison. Furthermore, it challenged the legitimacy of a new white officer like Lieutenant Bean, whose arrest of Sampson Goliah less than two weeks earlier had sparked the shipboard mutiny, itself rooted in the broad military protest movement initiated with the pay boycott.

When Ellsworth finally ordered Baker to begin the punishment, the private echoed Goliah and Morrison: "I won't stand to attention for you or any other damned white officer." Ellsworth grabbed Baker by the collar before he retaliated with two blows to the face. A desperate struggle unfolded in which both men traded blows until Captain Gordon intervened. Gordon dispersed the crowd that had gathered. Embarrassed and angry, Ellsworth seized Baker by the throat. Still, the private refused knapsack drill; he preferred confinement at the guard house.

Gordon convinced Ellsworth to agree. No sergeants appeared to take Baker to the guard house, and it fell to the two officers. The sergeants' refusal to escort Baker to the guard house probably manifested their own discontent with the lieutenant. Baker ended his mutiny confined at the guard house and bucked (tied so that he could not move) indefinitely.

What all of these mutinies in the 55th Massachusetts have in common is that Northern black soldiers believed they had certain rights because they were soldiers; these were rights that they could define; these definitions required defense; and that defense could include physical forms of protest. As a black Michigander of the 55th had explained at the year's opening, they had enlisted "for the love of our country, and the love of a free government based upon terms of equality. We . . . were told that we would be accepted by the U.S. Government, on the same terms as her other Regiments." Free government meant nothing to citizens in uniform if they could not have some say in their military lives. But if men in uniform did govern their own affairs, they might blaze a path for the entire race in mainstream society. Fighting in the Army served "not only to make men of ourselves, but of our colored brothers at home." Their civic manhood gained practical expression by exercising the attributes of "free government" enshrined in their soldier rights. Northern blacks like the Michigan citizen-soldier quoted above considered mutiny a legitimate means to secure such principles because "It is the principle . . . that made us men when we enlisted."[84]

The unjustified arrest of Goliah and his illegal restraint by a white civilian ran contrary to these expressions of self-governing citizenship and justified protests to defend that status. The general grievances of the Northern black military protest movement—unequal pay, commissions, and unfair treatment—enmeshed soldiers' specific complaints in the even older tradition of antebellum black activism on behalf of full equality for African Americans. Good evidence for this is the 55th Massachusetts's July 1864 petition drive. Individual companies submitted petitions to President Abraham Lincoln reiterating the soldier movements' well-worn grievances regarding equal pay. In it they contended that their complaints about violations of their soldier rights sprang from the status as loyal citizens of the republic. Enlisted as soldiers of the state of Massachusetts "in all respects as to pay on the footing of similar corps of the Regular Army" their lower rate of pay "was not according to our enlistment" and they were "enlisted under false pretence [sic]." Yet, they had left behind friends and kin "to fight for liberty, justice, and equality." Undeterred by the events described earlier, the petitioners felt emboldened enough to promise a "resort to more stringent measures" if their "demanding our pay from the date of our enlistment & our immediate discharge" was not answered.[85]

Much like the 55th Massachusetts, Company A of the 14th Rhode Island Colored Heavy Artillery served mostly on the war's margins, first on the Texas coast and later in Louisiana, in dreary garrison duty.[86] The movement of the Rhode Islanders from their home state to Matagorda Island on the Texas Gulf Coast had kept it in advance of any paymasters. The men had not seen any pay since their $300 state bounty at muster-in. While they knew quite well that other black soldiers in United States service were receiving $7 a month they had yet to undertake a pay boycott of their own, confident that the state would honor its 1863 call promising them the "same rights and privileges as are given to other soldiers."[87] An unexpected roll call on St. Patrick's Day 1864 led the men of Company A to suspect a conspiracy meant to trick them into publicly accepting lower pay. The sergeants remained silent to frustrate these supposed designs and the privates followed suit.[88]

While sympathetic, Major Joseph J. Comstock believed the "silent roll call" merited a firm response for the sake of the battalion's good order. Between March 23 and April 1, nearly all of the noncommissioned officers and privates involved received guilty verdicts to the misdemeanor charge of conduct prejudicial to good discipline. The privates forfeited any pay and did three months of hard labor on Matagorda Island; the "noncoms" not only lost their pay and rank, but earned hard labor for periods of six months to a year at Fort Jefferson on coral isles of the Dry Tortugas southwest of the Florida Keys.[89]

In the midst of these court-martial proceedings, a mutiny occurred on the afternoon of March 30, 1864. Officer of the day, Second Lieutenant Charles H. Potter, struck two inebriated soldiers with a strap of rawhide and threatened to shoot them if they did not follow him to the guard house. Soldiers stepped into the company streets to observe the commotion. Off-duty soldiers in the company streets looked on as a twenty-one-year-old waiter from New Jersey, Corporal Charles Cooley, rashly dared Potter to make good on his threat.[90]

As their voices rose and roused more soldiers from their bunks, Private William H. Smith overheard the officer boast that on Rhode Island soil he would have shot Cooley for his earlier remarks without hesitation. Cooley countered that he doubted Potter "would have any better right to shoot him in Rhode Island for nothing then [sic] he did here."[91] Potter rose to thrash the private, enraged by his response. Cooley grabbed the lieutenant's sidearm, but Potter fired a derringer into the back of his head and the corporal dropped to the ground. The gunshot brought additional men, like Corporal John Lane, out of their tents to witness Cooley bleeding out from the wound. He vowed, "If we are to be shot by our own officers I am willing to die now."[92] Sergeant William D. Harris questioned why white soldiers did not suffer such injustices. Smith, Lane, Harris, and others encouraged more men to occupy the company streets. Threats against Potter's life soon filled the air.[93]

Lieutenants Charles Chase and Rowland Hazard rushed from their quarters to calm the enraged soldiers who had gathered around. Concerned to prevent any violence, the subalterns worked hard to hustle the men back to their tents. Private William H. Smith told Lieutenant Chase, "We have stood this as long as we are agoing to, we are ready to die, and we will do it here." He and many others refused to leave the streets when ordered. Smith shook his fist at the officer and began to remove his uniform coat. "This ain't agoing to do, this work has gone far enough by God I am ready to die."[94]

News of the mutiny alarmed Gulf Department commanders enough that they marched a nearby regiment to Fort Esperanza to deter any further insubordination.[95] With the mutiny squelched, five privates, two corporals, and one sergeant faced general courts-martial on April 8th. The court found all of these men guilty of mutiny and they received sentences like that handed down to William Smith: five years of hard labor at Fort Jefferson and the loss of all pay. Brigadier General FitzHenry Warren subsequently reduced Smith's confinement to the end of his enlistment contract on August 13, 1866.[96]

Only two days before President Lincoln's assassination, Private Smith addressed to the Secretary of War a "petition to you for my release." By then incarcerated at Fort Jefferson nearly a year, this Ohio soldier profiled above made sure to contextualize his appeal within a framework of loyalty and allegiance. He had "vollunteered my service" as "my feble part to help crush this wicked rebellion" for the "maintainence of the nationality of our country."[97]

Potter's race, of course, distorted his relationship to black soldiers as fellow citizens in uniform. Perhaps more importantly, Company A had been Rhode Island's original heavy artillery unit; organized by specific direction of the War Department prior to authorizing an entire regiment. Although their company had since been brigaded, the soldiers nevertheless retained the integrity of their own organization. Defending these soldier rights in the military had enormous import for their claims to full citizenship in civilian life. In the wake of the ongoing courts-martial and burning with outrage over Cooley's shooting, Smith symbolically rejected his contract with the government and any further obligation to obey when he challenged Lt. Chase.

Smith retold his version of the Cooley shooting as a violation of their soldier rights. In so doing, it was exemplary of the very mentality Northern free blacks hoped military service would stamp out and against which their boycotts, disobedience, and mutinies pointed. "Any man who has been living under a free government" and "serving my country as a soldier" "knows what belongs to manhood."[98] Smith could have cited the twenty-fourth Article of War, which stated that "no officer or soldier shall use any reproachful or provoking speeches or gestures to another."[99] Even more, self-government meant they "cannot but help but say something against such mode of treatment" to "which our men have been subject since we have been in the service." That also included Potter's insulting presumption against the corporate rights of voluntary associations that he could lord his authority over the men despite holding command in an entirely different company.[100] Northern black soldiers refused to accept unjust authority or treatment. Their pay boycott and petitions, along with protest actions such as insubordination and mutiny, were all demands "to be treated in a manner by our officers, who pretend to coinside with us in this struggle, as men."[101]

Military protest actions should not be dismissed as only about issues of fair and equal treatment of soldiers. Black volunteers and their community consciously linked this service with the race's struggle for rights elsewhere, through the artifice of soldier rights made possible by that service to the nation. These soldiers' protests—by Northern and Southern black comrades—became early declarations of the civic personhood of all African Americans. As the scholar of black Civil War veterans, Barbara Gannon, has written, "African Americans never forgot their military service and never forgot that this duty occurred in a war that freed their race and made them citizens."[102]

The military protest actions within Northern black regiments paralleled Northern African Americans' efforts at home to push for emancipation and civil rights during the war. Northern African Americans and wartime escapees founded the National Equal Rights League in October 1864 to amplify the message of the antebellum convention movement through blacks' wartime service that had "fully earned" the suffrage as a "conventional right."[103] In September 1865, the League rested blacks' case for civil and political rights on the "loyalty, patriotism, and devotion displayed by colored soldiers during the conflict."[104] In addition to participating in associational culture, the League's members were stalwarts in the black freedom movement and were well aware of the modes of protest taken up by blacks against violations of their soldier rights. This reopens the relationship between protest and loyalty. Protest and service achieved black freedom and both stances rested on Northern blacks' fidelity to the nation's founding ideals.

William D. Forten, one of the most highly praised and well respected members of the black abolitionist cause, wove together self-government and loyalty when he addressed the League on the second day of its national convention in 1865. His insistence that African Americans across the country "must be a unit," "must rally," and effect "unison of action and intent" to "concentrate our energies and efforts with those of others whom we can influence" evoked the mutual protest efforts of Northern and Southern black soldiers. Only then could "those rights which are ours" through "the sacrifice of thousands of our brothers on our country's altar" be secured.[105] Toward this goal, he encouraged emancipated slaves to pursue self-improvement along the lines Northern blacks had for decades. He cited the "necessity" of "acquiring property," "educating their children and themselves," and "pursuing a course of conduct" that was respectable and would "elevate" them above their current station.[106] Forten coined the stirring, potent motto "Freedom to all, and all enfranchised" to encapsulate the need for a nationwide African-American movement for citizenship. To this end, the national League harnessed associational culture to assist the creation of local bodies in order to "resist the overriding tyranny of a united, powerful, and unprincipled majority." In the manner of an ardent associationalist, Forten declared that a national network of local leagues "embodies our desires, and gives force and pertinence to that resistance to tyranny, which it becomes us to make, as a people resolved to be free . . . and, in a word, makes us upright."[107]

Military protest actions and the actions of black civilians during the war revealed the complicated relationship between race and loyalty. Northern blacks came to the colors out of allegiance to the national government. This sense of loyalty stemmed from their participation in antebellum political culture. It had led them to see the possibilities of full citizenship within the web of associational rights and responsibilities under a federal Union. Nevertheless, loyalty to the country's founding ideals had established a long tradition of protest against inequality and disfranchisement. During the war, it turned them into critics of the national government's policies toward black soldiers. Northern black soldiers reared in this culture fixed on their status as loyal defenders of the republic to claim a particular body of soldier rights. Wartime also drew their recently emancipated comrades into league with them. Allegiance to the nation had bestowed the status of soldier, which carried with it an expectation of self-defined soldier rights. In Northern regiments, both free and freed African Americans risked charges of disloyalty to defend these rights. Thus, the associational logic attached to membership in the Army made possible military protest actions against the Army's policies and the unjust authority of its white officers. Northern black soldiers resolved conflicting loyalties to the national government and to the national creed through military protest.

Northern free blacks in and out of uniform contributed to carrying the Civil War beyond emancipation and abolition and implicated it in the longer American experiment with self-government. White veteran General John Logan, writing after the Civil War, characterized the American volunteer as "a soldier, a citizen, and a legislator."[108] These three identities are especially appropriate for Northern blacks who staged military protest actions made under the rubric of soldier rights and informed by their own antebellum culture of protest. Their actions contributed to tangible gains regarding pay, status, and treatment within the Army, gains that demonstrated African-American citizens in uniform not only serving on equal footing with white soldiers, but governing themselves like white soldiers always had. For this salient reason, military protest actions by Northern blacks should be seen as a crucial link in the chain between antebellum protest culture and the efforts for full citizenship in Reconstruction and beyond.

Notes

1. Charges and specifications, Colonel Alfred S. Hartwell testimony, Second Lieutenant Josiah Bean testimony, Privates David Wilkins and Charles C. Porter testimony in the general court-martial of Sergeant Sampson Goliah, 55th Massachusetts Infantry Regiment (Colored), May 7, 1864, NN2479, Court-Martial Case Files, RG 153 Records of the Judge Advocate, National Archives, Washington, D.C. (hereafter Goliah court-martial).

2. This essay accepts Christian Samito's contention that the legal rights extended to black soldiers in Army courts-martial formed an important basis for citizenship, but places added emphasis on the African-American military protest actions that gave rise to the achievements in the courtroom. See Christian G. Samito, *Becoming American Under Fire: Irish Americans, African Americans, and the Politics of Citizenship during the Civil War Era* (Ithaca, N.Y.: Cornell University Press, 2009) and "The Intersection Between Military Justice and Equal Rights: Mutinies, Courts-Martial, and Black Civil War Soldiers," *Civil War History* 53, no. 2 (June 2007): 170–203. It also rests on Keith P. Wilson, *Campfires of Freedom: The Camp Life of Black Soldiers during the Civil War* (Kent, Ohio: Kent State University Press, 2002), which identified points of cultural interaction among Northern and Southern blacks in folk music and religious practice as well as conflict over racial leadership and responses to discrimination within the military.

3. Edward A. Miller, *The Black Civil War Soldiers of Illinois: The Story of the Twenty-Ninth U. S. Colored Infantry* (Columbia: University of South Carolina Press, 1998); Joseph T. Wilson, *The Black Phalanx: A History of the Negro Soldiers of the United States in the Wars of 1775–1812, 1861–65* (Hartford, Conn.: American Publishing Company, 1890);

4. *War of the Rebellion: A Compilation of the Official Records of the Union and Confederate Armies*, 128 vols. (Washington: Government Printing Office, 1880–1901), III, IV,

1269–70; William Seraile, *New York's Black Regiments during the Civil War* (New York: Routledge, 2001), 2; J. Matthew Gallman, "'In Your Hands That Musket Means Liberty': African American Soldiers and the Battle of Olustee" in *Northerners at War: Reflections on the Civil War Home Front*, ed. Gallman, 234–39 (Kent, Ohio: Kent State University Press, 2010). Even my definition has limitations. Some free blacks had only escaped bondage very recently. Including the slaveholding border states is problematic, of course. In this essay, I have used some testimony from African-American soldiers born in St. Louis, Missouri. Although in a slave state, the antebellum metropolis was also a center of western antislavery sentiment and marked by its use of free labor and significant population of free blacks. See Adam Arenson, *The Great Heart of the Republic: St. Louis and the Cultural Civil War* (Cambridge: Harvard University Press, 2011); Louis S. Gerteis, *Civil War St. Louis* (Lawrence: University Press of Kansas, 2001). In all cases, I have used testimony of men whose military service records identified them as born in a free state or stipulated they were free before April 19, 1861.

5. Regimental Descriptive Books, 55th Massachusetts Infantry (Colored), vol. 1, Book Records of Volunteer Union Organizations, RG 94 Records of the Adjutant General's Office, National Archives, Washington, D.C. (hereafter, Descriptive Books, 55th Massachusetts). The 54th Massachusetts had similar percentages: Edwin S. Redkey, "Brave Black Volunteers: A Profile of the Fifty-fourth Massachusetts Regiment" in *Hope & Glory: Essays on the Legacy of the 54th Massachusetts Regiment*, ed. Martin H. Blatt, Thomas J. Brown, and Donald Yacovone, 21–24 (Amherst: University of Massachusetts Press, 2001). For the 14th RICHA, see the Compiled Military Service Records (CMSR) of the 11th United States Colored Heavy Artillery (USCHA), RG 94 Records of the Adjutant General's Office, National Archives, Washington, D.C. (hereafter, CMSRs, 11th USCHA).

6. Private William H. Smith CMSR. William H. Smith, age 10, Chillicothe, Ross, Ohio, page 49A, image 103, National Archives Microfilm Publication M432, roll 725, *Seventh Census of the United States*, 1850, RG 29 Records of the Bureau of the Census, National Archives, Washington, D.C. Judging by the birthplaces of William and his younger siblings recorded in the census, the family had resided in Ohio since 1844.

7. Fifty-two percent of the 55th Massachusetts's soldiers were farmers or farm laborers (Descriptive Books, 55th Massachusetts). In the 54th, it was 25 percent (Redkey, "Brave Black Volunteers"). In the 14th RICHA, only 17 percent were farmers (CMSRs, 11th USCHA).

8. Eugene D. Genovese, *Roll, Jordan, Roll: The World the Slaves Made* (New York: Random House, 1974), 5–6, 306–7, 597–98, 620–21; Peter Kolchin, *American Slavery, 1619–1877*, rev. ed. (New York: Hill & Wang, 2003), 111–18; Steven Hahn, *A Nation Under Our Feet: Black Political Struggles in the Rural South from Slavery to the Great Migration* (Cambridge: Harvard University Press, 2003), 17–33; John W. Blassingame, *The Slave Community: Plantation Life in the Antebellum South*, rev. ed. (New York: Oxford University Press, 1979), 195–96; Anthony E. Kaye, *Joining Places: Slave Neighborhoods in the Old South* (Chapel Hill: University of North Carolina Press, 2007), 162, 187–88; Stephanie M. H. Camp, *Closer to Freedom: Enslaved Women and Everyday Resistance in the Plantation South* (Chapel Hill: University of North Carolina Press, 2004), 1–4, 7–9. Solomon Northup, a free black from New York, sold into slavery in Louisiana, averred

that even the most ignorant and unschooled in the quarters possessed an "idea of freedom," *Twelve Years a Slave* (Auburn, N.Y.: Derby and Miller, 1853), 259–60.

9. Patrick Rael, "The Market Revolution and Market Values in Antebellum Black Protest Thought," in *African-American Activism before the Civil War: The Freedom Struggle in the Antebellum North*, ed. Patrick Rael, 288 (New York: Routledge, 2008), and again, "There were fewer more ardent apostles of . . . a rational, bourgeois public sphere than free African Americans in the antebellum North," 290. Contributions to the history of Northern black public culture include Benjamin Quarles, *Black Abolitionists* (New York: Oxford University Press, 1969); David W. Blight, *Frederick Douglass' Civil War: Keeping Faith in Jubilee* (Baton Rouge: Louisiana State University Press, 1989); Jane H. Pease and William H. Pease, *They Who Would Be Free: Blacks Search for Freedom, 1830–1861* (Champaign: University of Illinois Press, 1990); Gary B. Nash, *Forging Freedom: The Formation of Philadelphia's Black Community, 1720–1840* (Cambridge: Harvard University Press, 1991); James Oliver Horton, *Free People of Color: Inside the African American Community* (Washington: Smithsonian, 1993); Patrick Rael, *Black Identity and Black Protest in the Antebellum North* (Chapel Hill: University of North Carolina Press, 2002); Shane White, *Stories of Freedom in Black New York* (Cambridge: Harvard University Press, 2002); Leslie M. Alexander, *African or American?: Black Identity and Political Activism in New York City, 1784–1861* (Champaign: University of Illinois Press, 2008); Rita Roberts, *Evangelicalism and the Politics of Reform in Northern Black Thought, 1776–1863* (Baton Rouge: Louisiana State University Press, 2011); Stephen Kantrowitz, *More Than Freedom: Fighting for Black Citizenship in a White Republic, 1829–1889* (New York: Penguin Books, 2012).

10. *Proceedings of the Colored National Convention held in Rochester, July 6th, 7th and 8th, 1853* (Rochester, N.Y.: Offices of Frederick Douglass' Paper, 1853), 8.

11. James Oliver Horton, "Citizenship in Black Boston at Midcentury" in *Hope & Glory: Essays on the Legacy of the 54th Massachusetts Regiment*, ed. Martin H. Blatt, Thomas J. Brown, and Donald Yacovone, 16 (Amherst: University of Massachusetts Press, 2001).

12. Leonard Phenix, later a sergeant in the 14th Rhode Island, addressed the participants, "A Meeting of the Colored Citizens of Providence," *Weekly Anglo-African* (New York), November 9, 1859.

13. J. Matthew Gallman, *The North Fights the Civil War: The Home Front* (Chicago: Ivan R. Dee, 1994), 188; Reid Mitchell, "The Northern Soldier and His Community" in *Toward a Social History of the American Civil War: Exploratory Essays*, ed. Maris A. Vinovskis (New York: Cambridge University Press, 1990), 92. See also, Reid Mitchell, *Civil War Soldiers: Their Expectations and Their Experiences* (New York: Viking, 1988) and *The Vacant Chair: The Northern Soldier Leaves Home* (New York: Oxford University Press, 1993); Lorien Foote, *The Gentlemen and the Roughs: Violence, Honor, and Manhood in the Union Army* (New York: New York University Press, 2010); Steven J. Ramold, *Baring the Iron Hand: Discipline in the Union Army* (De Kalb, Ill.: Northern Illinois University Press, 2009); Earl J. Hess, *Liberty, Virtue, and Progress: Northerners and Their War for the Union*, 2nd ed. (New York: Fordham University Press, 1997); Ricardo A. Herrera, "Self-Governance and the American Citizen as Soldier, 1775–1861," *Journal of Military*

History 65, no. 1 (January 2001): 21–52; Thomas Rodgers, "Billy Yank and G. I. Joe: An Exploratory Essay on the Sociopolitical Dimensions of Soldier Motivation," *Journal of Military History* 69, no. 1 (January 2005): 93–121.

14. William J. Novak, "The American Law of Association: The Legal-Political Construction of Civil Society," *Studies in American Political Development* 15 (Fall 2001), 172, 174–75, 179; William J. Novak, "The Legal Transformation of Citizenship in Nineteenth-Century America" in *The Democratic Experiment: New Directions in American Political History*, ed. Meg Jacobs, William J. Novak, and Julian E. Zelizer, 10–19 (Princeton, N.J.: Princeton University Press, 2012). Once the war began, states felt compelled to explicitly instruct their volunteers that compliance with the military law governing United States forces would be expected. For an example, see "An Act to Provide for the Discipline and Instruction of a Military Force," Chap. 219, approved May 23, 1861, *Private and Special Statutes of the Commonwealth of Massachusetts for the Years 1860, 1861, 1862, 1863, 1864 and 1865* (Boston: Wright & Potter, State Printers, 1869), vol. 11, 235–40.

15. William C. Nell, *Services of Colored Americans in the Wars of 1776 and 1812* (New York: Prentiss and Sawyer, 1851), and *The Colored Patriots of the American Revolution: With Sketches of Several Distinguished Colored Persons: to Which Is Added a Brief Survey of the Condition and Prospects of Colored Americans* (Boston, Mass.: R. F. Wallcutt, 1855).

16. William Seraile, *New York's Black Regiments during the Civil War* (New York: Routledge, 2001), 7; "Colored Militia," *Frederick Douglass' Paper* (Rochester, N.Y.), August 3, 1855; on the hagiography of Crispus Attucks among Northern Blacks see Mitch Kachun, "From Forgotten Founder to Indispensable Icon: Crispus Attucks, Black Citizenship, and Collective Memory, 1770–1865," *Journal of the Early Republic* 29, no. 2 (Summer 2009): 249–86.

17. In May 1861, some New York City blacks rented a hall, which they used for a military drill even after a public meeting rejected petitioning the governor to form a militia company, Seraile, 17–18. Blacks in Providence held two public meetings in August 1862 to plan a regiment rumored to be sponsored by the governor. Their executive committee wanted assurances that the national government would accept black soldiers with the same pay and privileges as whites. If these terms of their service could not be met, they promised to disband the proposed organization, Westwood, 143–44. In September 1863, African Americans in Boston created The First Colored Militia of the Gallant Shaw in honor of the sacrifices of the 54th Massachusetts Infantry at Fort Wagner in South Carolina, "For the Christian Recorder," *Christian Recorder* (Philadelphia), October 3, 1863.

18. Alfred M. Green, October 19, 1861, *Weekly Anglo-African* (New York) collected in Alfred M. Green, ed., *Letters and Discussions on the Formation of Colored Regiments, and the Duty of the Colored People in Regard to the Great Slaveholders' Rebellion, in the United States of America* (Philadelphia: Ringwalt & Brown, 1862), 22.

19. Phillip S. Paludan, *A People's Contest: The Union and Civil War, 1861–1865*, 2nd ed. (Lawrence: University Press of Kansas, 1996), remains essential for dissecting the question of loyalty and dissent in the North. A newer study that considers the interplay of Northern sectional interest with nationalism is Susan Mary Grant, *North Over South: Northern Nationalism and American Identity in the Antebellum Era* (Lawrence: University Press of Kansas, 2000). For a prescient study that demonstrates the multiple, conflicting loyalties of Americans in East Tennessee, see Robert Tracy McKenzie,

Lincolnites and Rebels: A Divided Town in the American Civil War (New York: Oxford University Press, 2006). Paul Quigley, *Shifting Grounds: Nationalism and the American South, 1848–1865* (New York: Oxford University Press, 2011) finds evidence there that loyalty was always refracted through an individual's own group and regional memberships.

20. On defense of the Republic and citizenship, see Herrera, "Self-Governance and the American Citizen as Soldier," 23, 27; Joseph Allan Frank, *With Ballot and Bayonet: The Political Socialization of American Civil War Soldiers* (Athens: University of Georgia Press, 1998), 4. For a contemporary view of the subject, see John A. Logan, *The Volunteer Soldier of America* (Chicago: R. S. Peale, 1887), 1–13.

21. For the constitutional basis of these soldier rights, see Christian G. Fritz, *American Sovereigns: The People and America's Constitutional Tradition Before the Civil War* (New York: Cambridge University Press, 2008), 18, and also 45–46, 169, 182–84. See also, Larry Kramer, *The People Themselves: Popular Constitutionalism and Judicial Review* (New York: Oxford University Press, 2004), 106–7 and Kenneth M. Stampp, "The Concept of Perpetual Union" in Stampp, *The Imperiled Union: Essays on the Background of the Civil War* (New York: Oxford University Press, 1980), 28–29.

22. "Bay State" to *Weekly Anglo-African* (New York), April 30, 1864 in Noah Andre Trudeau, ed., *Voices of the 55th: Letters from the 55th Massachusetts Volunteers, 1861–1865* (Dayton, Ohio: Morningside House, 1996), 85; Sergeant Richard W. White to *Weekly Anglo-African* (New York), June 4, 1864 in Noah Andre Trudeau, ed., *Voices of the 55th: Letters from the 55th Massachusetts Volunteers, 1861–1865* (Dayton, Ohio: Morningside House, 1996), 102; "Picket" to *Weekly Anglo-African* (New York), July 30, 1864 in Noah Andre Trudeau, ed., *Voices of the 55th: Letters from the 55th Massachusetts Volunteers, 1861–1865* (Dayton, Ohio: Morningside House, 1996), 112; Resolutions of the 55th Massachusetts, October 10, 1864 in Sergeant Gabriel P. Iverson, 55th Massachusetts Infantry to *The Christian Recorder* (Philadelphia), November 12, 1864 in Edwin S. Redkey, ed., *A Grand Army of Black Men: Letters from African-American Soldiers in the Union Army 1861–1865* (New York: Cambridge University Press, 1992), 248.

23. Dudley Taylor Cornish, *The Sable Arm: Negro Troops in the Union Army, 1861–1865* (1956; New York: Norton, 1966); James M. McPherson, *The Struggle for Equality: Abolitionists and the Negro in the Civil War and Reconstruction* (Princeton, N.J.: Princeton University Press, 1964); Ira Berlin, Joseph P. Reidy, and Leslie S. Rowland, eds., *The Black Military Experience: Freedom: A Documentary History of Emancipation, 1861–1867*, Series II (New York: Cambridge University Press, 1983); Joseph T. Glatthaar, *Forged in Battle: The Civil War Alliance of Black Soldiers and White Officers* (New York: Free Press, 1990); Noah Andre Trudeau, *Like Men of War: Black Troops in the Civil War, 1862–1865* (Boston: Little, Brown and Company, 1998); Martin H. Blatt, Thomas J. Brown, and Donald Yacovone, eds., *Hope & Glory: Essays on the Legacy of the 54th Massachusetts Regiment* (Amherst: University of Massachusetts Press, 2001); Chandra Manning, *What This Cruel War Was Over: Soldiers, Slavery, and the Civil War* (New York: Knopf, 2007). The quote comes from Joseph P. Reidy, "The African American Struggle for Citizenship Rights in the Northern United States during the Civil War" in *Civil War Citizens: Race, Ethnicity, and Identity in America's Bloodiest Conflict*, Susannah J. Ural, ed. (New York: New York University Press, 2010), 231.

24. Stephen V. Ash, *When the Yankees Came: Conflict and Chaos in the Occupied South, 1861–1865* (Chapel Hill: University of North Carolina Press, 1995), 39–40.

25. Gallagher, 89–90; Joseph T. Glatthaar, *Forged in Battle: The Civil War Alliance of Black Soldiers and White Officers* (Baton Rouge: Louisiana State University Press, 1990), 169; Keith P. Wilson, *Campfires of Freedom: The Camp Life of Black Soldiers During the Civil War* (Kent, Ohio: Kent State University Press, 2002), 44. The monthly rate was $10 but $3 worth was paid in clothing.

26. Gordon S. Wood, "The Enemy Is Us: Democratic Capitalism in the Early Republic" in Paul A. Gilje, ed., *Wages of Independence: Capitalism in the Early American Republic* (Madison, Wisc.: Madison House, 1997), 143; Eric Foner, *Free Soil, Free Labor, Free Men: The Ideology of the Republican Party before the Civil War* (New York: Oxford University Press, 1972), 11–39; John Lauritz Larson, *The Market Revolution in America: Liberty, Ambition and the Eclipse of the Common Good* (New York: Cambridge University Press, 2010), 121–22; Rael, "The Market Revolution and Market Values."

27. "Bay State," 55th Massachusetts, Palataka, Florida, April 10, 1864, *Weekly Anglo-African* (New York) in Trudeau, ed., 86. Internal evidence in the letter marks him as a Northern black. Emphasis added. See also the former Boston cobbler, Samuel A. Valentine, 54th Massachusetts Infantry, Morris Island, South Carolina, *Christian Recorder* (Philadelphia), August 27, 1864 in Redkey, 66; and "Bought and Sold," a Pennsylvania draftee, 6th United States Colored Infantry, Yorktown, Virginia, February 8, 1864 in the February 20, 1864 *Christian Recorder* (Philadelphia) in Redkey, 237.

28. Campbell explained to a meeting of black men that equal pay should be rendered because black and white men both had equal responsibilities to their dependent wives and children. It took "as much money" to "clothe and feed the black man's wife" and "go to market for the black man's little boys and girls" as it did for white men. Address delivered at the Methodist Episcopal Sharp Street Church, Baltimore, Maryland, February 29, 1864, collected in Philip S. Foner and Robert James Branham, eds., *Lift Every Voice: African American Oratory, 1787–1900* (Tuscaloosa: University of Alabama Press, 1998), 428.

29. William Schouler, *A History of Massachusetts in the Civil War* (Boston: E. P. Dutton, 1868), 407, 410, 481. The 55th Massachusetts departed Boston on July 21, 1863.

30. Ira Berlin, Joseph P. Reidy, and Leslie S. Rowland, eds., *The Black Military Experience: Freedom: A Documentary History of Emancipation, 1861–1867*, Series II (New York: Cambridge University Press, 1983) (hereafter cited as Berlin, et al., *Freedom*), 362–65; Keith P. Wilson, *Campfires of Freedom: The Camp Life of Black Soldiers During the Civil War* (Kent, Ohio: Kent State University Press, 2002), 45; Susannah Ural, Introduction to *Civil War Citizens: Race, Ethnicity, and Identity in America's Bloodiest Conflict* (New York: New York University Press, 2010), 7.

31. "The Colored Regiment," *The Liberator* (Boston), August 22, 1862.

32. Howard C. Westwood, "Company A of Rhode Island's Black Regiment: Its Enlisting, Its 'Mutiny,' Its Pay, Its Service" in Westwood, *Black Troops, White Commanders, and Freedmen during the Civil War* (Carbondale, Ill.: Southern Illinois University Press, 1992), 145–46. The First Battalion, under the command of Major Joseph J. Comstock, comprised Company A, led by Captain Thomas W. Fry, and three other companies. The

invitation for Rhode Island (and Connecticut) to raise African-American regiments came the same month as Massachusetts's. Smith, "Let Us All Be Grateful" in *Black Soldiers in Blue*, ed. Smith, 24.

33. Gallman, "Battle of Olustee" in Gallman, *Northerners at War*, 239.

34. Richard M. Bayles, *History Of Providence County, Rhode Island* (Providence, R.I.: W. W. Preston & Co, 1891), 246. At a final ceremony on December 9, an association of women presented a hand-sewn flag to the battalion before Providence's black leaders addressed the soldiers.

35. The South Carolinians had actually received full pay for a few months early in 1863. Berlin, et al., *Freedom*, Documents 158A–E. The standard treatment of the Walker mutiny is Howard C. Westwood, "The Cause and Consequence of a Union Black Soldier's Mutiny and Execution" in Westwood, *Black Troops*, 125–41. Wilson, *Campfires of Freedom*, 47, 75, and Samito, *Becoming American*, 96–98 also discuss the Walker mutiny.

36. Jesse Stedman, "Letter to Hon. J. H. Lane," *The Liberator*, March 11, 1864. Sergeant George E. Stephens of the 54th Massachusetts, sensed the "utter hopelessness of the condition of slavery" even though he was "never a slave." Stephens feared that it was "the fixed determination of the people of the United States to maintain a line of demarkation between the white and black race, and to deny to the black equal rights and justice" (George E. Stephens to Robert Hamilton, March 6, 1864, in Donald Yacovone, ed., *A Voice of Thunder: The Civil War Letters of George E. Stephens* [Urbana: University of Illinois Press, 1997], 299).

37. William H. Chenery, *The Fourteenth Regiment Rhode Island Heavy Artillery (Colored) in the War to Preserve the Union, 1861–1865* (Providence, R.I.: Snow & Farnham, 1898), 20, 22; Westwood, 147–48.

38. On the greater amount of fatigue duty assigned to African-American soldiers and its effects, see Wilson, *Campfires of Freedom*, 39–40, 43–44. On black medical care, see Margaret Humphreys, *Intensely Human: The Health of the Black Soldier in the American Civil War* (Baltimore: Johns Hopkins University Press, 2008); Glatthaar, *Forged in Battle*, 187–95.

39. Noah Andre Trudeau, ed., *Voices of the 55th: Letters from the 55th Massachusetts Volunteers, 1861–1865* (Dayton, Ohio: Morningside, 1996), 18–21, surgeon quoted on 21.

40. The campaign had reached its climax with a bloody defeat at the Battle of Olustee, including the 54th Massachusetts, which returned to the Sea Islands two days before the 55th Massachusetts. See Noah Andre Trudeau, *Like Men of War: Black Troops in the Civil War, 1862–1865* (Boston: Little, Brown and Company, 1998), 137–51, 154; Gallman, "Battle of Olustee," 247–51.

41. Private David Wilkins and Private Charles C. Porter testimony, Goliah court-martial.

42. Second Lieutenant Josiah A. Bean testimony, charges and specifications, Goliah court-martial.

43. Sampson Goliah, 55th Massachusetts Infantry Regiment (Colored), Union Compiled Military Service Records, RG 94 Records of the Adjutant General's Office, 1762–1984, National Archives, Washington, D.C. (hereafter Goliah CMSR); Private Charles C. Porter testified that Goliah had "performed his duties faithfully," Goliah court-martial.

44. Goliah's words as related in the testimony of Privates Wilkins and Porter (Goliah court-martial). In his testimony, Bean claimed Goliah said "he would not go there for any damned white officer" (Bean testimony, Goliah court-martial).

45. Testimony of Captain William H. Nutt, Goliah court-martial.

46. "Bay State," 55th Massachusetts, Palataka, Florida, April 10, 1864, *Weekly Anglo-African* (New York) in Trudeau, ed., 87. Internal evidence in the letter marks him as a Northern black. Emphasis original.

47. Shorter was commissioned March 24, 1864, Trotter April 10, and Dupree May 30 (Trudeau, 62); Berlin, *Freedom*, 308, 337; Hartwell to Massachusetts Governor John A. Andrew, May 25, 1864, and Lieutenant Charles B. Fox's report to Hartwell, July 29, 1864, both in RG 94 Records of the Adjutant General, Book Records of Volunteer Union Organizations, 55th United States Colored Troops, Massachusetts Infantry, Regimental Letter and Endorsement Book, Vol. 3 of 5, National Archives, Washington, D. C. Trotter felt "my present *double* position is not pleasant," James M. Trotter to Francis Jackson Garrison, August 2, 1864, Folly Island, South Carolina in Trudeau, 143. The three black officers were not finally mustered in and allowed to take their place as officers in the regiment until July 1, 1865 (Trudeau, 181).

48. Josiah A. Bean, 55th Massachusetts Infantry Regiment (Colored), Union Compiled Military Service Records, RG 94 Records of the Adjutant General's Office, 1762–1984, National Archives, Washington, D.C.; Goliah CMSR; quotes come from "Picket," 55th Massachusetts, June 30, 1864, *Weekly Anglo-African* (New York) in Trudeau, ed., 113.

49. Testimony of Captain William D. Crane, Browning court-martial. Crane recalled a respectful, empathetic exchange with Browning. Crane believed Browning referred to a soldier shot by an officer at Readville, Massachusetts in 1863 and two others hanged after trial in February 1864 at Jacksonville, Florida for "heinous" crimes, in Crane's words. "Heinous" signaled in Victorian language crimes such as "murders, rapes, arson," for example as used in, "Juvenile Crime in New York," *New York Herald*, February 1, 1858. According to Trudeau, ed., *Voices of the 55th*, 19, in fact, three men were hanged at Jacksonville for raping a white woman. The regimental history prepared by its lieutenant colonel identifies Private Benjamin Hayes as shot at Readville for resisting a Lieutenant Kingston's orders. (Charles Barnard Fox, *Record of the Service of the Fifty-fifth Regiment of Massachusetts Volunteer Infantry* [Cambridge, Mass.: Press of J. Wilson and Son, 1868], 5.)

50. Nutt testimony, Goliah court-martial. Private John Posey of Indiana counted Nutt as "a good father to us" (December 2, 1863, to Mathias Embry, in Trudeau, ed., *Voices of the 55th*, 53). Nutt later acquitted himself to the satisfaction of the soldiers during the November 30, 1864 Battle of Honey Hill, South Carolina, braving numerous, costly assaults until his horse was shot out from under him (Sergeant William Scott to Burt G. Wilder, November 21, 1914 in Trudeau, ed., *Voices of the 55th*, 169). By 1865, Sergeant James Trotter classified Major Nutt as "very popular with the Regt and with everybody whose regard is worth anything" (Sergeant James M. Trotter to Edward W. Kinsley, July 1, 1865 in Trudeau, ed., *Voices of the 55th*, 184).

51. Some soldiers felt genuine affection, like Sergeant Trotter, who wrote, "Everybody is jubilant because of his arrival" from furlough for wounds. "I tell you, sir, that we

believe in Col. A. S. Hartwell! He is so true and such a perfect soldier" (James M. Trotter to Edward W. Kinsley, January 29, 1865 in Trudeau, *Voices of the 55th*, 177–78). See also, "Mon" to *Weekly Anglo African*, July 24, 1864, in Trudeau, 127; and anonymous to Edward W. Kinsley, June 2, 1864 in Trudeau, *Voices of the 55th*, 107.

52. Testimony of Colonel Alfred S. Hartwell, Bean testimony, Goliah court-martial.

53. Lorien Foote concluded that even in Anglo regiments "the frustrated officers of the Union Army, faced with continual resistance to authority and constant back talk from soldiers, often resorted to force immediately when a soldier was slow to obey orders" (*The Gentlemen and the Roughs: Violence, Honor, and Manhood in the Union Army* [New York: New York University Press, 2010], 156). Steven J. Ramold, *Baring the Iron Hand: Discipline in the Union Army* (De Kalb, Ill.: Northern Illinois University Press, 2009) argues that white soldiers "particularly targeted punishments they deemed too harsh or that lasted too long," 205. On white soldiers cutting down comrades tied up for punishment, see Ramold, 363.

54. Charges and specifications, Bean testimony, and Privates David Wilkins and Charles C. Porter testimony, Goliah court-martial

55. Charges and specifications, Bean testimony, Goliah court-martial.

56. Charges and specifications, testimony of Private Peter Adams in the general court-martial of Private Nelson Browning, NN2479, Court-Martial Case Files, RG 153 Records of the Judge Advocate, National Archives, Washington, D.C. (hereafter Browning court-martial).

57. Charges and specifications, Adams testimony, Browning court-martial. Foote, *The Gentlemen and the Roughs*, 164–65, rightly concludes that when white officers failed to appreciate the servile overtones of certain disciplinary measures against black soldiers, simple disobedience could escalate into mutiny. Except here the officer failed to appreciate how his discipline affronted blacks' convictions about their soldier rights as Northern freemen.

58. Private Nelson Browning, 55th Massachusetts Infantry Regiment (Colored), Union Compiled Military Service Records, RG 94 Records of the Adjutant General's Office, 1762–1984, National Archives, Washington, D.C.; testimony of Captain William D. Crane, Browning court-martial; Charges and specifications, testimony of John Lewis, Browning court-martial.

59. Hartwell testimony, Browning court-martial.

60. Charges and specifications, Bean testimony, Goliah court-martial.

61. Hartwell testimony, Crane testimony, Adams testimony, Browning court-martial.

62. Bean testimony, Goliah court-martial. The lieutenant thought that Goliah had begun to untie himself with his teeth, but it is clear from other testimony that he was freed with the help of his comrades. Bean's account of this confrontation with Goliah and his accusation of the cocking of the pistol—a threat of deadly force—used to convict Goliah remained unquestioned.

63. Bean testimony, Goliah court-martial. Hartwell relied on the noncommissioned officers not only from a sense of procedure, but also perhaps from an acknowledgement that having fellow African Americans summon him would make Goliah more compliant and hopefully diffuse the situation generally.

64. Nutt, Hartwell testimony, Goliah court-martial. Goliah claimed he told Nutt not to hit him because he was handcuffed and defenseless, but this is hard to know because elsewhere the officers said his handcuffs had been broken off when he escaped back below decks. And it seems from Bean's testimony they might have been removed when Goliah was tied (Goliah cross-examination of Hartwell, Goliah court-martial). In his final statement, Goliah insisted that he had raised his arms while in handcuffs to protect himself from Nutt, who drew his sword unprovoked (Goliah statement, Goliah court-martial).

65. Statement attributed to Young Gouch by Private Samuel Phillips in the general court-martial of Private Young Gouch, NN2479, Court-Martial Case Files, RG 153 Records of the Judge Advocate, National Archives, Washington, D.C. (hereafter Gouch court-martial).

66. John Lewis, 55th Massachusetts Infantry Regiment (Colored), Union Compiled Military Service Records, RG 94 Records of the Adjutant General's Office, 1762–1984, National Archives, Washington, D.C.; statement of John Lewis, testimony of Private Alfred Perry in the general court-martial of Private John Lewis, NN2479, Court-Martial Case Files, RG 153 Records of the Judge Advocate, National Archives, Washington, D.C. (hereafter Lewis court-martial).

67. Statement by the judge advocate, verdict and sentence, Goliah court-martial; verdict and sentence, Lewis court-martial; verdict and sentence, Browning court-martial; verdict and sentence, Gouch court-martial.

68. Colonel Alfred S. Hartwell to Lieutenant Colonel E. W. Smith, Assistant Adjutant General, Department of the South, April 23, 1864, RG 94 Records of the Adjutant General's Office, Book Records of Volunteer Union Organizations, 55th United States Colored Troops, Massachusetts Infantry, Regimental Letter and Endorsement Book, Vol. 3 of 5, National Archives, Washington, D.C (hereafter 55th Massachusetts Letter Book); Wilson, *Campfires of Freedom*, 53–58; Donald Yacovone, "The Pay Crisis and the 'Lincoln Despotism,'" in Martin H. Blatt, Thomas J. Brown, and Donald Yacovone, eds., *Hope and Glory: Essays on the Legacy of the Fifty-Fourth Massachusetts Regiment* (Amherst: University of Massachusetts Press, 2001), 45. Yacovone elsewhere in this essay gives the impression that Hartwell was an unsympathetic commander, a martinet, but that seems at odds with the soldier letters in Trudeau, the treatment of him by the historians Wilson and Samito, and his official correspondence in the records at the National Archives. Trudeau assesses him as "the best officer to lead the 55th," 244.

69. Colonel Alfred S. Hartwell to Lieutenant W. R. Dean, Acting Assistant Adjutant General, Department of the South, May 13, 1864, 55th Massachusetts Letter Book.

70. Colonel Alfred S. Hartwell to Massachusetts Governor John A. Andrew, June 12, 1864, 55th Massachusetts Letter Book.

71. Colonel Alfred S. Hartwell to Lieutenant Colonel E. W. Smith, Assistant Adjutant General, Department of the South, April 23, 1864, 55th Massachusetts Letter Book.

72. Colonel Alfred S. Hartwell to Massachusetts Governor John A. Andrew, June 12, 1864, 55th Massachusetts Letter Book.

73. Hartwell made these remarks in response to a question by the judge advocate, Captain James M. Walton of the 54th Massachusetts, as to whether there was any

"general dissatisfaction" in the regiment at the time, Hartwell testimony, Goliah court-martial; Nutt testimony, emphasis original, Goliah court-martial.

74. Trudeau, *Voices*, 9, 163n; Second Lieutenant Leonard Alden died of chronic diarrhea on October 5, 1863 and had been the first officer commissioned to the 55th Massachusetts, Second Lieutenant Leonard Alden, 55th Massachusetts Infantry Regiment (Colored), Union Compiled Military Service Records, RG 94 Records of the Adjutant General's Office, 1762–1984, National Archives, Washington, D.C. In October 1863, Governor Andrew had appointed the 23-year-old Ellsworth, previously a corporal in the 2nd Massachusetts, to the 55th. At the November 20, 1864 Battle of Honey Hill, Ellsworth risked his own life to drag the grievously wounded Colonel Hartwell to safety (Second Lieutenant Thomas F. Ellsworth, 55th Massachusetts Infantry Regiment [Colored], Union Compiled Military Service Records, RG 94 Records of the Adjutant General's Office, 1762–1984, National Archives, Washington, D.C.).

75. United States War Department, *Revised United States Army Regulations of 1861 with an Appendix Containing the Changes and Laws Affecting Army Regulations and Articles of War to 25 June 25 1863* (Washington: U.S. Government Printing Office, 1863), Thirty-Fifth Article of War; Wilson, *Campfires of Freedom*, 7, 10, 13–14; Ramold, *Baring the Iron Hand*, 365–68.

76. Mary P. Ryan, *Civic Wars: Democracy and Public Life in the American City during the Nineteenth Century* (Berkley: University of California Press, 1997), 31, 40; Leslie M. Alexander, *African or American?: Black Identity and Political Activism in New York City, 1784–1861* (Champaign: University of Illinois Press, 2008), 140.

77. Charges and specifications, Ellsworth testimony, and Morrison statement in the general court-martial of Private Richard Morrison, 55th Massachusetts Infantry Regiment (Colored), May 24, 1864, NN2479, Court-Martial Case Files, RG 153 Records of the Judge Advocate, National Archives, Washington, D.C. (hereafter Morrison court-martial). For a similar episode among whites, see Foote's discussion of the case of Private James Weir in the 5th New York, counted as "one of thousands" of similar episodes in the wartime Army, 154.

78. Article Thirty-Five, *Revised United States Army Regulations*, 481.

79. Charges and specifications, Ellsworth testimony, and Morrison statement, Morrison court-martial.

80. Gordon testimony, Morrison court-martial.

81. Private Richard Morrison, 55th Massachusetts Infantry Regiment (Colored), Union Compiled Military Service Records, RG 94 Records of the Adjutant General's Office, 1762–1984, National Archives, Washington, D.C.

82. White soldiers in the 133rd Pennsylvania requested their colonel, and ultimately the governor, to remove an incompetent lieutenant in their company (to whom they first served a petition) in favor of a man from the ranks with prior military experience (petition of August 22 and letters of August 23 and 26, 1862, 133rd Pennsylvania, Civil War Muster Rolls and Related Records, 14–4035 carton 81, RG 19 Records of the Department of Military and Veterans Affairs, Pennsylvania States Archives, Harrisburg).

83. Testimony of Privates Morris Carnell and Henry Call, respectively, in the general court-martial of Private Wallace Baker 55th Massachusetts Infantry Regiment (Colored),

May 17, 1864, LL2112, Court-Martial Case Files, RG 153 Records of the Judge Advocate, National Archives, Washington, D.C. (hereafter Baker court-martial).

84. "Wolverine," "A Letter from Our Soldiers," *The Christian Recorder* (Philadelphia), January 2, 1864.

85. "We, the members of Co. D of the 55th Massachusetts Vol." to the President of the United States, July 16, 1864, Folly Island, South Carolina in Trudeau, ed., 116–18. Seventy-four names are attached to this petition, including Nathan Lane, acquitted for his role in the mutiny.

86. Westwood, 160.

87. Westwood, 149.

88. Westwood, 149–51. A second call was announced after Major Comstock assured the men that it had nothing to do with the amount of their pay. All responded immediately. Westwood dismisses the notion that the mutiny centered on discontent with unequal pay. Westwood sees these incidents as illustrative of white racial attitudes toward African Americans that condoned harsh, peremptory treatment against "an alien breed." Yet Westwood's analysis fails to acknowledge the participants' concepts of soldier rights drawn from their participation in Northern political culture.

89. Westwood, 151–52, 154. For a contemporary description of Fort Jefferson, see "The Dry Tortugas," *Vincennes Weekly Western Sun* (Vincennes, Indiana), August 5, 1865.

90. Westwood, 152–53, Charles Cooley CMSR.

91. Smith to Stanton, appended to Smith court-martial, LL1891

92. Charges in general court-martial of William H. Smith, Lieutenants Charles Chase and Rowland Hazard testimony in Smith court-martial, April 14, 1864, LL1891, Court-Martial Case Files, RG 153 Records of the Judge Advocate, National Archives, Washington, D.C. (hereafter Smith court-martial); Chase and Hazard testimony in general court-martial of Private Sam A. D. Douglass, April 15, 1864, LL1891, Court-Martial Case Files, RG 153 Records of the Judge Advocate, National Archives, Washington, D.C. (hereafter Douglass court-martial). One witness during the subsequent trials of the men charged with mutiny claimed Cooley was shot in the back of the head (Westwood, 153, 158). Before war's end, Potter amassed quite a record of drunk and disorderly conduct himself (Second Lieutenant Charles H. Potter, 11th United States Colored Heavy Artillery, Union Compiled Military Service Records, RG 94 Records of the Adjutant General's Office, 1762–1984, National Archives, Washington, D.C.).

93. Sergeant William D. Harris, testimony in his general court-martial, 14th Rhode Island Colored Heavy Artillery, April 20, 1864, NN1688, Court-Martial Case Files, RG 153 Records of the Judge Advocate, National Archives, Washington, D.C. (hereafter Harris court-martial); Corporal John Lane, testimony in his general court-martial, 14th Rhode Island Colored Heavy Artillery, April 8, 1864, LL1830, Court-Martial Case Files, RG 153 Records of the Judge Advocate, National Archives, Washington, D.C. (hereafter Lane court-martial); Westwood, 155–56.

94. Charges, Lieutenants Charles Chase and Rowland Hazard testimony, in Smith court-martial.

95. Charges, Chase testimony, and Hazard testimony, Smith court-martial; Chase and Hazard testimony, Douglass court-martial. One witness during the subsequent trials of

the men charged with mutiny claimed Cooley was shot in the back of the head (Westwood, 153, 158).

96. Verdict and sentence, Smith court-martial; Brigadier General FitzHenry Warren review, April 22, 1864, appended to Smith court-martial; William H. Smith, 11th USCHA, Union Compiled Military Service Records, RG 94 Records of the Adjutant General's Office, 1762–1984, National Archives, Washington, D.C. According to Westwood, 156, the sergeant and one private had their prison sentences reduced to three months of hard labor on Matagorda Island.

97. Smith to Stanton, April 12, 1865, appended to Smith court-martial.

98. Smith to Stanton, April 12, 1865, appended to Smith court-martial.

99. Twenty-Fourth Article of War, United States War Department, *Revised United States Army Regulations of 1861 with an Appendix Containing the Changes and Laws Affecting Army Regulations and Articles of War to June 25, 1863* (Washington, D.C.: U.S. Government Printing Office, 1863), 489.

100. Second Lieutenant Charles H. Potter CMSR.

101. Smith to Stanton, April 12, 1865, appended to Smith court-martial.

102. Barbara Gannon, *The Won Cause: Black and White Comradeship in the Grand Army of the Republic* (Chapel Hill: University of North Carolina Press, 2011), 63, and further, 155, 162. Gannon's work sees the GAR as a biracial organization that preserved a Northern memory of the war linking Union and emancipation as a single "won cause." Contrast this with the earlier work of Stuart McConnell, *Glorious Contentment: The Grand Army of the Republic, 1865–1900* (Chapel Hill: University of North Carolina Press, 1992), which presented the veterans organization as a thoroughly white association, which mirrored the racial compromises of the postwar era.

103. Joseph P. Reidy, "The African American Struggle for Citizenship Rights in the Northern United States during the Civil War" in *Civil War Citizens: Race, Ethnicity, and Identity in America's Bloodiest Conflict*, ed. Susannah J. Ural (New York: New York University Press, 2010), 228; Ball, 170–71, 173.

104. Proclamation of the National Equal Rights League, 1865 in *Proceedings of the Black National and State Conventions, 1865–1900*, vol. 1, ed. Philip S. Foner and George E. Walker (Philadelphia: Temple University Press, 1986), 56.

105. Proclamation of the National Equal Rights League, 1865 in *Proceedings*, Foner and Walker, eds., 60–61.

106. Proclamation of the National Equal Rights League, 1865 in *Proceedings*, Foner and Walker, eds., 56.

107. Proclamation of the National Equal Rights League, 1865 in *Proceedings*, Foner and Walker, eds., 60–61.

108. John A. Logan, *The Volunteer Soldier of America* (Chicago: R. S. Peale & Company, 1887), v. Logan is an example of the celebratory veteran literature that appeared after 1880. Gerald Linderman (*Embattled Courage: The Experience of Combat in the American Civil War* [New York: Free Press, 1989]) calls this period until about 1910 a "revival," 275, that followed a "hibernation," 266, during most of Reconstruction. The period of revival saw the largest wave of veteran literature published, including battle accounts, memoirs, and regimental histories.

Contributors

Gary W. Gallagher is the John L. Nau III Professor in the History of the American Civil War at the University of Virginia in Charlottesville, Virginia. He is the author of numerous books, including *The Confederate War* (1997), *Lee and His Army in Confederate History* (2001), and *The Union War* (2011).

Judith Giesberg is Professor and Director of Graduate Studies in the Department of History at Villanova University in Villanova, Pennsylvania. She is the author of the recent title *Sex and the Civil War: Soldiers, Pornography, and the Making of American Morality* (2017). She is also the editor of *The Journal of the Civil War Era*.

Ryan W. Keating is Associate Professor of History at California State University, San Bernardino. He is the author of *Shades of Green: Irish Regiments, American Soldiers, and Local Communities in the Civil War Era* (2017) and *The Greatest Trials I Ever Had: The Civil War Letters of Margaret and Thomas Cahill* (2017).

Melinda Lawson is Senior Lecturer and Director of Public History at Union College in Schenectady, New York. She is the author of *Patriot Fires: Forging a New American Nationalism in the Civil War North* (2002.) She has published chapters in *An Uncommon Time: The Civil War and the Northern Homefront* (2002) and *Contested Democracy: Freedom, Race, and Power in American History* (2007), and articles in *Civil War History* and *The Journal of the Civil War Era*.

Julie A. Mujic is Adjunct Professor at Capital University in Columbus, Ohio. She is also a freelance indexer for scholarly monographs and serves on the Board of Trustees for the Columbus Historical Society. Her first book, *Why They Stayed: The Mind of Northern Men in the Civil War Midwest*, is forthcoming from Fordham University Press.

Timothy J. Orr is Associate Professor of History at Old Dominion University in Norfolk, Virginia. He is the author of several essays on politics in the Union army, editor of *"Last to Leave the Field": The Life and Letters of First Sergeant Ambrose Henry Hayward* (2011), and co-author of *Never Call Me a Hero: A Legendary American Dive-Bomber Pilot Remembers the Battle of Midway* (2017). For eight years, he worked as a seasonal ranger at Gettysburg National Military Park, and in 2013, he appeared on TLC's genealogy show, *Who Do You Think You Are?*

Thaddeus M. Romansky completed his doctorate in History in 2015 at Texas A&M University. He is currently the director of a Catholic radio network in College Station, Texas and has taught courses on U.S. History and African American History at Texas A&M and Sam Houston State University in Huntsville, Texas.

Robert M. Sandow is Professor of History at Lock Haven University in Lock Haven, Pennsylvania. He is the author of *Deserter Country: Civil War Opposition in the Pennsylvania Appalachians* (2009) and chapters in *Reconstructing Appalachia: The Civil War's Aftermath* (2010), *This Distracted and Anarchical People: New Answers for Old Questions about the Civil War–Era North* (2013), and *A Companion to the U.S. Civil War* (2014).

Sean A. Scott is Assistant Professor of History at the Indiana Academy for Science, Mathematics, and Humanities in Muncie, Indiana. He is the author of *A Visitation of God: Northern Civilians Interpret the Civil War* (2011) and a chapter in *Children and Youth During the Civil War Era* (2012).

Matthew Warshauer is Professor of History at Central Connecticut State University in New Britain, Connecticut. He was formerly editor of the scholarly journal *Connecticut History*. He is the author of *Andrew Jackson and the Politics of Martial Law: Nationalism, Civil Liberties, and Partisanship* (2006), *Andrew Jackson in Context* (2009), and *Connecticut in the American Civil War: Slavery, Sacrifice, and Survival* (2011), and editor of *Inside Connecticut and the Civil War: Essay on One State's Struggle* (2014).

Jonathan W. White is Associate Professor of American Studies at Christopher Newport University in Newport News, Virginia. He is the author of several books, including *Abraham Lincoln and Treason in the Civil War: The Trials of John Merryman* (2011), *Emancipation, the Union Army, and the Reelection of Abraham Lincoln* (2014), and *Midnight in America: Darkness, Sleep, and Dreams during the Civil War* (2017). He has published more than eighty-five articles, essays, and reviews, and was the winner of the 2005 John T. Hubbell Prize for the best article in *Civil War History*, the 2010 Hay-Nicolay Dissertation Prize, the 2012 Thomas Jefferson Book Prize for his *Guide to Research in Federal Judicial History* (2010), and the 2015 Abraham Lincoln Institute Book Prize.

Kanisorn Wongsrichanalai is Associate Professor of History at Angelo State University in San Angelo, Texas. He is the author of *Northern Character: College-Educated New Englanders, Honor, Nationalism, and Leadership in the Civil War* (2016), and coeditor (with Lorien Foote) of *So Conceived and So Dedicated: Northern Intellectuals in the Civil War Era* (2015).

Index

The North's Civil War
Andrew L. Slap, series editor

Anita Palladino, ed., *Diary of a Yankee Engineer: The Civil War Story of John H. Westervelt, Engineer, 1st New York Volunteer Engineer Corps.*

Herman Belz, *Abraham Lincoln, Constitutionalism, and Equal Rights in the Civil War Era.*

Earl J. Hess, *Liberty, Virtue, and Progress: Northerners and Their War for the Union.* Second revised edition, with a new introduction by the author.

William L. Burton, *Melting Pot Soldiers: The Union's Ethnic Regiments.*

Hans L. Trefousse, *Carl Schurz: A Biography.*

Stephen W. Sears, ed., *Mr. Dunn Browne's Experiences in the Army: The Civil War Letters of Samuel W. Fiske.*

Jean H. Baker, *Affairs of Party: The Political Culture of Northern Democrats in the Mid–Nineteenth Century.*

Frank L. Klement, *The Limits of Dissent: Clement L. Vallandigham and the Civil War.* With a new introduction by Steven K. Rogstad.

Lawrence N. Powell, *New Masters: Northern Planters during the Civil War and Reconstruction.*

John A. Carpenter, *Sword and Olive Branch: Oliver Otis Howard.*

Thomas F. Schwartz, ed., *"For a Vast Future Also": Essays from the* Journal of the Abraham Lincoln Association.

Mark De Wolfe Howe, ed., *Touched with Fire: Civil War Letters and Diary of Oliver Wendell Holmes, Jr.* With a new introduction by David Burton.

Harold Adams Small, ed., *The Road to Richmond: The Civil War Letters of Major Abner R. Small of the 16th Maine Volunteers*. With a new introduction by Earl J. Hess.

Eric A. Campbell, ed., *"A Grand Terrible Dramma": From Gettysburg to Petersburg: The Civil War Letters of Charles Wellington Reed*. Illustrated by Reed's Civil War sketches.

Herbert Mitgang, ed., *Abraham Lincoln: A Press Portrait*.

Harold Holzer, ed., *Prang's Civil War Pictures: The Complete Battle Chromos of Louis Prang*.

Harold Holzer, ed., *State of the Union: New York and the Civil War*.

Paul A. Cimbala and Randall M. Miller, eds., *Union Soldiers and the Northern Home Front: Wartime Experiences, Postwar Adjustments*.

Mark A. Snell, *From First to Last: The Life of Major General William B. Franklin*.

Paul A. Cimbala and Randall M. Miller, eds., *An Uncommon Time: The Civil War and the Northern Home Front*.

John Y. Simon and Harold Holzer, eds., *The Lincoln Forum: Rediscovering Abraham Lincoln*.

Thomas F. Curran, *Soldiers of Peace: Civil War Pacifism and the Postwar Radical Peace Movement*.

Kyle S. Sinisi, *Sacred Debts: State Civil War Claims and American Federalism, 1861–1880*.

Russell L. Johnson, *Warriors into Workers: The Civil War and the Formation of Urban-Industrial Society in a Northern City*.

Peter J. Parish, *The North and the Nation in the Era of the Civil War*. Edited by Adam L. P. Smith and Susan-Mary Grant.

Patricia Richard, *Busy Hands: Images of the Family in the Northern Civil War Effort*.

Michael S. Green, *Freedom, Union, and Power: The Mind of the Republican Party During the Civil War.*

Christian G. Samito, ed., *Fear Was Not In Him: The Civil War Letters of Major General Francis S. Barlow, U.S.A.*

John S. Collier and Bonnie B. Collier, eds., *Yours for the Union: The Civil War Letters of John W. Chase, First Massachusetts Light Artillery.*

Grace Palladino, *Another Civil War: Labor, Capital, and the State in the Anthracite Regions of Pennsylvania, 1840–1868.*

Christian B. Keller, *Chancellorsville and the Germans: Nativism, Ethnicity, and Civil War Memory.*

Sidney George Fisher, *A Philadelphia Perspective: The Civil War Diary of Sidney George Fisher.* Edited and with a new Introduction by Jonathan W. White.

Robert M. Sandow, *Deserter Country: Civil War Opposition in the Pennsylvania Appalachians.*

Craig L. Symonds, ed., *Union Combined Operations in the Civil War.*

Harold Holzer, Craig L. Symonds, and Frank L. Williams, eds., *The Lincoln Assassination: Crime and Punishment, Myth and Memory.* A Lincoln Forum Book.

Earl F. Mulderink III, *New Bedford's Civil War.*

David G. Smith, *On the Edge of Freedom: The Fugitive Slave Issue in South Central Pennsylvania, 1820–1870.*

George Washington Williams, *A History of the Negro Troops in the War of the Rebellion, 1861–1865.* Introduction by John David Smith.

Randall M. Miller, ed., *Lincoln and Leadership: Military, Political, and Religious Decision Making.*

Andrew L. Slap and Michael Thomas Smith, eds., *This Distracted and Anarchical People: New Answers for Old Questions about the Civil War–Era North.*

Paul D. Moreno and Johnathan O'Neill, eds., *Constitutionalism in the Approach and Aftermath of the Civil War.*

Steve Longenecker, *Gettysburg Religion: Refinement, Diversity, and Race in the Antebellum and Civil War Border North.*

Harold Holzer, Craig L. Symonds, and Frank L. Williams, eds., *Exploring Lincoln: Great Historians Reappraise Our Greatest President.* A Lincoln Forum Book.

Lorien Foote and Kanisorn Wongsrichanalai, eds., *So Conceived and So Dedicated: Intellectual Life in the Civil War–Era North.*

William B. Kurtz, *Excommunicated from the Union: How the Civil War Created a Separate Catholic America.*

Kanisorn Wongsrichanalai, *Northern Character: College-Educated New Englanders, Honor, Nationalism, and Leadership in the Civil War Era.*

Ryan W. Keating, *Shades of Green: Irish Regiments, American Soldiers, and Local Communities in the Civil War Era.*

Robert M. Sandow, ed., *Contested Loyalty: Debates over Patriotism in the Civil War North.*

Grant R. Brodrecht, *Our Country: Northern Evangelicals and the Union During the Civil War Era.*